APPLIED HUMAN RELATIONS:
AN ORGANIZATIONAL APPROACH

PRENTICE-HALL, INC., Englewood Cliffs, New Jersey 07632

Jack Halloran

Santa Barbara City College

Applied Human Relations

an Organizational Approach

Library of Congress Cataloging in Publication Data

Halloran, Jack,
    Applied human relations.

    Includes bibliographical references and index.
    1.   Organizational behavior.   2.   Communication
in organizations.   3.   Industrial relations.
4.   Personnel management.   I.   Title.
HD31.H235   658.3   77-17032
ISBN 0-13-040857-3

Printed in the United States of America

10   9   8   7   6   5

Prentice-Hall International, Inc., *London*
Prentice-Hall of Australia Pty. Limited, *Sydney*
Prentice-Hall of Canada, Ltd., *Toronto*
Prentice-Hall of India Private Limited, *New Delhi*
Prentice-Hall of Japan, Inc., *Tokyo*
Prentice-Hall of Southeast Asia Pte. Ltd., *Singapore*
Whitehall Books Limited, *Wellington, New Zealand*

Contents

v

FOUR HUMANS MUST FIT IN A SOCIETY

Preface

This book is an endeavor to approach some of the aspects of human relations as it is seen in action in organizations today. Since the field has so many general facets, such as communications, morale, motivation, and leadership, the material can only be treated as a basic course in the field of social science or business. Hopefully this book will generate interest and point the way for further study.

The topic of human relations, or organizational behavior, or psychology of business, as it is often known, is receiving more attention by companies from the assembly line to the board room. Since we spend more than a third of our daily lives at work, it should be meaningful. In an effort to find out what is meaningful, traditional theories and current reactions are blended into various categories for reading and discussion. The traditional avenues of motivation and morale are explored to see how they affect white collar and blue collar workers, as well as the more recent topics of employment discrimination, creativity, and intercultural relations.

This text is designed to meet the needs of popular courses taught in junior colleges, four year colleges, universities, adult schools, extension programs, and management training seminars. The direct, straightforward language attempts to emphasize the person in the organization, rather than the traditional theories of management philosophy. It is not a book on organizational theory, office management, or elements of supervision.

The material was written to develop thinking. To this end each chapter is introduced with a blend of two types of questions. Some questions can only be answered with personal opinions and are popular ways to start class discussions after the chapter has been read. Other questions are based on material that will be covered in the chapter and they provide clues to topics in the chapter. Throughout various chapters are exercises that can be done by the reader or by groups. Since human relations means self-discovery and interchange between persons, the more participative the class can become, the more the students can learn from the experience.

At the close of each chapter are summaries, footnotes, and bibliographies, as well as case studies that can be done during class or as outside assignments. Many case studies are real–life events of former students. The answers are not always easy to find, for the neophyte or for the experienced manager. Former students tested the case problems in groups of five and found them rewarding experiences. I hope they will be for you also.

The Student Activity Book, a supplement to this text, provides questions for review and many stimulating individual and group games.

An attempt has been made to write the text in the belief that individual differences are a blessing and that each man is unique. It is hoped that each person can build more confidence when he accepts his individual assets, even when he knows they are very different from those of others. Rapport can be built when people recognize their differences and respect them. The world is always in a state of flux, and many employees dislike facing change in their workplace. Therefore three chapters deal with the process of change—Creativity, Decision Making, and Resistance to Change. Such a presentation may help us accept change as a way of life and to understand those who resist change. Another topic that has received considerable attention is that of people under stress, such as alcoholics and drug abusers. Keeping employees who have been trained on the job by helping them with any serious problems is far better than firing them and having to train new ones. Such topics are covered in Personal Problems at Work.

My students during the past few years deserve a great deal of credit, as they were responsible for giving me the vibes that were necessary in trying out various methods with them. Their ideas, reports, and reviews of the manuscript helped to provide the catalysis for the textbook. To properly acknowledge all who have assisted in the development of the project is impossible. However, my thanks to Terri Dirlan, Ron Lewis, Bob Ruppert, Tom Nowak, Brian Mears, and Jim Ticer for their assistance in giving personal input and reactions. Also to Bea Willis, JoAnn Thomas, and Simone Woodcock, who proved themselves outstanding secretaries in their ability to decipher my rough drafts and smooth them into accurate manuscript copy. My thanks to old friends Robert Curtis and Rob Reilly for their assistance with appropriate photographs. My foreign friends Isaac and Esther Koyenikan of Nigeria and the Purvis and Brayne families of Surrey, England deserve a warm applause for providing me with the proper perspective on the Intercultural Relations chapter.

Certainly I would be remiss unless I acknowledged the college professors that inspired me to follow in their footsteps. Their dynamic leadership keeps me in the field of education. To Larry Erickson and Dr. Samuel Wanous of the University of California at Los Angeles I owe a great debt of gratitude. Dr. Ken Zimmer and Mrs. Madeline Strony, who were colleagues of mine while I taught at California State College at Los Angeles, gave me the courage to write a textbook.

As is true in any writing project, this effort would not have been possible without the assistance of many of my college associates, who read portions of the manuscript and gave valuable suggestions—especially John Bowman who gave me moral support during my heart attack. My thanks to the Board of Trustees, President Glenn Gooder, and Dean of Instruction Pat Huglin for providing the environment conducive to good teaching and a fertile ground to try many innovative ideas in the classroom—some of which are used in this textbook.

Countless contributions to the style and content were given by the editorial staff at Prentice Hall. Editor Bill Gibson and staff assistant Esther Koehn both kept me abreast of events at the publication end of the project. Stephen Cline, College Editor, who played the watchful eye of a "mother-in-law" during the critical stages of the manuscript, deserves a commendation for his assistance. Without his help the project would have taken longer.

My highest praise of course goes to my wife Kathy, who provided the instructurable support during the many times of fatigue and stress. I thank my children Mike and Karen for their patience. As I write this last page for the book I can still recall Karen's words, "Daddy haven't you finished that book yet?"

"Yes, sweetheart, now the book is finished."

JACK HALLORAN

APPLIED HUMAN RELATIONS:
AN ORGANIZATIONAL APPROACH

One
People
Are
Human

Introduction to Human Relations

" Where are We Going?" ■ ■ ■ ■ ■ ■ ■ ■ ■ ■

OBJECTIVES

After reading this chapter you should be able to:
1. Explain why there is a need for an interdisciplinary approach to human relations in business.
2. List the three main developments that led to an increased acceptance of the worker as a person with multiple needs.
3. Discuss both the goals and results of the Hawthorne Studies conducted by Elton Mayo and his colleagues for the National Research Council.
4. List five of the most common causes of problems in human relations and the ones you think you are more capable of handling.
5. List the four basic themes in human relations literature.
6. Discuss the shift that is taking place in the American value system, especially in relation to the concepts of ''success'' and ''failure.''

■ ■

Before you read this chapter or any chapter in the book you will read questions that are designed to stimulate your thinking. The answers to some will be found in the readings and the answers to other questions will depend upon your own personal opinion or experiences. Such open-ended questions are written to generate discussions and an exchange of ideas among people.

What is your definition of human relations?

Why would the study of human relations be more important to the supervisor than to the average worker?

Are traditional attitudes toward work changing today?

Is leisure, rather than work, the national preoccupation?

Has "scientific management" helped or hindered human relations?

What ways do we use to motivate people?

How can you explain that responsibility is a two-way street between the company and the employee?

DEFINITIONS AND PURPOSES

Human relations is the study of interaction among people

In its most general sense, the term "human relations" refers to all the interactions that can occur among people, whether they are conflicts or cooperative behaviors. By the time most people reach college age, they have developed a system of human relations in their social and personal relationships which satisfies their needs. Frequently, however, people who feel confident and socially secure in their personal relationships lack confidence and feel insecure in their business relationships. When people work together in groups to achieve a common objective, there is a great possibility that the differences among their individual viewpoints will cause conflicts. Many people do not know how to resolve business conflicts in a constructive manner. But, clearly, the person who does know how to work harmoniously even with those who hold different views or are motivated by different goals, has found an important clue to successful human relations in the world of work.

It is not uncommon for someone to be hired for a specific job because he or she has acquired the necessary training and skills in a particular field, but never to be promoted or advanced beyond that job. Most employers agree that the majority of those who fail in managerial positions do so because they lack skill in human relations, even though they may be competent in technical matters. Nor is it necessary for someone to be in a supervisory position to profit from a thorough understanding of human relations because such an understanding is useful for anyone who works with other people. The need to find new solutions to the day-to-day problems associated with modern job responsibilities and requirements has led to the development of human relations as a separate field of study, a modern discipline within the business curriculum.

The key to success in business is satisfying company needs and personal needs

From both the managerial and workers' point of view good human relations are necessary if people are to achieve economic, social, and psychological satisfaction from the work they do. *The study of human relations in business and industry is the study of how people can work effectively in groups in order to satisfy both (1) organizational goals and (2) personal needs.*

The chief subject matter of this book is the history of the continuing search for a set of valid theories and practices by which maximum production efficiency can be combined with the maximum satisfaction of workers' *multiple* human needs, for although the organization of any job can be divided into separate elements, people who do jobs cannot. They work for physiological well-being, for security and continuity, for the companionship and esteem of other human beings, and to establish an identity. In the modern world most people identify themselves

5

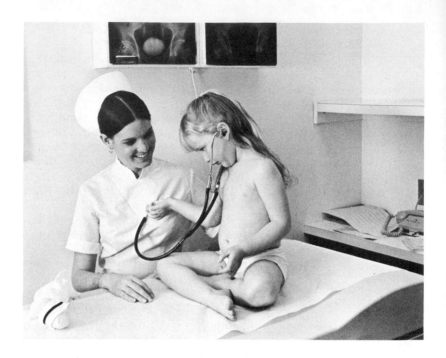

Figure 1–1. Human relations is a study of how people work together to satisfy personal needs and organizational goals.

Courtesy of Santa Barbara City College (Photo by Larry P. Johnson)

with their work. The question, "Who are you?" is usually taken to mean, "What do you do for a living?"

In much the same manner, the term *human relations* is usually taken to mean "getting along with others." But although the term does refer to relationships between human beings, in the context of business and industrial practice it is a far more complex subject than the question "How can I get along better with my fellow workers?" suggests. The term encompasses two entirely different sets of objectives—the goals of the organization and the goals of the people who work for the organization. Organizational goals such as productivity, growth, and profit maximization are influenced by nonhuman factors such as the organization's size, structure, complexity, and degree of technological sophistication. Human goals such as job satisfaction, recognition, and career advancement are influenced by many different kinds of social and psychological factors, as well as by the organizational condition of the work environment. Consequently, because human goals are affected by so many more variables than organizational goals, they are far more complex to deal with and more difficult to satisfy.

How to satisfy company goals and personal goals

Company goals are often growth, profit, and production

Human goals are often recognition and job satisfaction

6

The study of human relations in the world of work is *not* the study of human behavior for its own sake. It *is* the study of the practical attempts to achieve the two separate goals of (1) greater productivity at work and (2) greater human satisfaction within the organization. Patterns of behavior develop within groups of all kinds. For instance, parents and children interact in a special kind of group called the family; people jammed together at a football game are interacting in still another kind of human group. The focus in this book will be the *patterns of human behavior within organizations.*

THE INTERDISCIPLINARY ASPECT OF HUMAN RELATIONS

The theoretical basis of this book is that human relations is an integrated body of knowledge composed of various elements from several different disciplines. Human relations is an interdisciplinary field because the study of human behavior in an industrial or business setting must include the research of several social and physical sciences if it is to be coherent. The interdisciplinary approach requires an understanding of the separate contributions made by other disciplines and then the integration of that information into a unified whole.

For example, psychologists have done extensive research and experimentation on the relation of the individual to the work environment. They have conducted many valuable studies on job satisfaction, job placement, incentives, testing, training, counseling, and various other work-related areas. Sociologists, anthropologists, and social psychologists have made major contributions to human relations with their studies of group behavior and group dynamics. Their concepts of role behavior, status effects, and the influence of informal groupings have proved invaluable in understanding behavior in work environments. Political science has contributed useful information about the relationships between organizational structure, power struggles, leadership, and the processes of administration. Physiology has added useful data concerning the effects of monotony and boredom on production processes and total productivity. Economics has contributed both theories and information to a total theory of industrial relations. The science of semantics and the fast-growing new field of information theory have made enormous contributions to the practice of efficient communications in business and industry.

All these fields, and others, have added separate elements to our knowledge of human relations. Consequently, beginning with the brief history of the human relations movement below, the chapters on communication, motivation, leadership, decision making, etc., will be discussed with the understanding that they are important not only in and of themselves, but also as *parts,* or elements, of an integrated, interdisciplinary field of study.

A BRIEF HISTORY OF THE HUMAN RELATIONS MOVEMENT

Movement started after 1850

It is impossible to specify the exact date when the human relations movement began, but it is fair to say that not until the second half of the nineteenth century was much attention paid to workers' needs, nor was there any understanding of how those needs affect total productivity. Prior to that time, most managers and employers viewed the labor force as a commodity—to be bought and sold like any other commodity. Long hours, low wages, and miserable working conditions were the commonplace realities of the average worker's life. Labor unions were still struggling to exist and had not yet won the right to represent the labor force.

Frederick Taylor developed the theory of Scientific Management

Then, at about the turn of the century, Frederick Taylor and other less famous but equally important figures introduced and developed the theory and practice of *scientific management.* This theory held that greater productivity could be achieved by breaking work down into isolated, specific, specialized tasks. Not too surprisingly, this theory became popular at approximately the same time that mass production became feasible, and it helped to pave the way for the assembly line.

Scientific management has often been described as a series of techniques for increasing production rates through the means of better cost accounting procedures, premium and incentive payments, time and motion studies, and so on. But Frederick Taylor himself protested vigorously against this interpretation. In his view, utilizing these techniques did not in itself constitute scientific management, because, as he put it, the main objective of scientific management was "to remove the causes for antagonism between the boss and the men who were under him."[1] He believed that if employers and workers together concentrated on methods to increase production, if they would only "take their eyes off of the division of the surplus as the all-important matter, and together turn their attention toward increasing the *size* of the surplus,"[2] the surplus would become so huge that there would be no conflict about how to divide it. There would be more than enough for all.

Nevertheless, a great deal of legitimate criticism was directed at Taylor and his followers on the grounds that scientific management tended to exploit workers more than it benefited them. Early critics held that the theory emphasized control and discipline to the detriment of workers' morale. They accused the advocates of scientific management of seeing workers as mere economic tools, as separate, almost mechanical, parts of the production process, not as human beings with human needs. Later critics said that scientific management paid no attention to the complex social networks created by workers within the work environment. These critics held that it was precisely those complex social networks that had the greatest influence on production rates. But in spite of the validity of these and other criticisms, the introduction of scientific management practices in the world of work had far-reaching consequences for most industrial workers and managers, as well as for overall production processes.

New view proposed

Use of testing and job selection

With the spread of scientific management techniques, employers and managers, in order to improve job selection and placement procedures, learned to assess each worker's abilities as unique to the individual. By the 1920s the popular image of the worker had changed considerably from what it had been at the turn of the century. The new view held that all workers were complex, unique beings whose individual skills and abilities could be measured, tested, and trained. The individual worker came to be seen as a combination of various traits— traits that could be accurately measured and improved by appropriate training. During this decade many managers came to believe that testing could solve most if not all of the problems related to job selection, placement, and promotion.

The widespread use of testing in industry had one important effect that was not foreseen by even its most enthusiastic advocates: the tests demonstrated that worker's personal motivations influenced test performances. It became clear, as the popularity of tests increased, that a workers' skills and abilities could not be isolated from the individual's human interests, and that emotional and social forces, both within and outside the organization, influenced workers' interests. Just when sophisticated management had begun to believe that new testing methods could solve many traditional problems between labor and management, the tests themselves showed that more research had to be done to identify the forces that motivate workers.

Membership in unions increased at the start of the 20th century

At the same time that the new image of the worker was gaining popularity among employers and managers, unions were becoming an increasingly powerful force in industrial affairs. During the years from 1897 to 1904, membership in trade unions grew from 400,000 to 2 million.[3] And unions kept on growing. By 1920 trade unions throughout the nation had received a large measure of recognition from the owners and managers of industry.

Thus three separate developments—scientific management techniques, the struggles of the trade unionists, and the rapidly changing technology—all led to increased acceptance of the idea of the worker as a person with multiple needs. The same three developments also led large numbers of managers to reexamine their own image. They took a fresh look at themselves and began to question the wisdom of their traditional views of leadership and decision-making styles. "The mind of management is also an integral part of human relations in industry," said one writer in 1924. "Now that the American worker's mind has been explored, one might be led to expect a similar exploration of the mind of management."[4]

A popular theory of that time that is still influential held that great leaders are not only born, they can also be trained—by appropriate training procedures. The theory gained credence as the understanding grew that there are bad managers as well as good ones, and that proper management techniques can be taught. In the 1840s the characteristics of a good employer were said to be "industry, arrangement, calculation, prudence, punctuality, and perseverance." One hundred years later, a group of successful managers listed the personal qualities they felt had contributed the most to their success as, "personal appearance, intelligence, willingness to assume responsibility, self-control, broadmindedness, and decisiveness."[5] The inclusion of such items as broadmindedness and personal appearance indicates that the ability to succeed socially has become far more important to managerial success than it used to be. As vague as these "ideal" qualities of a good manager are, compared with the earlier list they show a clear shift in the direction of a humanistic, as opposed to an autocratic, approach to managerial theory.

In the mid-1920s the focal point for the humanistic approach in business and industry was the famous Hawthorne Studies conducted by Elton Mayo and his colleagues for the National Research Council in arrangement with the Massachusetts Institute of Technology. Mayo's group began their work by studying the effects of illumination, ventilation, and fatigue on the workers of the Hawthorne Plant of Western Electric.

In one area of study two groups of employees working under similar conditions and doing similar types of work were selected and output records were kept for each group. The intensity of the light under which one group worked was systematically varied, while the light was held constant for the second group. The intensity of the light of the first group was increased. The general result was that the productivity of the group increased each time the intensity of the light increased. This fact was anticipated; however, decreasing the intensity of the light under which employees worked also increased productivity. In fact, the productivity of the group continued to increase as the level of illumination was lowered and one of the highest levels of productivity was recorded during an extremely low level of illumination. Obviously some other variables were contaminating the effects of the experiment.

The employees themselves provided a clue to the changes in the output. They stated that it was easier to work faster, because work in the test room was fun and there was little regular supervisory control. In effect, the employees were saying that their productivity increases were attributable to greater freedom and a feeling of importance.

Personal attention can affect morale

After a few years of experimentation, it became clear to the researchers that group morale and personal motivation factors were so important that they completely obscured the effects of the illumination, ventilation, and fatigue factors under investigation. The Hawthorne Studies conclusively showed, by quantitative measurements, that normal interactions of workers at work *always* create a social network called the *informal organization,* which exerts tremendous influence over workers' behavior patterns. These particular studies also showed that the informal organization at Western Electric frequently countermanded official orders passed down through the formal organization and consequently played a determining role in setting production rates.

The informal group can have as much influence as the formal organization

From that point on it was no longer possible for management to view workers as mere economic tools, or as isolated units in the production process. They had to be seen as complex human beings whose normal human interactions were bound to affect total production output, no matter how sophisticated the technological processes employed were. Mayo's findings helped to develop the image of both workers and managers as whole persons, creatures of sentiment, whose basic human desires and conflicting personal motives often resulted in complex outcomes to problems, outcomes which cannot be predicted in a purely technological, theoretical framework. Much criticism has subsequently been levied at Mayo's methodology, but the light shed by the Hawthorne Studies still shines in the field of human relations.

Interest in human relations decreased during the Depression

Interest in human relations diminished in the 1930s during the early part of the Great Depression. With the passage of the Wagner Act, however, and the reemergence of militant unionism, business leaders turned again toward meeting workers' needs—particularly as those needs influenced total productivity. The industrial and business expansion during World War II and the prosperous postwar period stimulated and encouraged a deeper understanding of the relationship between productivity and worker satisfaction. Countless studies were published by business theorists and social scientists. Two of the most important were Douglas McGregor's paper on traditional management theory, which he called Theory X, as opposed to the humanistic approach to management called Theory Y, and Abraham Maslow's studies on the hierarchy of human needs. Both sets of theories were milestones in human relations studies and still exert considerable influence.

Interest in human relations reappeared in 1940–1970s

Contributions to the fast-growing discipline greatly increased during the forties and fifties. Studies were done by such psychologists as Carl Rogers and Kurt Lewin; sociologists Daniel Bell and C. Wright Mills; and managers of giant corporations such as Chester I. Barnard. In the sixties and seventies, both by choice and necessity, corporate employers and managers in the developed nations have come to value the importance of these theoretical and experimental contributions. Human relations has become a body of knowledge no student of business can afford to ignore.

THE SCOPE OF HUMAN RELATIONS

When someone's abilities and ambitions match the demands of a particular job, the job will be done well and a great deal of personal satisfaction may be obtained by the person doing it. If the demands of the job exceed that person's abilities or ambitions, the job will not be done well and personal frustration will result. If the drives and abilities of the person far outweigh the job demands, he or she may experience boredom, and the job may be done carelessly.

Similarly, different kinds of jobs demand different kinds of human relations skills. A salesperson for a small retail store will have an entirely different set of human relations problems to deal with than will someone working on the assembly line or in a typing pool of a large corporation. The personnel manager of that corporation will, of necessity, have to cope with very different kinds of human relations than a finance officer of the same firm. The procedures and rules used to govern workers' activities in large corporations are generally stricter and more formalized than those found in small businesses. Yet some people find it easier to work for large, impersonal organizations than to work under the constant watchfulness of a small shop owner.

Human relations problems have many different causes. Five of the most common are:

Your talents

1. Every person brings a unique set of talents, ambitions, and work experience to a job. These personal attributes change over time, often as a result of the degree of success or failure the person experiences in the work world. Matching so many unique sets of

personal qualities to a standardized technology can create problems.

Company needs

2. The organizational aspects of a company, such as its size, geographic location, economic health, and degree of automation, define the scope of work and the activity in each work division. These frequently arbitrary structural definitions often cause difficulties in human relations.

Growth of technology

3. Innovations in technology and production methods generally require the restructuring of job roles and responsibilities. Radical changes in basic organizational structure can cause severe strains between workers and management and thus create intense problems in human relations.

Need for responsibility

4. Promotions of individuals to positions of greater responsibility and authority generally create a need for changed behavior patterns between the new supervisors and their former peers which, in turn, can create human relations problems.

Young inexperienced workers

5. Inexperienced or young workers may not be able to perform their roles or tasks in work groups in a competent manner. The time they take to adjust can not only create problems with production schedules, it can also create particular kinds of human relations problems between them and their coworkers and supervisors.

Since human relations problems have many different causes and perspective, it might be interesting to see where your feelings are at this time in relation to the five named above causes. Afterwards it might be interesting to share them with members of your class. The idea of writing down your immediate feelings may help develop your own value clarifications as to your place in the working world.

1. Every person brings a unique set of talent, ambitions, and experience to a job. What are the three most outstanding things you feel you can bring to a job position?
   a. _____
   b. _____
   c. _____
2. Organizational aspects of a company.
   a. What size company would you like to work with?
      (1) 10–50 employees   (2) 50–150 employees   (3) over 150
   b. Where would you like your company located?
      (1) locally   (2) within 100 miles of home   (3) Anywhere in the U. S.   (4) Outside the U. S.
3. Do you enjoy changes at work?
   (1) Look forward to change.   (2) Occassionally enjoy changes.   (3) Seldom like to see change.   (4) Change makes it difficult to get one's work done.

4. Promotions mean greater responsibility and authority. In my next job I would like to see a promotion in (1) 3 months   (2) 6 months   (3) 1 year   (4) When I deserve it.

5. One way to handle untrained and inexperienced workers is to (1) Have training classes frequently for new employees.   (2) Only hire experienced employees.   (3) Have a trainee work with you to learn the trade.

Your ideas may change in a few months or remain the same. In any case if you compare your answers with others and share your feeling about your answers you may clarify some of your attitudes about work and discover some of your expectations of a career.

This variety of causes of human relations problems inevitably leads to the conclusion that no one program or single approach can create conditions for good human relations. Since so many different factors can be shown to cause trouble, many different kinds of programs are necessary to deal with different sets of problems. The work of the past fifty years has demonstrated conclusively that short-term solutions, no matter how popular they may be, do not solve complex human relations problems. Such problems demand carefully thought-out measures which must be given enough time in actual practice to prove or disprove their worth.

Short-term solutions do not solve long-term human relation problems

It is nonproductive for managers to be too hasty in adopting faddist human relations theories before the value of those theories has been demonstrated. Recent human relations fads have ranged from rotating jobs to providing brightly painted work environments and piped-in music. Certainly providing workers with a pleasant work environment, or some form of recognition of their worth and human dignity often leads to higher group morale. But it should be remembered that high employee morale does not always result in high productivity. Sometimes the methods used by managers to achieve high morale have questionable productive value. Flattering an employee, for example, for accomplishing a task that is a regular part of his or her job is not automatically going to raise production rates.

The Hawthorne Studies led to simplistic solutions, of little use in meeting either organizational goals or employee needs. For example, in some companies the idea of the productive value of teamwork developed by Mayo and his colleagues was translated into a "magic formula" that was supposed to cure all kinds of morale and production problems. In these companies the idea of teamwork was blown all out of proportion. It became a tool used to pressure employees to conform to rigid behavioral standards. Of course, businesses must institute controls to govern time, production, and quality standards; but excessive con-

There are no magic formulas

trols on employee freedom will *reduce* motivation and lower morale. Excessive controls masquerading as "teamwork" have damaged individual creativity and initiative. An organization chart can look very logical and efficient, but conformist "teams" seldom produce creative solutions to difficult problems, and creative solutions to production bottlenecks and troublesome organizational relationships are essential if a company is to survive and prosper.

Implementing creative solutions is often harder than thinking of them. Some managers prefer to sidestep such difficulties by reaching for the latest fad in the human relations movement. When the fad fails to solve a specific set of problems, such managers then feel free to ignore or reject all human relations theories and practices. But a closed mind is of no more value to managers than a naive one is. Organizational employees, whether top executives or hourly workers, do more work and get greater job satisfaction when they approach new ideas, systems, and technologies with an open mind and a certain degree of caution. Satisfied, productive employees from vice-presidents down to stock clerks understand that there are no ready-made magic formulas suitable for solving all human relations conflicts.

BASIC THEMES IN HUMAN RELATIONS

The student of human relations will find four basic themes recurring in the literature. They are the necessity to (1) *communicate* effectively with others; (2) *motivate* oneself and others; (3) exercise *responsibility* in a just and satisfactory manner; and (4) *empathize*, or understand and make allowances for other people's needs and desires. Following is a summary of this book's approach to these themes.

Communications

In modern organizations, all other functions depend on communication. It is the way in which information and understanding are transmitted; it unifies group behavior; and it provides the basis for group cooperation. Without effective communication procedures no business can survive, much less prosper. If managers cannot communicate effectively with employees, they cannot motivate them, nor can they exercise the functions of leadership. If workers cannot communicate well with management, they cannot perform their jobs properly, nor can they receive adequate recognition for their work. If communication in an or-

ganization is not good, then there is no way that the human relations in that organization can satisfy the people who work
there.

Chapters 2 and 3 deal exclusively with communication
principles and processes—first on the interpersonal, face-to-face
level, and then on the organizational plane. Chapter 2, "The
Language of Communication," presents a number of abstract
principles and communication behavior patterns, the mastery of
which will lead to more effective communication behavior.
Chapter 3, "Communication in Organizations," describes the
interlocking relationships that exist between an organization's
structural forms and its communication procedures. Chapter 6,
"Personal Problems at Work," also discusses an important communication skill: the theory and principles of active listening.
The importance of effective communication is implicit throughout this entire text.

Motivation

Although human relations is a vast and complicated subject
composed of and influenced by many variables, it can be simply
described as the total response of individuals to various motivating forces. In other words, people in organizations relate to
each other in the ways they do because they are driven by psychological, social, and economic forces that have the power to
motivate them to behave in particular ways. The way people behave when they experience conflicting motives within and
among themselves is a major source of organizational strife. It is
well established that in most circumstances proper motivation
on the part of leadership can increase overall productivity.

Chapter 4, "Motivation," introduces some of the theoretical
and experimental approaches to motivation that have been influential in the human relations movement. McGregor's Theories
X and Y are discussed in this chapter, as is Maslow's hierarchy
of human needs. Like communication, motivation is a pervasive
theme throughout the book and surfaces everywhere—most notably in the chapters on morale, resistance to change, status and
the work force, and appraisals and rewards.

Responsibility

In a very real sense, the history of the human relations movement is the history of responsible leadership. A leader's fundamental responsibility in any kind of work organization is to get
work done through the combined, cooperative efforts of others.

A leader must communicate with and motivate his or her subordinates in a just and satisfactory manner or work will not get done. The human relations function is not, of course, the only responsibility a leader must discharge. Planning, coordinating, and controlling the organization's affairs from finances to work flow are equally, if not more, important. But good human relations with subordinates appears to be necessary if leaders are to handle these other functions well.

The theme of the exercise of responsibility in a satisfactory and just manner is discussed from the managerial point of view in the chapters on leadership, resistance to change, and making decisions. The focus of the theme shifts to the workers' point of view in the chapter on morale. In "Personal Problems at Work," the theme is expressed in terms of the reciprocal responsibilities workers practice with each other to achieve good human relations. And, as with the themes of communication and motivation, the notion of responsibility underlies many of the concepts and practices discussed elsewhere in the text.

Empathy

Empathy is the ability to put yourself in someone else's place, and to feel sympathy for that person's motives and point of view. Lack of empathy is a primary cause of conflict in organizations. Empathy is the chief quality mediators of labor disputes must have, and successful salespersons are usually empathic to a very high degree. Empathy is an important element in leadership, and its absence can create insurmountable barriers to communication.

The theme of empathy, in the form of understanding and making allowances for other people's needs and desires, is *the* integrating and unifying theme throughout this book. It is particularly stressed in the first chapter on communication, and it is basic to the discussions in the chapters on creativity, unions, discrimination, and intercultural relations.

Let us try another experiment. Of the four basic themes mentioned here, which one of the four do you feel most adept at performing. (1) Do you feel you can communicate to others your ideas, feelings, and thoughts better than the other three themes? (2) Or do you feel you are best at giving "pep talks," encouraging people to pursue their personal goals, and have a strong sense of direction and goal in life? (3) Perhaps responsibility and the desire for leadership are some of your strongest characteristics? Do you feel you could with a little time lead a group of five students in a group discussion? (4) Finally, is the ability to empathize one of your strongest abilities? Do you feel that you really know how others feel and can place "yourself in their shoes." Do people come to you for counsel and help on personal matters?

Which is *your strongest area* in the human relations field?

1. Ability to communicate _____
2. Ability to motivate yourself and others _____
3. Ability to accept responsibility and lead others _____
4. Ability to empathize with others and understand their problems.

Now that you have selected an area that best fits your background, think of an example or two that demonstrates that strength. After a few minutes of individual thought the class could be divided up into groups of five to discuss everyone's decisions and feelings.

HUMAN RELATIONS IN PERSPECTIVE

Success can be measured by public or personal standards

As the United States settles into the seventies and looks to the decades ahead, many people appear to be redefining the concept of "success" and "failure" as fundamental motivating forces. More and more people are becoming aware that success can be measured by personal standards as well as by public ones. Some of the personal standards that are gaining importance as measures of a successful career have been advocated by the human relations movement for at least three decades. For example, employees of firms that allow them to participate in company decision-making policies have said that that aspect of their jobs is as important to them as good pay. Recognition for work well done and a sense of the relevance of one's work are two other human relations "issues" whose value as "success" indicators is rising.

Significant numbers of people have begun to view the exclusive pursuit of profit as *destructive* to the fulfillment of their other human needs. Even the high value that used to be given to the notion of unchecked economic growth on the national level is changing. The twin problems of pollution and the limited energy resources of the planet are causing many people to reexamine their thoughts on such basic issues. In the last ten years, the managers of several American industries have had to cope with an entirely new human relations problem: the general public's concern and growing anger about pollution and inflationary profits.

In view of these and several other indicators, it appears

There may be a shift in value systems

A system based on people — not things

that a major shift is taking place in the American value system. The positive value given to the pursuit of power and profit is diminishing. The value placed upon creativity, full communication, and personal involvement and responsibility is increasing. The new value system seems to be based upon people — not things. It is still so new that its outlines are barely perceptible, and it is impossible to predict the direction it will take. But current trends suggest that person-centered work environments, and better human relations between managers and workers are gaining more and more advocates throughout business and industry.

Recent surveys and interviews conducted by advocates of the human relations movement indicate that significant numbers of white- and blue-collar workers are usually dissatisfied with their work. A common complaint is that they feel alienated from their jobs and lack motivation to work efficiently because they have little or no voice in making the decisions that affect their work lives. The managers of some businesses have begun to create programs to combat worker alienation by allowing them to participate in decision-making policies. These managers have understood the basic human relations dictum that an alienated work force *cannot* operate at peak efficiency, particularly if alienation takes the form of tardiness and absenteeism.

This is readily apparent in the automobile and steel industries, where the rising rates of tardiness, absenteeism, and job accidents have seriously affected production output. In 1972, Bureau of Labor statistics showed that "absenteeism had soared 35 percent since 1961, and annual turnover in the auto industry . . . has topped 100 percent (costing General Motors at least $79 million per year). . . ." [6] Some concerned managers in these industries are appealing to the human relations movement to find new ways to remotivate these alienated industrial workers. Some human relations theorists believe that precisely because huge corporations are miniature versions of the larger society they are the ideal places in which to experiment with new ideas in human relations — ideas that will reflect the new value system: "people not things."

Modern industry was built on the concept of fragmenting work and breaking it down into its smallest components, so that, ideally, managers could control workers and production more or less mechanically. But the study of human relations in the past century has pretty well established that treating workers mechanically causes them to feel alienated. On the other hand, treating workers as whole persons, people with traits and skills, and motivated by multiple needs, effectively combats the depersonalized alienated atmosphere so common in industrial environments.

19

In this third decade of the Atomic Age we are emerging from the last phase of the Industrial Revolution. We have designed and created an extraordinary technological system to mass produce and distribute all manner of goods. We have provided an unparalleled standard of living for an unparalleled number of people. It now remains for us to find effective ways to accommodate the individual to the technology as a *whole* person — not as an interchangeable part of the production process.

We have hired the "whole man" in the work force.

THE FUTURE OF HUMAN RELATIONS

Our rapidly changing technology, including the phenomenal growth of automation, our less rapidly but nevertheless changing value system, and the depletion of what was once thought to be an inexhaustible supply of natural resources, have led one writer to claim that the degree of change America has experienced in the past few decades has caused an entirely new form of social maladjustment, which he calls *Future Shock*.[7] Other writers have a less gloomy view of what is happening in these early years of the Atomic Age.

Suzannah Lessard, for example, has suggested a new way of interpreting the human life-cycle in relation to the problems of work.[8] She says that one of the cornerstones of our present-day value system is the belief that life is *naturally* divisible into three stages — education, work, and retirement — and that we believe there should be little or no overlap among these three stages because (1) people should go to school when they are young so that they can work when they are in their prime; (2) that people in their prime have the most to contribute as workers, because that is when human talents and energies are at their peak; and (3) that when people become old they become less productive, because they are physically weaker.

Life-cycle of education, work, and retirement must change

When we think this way, however, we are ignoring masses of information gathered by human relations scholars about how human energies and talents actually work. The rigid programming of three distinct stages — education, work, retirement — leaves no room for slowly evolving psychological change; no room for renewal and reorientation; and certainly no room for the continuous growth throughout life that writers such as Abraham Maslow and Carl Rogers believed possible for all human beings.

Education, work, or retirement can come at any time in life

People of all ages go through periods of tremendous productivity and creativity — and then must sit back and take a break, take the time to reset and recharge their energies, take the time to think about their work, or take the time to expand

and enrich their knowledge. Periods of great productivity are as likely to occur at age 65 as at age 45. The need for education can be even more urgent at 55 than it is at 20.

It is axiomatic in our present-day value system that as a person grows older his or her capacity for growth declines, but studies in human relations have clearly proven that anyone working at the same job for twenty years is bound to go stale and that the best way to restore interest, imagination, vigor, and the capacity for growth to those who are stagnating is to allow such people to take long breaks—to rest, to study, and possibly to change fields.

With concepts such as these gaining wide attention, a more flexible kind of life programming may be in store for us in the future. Of course, such theorizing can easily be dismissed as a "pipe dream." But wouldn't the conditions of life in a fully automated factory have sounded like a pipe dream to the workers in the Chicago meat factories in 1900? Who is to say that the next seventy years will not bring about even more remarkable changes in the world of work than we have experienced in the last seventy? We would probably have more trouble believing descriptions of the world of 2050 than the people of 1900 would have had believing descriptions of our world.

"HOW DO I FEEL TODAY?"

Individual Case Study #1

It is always exciting to see how you feel today and the attitudes you express at the beginning of a course. At the end of the course look back and see if your feelings about certain ideas on life have changed. These questions will be hard to answer, but put the first ideas that come to mind down on paper. This will be a study of value clarifications that will start you thinking about these questions long after you have answered them.

1. Which is more important, "team spirit" or individual achievement? _____
_____

2. Is today's fun more important than future accomplishments?___
_____

3. What do you regard as your greatest personal achievement to date? _____
_____

4. What is one thing that other people can do to make you happy? _____
_____

5. What do you regard as your own greatest personal failure to date? _____
_____

6. What two things would you most like to be said of you if you died today? _____
_____

Terms and Concepts Students Should Know

human relations
individual goals
scientific management
trade unions

growth of technology
Hawthorne Study
communication
motivate

responsibility
empathize

Bibliography

1. DAVIS, KEITH, *Human Behavior at Work*, 5th Edition, New York: McGraw-Hill Book Company, 1977.

2. DUBIN, ROBERT, *Human Relations in Administration*, 4th Edition, Englewood Cliffs, N.Y.: Prentice-Hall, Inc. 1974.

3. HUNERYAGER, S.G., and I.L. HECKMAN, JR., *Human Relations in Management*, 3rd Edition, Cincinnati: South-Western Publishing Co., 1972.

4. KOSSEN, STAN, *The Human Side of Organizations*, New York: Harper & Row, Publishers, Inc. 1975.

5. SANFORD, AUBREY, *Human Relations, The*

Theory and Practice of Organizational Behavior, 2nd Edition, Columbus, Ohio: Charles E. Merrill Publishing Company.

6. SHEEHY, GAIL, *Passages, Predictable Crises of Adult Life,* New York, E. P. Dutton & Co., Inc. 1976.

7. TAYLOR, FREDERICK, *Scientific Management,* New York, Harper, 1947.

8. TOFFLER, ALVIN *Future Shock,* New York, Random House, 1970.

Footnotes

[1] Frederick Taylor, *Scientific Management* (New York: Harper, 1947), pp. 128–29.

[2] *Ibid.,* pp. 29–30.

[3] W. G. Sumner, *What Social Classes Owe Each Other* (New York: Harper, 1883) pp. 91–92.

[4] *American Management Review, XIII* (1924) pp. 6–7.

[5] Reinhard Bendix, "Managers, Workers, and Ideas in the United States," in *Research in Industrial Human Relations,* edited by Conrad M. Ahrensberg, (New York: Harper & Brothers, 1957) p. 10.

[6] Daniel Zwerdling, "Beyond Boredom—A Look at What's New on the Assembly Line," *The Washington Monthly,* July/August 1973, p. 82.

[7] Alvin Toffler, *Future Shock* (New York: Random House, 1970).

[8] Suzannah Lessard, "America's Time Traps: The Youth Cult, The Work Prison, The Emptiness of Age," *The Washington Monthly,* February 1971, pp. 26–37.

Language Of Communication

"What Will I Say?" ■ ■ ■ ■ ■ ■ ■ ■ ■ ■

2

OBJECTIVES

After reading this chapter you should be able to:

1. Restate in your own words the idea that "meanings are in us, not in messages."
2. Describe the importance of the following elements in communication:
   A. Attitudes
   B. Emotions
   C. Roles
   D. Nonverbal behavior
   E. Feedback
3. Describe why listening is an active, not a passive activity.
4. List five general guidelines for more effective listening.
5. Define the four basic levels of communication and give examples of each:
   A. Conventional
   B. Exploratory
   C. Participative
   D. Confrontive

■ ■ ■ ■ ■ ■ ■ ■ ■ ■ ■ ■ ■ ■ ■ ■ ■ ■ ■

Here are a few questions you might think about as you read this chapter. The answers to some of these questions can be found in your reading and others can only be answered based on your own experiences. Your feelings and ideas about these questions might well be shared with others.

Is it easier for you to speak or to listen?

Does body language contradict your verbal messages?

What are some of the examples of how we visually communicate our feelings?

What is the mysterious "Inner circle" and is your "inner circle" larger than that of your friends'?

Do you believe in E.S.P.?

What are ways to make the written word easier to read?

What are some of the international symbols that all people seem to understand?

A LOOK AT COMMUNICATION

A study showed that an average American spends approximately 70 percent of his active hours communicating verbally—listening, speaking, then reading, or writing, in that order. This amounts to ten or eleven hours a day.[1] With so much practice it is surprising that we don't do a better job.

Regardless of the type of business—sales, manufacturing, or service—all firms have one problem in common: how to communicate more effectively and efficiently. Profit and the actual survival of a company is dependent upon how well people sell or motivate their employees. A successful conversation can make a friend, build good will, or sell a product. A poor message can create misunderstandings and that will lose time, money, or a business. In general, it might be said that to be an effective communicator, an employee must be able to adequately give facts, ideas, and opinions, with a minimum of effort and the maximum of skill.

In today's world, as foreign companies invade our soil, and competition becomes greater, the necessity to effectively communicate is more apparent. Companies, as well as colleges, are offering courses in public speaking, speed reading, and effective writing. Even Xerox has developed an effective listening program for businesses and colleges.

THE MEANING OF MEANING

There is an old story about three Englishmen riding on a bus. The bus stops. The first man says, "I say there, is this Wembley?" "No," says the second man. "This is Thursday." "So am I," says the third, "let's have a drink." Moral: All too often we hear only what we want to hear!

Communication is the process of transferring information and understanding *from* one or more people *to* one or more people. In the simplest form of communication, one person transfers information to another. In more complex kinds of communication members of a group transfer information to other members of a group. Comprehension is the only test of a message's success as communication. If the message is *understood*, communication has succeeded. If it is not, communication has failed.

How many times have you asked someone, "What do you mean by that?" How many times have you had to answer that question yourself? How do you answer it? Consult a dictionary? Probably not. Most people confronted with that question assemble their thoughts into new combinations of words and

**The meaning of words
exists within ourselves**

phrases and try to get the meaning across in different words. The meaning doesn't change, but the words do. *Meaning exists within ourselves,* not in the words we use to express that meaning. The meaning of a message is also called its *semantic* content.

Meaning is that which is intended to be understood. Except in the case of all mathematical and some scientific communications, meaning is always *subjective. Objective* meaning in mathematics and science can be communicated because in those "language systems," one term is never allowed to have more than one meaning. Nor can a term have an ambiguous meaning. "Plus" can never mean "minus," nor can it ever imply "equal to." The rules of mathematical language leave absolutely no room for disagreement, but the word "happy" can mean 100 different things to 100 different people. It can also mean ten different things to the same person in ten different sets of circumstances. What makes one person happy can cause another to become sad, but "two and two equals four" always means the same thing to everyone.

When a dictionary is written, at least a half a dozen experts must agree on the meanings of the definitions. Such agreement is frequently hard to come by and heated arguments are not unusual. Nevertheless, the dictionary is the authority we usually turn to when we don't know the meaning of a word or are unsure of it. Dictionary meanings are as close to being *objective* as it is possible for nonmathematical meanings to be.

A word's *subjective* meaning is the personal *significance* that word has for an individual. To some people, "rock music" means stimulating, exciting rhythms, singable melodies, and amusing or provocative lyrics. To others, it means a noisy assault on human ears, with no discernible melodies and inaudible or asinine lyrics. Almost every word we use has different emotional and intellectual meanings for each of us. Even the most ordinary, everyday term will have an astonishing variety of meanings attached to it because *the meaning attached to any object or experience is always personally experienced.* Julius Laffal put it this way:

> Relationships between words and things exist only by virtue of and within the minds of the people who use the words.[2]

Meanings are in us, not in messages. Messages are transmittable, but meanings reside in the message-users. When we transmit a message we hope that the other person's "meanings" will overlap or be similar to our own, and that we will be understood.

The more our messages relate to and overlap the other person's mental and emotional experiences, the more effectively we communicate with each other. And, just as experiences are constantly changing, so are meanings. Thus, meaning can never be permanently fixed. Since no two people can ever give *exactly* the same meaning to anything, good communication demands a high tolerance for ambiguity, especially because the more abstract the term, the more meanings it can have. Consider some of the different meanings words such as "justice," "freedom," and "faith" have for different people.

Because so many words have such ambiguous meanings, to fully understand someone's meaning requires paying as much attention to the *person* speaking as to the words being spoken. Voice tones, facial gestures, and body language communicate as much or more meaning than words do. Effective communicators are *person oriented, not word oriented.* They know that although one word may have many meanings, people always give their own meanings to all words.

Words are used to shape people's beliefs, fears, prejudices,

Communication—The Exchange of Ideas

How Fast Can You Read

Time—10 Minutes

Here is a test to see how fast you can read and comprehend. Read the following directions and do as it says.

1. Read all of the items from one to ten first.
2. Draw a square to the left of number five.
3. Circle number one in this list.
4. Write the letters WYZ at the bottom of this page.
5. Write the total of $5 + 7 + 32 =$
6. Write the author of the "Gettysburg Address" in the margin.
7. Stand up and repeat 1, 2, 3, 4, 5, very fast and then sit down.
8. Write your name on the line shown below.
9. Do the following problem and write the answer $(42 + 7) \times (36 + 6) =$_____
10. Now that you have just read all the items, write only your name at the bottom of the page and wait for the others to finish.

_____
Name

To reemphasize, *the meaning is in us, not in the words.* If this experiment was done in class, there is little that needs to be said.

ideals, and aspirations. They are used to arouse indignation, loyalty, awe, and horror. They are a profound means of influencing the thought and behavior of individuals, groups, and nations. As ambiguous and unsatisfactory as words frequently are, they are the basic units, the building blocks of human communication.

THE COMMUNICATION PROCESS

Speaking and Listening

We speak fast, but think faster

It has been estimated that we think at the rate of 1,000 to 2,000 words a minute. After digesting that figure, consider the implications of the fact that we can speak no more than 100 to 200 words a minute.[3] It means that in order to speak coherently, we select 10 percent of the words and thoughts in our minds and discard or "put on hold" the remaining 90 percent, *at the same time* that we are speaking. It is an amazingly complex process.

When we listen, we can hear and comprehend at least double the number of words that we can speak. John Keltner says that in general "we can listen effectively to spoken words produced at about three times the normal speech rate."[4] Therefore, it would seem that listening to and understanding a message would be easier than speaking it, because listening requires less mental activity than speaking. However, in our culture, it is well known that verbal messages, more often than not, are inaccurately received, poorly understood, and garbled in the retelling.

The game of rumor distorts the message

In the United States it is axiomatic that if the accuracy of a message is considered important, then it is necessary to "get it in writing!" There is even a popular game called "rumor" that teachers play with young children to illustrate how inaccurate verbal communication can be. In this game the teacher whispers a message to one child and asks the child to whisper the *same* message to another child. The second child repeats the whispered message to a third, and so on, until everyone in the class has heard it individually. The teacher then asks the last child hearing the message to stand up and repeat it out loud for all to hear. Invariably, the words the child speaks have little or no relation to the words of the original message.

In primitive societies, where writing is unknown and *all* messages are transmitted by speech, the accuracy of the transmission is much higher than in countries with high literacy rates. This indicates that illiterate people know how to listen and remember messages better than literate people do. David Riesman says:

> For these tribesmen, words are like buckets in a fire brigade, *to be handled with full attention, while we feel we can afford to be careless with the spoken word,* backstopped as we are by the written one.[5]

We can overload our listening circuits

Perhaps some of our listening difficulties are due to "overload" from too much message input. Just as electrical circuits break down when they must carry more messages than they have been built to receive, so too our "listening circuits" may break down when we are receiving more messages than we can handle comfortably. Most of us are "receiving stations" for auditory messages coming in all day long from radio and television. Our eyes automatically decode visual messages such as traffic signs, billboards, and movie marquees. These messages are all *one-way forms of communication,* demanding our attention. *They are the one-way messages because there is no way to respond to them and be heard.* Many of us are unwilling to give our full attention to a constant barrage of one-way communication, so we learn to listen with only "half-an-ear."

Listening with only half-an-ear to used-car commercials has undoubtedly had a certain survival value. Without such skill we might all have been driven mad long ago. The habit of tuning out singing commercials makes driving a car with the radio on supportable. Unfortunately, the same habit—tuning out incoming messages—carries over into *conversation, which is a two-way form of communication,* in that appropriate responses, or feedback, are indispensable to the process. Whatever name it goes by, not paying full attention, listening with half-an-ear, or tuning out messages, this habit can wreck communication, and ruin a conversation.

Keltner has estimated that speaking and listening activities account for 74 percent of the time people spend interacting with one another.[6] Given all the time that is spent in "rapping," one might think good communication is frequent. In far too many everyday conversations, messages are short circuited, meanings are distorted, feelings are hurt, and communication is poor or nonexistent. If the basic purpose of communication is to transfer information and understanding *from* one or more people *to* one or more people, and to have the message go from sender to receiver with as little distortion as possible, what causes all the distortion that we experience when we communicate with each other?

One way to find out what takes place during any changing process is to construct a model of the process. A model is a visual representation that names, describes, and classifies the separate parts of the process. It also shows how the separate parts connect, interact, and influence one another. Figure 2–1 shows a simple model of the communication process. In it a speaker (sender) transmits a message to a listener (receiver), who sends back another message.

This simple model omits so many parts of the communication process it could be applied just as logically to a temperature control system. Figure 2–2, although still quite simple, shows a more sophisticated model of human communication. In Figure 2–2 the clarity of the transmission is shown as a function of the listener's attitudes, emotions, role relationships with the speaker's words, and nonverbal behavior. Similarly, the clarity

Figure 2–1. Simple communication.

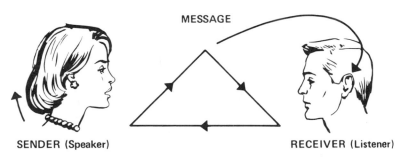

Figure 2–2. Complex communication.

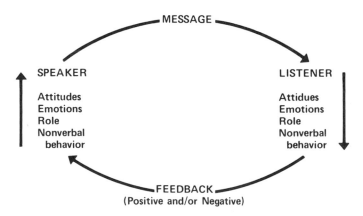

or the reception is shown as a function of the listener's attitudes, emotions, role relationships with the speaker, and nonverbal behavior. Additionally, the listener is shown as responding to the message by means of either positive or negative feedback, or by a combination of both.

Feedback

Feedback connects, influences, and interacts with all of the other parts of the communication process. Originally the term *feedback* was used by engineers to refer to the transfer of electronic energy from the output to the input of the same electrical circuit. In computer technology, the term is used to describe a computer's coded responses or answers to messages. These responses are usually very simple. "Correct," "incorrect," and "not enough data" are the most common. In this manner the computer "tells" the source of the message whether the message has been received accurately or not. In similar fashion, people tell one another whether their messages are being correctly received or not.

Feedback is verbal and visual
In face-to-face communication, both the listener and the speaker continuously give feedback to each other in a variety of ways: nonverbally, by nodding agreement or disagreement, frowning or smiling, yawning or engaging or avoiding eye contact; verbally, by the relevance of their questions, and responses in relation to what is being talked about.

Those responses likely to be perceived as rewarding (smiles or nods of agreement) are called positive feedback. Those perceived as punishing (yawns, signs of inattention) are called negative feedback. Feedback enables us to recognize misunderstandings while they are happening so that the messages can be modified and redefined until the confusions are cleared away.

Feedback in its broadest usage includes *all* the verbal and nonverbal responses to a message that are perceived by the sender of that message. In its narrow usage, feedback means only those specific responses that correct misunderstandings. The following conversation illustrates corrective feedback rather neatly:[7]

> Transmitter: Feedback is a process of correcting miscommunication.
>
> Receiver: Are you saying that feedback is simply a process of correcting errors?
>
> Transmitter: No, that is not what I mean entirely, although that is a part of it. I mean that it is a way of being sure that what one person says

to another person is adequately perceived by the other.

Receiver: Now you are more complicated than before. How do you know what "adequately perceived" means?

Transmitter: Well, to me, "adequately perceived" means that you get the idea as I want you to get it.

Receiver: Oh, then you mean that feedback is a way of checking as to whether or not I got the idea as *you* wanted *me* to get it.

Transmitter: Precisely.

Receiver: Have I used feedback effectively?

Transmitter: What do you think?

In effective communication, feedback can be both positive and negative, but for complete effectiveness it should be interpreted *during* the time of the exchange. If two days *after* a conversation has taken place, someone strikes his forehead and says, "Oh *that's* what she meant!" the chances are good that the feedback process was not operating well that day. If the speaker asks the listener to repeat the message so that the speaker can correct any misinterpretation, and the listener can reproduce the message accurately, without any need for further correction, then feedback is being used properly and communication is good.

Listening

Henry Thoreau once wrote, "It takes two to speak the truth— one to speak and another to hear." Sometimes people think they are communicating when all they are really doing is talking a lot and taking some time to get the feedback on what they have said. This has been called the "echo-chamber approach to communication."[8] Feedback is important, but there is much more to listening than just feedback.

The "echo-chamber" is not worthwhile feedback

Many people fail to realize that listening is an active, not a passive activity. Listening can be described as a combination of (1) *hearing*—the physical reception of sound; (2) *comprehending*— the interpretation and understanding of the message; and (3) *remembering*—the ability to retain what has been heard.

How many times have you had a conversation with someone and not heard a word that was said? Have you ever wanted to shake anyone and force him or her into "paying attention" to you while you were speaking? Most people have these experiences from time to time. Listening is a form of *paying attention*, which is an active process involving much more than hearing and seeing. When we pay attention to each other, we are *focus-*

Good listening is paying attention to what is said

ing our awareness on what is being said and excluding other external and internal stimuli. This is not always easy, since our senses are constantly scanning the environment for incoming stimuli, much like switched-on radar screens, and our minds are often preoccupied with our own thoughts.

The deluge of daily words dulls the brain

All day long, words hit us from all sides. Hundreds of advertisements bombard us with suggestions. Words, a deluge of daily words, crash over us in waves. Even when we stroll down the street, minding our own business, our poor brains jerk under the impact of instructions (Walk—Don't Walk); threats (Trespassers Will Be Prosecuted); and cries from the newsstands ("32 Killed in Plane Crash"). Our mind goes numb and we stop listening. A national proclamation may have little more effect than the notice on a book of matches: PLEASE CLOSE COVER BEFORE STRIKING. All day long, we are really practicing how *not* to listen.

An example of nonlistening

An example of nonlistening is shown in the "Unheard Conversation" by a mother and her son:

"Hi Mom. At school we saw this really tough movie."

"Oh, that's terrible. Would you please put the clothes in the dryer?"

"And we've got this new girl at school and she's really cute!"

"Oh, you ought to invite him over sometime."

"Mom, I'm hungry."

"I'm glad you offered to mow the lawn."

"Is there something I can eat?"

"Yes, I really think you should make your bed."

"Mom, you're not listening."

"Oh, that's nice."

"I think I'll go eat the grass."

"That's a good idea."

Preconceived notions

Other reasons why some people are poor listeners are easily identified. Some people have *preconceived* notions about what will and won't interest them, and they are so self-centered they can't believe that anyone would have anything of interest to say to them—so they don't even try to listen. Some people are so insecure they are afraid that if they listen long enough, eventually they will be bound to hear unpleasant remarks about themselves—so they don't listen. Some other people are just too busy. They know that successful listening requires a lot of time and energy, and they think the return will not justify their investment—so they don't listen either.

When people find themselves in a conversation, unable to attend to what is being said, it is a good idea if they try to understand why. Pinpointing why they can't listen is often the first step toward being able to listen more attentively.

© 1973 United Feature Syndicate, Inc.

There are no specific rules for effective listening, because what might work well for one person might not for another. There are, however, some general guidelines that will help you to construct your own rules for more successful listening.

GOOD LISTENING HABITS

1. LISTEN WITHOUT EVALUATING.   Listen as well as you can without passing judgment. A listener who is not critical, evaluative, or moralizing creates an atmosphere of understanding, acceptance, and warmth.

2. DON'T ANTICIPATE.   Sometimes we think we know what people are going to say before they say it—and we say it for them. Often we are wrong. Don't jump the gun by anticipating the next moment; stay in the present and listen.

3. DON'T TRY TO "GET" EVERYTHING.   Listen for the major points being made. Don't try to memorize details as you listen.

4. DON'T FAKE ATTENTION. The same time and energy that are used to fake attention can be put to good use by *really* paying attention. Actually, it takes less energy than faking does. Acting is hard work.

5. REVIEW.   Periodically review the portion of the talk given so far.

PERCEPTIONS

Remember the story of the three Englishmen at the beginning of this chapter? Too often, too many of us hear only what we want to hear. When we are unable to focus our attention, it may be that some hidden motive is working at cross-purposes and preventing us from hearing what is actually being said. If we are expecting someone to be angry with us, we will probably interpret whatever is said to us as angry talk. We should constantly check and recheck our expectations against the reality of our experiences. Feedback is the most effective tool to use for "reality checking."

Feedback is reality checking

Four stages of listening

Fred Carvel has classified listening behavior into four stages.[9] In the first stage all the listener does is to distinguish the sender's words and pays no attention to meaning. When we read and listen to the radio at the same time, we are listening in this manner. In the second stage the listener pays undivided attention to the sender. This is when understanding begins. This is also when misunderstandings begin. Carvel calls the third stage *evaluative* because this is when factors such as taste, experience, prior knowledge, and intelligence come into play. The fourth stage is called the "highest" because it requires the most in listening skill and concentration. The dimension of *empathy* has been added. *At this stage the listener understands what is being said from the speaker's own point of view.* This is the rarest kind of listening and the one most conducive to stimulating effective communication.

Some of you may feel that you listen very well and that none of the foregoing applies to you. Test yourself. The next time you get into an argument with someone, stop the argument for a minute and try Carl Rogers' famous communication game.[10] The only rule in this game is that each person can speak up only after *restating* the ideas and feelings the other person has expressed during the argument, to the other person's satisfaction. In other words, you have to present the other person's point of view in terms that will be acceptable to him or her.

Carl Rogers' communication game

Sounds easy? Try it. It's very difficult indeed.

Once you can state the other person's point of view satisfactorily, you may find that you have to revise your own responses drastically. And the emotional intensities of the argument will decrease quite a bit. It takes courage to play this game because you run the risk of having to change your mind, and for most of us that can be, although it shouldn't be, a humiliating experience. When you can play this game successfully, you are really communicating. You may not reach an agreement — communication does not always bring agreement in its wake — but you are communicating, fully and effectively.

Here are two topics that might develop some strong contrasting feelings between people. Pair off with another student and take opposite views on the topic. Argue for five minutes for your special viewpoint, then engage in the Carl Rogers' *Repeat My View* game. See if you don't develop a new appreciation or understanding for the other person's point of view.

A game of understanding

1. Thousands, perhaps even millions, of illegal aliens are in the United States and many are working in our industries. They are depriving our citizens of potential employment;

they are not paying taxes and are receiving welfare. Many businesses feel that they must compete with the open market place. If they can pay the illegal alien less than the prevailing wage rate, they can in turn sell the product cheaper to the public. The public benefits. It is cheaper than sending the work to a foreign country to produce and shipping it back. Are you for or against illegal aliens in the United States?

Should we keep illegal aliens?

2. Is nudity pornographic? Do you consider a nude model in an advertisement to be in bad taste? A well-known cosmetic company is trying to sell a beauty-skin product. The ad tells women to compare facial skin to breast skin. Further it explains that women should use their skin product. The ad claims to use the "adult approach" and it is above sexiness. Here we have a beauty product company employing nudity in their campaign. Is it pornographic? Should it be used in family magazines? Where do you stand?

Is nudity pornographic?

Attitudes

SENSITIVITY TO OTHERS

Sensitivity to others has been defined as the one absolute requirement for good speech communication.[11] Such sensitivity begins with the *desire* to communicate, which involves the desire to perceive other people's meanings as well as the desire to express one's own. Sensitive people are willing to make the necessary effort to try to understand other frames of reference and other sets of values. Sensitivity to others also requires the ability to recognize and identify one's own responses and perceptions as well as those of others. It is impossible to be sensitive to other people, if you are not sensitive to yourself.

SELF-DISCLOSURE

When people communicate with each other, especially face-to-face, their physical and emotional states of being are to some degree exposed. This exposure is sometimes disturbing, because our culture places a high value on self-concealment. In a competitive society, concealment is frequently more useful than self-exposure or self-revelation. Communication scholars believe that if we revealed more of ourselves to each other, we would *understand* each other better.[12]

When people wish to reveal themselves to each other, they talk about *personal* matters such as loves and hates, beliefs and fears, worries and anxieties, perceptions about work, about themselves, and about each other. Can satisfying communication take place if at least a few of these subjects are not discussed? Of course the atmosphere for self-disclosure must be one of mutual acceptance and good will or mutual self-defense systems will automatically switch our psychic "early warning systems" on to "red alert," thereby "defensive barriers" will be raised, and communication will be short circuited.

Emotions

DESIRE

Perhaps the most important emotional factor in good communication is desire. If the desire to understand oneself and others is strong, then understanding usually results. However, one of the largest drawbacks to effective communication is that, as humans, we do not separate ourselves from our emotions. In fact we identify with them. We *become* our emotions. We say, "*I* am angry" or "*I* am sad." The intensities of our feelings color everything we think and talk about. When we talk about a problem we cannot help seeing it in terms of our own past experience and in terms of how we feel at that very moment. Naturally, this can make it more difficult to see the other person's point of view—especially if he or she is also in the throes of some strong emotion.

Our emotions color our communication

Emotions can make it hard to listen accurately

MIRRORING

When two or more people are talking together, each person's emotions influences the other's, and these in turn affect communication. If we parade our tastes, biases, and prejudices as proof of our moral superiority, such behavior is often felt as threatening and serves to distort understanding and cut off communication. A threatening sender automatically puts the receiver on the defensive. When defenses are raised, arguments or silence follow. In either case, good communication ceases.

If we believe that our messages are being received with warmth, respect, and concern, we tend to become more relaxed and more articulate. If our messages are received with signs of coldness, disrespect, and indifference, we tend to tense up, and it becomes more difficult to express our thoughts. Face-to-face communicators tend to *mirror* each other's moods.

VOICE TONE

Often the tone of our voices will indicate our emotional states to others even if we are not aware of them ourselves. To those who know how to listen to them, voice tones can transmit as much or more emotional information as words do. Loudly pitched

Figure 2–3. If we believe that our messages are being received with warmth, respect, and concern, we tend to become more relaxed and more articulate.
Courtesy of Chino Valley Bank (Photo by Robert Curtis)

voices can communicate anger no matter how emotionally neutral the dictionary meanings of the shouted words might be. Anger also can be conveyed by very intense whispering. The same emotion can be expressed in different tones of voice at different times, and people differ in their reactions to tones of voice. It should be noted that in some subcultures loud voices often indicate good fellowship and cheerfulness.

Roles

According to John Keltner, any effective speech communication must be consistent with "the image, conditions, the role expectations, the requirements of the particular setting and of the particular circumstances under which it is taking place."[13] If all of these elements are ignored, the chance of successful communication is very slight.

ROLE BEHAVIOR

Each of us plays many different roles in our daily lives. The role one plays at work or school is different from the role played within the family or with friends. Because role behavior structures our social interactions, it helps to make life more predictable. Without established role behaviors, we would never know what kinds of responses to expect from other people and we would be unable to test our own perceptions about our own behavior.

The same role cannot be used for all situations because different people perceive us in different ways. If we are to communicate, we must make room in our own minds for their perceptions of us. Effective communication depends in large measure upon our ability to "see ourselves as others see us."

ROLE EXPECTATIONS

In all formal groups or organizations, roles are ranked according to status. Some roles are assigned more power than others and the people playing these roles learn to expect certain messages of esteem and prestige to be communicated to them. However, too often people accept role expectations as substitutes for communication.

Policeman's uniform creates a role expectation

A policemen's uniform, for example, creates certain role expectations which can cut off spoken communication. In an experiment conducted by the officers of a police department, the regular uniform of the cop on the beat was exchanged for civilian dress. The officers carried their guns in their pockets instead of displaying them, and they did not carry night sticks. An impartial observer reported that:

> Stripped of their usual sources of authority the police department had to find its support in the community. They developed new styles of communications and new patterns of relating to the community both on and off the job.[14]

The uniform and the role expectations attached to it controlled all the interpersonal patterns and structured almost everyone's perceptions, attitudes, and emotions. Communication became much more open and flexible when the uniform was not worn.

Nonverbal Behavior

BODY LANGUAGE

Body Language or its more scientific name, Kinasic, is using your eyes to understand how a person feels without using verbal communication. Any nonflexive or reflexive movement of the body can communicate something to the outside world, and often more honestly than verbal communication can.

Body language can convey the opposite of our words

In face-to-face communication our nonverbal, physical behavior transmits as much information as our verbal messages do. Nonverbal behavior can take many forms and guises, from how many minutes late someone arrives for an appointment to how far apart people stand from each other when conversing. Nonverbal behavior includes unintentional as well as in-

Nonverbal cues are more honest than verbal cues

tentional messages. It can convey messages that are the exact opposite of the meaning intended by the words being spoken. Unlike verbal behavior, nonverbal behavior seldom lies. To put it another way, it is much harder to tell a successful lie using body language than it is using words. One study reports that when the message transmitted by nonverbal behavior contradicts the verbal message, the nonverbal message will receive greater attention.[15]

According to Randall Harrison, "in face-to-face communi-

Figure 2–4. Body language
Source: By Julius Fast M. Evans and Company, Inc., New York 1970

cation no more than 35 percent of the social meaning is carried in the verbal message."[16] Our eyes, and hands, and bodies send and receive communication signals constantly. Some thirty-three separate major head and facial movements that communicate specific messages have been isolated.[17] When engaged in non-flirtatious conversation, nearly all men and women and boys and girls tend to imitate the sitting and standing postures of someone they admire. People may cross their arms and legs and orient their bodies in specific "withdrawal" postures to shut out people who are perceived as threatening. And most people regardless of sex or age will touch each other when they are deeply moved by strong emotions. An example, cited by Julius Fast, author of *Body Language,* is one in which a family is all seated and the mother crosses her legs with the family unknowingly following suit. She is actually the family leader even though she and the family may not admit it. Mr. Fast brings up the idea of space as a form of communication. There are two types, social and public. In the social phase the contact between a housewife and a repairman or the distance in a normal business transaction would be four to six feet. This distance is used for casual social gatherings, but it can be used as a manipulative tool, by a salesman. As the salesman steps closer to the client, he invades his inner circle, making the customer feel uncomfortable. The salesman psychologically pressures the client into a sale. The social space of six to twelve feet is used for more formal business relations. It is the distance between the "big boss" and you—a way of showing his authority. This distance also allows other activity with another around without being rude. Public space of twelve to twenty-five feet, as in a teaching situation, allows many to focus their attention on one or more persons.

Eye Contact

Everyone knows that a few seconds of eye contact can transmit meanings that might require hundreds of words if spoken. Idioms such as "to make eyes at," "to keep an eye on," or "if looks could kill," reflect the importance of eye contact in many kinds of communication. Someone who sits at a crowded luncheon counter looking straight ahead, or an airplane passenger who sits with tightly closed eyes, are both communicating that they do not want to speak or be spoken to. And their message is usually interpreted correctly without any need for words. In our culture, women are said to use fewer hand gestures than men do, but engage in more direct eye contact.[18] But both men and women will refuse to meet the eye of someone glaring at them angrily.

Touching

Certain kinds of nonverbal behavior seem related to sex differences, although no one has yet shown whether these differences are innate or conditioned. For example, the function of touching in the communication process has just begun to be explored by serious researchers. In our culture, we are taught very early to avoid touching each other except under strictly defined circumstances. The nontouching rules are stricter for boys than for girls, except for handshakes and the backslapping of the athletic field. But even for girls, relative to other parts of the world, touching has many taboo connotations. However, in recent years, the nontouching taboo has lost much of its strength. Encounter groups and sensitivity-training classes in schools and industries have emphasized touching as a way of breaking down communication barriers.

Touching rules are more strict for boys than for girls

When we allow ourselves to touch and be touched, we become more open and vulnerable to each other. This openness, in turn, creates a sense of greater receptivity, and, consequently, a greater willingness to listen attentively and to try to understand the other person's point of view.

There is an interesting relation between the words "touch" and "tact." The word tact derives from the Latin word for touch. The psychological relationship between the two terms has not been altogether lost, for even today we say of a tactless person that he or she has a "heavy touch." We do not *trust* tactless people because they are likely to wound or betray us. We do trust those whom we allow to touch us and those whom we feel it is safe to touch. Trust, or the lack of it, often determines the kind of feedback that is generated during a conversation.

We trust those more whom we allow to touch us

Sixth Sense

Much has been said in recent years about E.S.P. or extra sensory perception as a method of communication. Interestingly, it is perceived by most businessmen as a manner in which information can be received rather than transmitted. A chief executive of an oil drilling company felt the bid he submitted on an offshore proposal was high, so he changed it at the last minute to $72.3 million. He won the bid by a scant $200,000. Even with the availability of a super computer analysis system executives admit that they make decisions on pure hunch. Is it open rebellion of the report, the ability to read symbolic or nonverbal communication, or a sixth sense? In a study done with businessmen about 80% surveyed believed in some form of E.S.P. Further, the study showed that a dynamic attitude is important and people who have a dynamic attitude generally possess a higher level of E.S.P. A test was conducted to see how many

Is intuition a sixth sense or E.S.P.?

could predict a random selection of digits from 100 digits. The executive who had doubled profits in the past five years scored an average of 12.8, the total group averaged 10.17, and those who did not earn a profit scored 8.3. Does precognition deserve a "place" in a testing battery for hiring recruits in the management program? *Should employees be tested for E.S.P.?*

MEDIUM OF COMMUNICATIONS

In business there are so many ways to communicate with employees or clients. The impact of the communication often depends on the media selected. Marshall McLuhan states a very startling point in a title of one of his books, *The Medium is the Message,* meaning the emotional effect of the medium may carry the message better than the words. In some cases the medium influences the receiver in a different way from that intended. The propagandist has discovered how media influences the public. The counterculturists have discovered the impact individual words have through screaming. The catch phrases then act like Pavlov's bells in order to produce saliva. The movement propagandist rings his chimes (Fascist! Pig! Honky! Male chauvinist!) to produce emotional reactions rather than positive actions. The use of stammer rather than grammar can put inarticulate phrases to fantastic advantage.

Written Word

What Have You Learned About Reading and Actions Taken by People?

SPOT THE "F's"

Read this sentence aloud and see how good you are at counting the number of F's in the sentence.

"Fouled up files are the result of years of foolish secretaries and office personnel combined with years of scientific nonsense."

Did you count nine "f's? Try again if you didn't find all nine. Why did you miss a few of them?

In the sample above it is easy to overlook the F's in the words "of". An unimportant detail, you may say, however it is easy to overlook significant details just as easily in written documents. In human relations problems you can't afford to overlook 33 percent of the relevant details.

The most durable of all media of communication is the written word. Perhaps when facts need to be presented nothing surpasses the written word, for it provides an historical document for future reference. A few factors used to determine the readability of material are based on studies by Dr. Rudolf Flesch in his book *The Art of Plain Talk,* and Robert Gunning in his book *The Techniques of Clear Writing.* The more words in a sentence, the more difficult it is to read and to understand. The more personal references in a passage the easier it is to read. Considering these studies The Prudential Insurance Company developed guideposts for more effective writing. Shorter sentences do not mean duller or degrading sentences, but sentences that are more easily understood by more people.

The average sentence should be 17 words long

The three averages are applied to a scale which gives the reading-ease score. For example, an average sentence length of 17 words, with about 150 syllables for each 100 words, and 6 personal references per 100 words would be considered average. How would you classify this textbook? Take any page at random and add the number of words on a page and divide it by the number of sentences to arrive at the average sentence length. The second step is to count 100 words and then count the number of syllables in those 100 words. Then divide the number of syllables by the number of words. The standard category should be satisfactorily read and understood by at least 83 percent of the adults in the United States. Research shows that a great deal of company literature is more difficult than the standard readability level. Can you determine why?

Visual Symbols

Besides the written word, we communicate in other graphic ways—and more universally. The world speaks a babel of a thou-

Table 2–1. Guidepost for Effective Writing[19]

READING LEVEL	FAIRLY EASY	STANDARD	FAIRLY DIFFICULT	DIFFICULT
Average Sentence length in words	14	17	21	25
Syllables per 100 words	142	150	158	166
Personal references per 100 words (I, you, us)	10	6	4	3
Typical Publications	Newspaper	Magazine	Literary	Scholarly

sand tongues, but wouldn't it be nice to travel anywhere in the world and be able to find the restroom or the ticket agent in any airport? Or wouldn't it be nice for a three-year old in Gambia and a three-year old in Santa Barbara to visually see "Danger—Don't touch!" instantly? Some signs are to us "instant communications." The biological symbol for man and woman are known in many countries. The symbol of a man is a circle with an arrow going up, easy to remember if you think of Mars, as a shield and a spear. The symbol of a woman, the circle with a cross going down, is Venus or a woman with a hand mirror. However a figure in a skirt and a figure in pants are usually used on restrooms. Henry Dreyfuss is working on pictographs for a dictionary that can be used the world over for international understanding. How would a pictograph of a man in trousers and a woman in skirt go over in India, where men often wear skirts and women trousers?

Traffic symbols are more or less standard in Europe,

Figure 2–5. International symbols help people communicate. The United States are now using symbols the rest of the world has been using for decades.

INFORMATION   HOTEL INFORMATION   NO SMOKING

RAIL TRANSPORTATION   COFFEE SHOP   TOILETS

thanks to an intercountry agreement that makes it possible for a stranger to drive from Italy to Denmark with nothing more than a smile and a map. But there are still some problems worldwide. A triangle—which means "caution" in France, means "stop" in England, "yield" and "helicopter landing" in America, and "birth control" in India. A Japanese plane may fly through nine language barriers. If they tried to say "fasten your seat belt" or "no smoking" in all those languages, the plane would be one big classified ad section.

We find that we react to symbols or pictures and draw certain inferences from them. The color red or black may derive positive or negative sensations to us. The use of such in a sign may invoke actions that were not intended by the signmaker.

LEVELS OF COMMUNICATION

There are four levels of communication (Figure 2–6). We communicate with strangers and casual acquaintances on the *conventional level*. Conversation on this level is fairly impersonal. It consists of conventional attempts to be polite or get acquainted to fill silences, or to seek or convey incidental information or relieve tensions. Remarks like: "Hi, there!" "Do you have the time?," "Good morning, Homer." show only that we acknowledge the presence of the other person. They may open the door to further communication, but they are not true attempts at communicating.

The first level is to get acquainted

On the second hand, *exploratory* level, communication is fact and problem-oriented. Here, too, conversation is usually

Figure 2–6. Levels of Communication.

Fourth Level
CONFRONTIVE

Third Level
PARTICIPATIVE

Second Level
EXPLORATORY

First Level
CONVENTIONAL

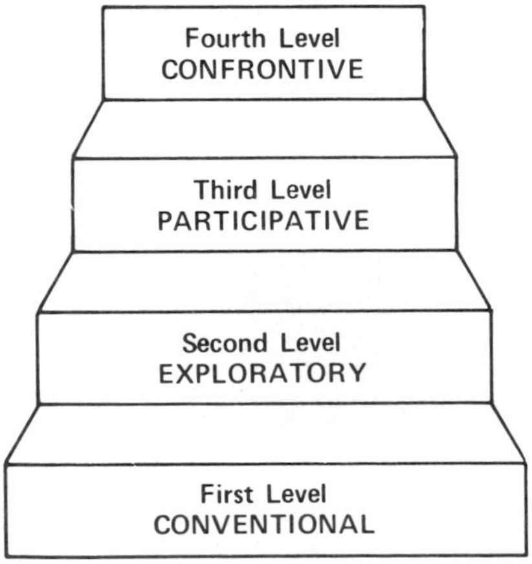

The second level is for lecture

impersonal. Things, people, theories, definitions, and incidents are discussed. Classroom lectures are usually conducted on this level. Often in personal transactions a relationship must be established on this level before the participants can move on to the third level.

The third level is for self-disclosure

The third level is *participative.* Here people talk about themselves and engage in self-disclosure. They express their own feelings, describe their own experiences, and discuss their own ideas. While these are *personal subjects,* they are expressed in fairly *safe ways:* "I feel happiest with people my own age." "I would say I am more conservative now than I was five years ago."

The fourth level is for intimate conversations

The fourth, *confrontive,* level we reserve for only a select few. Here again people reveal themselves, but now they expose themselves intimately to one another in ways that involve *risk.* "I get the feeling you don't really care about me." "I want you to know I've been on drugs." Intimate relationships are characterized by communication of this kind, which evolves from deeply felt mutual understanding. Fourth-level communication is rare except between close friends, lovers, and married couples.

SUMMARY

Communication is the process by which information and understanding are transferred from one person to another. Effective communication enables people to exercise control over their environment. It is an essential tool for the establishment and maintenance of good social and working relationships. If the messages being communicated are not understood, then communication is poor or nonexistent. Effective communication is a dynamic process that involves constant change and interaction between all the elements that comprise it.

The meaning, or semantic content, of a message is always subjective, because meanings reside in people, not in words. A word's meaning is the significance that that word has for both speaker and listener, and that significance is likely to vary greatly from person to person. Good communication requires paying as much attention to the person speaking as to the verbal message itself, because so many words have such ambiguous meanings.

In cultures without writing, verbal messages are transmitted more accurately than in highly literate ones, perhaps because of the constant barrage of one-way messages typical of highly developed nations. Tuning out radio commercials and billboard signs may have detrimental effects on listening and communication skills.

Listening is an active, not a passive, activity. Effective

listening depends on paying attention and focusing. Although there are no specific rules everyone must follow to become a good listener, there are some general guidelines for acquiring good listening habits.

The communication process can be described in terms of a model in which attitudes, emotions, roles, nonverbal behaviors, and feedback are constantly interacting.

There are four levels of communication that depend on the degree of intimacy existing between speaker and listener. They are: conventional, exploratory, participative, and confrontive.

TALKING OVER THEIR HEADS
Case Study #1

Ray Duncan is the Program Director of the Riverbend Summer Camp for Boys. The camp works in conjunction with juvenile homes in the neighboring counties, and is in operation for ten weeks each summer. Counselors who work at the camp are concerned citizens from the local area and all work with the boys on a volunteer basis.

Bob Moreau is a concerned volunteer. He works in the arts and crafts room with the boys on a rotating schedule, and has been doing so since the camp opened for its summer session three weeks ago. Unfortunately though Bob and the boys are having trouble communicating.

Ray Duncan is aware of these difficulties. On more than one occasion he has overheard conversations among the boys concerning Bob. A comment in particular that he remembers hearing went like this: "He always knows the best way to do something, regardless of what anyone else thinks. He wasn't even listening to my idea. And how about all the Greek he throws at you? Half the guys sit there and act like they understand him. Who are they kidding?"

As a result of these comments, Ray sat in on one of Bob's sessions. He soon realized that there was indeed a problem. As he observed Bob instruct a group on woodcarving techniques, he noticed that Bob would tend to be a little impatient with the questions he felt were not reasonable. In addition, the way Bob carried himself seemed to portray a rather stern and withdrawn character. The boys probably felt this. Furthermore, Bob's use of vocabulary was at times far beyond the boys understanding. Putting himself in the boys position Ray could understand some of the hostility they felt towards Bob.

Ray quite naturally feels that it is necessary to talk to Bob about this problem. The main purpose of the camp is to provide a pleasant and friendly atmosphere for the boys. Although Bob feels friendly toward the boys and is very interested in working with them, there are definitely problems that must be cleared up.

If you were Ray how would you handle this problem? How would you communicate this problem to Bob?

1. What is the general problem that Bob has in communicating with the boys?
2. What steps can Bob make to improve his method of communicating?
3. How would you approach Bob?
4. Should this problem be discussed personally with Bob or as a general topic to bring up during a staff meeting with the counselors?

VISUAL COMMUNICATIONS SPEAK LOUDLY IN THE ESCROW OFFICE

Case Study #2

An escrow department of a large national bank firm recently hired a new employee. Monica Chatman is twenty-five years old, single, and prior to being hired as an escrow officer worked as a teller and later as a secretary of an escrow office in another firm. Before leaving her former location Monica was given some training in escrow procedures. Monica is an attractive looking woman and this highlighted by her stylish, yet conservative method of dress, as seen in her preference for sharp coordinated pantsuits and dress suits.

Although Monica has had previous on-the-job training in escrow, she has not yet reached complete proficiency. In some areas she is still in need of further training and advice. The person closest to Monica, both in physical distance and job responsibilities is John Baxter,—the only other escrow officer. When Monica was hired she was informed by the department supervisor that John would be the person to go to for help and advice, primarily because both she and John would be working on the same tract of homes for some time.

Being a rather shy person Monica has not made a habit of asking John for his help. She has tended to keep to herself for the most part and John has not gone out of his way to help break the ice between them. At any rate, Monica doesn't really know if John is capable of giving her any worthy advice, let alone taking the time to help her. From all appearances she feels John is a pretty sloppy individual both in appearance and in his work. He seems to have trouble handling his own duties. It looks as if he is always a week behind in his work. His desk is constantly a mess. Besides, John's clothes look almost as if he has slept in them. To Monica it seems that John has enough trouble taking care of himself—let alone helping train someone else.

In spite of his overly casual appearance and method of handling his work, John is competent and qualified in the escrow business. When Monica began working in the department a few weeks back John had planned on giving her any assistance she would need in handling her new position. However, John soon began to feel that Monica really didn't want his help. Although seemingly shy, John believes that Monica is more stuck up and cold than anything else. This he finds a little hard to swallow, especially considering the fact that Monica is not only the new person in the bank, but also a woman. To friends, John will readily admit that he is a little chauvinistic when it comes to women, and he has admitted to a close friend in the bank that he is somewhat jealous of Monica's promotions all the way from teller to escrow officer by the age of twenty-five. He also finds it irritating that Monica manages to type so quickly and has her desk clean at the end of each day. It is also John's opinion that Monica looks down upon his appearance. As a family man he cannot afford the quality of clothes that Monica, as a single woman, wears each day. As far as John is concerned at the present time if Monica wishes any help from him, she will have to come and ask for it.

As the supervisor of the escrow department you have become aware of the problem existing between Monica and John. They should be working together and yet they are not.

1. Given the information supplied, what would you identify as the main problem?

2. What steps would you take to improve the situation?

3. By the above description of Monica, what other assumptions might you decide about her personality? Could these assumptions lead to faulty conclusions?

4. By the above descriptions of John, what other assumptions might you decide about his personality? Could these assumptions lead to faulty generalizations?

5. How can you, as the supervisor, help both Monica and John overcome their misconceptions of each other?

Terms and Concepts Students Should Know

the meaning of meaning	self-disclosure	sixth sense
"overload" circuits	"mirroring"	guidepost for writing
perceptions	role expectation	levels of communications
feedback	body language	

Bibliography

1. ADLER, RON and TOWNE, NEIL *Looking Out, Looking In,* Rinehart Press, Corte Madera, CA, 1975.

2. BERLO, DAVID *The Process of Communication,* Holt, Rinehart and Winston, New York, N.Y., 1960.

3. CARVEL, FRED *Human Relations in Business,* Toronto: The Macmillan Co., 1970.

4. FAST, JULIUS *Body Language,* M. Evans and Company, Inc., New York, 1970.

5. FLESCH, RUDOLF *The Art of Plain Talk,* New York, Harper & Row, Publisher, 1946 and *The Art of Readable Writing,* New York, Harper & Row, Publisher, 1949.

6. GUNNING, ROBERT *The Technique of Clear Writing,* New York, McGraw-Hill Book Company, 1952. (Developed the "Fog Index").

7. JOHNSON, BONNIE MCDANIEL, *Communication: the Process of Organizing,* Boston, Allyn and Bacon, Inc., 1977.

8. ROSENFELD, LAWRENCE and CIVIKLY, JEAN *With Words Unspoken, the Nonverbal Experience,* Holt, Rinehart and Winston, New York, 1976.

Footnotes

[1] David Berlo, *The Process of Communication,* (New York: Holt, Rinehart and Winston, 1960) p. 1.

[2] Julius Laffal, *Pathological and Normal Language* (New York: Atherton Press, Inc., 1965), p. 272.

[3] Fred J. Carvel, *Human Relations in Business* (Toronto: The Macmillan Co., 1970), p. 290.

[4] John W. Keltner, *Interpersonal Speech Communication* (Belmont, Calif.: Wadsworth Publishing Co., 1970), p. 172.

[5] David Riesman, "The Oral and Written Traditions," in *Explorations in Communication*, edited by Edmund Carpenter and Marshall McLuhan, (Boston: Beacon Press, 1960), p. 111.

[6] Keltner, *Interpersonal Speech Communication*, p. 12.

[7] Keltner, *Interpersonal Speech Communication*, p. 92.

[8] William F. Dowling, Jr., and Leonard Sayles, *How Managers Motivate: The Imperatives of Supervision* (New York: McGraw-Hill Book Co., 1971), p. 223.

[9] Carvel, *Human Relations in Business*, p. 291.

[10] Carl Rogers, and F. J. Roethlisberger, "Barriers and Gateways to Communication," *Harvard Business Review* 30, no. 4 (July–August 1952), p. 48.

[11] Keltner, *op. cit.*, p. 17.

[12] *Ibid.*, pp. 53–59.

[13] *Ibid.*, p. 59.

[14] Michael Burgoon, *Approaching Speech Communication* (New York: Holt, Rinehart and Winston, 1974), p. 189.

[15] Albert Mehrabian, "Orientation Behaviors and Nonverbal Communication," *Journal of Communication* 17 (December 1967): 331.

[16] Randall Harrison, "Nonverbal Communication: Exploration into Time, Space, Action, and Object," in *Dimensions in Communications*, edited by J. H. Campbell and H. W. Hepler, (Belmont, Calif.: Wadsworth Publishing Co., 1965,) p. 161.

[17] Burgoon, *Approaching Speech Communication*, p. 128.

[18] *Ibid.*, p. 126.

[19] Rudolf Flesch, *The Art of Plain Talk*, (New York: Harper & Row, Publisher, 1946,) and *The Art of Readable Writing*, (New York: Harper & Row, Publisher, 1949.) See also Robert Gunning *The Technique of Clear Writing* (New York: McGraw-Hill Book Company, 1952), (more often known as the "Fog Index" made popular by Robert Gunning).

Communication in Organizations

"What Did They Say?"

■ ■

OBJECTIVES

When you finish this chapter you should be able to:

1. Show how communication is the foundation of modern work organizations.
2. Describe the kind of information that vertical communication usually conveys, both upward and downward.
3. Describe the basic elements involved in improving upward and downward communications.
4. Outline at least five company benefits of good upward communication.
5. Explain the importance of good horizontal communication in coordinated group effort and how it can be improved.
6. Define the difference between formal and informal communication channels in business.
7. Argue for the importance of the "grapevine" in business organizations and describe:
   A. The people who use it,
   B. Its accuracy,
   C. Its uses.
8. State the difference between staff and line personnel in the traditional division of labor.
9. Understand the behavior of committees and how the make-up of the committee affects the communication of its members.

Here are some more questions to challenge your reading and to stimulate your thinking. Not all of the answers to these questions will be found in the chapter. Some can only be answered from your own perspective.

How do formal communications differ from informal ones?

Have you ever wondered why it is easier to accept a "no" from one person than another?

Are the contents of vertical messages likely to be the same if they are moving up or down?

Why do some supervisors distort messages?

How do they use the "positive sandwich" technique?

Have you ever wondered when employees are most truthful with one another?

Should companies try to "stamp out" the grapevine?

Can the grapevine have any useful purpose? Is it ever accurate? Does it serve any useful purpose?

What are staff and line functions, and why are they sometimes confused with each other?

COMMUNICATION
IN ORGANIZATIONS

In prehistoric times, because small groups of hunters were able to communicate and cooperate, they were able to trap and kill large animals for food, using only the simplest of tools. First they tracked the animals down. Then they dug large pits, which they camouflaged with slender branches, dirt, and leaves. Then, by shouting and throwing small objects at the animals, they were able to herd and drive some of them into the pit-traps, where the animals died of hunger or injuries. Judging from the numbers of animal bones found at some prehistoric sites, these early people were quite successful hunters. Their success resulted from their ability to communicate and cooperate. Today, although technology and science have changed the very face of the planet, the need for effective communication and cooperation is stronger than ever.

If a group is to cooperate to accomplish a common purpose, that purpose must be known to all group members, and to be known to all it must in some way be communicated. All cooperative activities take place within a framework of communication. Without effective communication there is no cooperation.

An organization comes into being when (1) there are individuals able to communicate with one another (2) who are willing to act (3) to accomplish a common purpose. These are the three basic elements necessary for any organization, and all are equally important for the effective functioning of the organization.

Good communications unify group behavior

In modern work organizations, communication is the foundation upon which all other functions rest. Communication serves not only to *transfer information and understanding among individuals and groups,* but it also *unifies group behavior.* Unified behavior provides the basis for *continuous* group cooperation. Therefore the efficient functioning and continuous existence of any organization depends on how well its communication channels operate.

Communication Channels

Formal communication is a part of all organizations

Communication channels are the paths along which messages travel either from one person to another, or from one group to another, or both. All organizations use both formal and informal channels of communication. Formal channels are the communication chains and networks that determine the direction and flow of official messages among all of the different members and

58

divisions of an organization. *Formal communication channels are an integral part of organizational structure.* They stem from the rules and customs that govern the distribution of authority, rank, and type of work within the organization.

Informal channels consist of the informal communication chains and networks created by friendships and social associations within the work environment. The channel known as the "grapevine" is perhaps the most important informal communication channel in any organization.

The grapevine is part of the informal channel of communication

Communication channels have been compared to the nervous systems of organisms because they perform the same function. Both carry messages, or impulses, from one place to another to keep the organism, or organization, informed about any changes taking place in the environment. "These impulses carry the signals from one portion of the complex system to another and to a central coordinating agency through which the entire system is kept in balance and functioning."[1] But transferring a message along an organization's communication channels is not always accomplished as efficiently as the transfer of impulses along a nervous system generally is. In organizational communication, contrary to face-to-face communication, comprehension is *not* the only test of a message's effectiveness. In an organization a message must pass *three* tests: (1) it must be *understood*; (2) it must be *believed*; (3) it must be *accepted*; (4) and action must take place.

Not all the messages that are transmitted in complex organizations pass these tests because, for one reason, some of the formal channels used to convey messages are essentially one-way forms of communication, and opportunities for feedback are minimal or nonexistent. In large organizations, a great deal of communication is transmitted in writing. Even when provisions are made for written feedback, which is often not the case, the feedback is necessarily not immediate. And in organizational communication, as in face-to-face conversation, *immediate* feedback is the best tool for achieving understanding, credibility, and acceptance.

Organization Charts

A chart or table showing an organization's structure is a kind of anatomical drawing indicating the formal, *official* channels messages must travel by, as shown in Figure 3–1. Flowing around the formal structure are complicated, everchanging networks of informal, *unofficial* channels. Informal channels are not shown on a table of organization because they are by nature *unstable*, whereas the structure of an organization is more often stable.

Organization charts show the formal channel of communication

An organization chart cannot indicate *all* the formal chan-

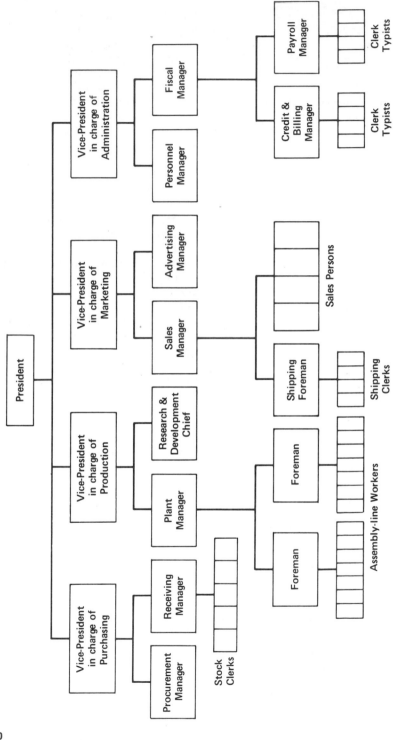

Figure 3–1. Organizational structure of an industrial plant.

nels, only the *major* ones. A chart that showed all the formal paths messages must travel would look more like a maze or a Chinese puzzle than a chart. For example, secretaries and receptionists are seldom shown on charts, but in large organizations most messages are routed through these individuals. The efficiency of a communication system often depends on how well or badly the secretaries of vice-presidents are relating to one another. Sometimes the ways in which secretaries transmit information formally can be very funny.

> When Queen Elizabeth visited America in 1957 the Mink Breeders Association sent her a mink coat—with very long sleeves. When the Queen first wore the coat, the sleeves almost covered her hands. The sleeves were meant to be turned back in cuffs, but nobody could get in touch with the Queen to tell her so. The news had to filter through press secretaries, undersecretaries and a lady-in-waiting before the Queen found out how her coat ought to look.[2]

FORMAL CHANNELS

Figure 3–1 is an organization chart illustrating the internal structure of a complex factory in terms of its work divisions and power hierarchies. It also illustrates the formal channels official messages must travel between and within the separate divisions. Official communications usually move along structural paths.

In complex organizations, there are usually several levels of management, but only one or two workers' levels. Management levels tend to increase in number and complexity, but worker levels tend to remain stationary. Communication problems are often intensified when businesses achieve success. The more managers there are, the longer the communication chain grows, and the possibilities for communication breakdowns become more numerous. Because of this problem, some companies have been trying to reduce the number of their intermediate management levels.[3]

The taller the organizational structure, the greater the chance of a message being filtered. The fewer levels of management, the better the chances are of accurate information being transmitted. This in turn usually means that each supervisor is responsible for more people. Considering the same number of persons in an organization the axiom seems to be: the taller the structure or the greater the number of levels of management, the poorer the communication, and the flatter the structure or the fewer the levels of management, the better the chances of good communication (see Figure 3–2).

The taller the organizational structure, the poorer the communications

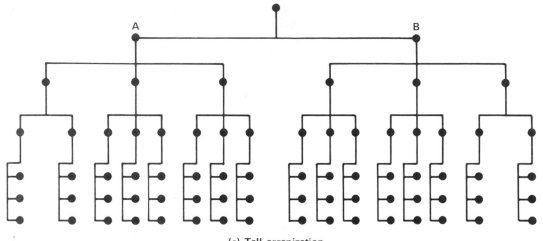

(*a*) **Tall organization**
(Maximum span of management: 3. Four levels of management)

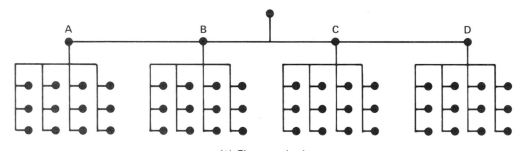

(*b*) **Flat organization**
(Maximum span of management: 12. Two levels of management)

Figure 3–2. Organizational differences caused by different spans of management for the same number of operative employees (forty-eight).

Although formal channels have many shortcomings, they *do* provide orderly, predictable routes for the necessary information to reach the right people in time for decisions to be made and actions taken. For example, sales orders sent to factories by traveling salespeople must be processed to make sure that the customers who placed the orders will receive them. Figure 3–1 illustrates some of the routes that such processing would probably have to travel: (1) The sales manager would have to be notified by the salesperson of the sale. (2) The sales manager would then have to inform the shipping foreman to have the goods packed and shipped. (3) The shipping foreman would have to send the necessary information to the credit and billing manager so the customer

could be billed. (4) Either the sales manager or the shipping foreman might have to notify the plant manager in the production department to replace the goods that were sold. (5) If sales are very
good, some shipping or stockroom clerks might have to work
overtime; and the payroll manager in the finance office will have
to be notified to readjust employees' paychecks for overtime pay.

In complex organizations, the flow of formal communications never stops. A remarkable variety of messages travels from
department to department, many of which are far more complex
than the processing of sales orders described above. Communications moving *between* divisions such as sales and production
are called *horizontal* because messages flow in a horizontal direction, as can be seen on the chart.

Communications must also be continual between people of
different rank in the same department, such as the sales manager, the shipping foreman, and the shipping clerks. These are
called *vertical* routes because messages travel *up and down* according to organizational rank, as can also be seen on the chart.

VERTICAL CHANNELS

**It is easier to
communicate downward
than upward**

Messages moving along vertical channels flow in two
directions, up and down. However, although downward and
upward communications travel along the same paths, the content, nature, and problems of the two vary considerably. The
differences between them can be compared to the force of water
when it flows up or down. Downward communication is like
water streaming down from a waterfall or a showerhead. It
pours down easily with great force and wets a large area, while
upward communication is like a small spurt of water shooting
up from a fountain *against* the pull of gravity. The higher it travels, the more it loses its force. Official top-to-bottom communication channels flow down with great force and reach a great
many people, but official bottom-to-top channels flow up with
difficulty, and reach relatively few people.

Downward Communications

The channels that carry orders, information, and work-related
questions from the president's office to rank-and-file assembly
workers travel down. Whenever anyone in a higher position
communicates orders, information, or questions to someone
lower in the organization's hierarchy, the message travels downward. If the president of a company calls a semiannual meeting
of vice-presidents to inform them about recent financial

changes, or the supervisor of a steno pool calls a weekly meeting of typists to inform them of the week's typing schedules, both meetings are held to transmit information. If a plant manager orders a foreman to work overtime, or a finance manager requests information from an accountant, both messages move in a downward direction.

The content of downward communications is usually informative or directive in nature to initiate action on the part of the subordinates. Downward communication is the fastest form in the vertical chain of communication, is accepted more at face value, and is reacted to more vigorously.

Matters that affect employees directly, such as salaries, job security, and fringe benefits, are of real interest to them. Studies show that this type of information ranks highest with employees whether they are managers, supervisors, or shop workers. Therefore, a basic approach toward more effective communication is to use words which are understandable and simple.

The sender should use language which the receiver will actually understand, for what we perceive has been said is more important than the technical impressive jargon that is used. Using the phrase from a sign in the president's office, "Keep it simple, friend," is good advice. Another sign I have seen in police offices where reports were being typed and in technical writing laboratories of the electronic firms is the famous: "Remember the *KISS*" (which stands for Keep It Simple, Stupid.)

Another problem of downward communiques is that many managers think they understand the problems of their employees; however, their employees are not likely to agree. This fundamental difference in perception tends to exist at each level in organization, thereby making communication more difficult. By illustration, one study gave the following results: 95 percent of the foremen said that they understood their employees' problems well, but only 34 percent of their employees thought their supervisor did.[4] These perceptions cause downward communicators to be overconfident and probably to take less care with their downward communications.

Downward information is usually to inform or command

Downward communication is the fastest form of communication

Managers only think they know the problems of their employees!

WRITTEN

Written communications traveling along downward channels range from handwritten messages pinned to bulletin boards, to typed interoffice memos, to printed job descriptions, circulars, handbooks, and job manuals. In the United States and Canada, about 6,000 company publications, called house organs, are addressed exclusively to employees.[5] The combined circulation of internal publications, (meant for employees only) and external publications (addressed to customers, the public, and employees) is more than double the circulation of all the daily newspapers in the United States.[6] Bulletins, newspapers, and magazines are published regularly by different industries to communicate information downward.

Many companies also issue annual reports to their employees, but the most popular vehicle to transmit a communication downward appears to be the lowly pay envelope. It is widely believed that enclosing a letter or circular in the pay envelope is the surest way to transmit information down *that will be read.*[7]

Messages pinned to bulletin boards, typed memos, printed circulars, and annual reports can be excellent forms of downward communication—*when* and *if* they are read. A great deal of research suggest that those who rely principally on memos, letters, manuals, and other written materials to communicate messages downward not only fall short of achieving understanding, credibility, and acceptance—they actually contribute to new problems of misunderstandings, disbelief, and rejection.

Top managers like to write; foremen like to "tell it to them"

In 1959, Rensis Likert found that upper-level managers preferred written communications, but at the foreman level, more than 80 percent preferred to receive their supervisors' policy explanations orally.[8]

Ten years after Likert's study, it had become clear that American businesses were drowning in a sea of paper. Today, many managers prefer oral messages to written ones. The problem of the unread report has become one of the gravest problems in the American economy. For example, the annual report of one Minnesota company revealed that the company had spent nearly a million and a half dollars on communications the preceding year. One entry was extraordinary.

> It indicated that the firm had used *3,400 different memorandum forms* for inside-the-firm communication during the previous year. One could but wonder, "How on earth can the human brain ever dream of 3,400 different kinds of memorandum forms?"[9]

Today, it is quite clear that incredible amounts of time, money, and materials are wasted on written communications that serve little purpose.

Some employees are best informed in writing, some orally, and some both in writing and orally. And there are those who must be told repeatedly in order to have any substantial impact. Any tender topics are best handled orally rather than in writing.

When emotions are "high," tell it to them

The firing of an employee or arbitrating conflicts among workers is best handled in person. When emotions are high or financial stakes are great, face-to-face communications are a must.

"Talk it over" replaces "jot it down"

In this decade, many companies have begun to change their basic views about internal communication systems. One corporation banished the famous "Never Say it—Write it!" slogan, and replaced it with "Talk it over—Jot it down."[10] New York City's superintendent of public schools ordered a temporary moratorium on written reports, explaining that, "The number of unnecessary—and often unread—reports is beyond belief."[11]

No one denies that written, downward communication serves an extremely important function when complex, hard-to-remember facts and details must be precisely transmitted and carefully preserved. But paper is often the wrong medium for the "getting-things-done" kind of message that demands quick decisions in response. In today's rapidly changing world, written communications are often the slowest, most expensive, and least effective means to transmit information, orders, or questions downward.

Oral messages for quick decisions

Downward oral communications can occur in face-to-face conversations, in group meetings or conferences, by telephone, tape recordings, and telecasts. Often, oral messages are conveyed in conjunction with visual aids such as slides and movies. In some states, the General Electric Company uses two-way closed circuit TV for communications between its home and branch offices. For some years now, its Apparatus Sales Division has used semimonthly newsreels to introduce new products and manufacturing methods to its officials.[12]

Today, managers are finding that making a few three-minute phone calls to subordinates is much less expensive than dictating, typing, and distributing a memorandum would be. Phone calls can achieve quicker, more effective results. The chief advantage of oral communication is that the sender receives immediate feedback on the message's effect.

Oral messages are cheaper and faster

IMPROVING DOWNWARD COMMUNICATIONS

Chester I. Barnard was both an extremely successful executive manager and a theorist of modern managerial processes. At various times he was president of the New Jersey Bell Telephone Company, and president of the Rockefeller Foundation. In his book, *The Functions of the Executive*,[13] he described the conditions he thought downward communications must fulfill if they are to be believed and accepted. He said that people will accept the *authority* of downward communications only when the following four conditions are met:

1. The employee must clearly understand the communication. A message that cannot be understood carries no authority. A great deal of administrative time is wasted interpreting and reinterpreting and trying to apply vaguely worded orders to concrete situations. It must be written at the reader's level of comprehension.

2. The employee must believe that the communication is consistent with the purposes of the organization. If orders are seen as incompatible with the organization's purposes, they will not be carried out. Conflicting orders from different supervisory personnel are not rare. If an employee is issued an order that conflicts with a previous order, he or she must be given a reasonable explanation, or the order will not be accepted.

3. The employee must also believe that an order is consistent with his or her personal interests. If orders are issued that are believed to be incompatible with personal interests, they will not be obeyed. Resignations, malingering, and sabotage are common responses to orders viewed as inconsistent with personal interests.

4. The employee must be able to comply with orders—mentally and physically. Ordering someone to "sink or swim!" is a metaphor, but some orders fall just short of that because they ask the impossible. Orders that *cannot* be obeyed, *will* not be obeyed.[14]

Those desires and beliefs must travel *up* the formal channels of communication. Like a spray of water spurting upward, messages traveling up vertical channels don't move very fast or get very far. It is far more common for managers to spend large amounts of time and money on downward systems than on upward ones.[15]

Managers are frequently called on to transmit negative messages, such as denying salary raises, job promotions, or transfers.

The "positive sandwich" is bad news between two slices of good feelings

Basically, the "positive sandwich" technique should be used in handling negative news. Start with a good slice of bread spread generously with good news and information that is true and supportive. Then express the bad news quickly and simply as a slice of thin ham, followed up with another piece of bread bearing supportive reasons and assurances. For example, if a subordinate's request for a new assignment has been turned down he should be told why. However, it is wise to prepare him by telling him of his assets. Such information will "buffer" the denial. Then he can be informed of the bad news. If a more experienced person is selected he can be told, and should he acquire more experience to better prepare him for a position, then this supportive attitude can follow.

Whether the message is written or oral, you have to prevent the disappointing news from turning your subordinate against you. So make him as favorably disposed toward you as possible before you give the bad news. The opening sentences should strengthen whatever good feeling exists. Certainly, by asserting the bad news right at the beginning, you would be giving too much emphasis on it, and jeopardizing existing goodwill. The refusal of the promotion should be clear, however, and not leave the employee guessing as to what was really meant. Equally vital to a bad-news situation is the latter half of the positive sandwich—a positive ending. A positive closing can tip the scales toward the retention of the employee's goodwill. Here is an example of a letter sent to an employee:

> We are glad you applied for the position, Ken, because that shows you have ambition and fortitude. You have been an enthusiastic employee, always on time, and willing to work hard. However, I feel you need more experience in company operations, and particularly in your position. We have selected someone with more experience. Although we cannot, at present, consider you for the position, it does not mean we cannot consider you for other positions in the future. I want you to know we consider you a valuable employee and a real member of the team.

Upward Communications

Upward communication occurs when someone in a lower position in the organizational hierarchy communicates information, ideas, suggestions, opinions, or grievances to someone higher. When a typist drops a suggestion in the company suggestion box, or a foreman reports a breakdown in the machinery to the plant manager, or a copy editor suggests a sales campaign to the advertising manager, or the results of a survey about workers' attitudes are distributed to the vice-president—all of these communications travel by upward routes.

In many studies undertaken to find out how well managers understand their employees, the evidence repeatedly shows that managerial staffs hold many false ideas about what employees really think. For example, a recent study of twenty-four industrial plants revealed some interesting findings.[16] In the early stages of the study, the researchers selected the ten separate elements they thought were the most important for high employee morale. The managers of the twenty-four plants were asked to rank these ten elements in the order they believed their employees would judge the most important. The managers placed the following three factors in the lowest ranks.

8. Full appreciation of work done.
9. Feeling "in on things."
10. Sympathetic help on personal problems.

Then the researchers asked the hourly workers themselves

to rank the ten elements in the order *they* perceived as most important. They ranked the top three as follows:

We like to know we are doing a good job

1. Full appreciation of work done.
2. Feeling "in on things."
3. Sympathetic help on personal problems.

It seems incredible that the managers of twenty-four large industrial plants would guess exactly wrong, but they did.

The house organs of some large companies carry question-and-answer columns and print many letters from low-ranking employees along with managerial responses.

For upward communications to be effective, managerial staffs and their subordinate employees must work together in a spirit of trust and goodwill. Suppose that a company maintains a conspicuously placed suggestion box which gets a great deal of use, but that the employees never receive managerial feedback on any of their suggestions: they will probably take a cynical view of management's sincerity. On the other hand, when workers know that their messages are treated with respect and attention, the company benefits in at least five important ways:

1. Effective upward communication reveals to management the degree of acceptance and credibility that company policies have among employees. When a message can move up the line easily, managers can learn exactly how effective *downward* communications really are.

2. Free, open upward communication stimulates employees to work more enthusiastically and encourages workers to participate more actively in the operations of their departments. Employees support company policies more wholeheartedly when they have some say in planning or evaluating those policies.

3. Employees often have valuable ideas and suggestions about increasing product quality and production rates. When upward communications are good, many managers find that the research and design department does not have a monopoly on all the good ideas.

4. When messages travel up easily, managers can stay informed about potentially troublesome situations. If upward channels had been operating efficiently, many unexpected "wildcat strikes" would not be quite so unexpected.

5. If a subordinate wishes to speak to a supervisor about a personal problem affecting his or her job performance, and the supervisor listens attentively and sympathetically, then the worker's sense of personal value is enhanced. By listening attentively, the supervisor satisfies the worker's need for respect.

One study indicated that employees view communications with superiors as the most satisfying and important kind of communication in the work environment.[17] But the study also indicated that these are precisely the kinds of communication that employees are *least able to initiate*. In another study, some professors at Loyola University spent eighteen months selecting the essential attributes a good manager must have.[18] They found that the ability to listen well is the most important. Since attentive listening is the best way to stay in touch with everything that is going on, such managers are invariably well informed. Good listening, in addition to keeping managers well informed, also promotes good human relations. When workers who thought highly of their supervisors were asked, "Why?," they always responded with variations on the following theme: "I like my boss because I can talk to him," or "She listens to me, and cares about what I have to say."

Listening supervisor gets the highest rating

THE OPEN-DOOR POLICY

In the "good old days" many company presidents made it their business to know everyone on their payroll personally. They took great pride in knowing all of their employees by name. A certain part of their work day was spent walking through the plant and engaging the hourly workers in face-to-face conversation. But then the twentieth century came along, and with it growth, and mergers, and giant corporations, and that kind of old-fashioned, daily, informal, upward communication went out with the horse and buggy.

In recent years, many companies have tried to revive that tradition with what is called the "open-door policy." Theoretically, this policy allows low-level workers the privilege of walking into any manager's office, up to and including the president's, to register a complaint or to make a suggestion. In most cases, however, the policy exists only on paper. The door may be open, but somehow, hourly workers are seldom seen crossing the threshold.

There are several reasons why the open-door policy works better in theory than in practice:

Physical walls isolate supervisors and communications

1. The physical layout of most modern industrial plants isolates supervisory personnel in inaccessible offices, remote from the hourly workers. Should a low-level worker brave the trip from the factory floor to the carpeted office of a vice-president, he or she would undoubtedly find the way barred by a receptionist whose duties include screening out unexpected visitors.

2. Norman Maier, an industrial psychologist, says that workers or managers who try to *bypass* or skip over the supervisor ranked immediately above them are frowned on by top management be-

cause bypassing is viewed as a violation of authority and "makes locating responsibility difficult for all parties involved."[19]

It seems, therefore, as if the most practical open-door policy today would be one in which managers tried to recreate some of the conditions of the nineteenth century. The open door appears to work most effectively when supervisory personnel walk through it *out* to the workers, instead of waiting for the workers to come in to them. Managers should make it an integral part of their business to stay as well informed as possible about their workers' grievances and suggestions.

HORIZONTAL CHANNELS

Horizontal, or lateral, channels are used when members at the same level in the hierarchy of authority communicate with one another: that is, one worker to another, or one manager to another. Horizontal channels operate both formally and informally, both officially and unofficially. A sales manager who tells a plant manager to increase production next month because a clever advertising campaign has paid off and sales are pouring in, would use formal channels for the message. But the plant manager might have given the sales manager the great idea for the advertising campaign over a drink at lunch a few months previously—surely an informal situation. Many workers and managers use informal horizontal channels often and with great success. They rely on friendships and favors given and owed as a way to ignore or expedite requests, to evade rules, or to change the work flow.

Some companies have recently initiated innovative organizational programs to create better horizontal communications between departments. Such programs include:

PROJECT TEAMS OR MATRIX ORGANIZATIONS

Teams of people are brought together from different departments to work on a single specific project. The project manager may have no permanent authority in the organizational structure, but be an expert in the specific project and as such coordinate, direct, and control the various members of the project team. In effect, a matrix organization is a second form of organization overlaid on the line chain of command (Figure 3–3). Computer engineers, who install electronic data processing equipment (EDP) or automated machinery, often function in this capacity. As short-term programs are established, special groups are created to handle them.

Under a team project a man may have his boss report to him

The chairman may find he has persons reporting to him

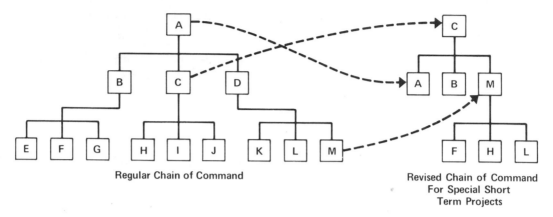

Regular Chain of Command

Revised Chain of Command
For Special Short
Term Projects

Figure 3–3.

who are above, below, or at the same hierarchal level as he. Temporarily, for only hours a day, or for months at a time, a person may find that he has a superior from another department working under his direction. This can put a strain on the relationship or can help break down the rigid barriers of formal communications.

Integrated machine production and data processing can be developed into what might be called a "horizontal plane." Such a combination of two different units into a workable team cuts across superior-subordinate relationships, affecting the jobs of employees in different areas. This new matrix plan superimposes a new vertical structure whose chain of command can help or cause obvious difficulties.

Project managers who have to solve *new* problems must learn to deal horizontally with their peers and diagonally with workers at different levels. Following established, formal, vertical routes is costlier, takes more time, and is too disruptive.

Improving Horizontal Communications

The problems associated with horizontal communications seldom stem from a lack of messages among individuals or groups, but on the contrary from the large numbers and varied types of messages that are sent and received. Work is often unnecessarily duplicated or inordinately delayed because information needed in one department is available only in another, and sometimes no one in the department needing the information knows it exists.

In some companies, lengthy written reports have been re-

72

placed by efficiently organized conferences. The managers who run these conferences frequently employ a great many sophisticated audio-visual aids. Some companies have begun to transmit routine, daily reports by recording the information on tape. The tapes are plugged into the telephone systems within the plant. Anyone needing the report can get it by dialing a pre-arranged number. Such reports were formerly written, reproduced, and distributed by many more people than are needed to run the tape system.[20]

Dial your report, don't read it

Informal Channels

"Although informal organizations are bound by no chart on the wall, they are bound by convention, custom, and culture."

Informal communications grow out of the *social* interactions among people who work together. These communications do not appear as formal patterns of relationships on organization charts. Most theorists believe that informal relationships cannot be charted because they change so rapidly and are so complex. One of the major functions informal channels serve is to provide communication routes for members of small groups. Every successful business has at least one healthy, if invisible, communications channel to conduct the messages of the informal organization, "that mysterious entity . . . which is the *real* organization" because "*It* is how things get done."[21]

Occasionally, communication channels in an organization may appear to be informal when in truth they are not, for example, the so-called informal contacts that supervisors are sometimes *required* to maintain with subordinates. When supervisors are formally *ordered* to associate with workers *socially*, as a part of their job, a true informal channel seldom emerges, and communications remain formal and perhaps even more stilted than they need be. However, a supervisor's success often depends on the degree to which he or she accepts and uses the existing informal channels.

Suppose a secretary in the personnel manager's office is a link in the formal channel for receiving information about job openings. The secretary is also a link in an informal friendship clique of other secretaries throughout the entire organization. When a job requisition comes in to the personnel manager's office, the secretary might process it through to the personnel manager along the formal route. Then again, she might not. The secretary might decide to notify the people in the friendship clique about the job opening first, before telling the personnel manager about it. If the personnel manager goes along with the

The secretary's friend gets the job

use of the informal channel and accepts the candidates who appear for the job via the friendship clique without using formal job recruiting techniques, such as placing an ad in the help-wanted section of the newspaper, then the informal channel has become a part of the organization's formal communication processes.

Transmitting Informal Messages

Informal communications about work-related matters can be transmitted in a variety of ways. In addition to the usual modes of speech and writing, two other techniques are frequently used. They are (1) gesture and (2) silence.

GESTURE.　Charles Redfield tells the story of a machinist who once opened his locker at lunch time and found his lunchbox had been painted yellow by his coworkers. By this "gesture," or symbol, he understood that he was being told not to work so hard or so fast. On the use of such symbolism, Redfield has this to say: "if painting lunch-boxes yellow were an *established* communication device of a labor union, it could no longer be regarded as informal communication."[22]

SILENCE.　"The silent treatment" is a common tool used to punish a worker who has offended most of the members of his or her informal work group. Being ostracized can be very painful. Few workers will risk rebelling against the "rules" of the informal organization if they fear being ostracized.

WRITTEN MESSAGES.　Most written messages that travel along informal channels are letters, and are often marked "Personal," or "For Your Eyes Only!"

The informal group sets the "standard"

ORAL MESSAGES.　Oral communications about work-related matters are often transmitted at the same time that social matters are being discussed. Suppose, for example, a young man is a speed demon when working with his own lathe at home in his own workshop. Suppose further that he gets a job running a lathe at a machine shop. It takes him exactly twice as long to perform a task at work as it does at home. What might be the reason? It's more than likely that one day, probably during lunch hour or on a coffee break, some of his coworkers "wised him up" with this message or a variation of it: "There's no sense in killing yourself, kid. A fair day's work around here, for your job, is twenty to twenty-five borings an hour."[23]

The young man not only got the message—he took it seriously. His production rate will not deviate from the norm set by the informal organization because his coworkers are also his friends, and he wants them to stay friendly.

The Grapevine

The grapevine is the unofficial news carrier

The term "grapevine" is believed to have come into use during the Civil War when the first telegraph lines, used to carry military intelligence, were strung from tree to tree in the pattern of a grapevine. Often messages were garbled or interfered with, and so all rumors, or unofficial messages, came to be known as carried "by the grapevine."

In a sense the grapevine is universal. Messages have always been transmitted by unofficial means. The graffiti written on ancient Roman walls and modern buildings and the messages prisoners have always exchanged by tapping on prison walls can all be said to be carried by a kind of grapevine.

The communications chains formed by friendship cliques or casual associations, which carry daily gossip and news of work, are more frequently used forms of the grapevine. In a complex organization, depending on its size, there can be dozens or hundreds of grapevines. They carry information that is not, or cannot be, transmitted by formal means. Information of this sort: "I wouldn't ask for that raise today, if I were you. The boss is in a foul mood, and you'd better wait until her mood changes."

You can't eliminate the grapevine

However, it is impossible to predict the direction, speed, accuracy, or final content of a message carried by the grapevine. Messages may be abbreviated, magnified, restructured, elaborated, or generally twisted all out of shape. Sometimes official messages must be issued to counteract the inaccuracies of the grapevine. At other times it can spread information very quickly and accurately. No matter how well it "works" or doesn't, it can *never* be eliminated. It cannot be controlled, and it cannot be systematized, although some managers have made unwise efforts to do so. The best thing that can be done is to try to understand it.

PEOPLE WHO USE THE GRAPEVINE

Some people become very active on the grapevine when the organization is undergoing periods of instability or excitement. Layoffs and rumors of impending automation or electronic data processing tend to start the grapevine working overtime. At such times, managers should take care to "feed" the grapevine accurate information to keep the rumor level down from the fever pitch that can interfere with morale or production rates.

Some people become active on the grapevine only when their personal feelings are involved. If Joe gets a promotion, his friends Manuel and Isabel will want to know about all the details. If Joe doesn't have time to fill his friends in as soon as news of his promotion comes to them, they may do a lot of speculating—to one another and to other individuals.

Most grapevine messages are short-lived. People become easily bored by stale gossip. Some people, however, always have the latest "dirt." They are the central transmitters on the grapevine line and sometimes the ones to consult when it is necessary to find out "what is really going on." Such people are the "stars" of the grapevine channel. Of course, some are stars because they possess such vivid imaginations. On the other hand, some grapevine stars do manage to collect and disseminate remarkable amounts of reliable information. Time and experience are the only tools available to distinguish the first kind of star from the second.

HOW ACCURATE IS IT?

Three-fourths of the information is accurate

One study showed that in normal *noncontroversial* work situations, a little over three-fourths of all the messages carried by the grapevine were accurate.[24] When there were errors, they tended to be dramatic ones and people remembered them very well. But this study, and others, indicate that for day-to-day routine matters, the percentage of accuracy for grapevine messages is very high. Some companies keep their publication staffs working all night long when new labor contracts are signed at midnight. They do this to have an accurate bulletin ready to hand out or to post on bulletin boards early the following morning to match the grapevine's speed and to *ensure* its accuracy.

It is easy to see why grapevine messages can become so distorted. The message invariably carries the personal impressions and emotional reactions of each person on the communication chain, as well as the information. Some managers view the grapevine as a demoralizing influence that leads to irresponsible behavior and lowered production rates and sometimes destroys morale and reputations. But if this is so, it is usually due to inadequate channels of communication.

Rumor has no standard of evidence, no bases but feelings

Rumor, a term that is sometimes used as a synonym for the grapevine, is a message transmitted along the grapevine having no *secure* evidence or a *reliable* person's word behind it. Rumors can be correct, but more often they are not. Generally, rumors are spread by people who are very interested in the subject. In the course of a day, the details of a rumor may change, but the theme will remain the same. Sometimes rumors are agents for wish fulfillments. Why would Mary and Herman start a rumor that everyone in the office is going to get a $25 monthly raise?

Rumor is more often untrue

Probably just saying it out loud makes them feel good, and they may think that if the words are said long enough and loud enough to enough people—it just might come true. The problem with rumors is that they are especially subject to distortion because people *are* interested in the subject matter, and they filter and distort those details that don't interest them and enlarge and elaborate the ones that do.

Stop rumors quickly

Managers wishing to stop rumor-mongering should try to stop only those that are important—rumors that affect morale and productivity. Those should be nipped in the bud as quickly as possible. Face-to-face conversation or group meetings are the best methods for stopping dangerous rumors from spreading. But the person denying the rumor must be known for honesty and be willing to answer questions on the subject.

Official word combats rumors

Dowling and Sayles say that people are less likely to believe official denials of a rumor if they have heard the rumor *first*. Therefore, it would seem that the best way for managers to transmit important information is to get the truthful message out as soon as a decision is reached, and then let the rumor mill go to work as it will. "A message is more likely to be understood and accepted if it is not competing with another, and potentially conflicting message."[25]

Rumors express a feeling—maybe insecurity

It is also true that upwardly moving rumors can provide managers with an understanding of the emotional feelings among the work force. Managers who learn to ask questions such as, "What does that rumor mean—is someone insecure and afraid of being fired?" or "Is someone really quitting?" are often provided with truthful answers via the grapevine. Labor relations mediators always make it their business to listen to the rumors union officials and company officials spread about each other. They believe that such rumors are projections of fears, and that if they can learn what each side is afraid of, they can achieve a better understanding of complex issues.

THE USE OF THE GRAPEVINE

Even though the grapevine's reliability can never be determined with complete certainty, it does serve some useful functions:

1. It satisfies a need employees have to enjoy friendly relations with their fellow employees.
2. It helps workers to make sense out of their work environment, especially in interpreting unclear orders from supervisors.
3. It acts as a safety valve. When people are confused and unclear about what is going to happen to them, they use the grapevine to let out their anxieties. When they feel powerless to direct their destinies, passing a rumor along the grapevine is a way of expressing and releasing negative energy.

4. When people gossip about someone who is not present, they often pass judgments. Some people pass judgment on others to find out where they stand. It is a way of dealing with self-doubt and insecurity.

GRAPEVINE'S CHARACTERISTICS

Company grapevine usually operates at work only

Keith Davis spent some time studying the way the grapevine worked at a company he called the Jason Company, a manufacturer of leather goods. The Jason Company employed sixty-seven people in management, from top executives down to line foremen, and 600 hourly employees. The company was located in a rural town of some 10,000 population. In his study, Davis isolated four characteristics that he considered essential for understanding how the grapevine works.[26] They are:

Word travels fast

1. SPEED OF TRANSMISSION. When employees are interested in the affairs of their coworkers, messages will travel with astonishing speed. For example, one day the plant manager's wife had a baby at 11:00 p.m. By 2:00 p.m. the next day, 46 percent of management personnel had heard of the event via the grapevine.

2. DEGREE OF SELECTIVITY. Those who use the grapevine exercise discretion and intelligence about whom to pass information to. For example, the company president decided to have a picnic, and only thirty-six of the managerial staff were invited. Invitations were transmitted *orally*, not in writing. Of course, the grapevine was activated, but only two people of the thirty-one managers not invited had any news of the picnic. The grapevine communicators understood the invitation to be confidential, and they told only those whom they thought would be invited. Apparently their selective guessing was very nearly perfect.

3. LOCALE OF OPERATION. Contrary to what Davis expected to find, most information was transmitted at the plant itself. Although the Jason Company was in a small town and most of the people who worked there knew each other socially, people did not pass grapevine messages to each other in their homes but only at work. When the president made plans to go away for a two-week vacation, the top executives learned of his vacation plans when everyone else did — at the office. Davis says that the significance of this is:

> Since management has some control over the work environment, it has an opportunity to influence the grapevine. By exerting such

influence the manager can more closely integrate grapevine interests with those of the formal communication system, and he can use it for effectively spreading more significant items of information than those commonly carried.[27]

Grapevine doesn't take the place of formal messages

4. RELATION TO FORMAL COMMUNICATION. At the Jason Company, Davis found that the formal and informal communication systems worked together—or not at all. When formal systems were not active, the grapevine did not rush in to fill the information gap. There were just no communications on the subject at all. When there was effective formal communication, there was also an active grapevine.

STAFF AND LINE COMMUNICATIONS

The words "staff" and "line" are the classical terms for the traditional divisions of labor in complex organizations. They stem from nineteenth century military usage and are still employed by the military. In business and industry, generally speaking, a line function is one that contributes directly to the main activity of the business; a staff function is one that assists the line function in an advisory or administrative capacity. Today, as far as some management theorists are concerned, distinguishing between the two is a purely academic matter, because organizational titles are frequently interchangeable and misleading. What one company views as staff, another will see as a line function.

Nevertheless, the *type* of business a company is engaged in usually furnishes sufficient clues about who are "line" and who are "staff." For example, manufacturing firms whose prime activities are to produce goods always view certain functions as staff, i.e., finance, legal, secretarial, personnel administration, and public relations. However, for a finance company whose primary activity consists of taking in and paying out loans, the finance office is a line function: because the *business* of the business is finance. Sweeping the floors and washing the windows at the finance company would obviously be a staff concern. For a janitorial service company, sweeping floors and washing windows constitutes their main business activity and as such is viewed as a line function.

There are two separate types of staff—general and specialized. General staff personnel usually assist division managers in a *variety* of ways. Specialized staff usually contribute specific skills in very *narrow* areas of expertise.

Staff persons must be better informed and usually are

General staff are much more mobile than line personnel because of the nature of their jobs, especially in factories. Their jobs tend to cut across horizontal divisions and consequently they are much better informed about company affairs than line managers. At the Jason Leather Goods Manufacturing Company, for example, more staff executives usually knew about a company event than line executives did. When the president of the company made a trip to Washington to try to persuade government officials to increase allotments of animal hides so that the factory could continue to operate at maximum capacity, 25 percent of staff personnel knew why the president had gone, whereas only 4 percent of line managers knew why.[28]

Staff persons are greater motivated to communicate

Staff must sell ideas not give commands

Specialized staff personnel often find themselves in conflict with line managers because the line managers fear that new production methods will render their jobs obsolete. Poor communications, hostility, and even sabotage are not uncommon between line and staff personnel. While many specialists lack command or line authority, they have greater motivation to communicate because they realize that their success is dependent upon selling their ideas to others. A specialist has a shorter communication chain to higher management which, as a result, usually gives him more mobility than operating workers (see Figure 3–4).

It has been claimed that violations of the chain of command reduce employee satisfaction and increase stress, because of role conflicts. However, present evidence shows that multiple command relationships can be beneficial and satisfying. The nature of the activity and the type of interpersonal relations involved appear to play a deciding role. In one organization, 28

Figure 3–4. Types of staff positions.

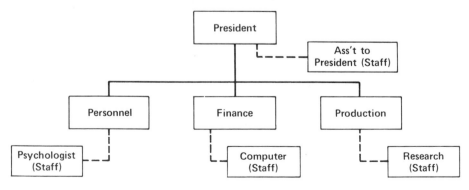

out of 30 supervisors who received instructions from five executives enjoyed the close association, because they felt they knew what was going on.[29]

Such functional groups have proved to be effective at establishing sound human relations because they stimulate and encourage open and full communication. They also encourage democratic participation in the planning, implementing, and evaluation of change. In many modern businesses, integrated functional groupings have proven a far more useful organizational tool than classical staff and line divisions.

The concept of group work teams has become an important aspect of modern organizational theory. Traditional organizations utilized a pattern of one-to-one relationships between organization members in which supervisors dealt with subordinates individually. Modern concepts emphasize group relationships and task-force teams in accord with the new emphasis on better human relations and fuller participation between and by all employees. Learning how to organize and monitor these groups, however, is in itself an art. The manager must have a good grasp not only of group dynamics but of each person involved.

Group participation is, in fact, sometimes referred to as human relations because its primary function is to give employees a voice in what they do and how they do it. The available evidence indicates that when a solution to a problem is worked out by the group to be affected by the change, it is accepted much more wholeheartedly than when it is superimposed from above.

SMALL GROUP COMMUNICATIONS

Groups satisfy needs

Most people spend a great deal of time communicating in small groups. Our lives revolve around our families, classes, work teams, athletic teams, and committees, and this list could be extended much further. The groups that most influence peoples' behavior become their reference groups: the groups with whom values, attitudes, and beliefs are shared. Groups also provide people with opportunities to satisfy their needs for recognition and achievement. They satisfy other wishes too, such as those for dominance and autonomy.

Small-group communication has been defined as "face-to-face interaction by a number of individuals who regard themselves as a group."[30] Like face-to-face communication, small-group interaction is dynamic and involves a lot of feedback. The social relations within a small group influence the kind of communication that takes place, and, in turn, the nature of the communication will influence social relations. For example, a person who has high credibility will have much more influence than someone of high status but of low credibility. High credibility confers a kind of power on the person who has it.

A person with high credibility has great influence

In business organizations especially, the power relations within a group determine to a large extent the kind of communication that exists. When power is concentrated in too few high-status people, lower-status group members will feel their needs are not being met, and communication will be less than effective. Communication is also affected within a group by the degrees of cooperation and competition among the group members.

Behavior of Committees

The behavior that goes on in a committee can be viewed as positive and negative reactions to questions and answers. Such negative reactions include: showing disagreement, tension, or antagonism. The positive reactions include: showing agreement, tension release, and friendly solidarity.

A successful meeting needs a balance between positive and negative reactions

There are about twice as many positive reactions in most meetings as there are negative reactions. One might suppose that the more successful the meeting, the more positive reactions one would find. But evidence does not support this view. Rather, there appears to be a kind of optimum balance between disagreements and agreements. Too few disagreements may be an indication of the lack of involvement and interest in the task, or the atmosphere is so inhibited and constrained that nobody dares disagree. When ill feelings rise about some critical point, a chain reaction tends to set in and logical or practical demands of the task may cease to be governing factors.

TASK LEADERS OR SOCIAL LEADERS

When people are active in a group meeting they may be characterized by actions of two types: the task leader and the social leader. The *task leader* feels that the accomplishment of the task is important. The ability to define the problem, the best way to handle it, and the time restriction become of paramount importance to him. The feelings of the individual members are of lesser concern to him. He is willing to "forgive and forget" if he hurts anyone's feelings or if someone tramples on his emotions. The accomplishment of the goal, success, and self-ego are his trademarks. The *social leader* is interested in the feelings of each member and that each has an opportunity to participate. An agreement on a solution to a problem is only possible if there is

A task leader wants to get the job done

A social leader is interested in the people in the group

compatibility among the members. The social leader will resent the "take-over" tactics of the task leader. The social leader will sense if the group is being moved too fast along the trail by the task leader, and will move in for a reassessment, compromise, or evaluation.

HIDDEN AGENDAS

People have hidden feelings that affect the meetings

"Groups work simultaneously and continuously on two levels," says Dr. Leland Bradford, director of the National Training Laboratories. One level is for the formally advertised purpose of the group. The private feelings of the individuals is the second level. Here are the aspirations and emotional reactions of the individual members. An employee may not admit he is afraid of losing his job, but he will fight to keep it and say strange things that would seem reasonable if we knew his hidden agenda.

We all bring hidden agendas to meetings

Approaches to handling hidden agendas:

How can we handle hidden agendas?

1. Recognize their presence.
2. Don't expect fast action on the surface of tasks assigned, as many problems of personalities may be gnawing at each other underneath.
3. Hidden agendas are only discussed when the people involved feel comfortable.
4. Don't get angry at people for their hidden agendas; you have one, too.
5. Help members develop ways of handling their hidden agendas, just as they handle surface agendas — by resolving the problem.

Hidden agendas are neither good nor bad, but they are as real as surface problems, and seem far more important to the individual concerned.

Size of Committees

The ideal size of a committee is from 5 to 7 persons

The size of the committee is important, and the desirable number seems to be five, although some experts would say it is seven members. Below five, for the most part, each person in the group says something to each other person. In groups over seven, the low participators tend to stop talking to each other and speak more to the leader. Subconsciously this situation becomes more formal and real interaction tends to drop. The tendency for stronger directive leaders tends to increase rather powerfully as size increases.

Successful communication between the different members of a group depends on something more than a common language. Experts trained in using precise technical vocabularies have difficulties in communicating with laymen. Even in ordinary everyday language, different words have different meanings for different people. The ways in which a skilled tool maker thinks will differ from the ways in which a nonskilled worker thinks, and their thinking will differ from the ways in which accountants, salespeople, and engineers think. If there is to be successful communication in groups composed of many different kinds of people, there must be recognition of these different modes of thought. There also must be recognition by each group member that each way of thought has its own validity. The failure of group members to grant these recognitions to each other inevitably results in the failure to communicate.

Primitive people were able to accomplish extraordinary feats because they communicated with each other for the purposes of cooperation. If modern business organizations are to survive and flourish, some of the competitive uses to which communication has been put will have to be transformed again to serve cooperative functions for the common good.

SUMMARY

If effective cooperative behavior is to exist in organizations, communications must be understood, believed, accepted, and acted upon. Two kinds of communication channels serve to accomplish these ends—formal and informal. Formal channels are the official paths by which official messages travel. They are called the vertical and horizontal channels because they relate to and grow out of the vertical and horizontal relationships pictured on an organization's structural chart. Informal channels stem from the unofficial, social relationships existing between individuals who work together, and they serve to transmit unofficial messages.

Although the downward and upward channels both move vertically, the nature, content, and sheer amount of messages going up or down are completely different. The downward channel is dominated by orders from above dealing with policies and procedures. Vast amounts of printed matter are generated in the top-down channel as memos, reports, and house organs. In recent years, modern organizations have begun to emphasize speech communication as a more effective way of sending messages down.

The channel that carries information and grievances up to top management from the rank and file has fewer resources than the downward one. Some companies take regular surveys of workers' opinions and attitudes, but many studies indicate that top management is frequently out of touch with what workers are thinking and feeling about work-related matters. Some companies have instituted the use of grievance and rumor boxes as well as the more traditional suggestion boxes. But union grievance committees still remain one of the most potent upward channels available to workers. The open-door policy would be more effective if more managers would walk through it to the factory floor—instead of waiting for workers to walk through it to see them.

Horizontal channels exist for members of the same organizational rank to communicate with one another. Horizontal communications can be observed on a formal organization chart, but they also exhibit a number of characteristics associated with the informal modes of communication. It has been demonstrated that open horizontal communication is essential for the success of any complex organization, from the managerial level to the assembly line.

In the informal channel, the major modes of communication are the friendship clique and the grapevine. Friendship cliques are important because they generate and sustain loyalty to the larger organization and because they are the area in which natural leaders develop their talents for leadership.

The grapevine is used by nearly everyone in an organization at one time or another. It can carry accurate messages with amazing speed. It can also distort and filter messages beyond recognition. Rumors as well as facts are carried by the grapevine. Good managers pay attention to grapevine communications as a way of staying in touch with workers' thoughts and feelings. Such managers also learn how to stop troublesome rumors before they assume too much importance.

Traditional concepts of staff and line have changed in recent years. With those changes have come innovations in communication techniques between the divisions. Integrated work teams composed of both line and staff personnel create much better human relations between employees and contribute greatly to better small-group communications.

HOW CAN THE STAFF COMMUNICATE MORE EFFECTIVELY WITH LINE PERSONNEL

Case Study #1

Good communications between staff and line personnel is important in all organizations, and it can be said that effective communications plays a significant role in determining the overall success of any organization. However, when the communication process between staff and line personnel is less than effective, problems can develop as seen in the following illustration.

Jay Galler, who manages the personnel department of a large industrial plant of about 200 employees, recently distributed to all employees a detailed questionnaire that required the employees to fill in information about their job title, amount of years with the company, salary rate, and a description of their job responsibilities. The form stated that the purpose of the questionnaire would be to provide management with an update material concerning personnel classifications. The form stated that all employees should return the form on or before the coming Friday, which gave the men five days in which to fill all of the information needed. Jay announced to each department that he would tour the plant on Friday morning and pick up all of the forms that had not yet been turned in to the Personnel Department.

The updating of the personnel classifications was requested by the Plant Manager. The reason was to review all the job duties with the possibility of reclassifying some of the positions. In some cases to provide a more equitable pay rate—that would mean a pay raise for some.

At the end of the week, before Jay's tour of the plant, less than 20 percent of the questionnaires had been returned to the Personnel Office. After touring the plant, Jay had collected only an additional dozen forms. After requesting that the men get the forms in as soon as possible, Jay went to see the Plant Manager and other management officials. They were waiting to see all of the completed forms. Obviously, an accurate study of the wages and salary schedules could not be done because of the lack of necessary data. There appears to be a problem between line and staff, more specifically the passing of information from the line personnel to the staff. A common problem.

1. How will the line personnel suffer as a result of not filling out the questionnaire?
2. How could Jay have made his communication more effective?
3. Was Jay's method the best way of distributing the forms? Is there a better way? Should Jay have departmental meetings to discuss the form?
4. What information should be included on the memo regarding the questionnaire?

THERE'S A RUMOR ABOUT MY PROMOTION

Case Study #2

Bill Hackaday has worked for the Denver Branch of the Tamlon Corporation for three years and is now a junior executive in the Engineering Department. Bill has just returned from a two-week vacation.

This morning Randy Meyers, a coworker and good friend, stopped Bill on his way into the building. "Congratulations Bill, from what I hear, you will apparently be in your own office soon."

"What are you talking about, Randy? I'm not due for a promotion yet."

"I didn't think you were, but the rumor is that Mr. Lundquist is going to promote you."

This information has Bill puzzled. He knows there are others in line for promotion before him. But then again, he knows his work is good and a promotion at this time would be ideal for he is about to be married. With the promotion he could consider purchasing a new home.

When Bill entered the plant, he was not approached by anyone else about the promotion. When he passed Mr. Lundquist in the hallway he mentioned nothing about a promotion. That evening, as Bill prepared to leave work, Mary Stewart, a coworker in the department, asked, "Is it true that you'll be leaving us soon, Bill? I heard that you were being transferred to the Atlanta Branch this summer."

"I haven't been told anything about it. Where did you hear about it?"

"Oh, I don't know; someone mentioned it last week and said to keep it quiet until you got back. The word is that either you'll be promoted or transferred to the Atlanta Branch."

"But don't you think someone would have said something to me by now?," inquired Bill.

"It sure seems so. I suppose it could be another false rumor. Do you remember the one that was going around last month?"

This information has Bill concerned. He'd like a promotion, but the last thing he wants right now is a transfer. What would you do if you were Bill?

1. Ask Mr. Lundquist directly about the rumor?
2. Should you ignore the rumor and go ahead with your future plans?
3. Would you try to track down the source of the rumor?
4. Would you discuss your personal plans with Mr. Lundquist?
5. Are there other ways of checking the validity of the rumor?

Terms and Concepts Students Should Know

formal communications	task leaders	rumor
tall organizational structure	hidden agendas	behavior of committees
vertical communications	informal communications	social leaders
"positive sandwich"	flat organizational structure	committee size
grapevine	horizontal communications	
staff and line communications	project teams	

Bibliography

1. DUBIN, ROBERT, *The World of Work*, Englewood Cliffs, New Jersey, Prentice-Hall, Inc., 1958.

2. BITTEL, LESTER, *What Every Supervisor Should Know*, Third Edition, New York, McGraw-Hill Company, 1974.

3. REDFIELD, CHARLES E., *Communication in Management*, University of Chicago Press, 1958.

4. ROBBINS, STEPHEN, *The Administrative Process*, Englewood Cliffs, New Jersey, Prentice-Hall, Inc., 1976.

Footnotes

[1] Robert Dubin, *The World of Work* (Englewood Cliffs, N.J.: Prentice-Hall, 1958), p. 336.

[2] Charles E. Redfield, *Communication in Management* (Chicago: University of Chicago Press, 1958), p. 1974.

[3] Keith Davis, "Channels of Communication in Organizations," in *Studies in Personnel and Industrial Psychology*, edited by Edwin A. Fleishman, (Homewood, Ill.: Dorsey Press, 1967), p. 458.

[4] Resis Likert, "Motivational Approach to Management Development," *Harvard Business Review*, July–August 1959, pp. 75–82.

[5] Redfield, *Communication in Management*, p. 22.

[6] Carl Heyel, *How To Communicate Better with Workers: The Open Door to Employee Cooperation* (Concordville, Penn.: Clemprint, 1973), p. 179.

[7] Redfield, *Communication in Management*, p. 22.

[8] Likert, "Motivational Approach to Management Development," pp. 75–82.

[9] Ernest G. Bormann, William S. Howell, Ralph G. Nichols, and George L. Shapiro, *Interpersonal Communication in the Modern Organization* (Englewood Cliffs, N.J.: Prentice-Hall, 1969), p. 10.

[10] *Ibid.*, p. 15.

[11] *Ibid.*

[12] Redfield, *Communication in Management*, p. 21.

[13] Chester I. Barnard, *The Functions of the Executive* (Cambridge, Mass.: Harvard University Press, 1938), pp. 165–166.

[14] *Ibid.*

[15] Fred J. Carvel, *Human Relations in Business* (Toronto: The Macmillan Co., 1970), p. 30.

[16] Bormann, *et al.*, *Interpersonal Communication in the Modern Organization*, p. 190.

[17] Norman H. Brekowitz and Warren G. Bennis, "Interaction Patterns in Formal Service-Oriented Organizations," *Administration Science Quarterly*, June 1961, p. 49.

[18] Bormann, *et al.*, *Interpersonal Communication in the Modern Organization*, p. 191.

[19] Norman Maier, *Psychology in Industry*, 3rd ed. (Boston: Houghton-Mifflin Co., 1965) p. 191.

[20] Redfield, *Communication in Management*, p. 17.

[21] Harold Steiglitz, "What's Not on the Organization Chart," in *Readings in Industrial and Organization Psychology*, edited by Edward L. Deci, B. von Haller Gilmer, and Harry W. Karn, (New York: McGraw-Hill Book Co., 1972), p. 116.

[22] Redfield, *Communication in Management*, p. 10.

[23] William F. Dowling and Leonard R. Sayles, *How Managers Motivate, The Imperatives of Supervision* (New York: McGraw-Hill Book Co., 1972), p. 77.

[24] Eugene Walton, "How Efficient is the Grapevine?" *Personnel*, March–April 1961, p. 48.

[25] Dowling and Sayles, *How Managers Motivate*, p. 220.

[26] Davis, "Channels of Communication in Organizations," pp. 454–455.

[27] *Ibid.*, p. 455.

[28] *Ibid.*, pp. 546–557.

[29] Woodward, *Industrial Organization Theory and Practice* (London: Oxford Press, 1965).

[30] Michael Burgoon, *Approaching Speech Communication* (New York: Holt, Rinehart and Winston, 1974), p. 209.

Human Motivation
" What Makes People Move? "

4

OBJECTIVES

When you finish reading this chapter you should be able to:
1. Restate in your own words the meaning of motivation.
2. Explain how the individual's need to be motivated may be different from the company's need.
3. Explain the difference among fear motivation, incentive motivation, and attitude motivation.
4. Describe the five elements of Maslow's heirarchy of needs.
5. Contrast the differences between Herzberg's hygiene or maintenance theory and motivators.
6. Contrast intrinsic motivators from extrinsic motivators and be able to list several of each type.
7. Contrast the difference between the foreman's view of motivation and the subordinate's view of motivation.
8. Summarize some of the important methods of job enrichment.

■ ■ ■ ■ ■ ■ ■ ■ ■ ■ ■ ■ ■ ■ ■ ■ ■ ■ ■ ■

Here are a few questions that might stimulate your thinking. The answers to some may be found in the reading and others may be found in the recesses of your experiences and personal opinions.

Why do people work when they don't need the money?

Is money the most important incentive, or are there other incentives equally important?

What makes some people work harder than others?

Does everyone have the same needs?

How does basic needs affect work performance?

What makes a job satisfying or dissatisfying?

How can routine jobs be reorganized to be more satisfying?

WHAT IS MOTIVATION
ALL ABOUT?

If work is defined as any activity or effort undertaken to accomplish a goal, then work is natural, because no one can accomplish anything without effort. Work is central to human life. Human beings invented tools, thus increasing their capacity for work, and humans have always defined themselves by their work.

**A motivated person
wants to work**

In the business world, the word *motivation* is used to describe the drive that impels an individual to work. A truly motivated person is one who *wants* to work. Both employees and employers are interested in understanding motivation. If workers know what strengthens and what weakens their motivation, they can often perform more effectively to find more satisfaction in their jobs. Employers want to know what motivated the employees so they can get them to work harder. The motivation to work is integral both to successful, profit-making business and to job satisfaction. Thus, both employees and employers must understand it better.

Motivation and Behavior

When a psychologist uses the word motivation, he thinks of it as something stemming from *within* a person. Part of motivation is an internal feeling in the individual. Motivation is an internal need that is satisfied through an external expression. The achievement of the goal or obtaining the incentive is the external factor the public sees, but the reason why people are moved or motivated to achieve it may not always be obvious.

**Motivation is an internal
need satisfied by
external expression**

People are motivated to perform similar actions by very different internal drives. Imagine, for example, two employees working hard to get raises. To one, the raise is important because it will provide more money; to the other, the higher status that the raise signifies is a stronger motivation than the money.

Also, similar internal motivations can have different results. Two employees who feel a strong need for job security may handle their needs in very different ways. One might decide to work hard, but never to "rock the boat" for fear of being fired. The other chooses to be innovative, even at the risk of being controversial, as a way of becoming indispensable.

When actions contradict statements of personal goals, unless deceit is involved, unconscious motivations are the governing forces. A man may say he doesn't want to work any harder, yet take on even more work. Perhaps he seeks more status, which he believes can be gained by assuming more responsibilities. Perhaps he unconsciously fears a financially insecure fu-

93

ture, which he hopes to prevent by working harder and making more money. Some employers are well aware of these motivational variables. "How," they ask, "can we be sure to offer the right motivators, ones that will cause workers to work?"

Motivation and Organizations

Management often refers to employees as "resources" or "assets," which means that employees are valuable, profitmaking parts of a business organization. Studies of motivation try to discover what incentives will cause workers to work and increase their value as assets. Managers are usually not particularly interested in their workers' personal motivations as such, but they do care about personal motivations as they affect production rates. Therefore, management tries to structure or manipulate, by incentive systems, the motivations of workers.

Management may try to manipulate motivation

The organizational structure evolved by management to facilitate achievement of goals such as profitmaking is also the framework in which workers must try to fill their own needs. (Figure 4–1). Chris Argyris has examined the proposition that individual growth needs and organizational needs are often in conflict. He found that as people mature, they grow more independent and want to make more decisions for themselves. They want to take on more responsibility, to become more competent. He also found that some organizations exert pressures that directly oppose these patterns of self-actualization. In the interests of efficiency, organizations require employees to submit to

Figure 4–1. The motivation process.

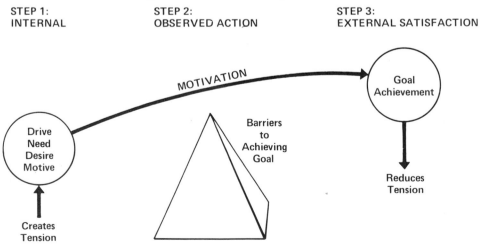

STEP 1:
INTERNAL

STEP 2:
OBSERVED ACTION

STEP 3:
EXTERNAL SATISFACTION

MOTIVATION

Goal
Achievement

Drive
Need
Desire
Motive

Barriers
to
Achieving
Goal

Reduces
Tension

Creates
Tension

rigid forms of authority, demand few skills of them, and make as many decisions as possible for them. Some of the most positive personality traits necessary for individual growth may be the least functional in organizational systems. However, Argyris also believes that the "incongruence between the individual and the organization can provide the basis for a continued challenge which, as it is fulfilled, will tend to help man to enhance his own growth and to develop organizations that will tend to be viable and effective."[1]

Motivation is a process that can be understood in its simplest form as a three step process. Number one: there is an internal need; two: a behavioral action or direction to satisfy that need; and three: the accomplishment or the satisfaction of that need. Let us review a simple example. You feel a hunger pang, developing a deep desire for food, a need you want to satisfy. You therefore display certain observed behavior in the ways you wish to satisfy that need. Until you satisfy your hunger need by eating the tension will build; and the desire to satisfy your hunger need will become more important. Your action or behavioral direction can be one of many. You may satisfy your immediate need by grabbing a snack or waiting several hours for a good meal.

The achievement of a goal is very satisfying and the tension release is gratifying, but the feeling of satisfaction is usually short lived. The "glow" of achieving a goal lasts but a few minutes to an hour, and seldom more than a day.

Three Motivating Sets

Each of us has our own sets of needs, and they vary considerably from person to person. Yet Mr. Paul Meyer, of Success Motivation Institute, believes that there are essentially three types of motivation that effect us all: fear, incentive, and attitude.

Fear motivation is used and causes us to act in a certain way, because we are afraid of the consequences if we don't. We were introduced to fear motivation very early in life. If we disobeyed our parents, we were spanked. The next time we were tempted to disobey, the fear of the possible results motivated us to suppress our desires. There are many forms of fear motivation at work in our society. The laws of our land impose the fear that if we don't obey the various codes we will be arrested. Members of the FBI have said that the crime rate would be greatly reduced if every potential lawbreaker knew for certain that he would be caught and punished. Even the method of withdrawing privileges is a way of using fear motivation.

Fear can motivate us to obey the law

Incentives motivate us to work for tokens

Incentive motivation is a tangible or intangible reward for a simple action. As adults we work for incentives in forms of the four P's of motivation: *praise, prestige, promotion,* and the *paycheck*. It may be in the form of accolades, social acceptance, and commissions.

We all know the story of how the donkey was motivated by the carrot. The carrot dangled on a stick in front of the donkey to encourage him to move, and there is no doubt that the donkey will move provided the stick is short enough, the carrot is big enough, and the donkey is hungry enough.

Incentives "pull" to rewards

Fear "pushes" us

Incentive motivation is the "pull" mechanism and the fear motivation is the "push" mechanism. Or to describe the comparison in another way, which does your company use, is it the KARROT approach, or the K.I.T.A. (Kick in the A−−) approach (Figure 4−2)?

The philosophy of *attitude motivation* or self-motivation is

Figure 4–2. Negative motivators and positive motivators: mental or physical K.I.T.A. (Kick in the A..) or Karrot (incentives).

"THE POSITIVE AND NEGATIVE FORMS OF MOTIVATION."

based on the understanding of human nature. Attitude motivation is a personal set of goals, not goals set by others. It is important to crystallize, to actually commit yourself to a specific goal by writing it down. Next set a deadline, a date that you will reach that goal. It is easy to procrastinate and put off the accomplishing of the goal and really it only proves to yourself the goal was not that important. The desire and determination must be like the zeal of a crusader to become a part of the striving for success. Develop a supreme confidence, while focusing on your strength, not your weaknesses. One way to enforce such desires is to commit yourself to others by telling them of your desire. Once we let others know of our goals it becomes an additional reason to fulfill the expectations that we and others have for us.

Here is an exercise that will help you zero in on goal setting. Below write down something you personally would like to accomplish in three months.

MY GOAL FOR THREE MONTHS _____

By writing something down you have committed yourself and established a deadline. Don't procrastinate—work for it. Now list something you would like to accomplish in three years.

MY GOAL FOR THREE YEARS _____

Neither goal should be so easy that you will naturally reach it through the course of events. You should have to make a few sacrifices to achieve them. If you have enough stamina you will write your goals on the cover of your notebook as a constant reminder of what you are striving for. If you have enough self-confidence you will share your goals, not dreams, with others in your class.

"Management by objectives" is an example that is being practiced in industry. The supervisor and the employee together develop some realistic goals for the employee to accomplish by some future date, usually six months to a year.

The employee's next appraisal or review is based on how well he has met the goals they have established. In some firms it becomes a method by which employees can set their own goals and recognize how they will be evaluated later.

Complexity of Needs

If we were able to deal with a single motivating force within us one at a time we would be able to make logical decisions more easily. However, life is not that simple; we must handle many problems simultaneously, immediate needs of hunger, sleep, shelter, as well as long-range personal goals of job security. Personal needs vary in intensity from person to person and vary daily within the same person. Our needs tend to develop and enforce attitudes about ourselves and the world.

For some people this complexity of needs makes an exciting life; for others it makes life too burdensome and difficult. Regardless of the complexity, the challenge, or the intensity, our needs can become hidden from our conscious recognition. Motivating drives can be summed up in five fairly clear ideas.

1. They are strongly conditioned by past experiences.
2. The intensity varies among persons.
3. More than one need operates at a time.
4. They are often hidden from the conscious recognition.
5. They are nebulous feelings, and are only as logical as our feelings let us be.

MASLOW'S BASIC NEEDS

While industrial engineers were busy streamlining production performance, psychologists and behavioral scientists were concerned with discovering what the workers themselves got out of their jobs.

For a long time there was little if any interest on the part of employers in what the psychologists and scientists were finding out. Today, however, employers are becoming increasingly aware that the intelligent and meaningful structuring of work methods and environments depends as much on identifying basic human needs as it does on developing more efficient techniques.

Identifying Needs

Abraham Maslow conjectured that basic needs are the same for all human beings.[2] He found that while different cultures satisfy these needs in different ways, the needs themselves remain the same. What are these basic needs or instincts that motivate people to act in the ways that they do?

Identifying needs in one's self and in others can be difficult for a variety of reasons. First of all, while five basic needs have been defined, they result in endlessly varying activities. The expression of these needs is influenced both by a person's present surroundings and past experiences, and is different in different individuals. To further complicate matters, basic needs are often more unconscious than conscious. How can the many and changing needs of individuals be made relevant in a working situation, and how, for instance, do they influence a large group of people in an organization?

Needs cannot always be matched to behavior, but observing the choices someone makes will often indicate which needs are operating. Needs often compete for attention and become mixed up with each other. For example, someone who feels hungry and eats to satisfy that "felt" hunger may actually be needing love or security.

Physiological Needs

Maslow's five basic needs start with the physiological need

Not much can motivate a person who has not reasonably satisfied his basic physiological needs. As Dr. Maslow said, "For the man who is extremely and dangerously hungry, no other interest exists, but food. He dreams of food, he thinks about food, he emotes only about food, he perceives only food and wants only food." Gandhi put it another way, "Even God cannot talk to a hungry man except in terms of bread."

The physiological needs are for things that keep the body functioning in a healthy manner. They include such basics as food and drink, sleep, clean air, satisfactory temperature, and protection from the elements by clothing and shelter. When the primary physical needs are satisfied, other physical instincts may take their place, such as sexual desires and the sensual desires of taste, smell, and touch. For most Americans, the physical needs are indirectly satisfied with the money earned from the work they do. Most people in the United States work to earn the money necessary to take care of the basic needs of adequate food, housing, and medical care.

Safety or Security Needs

Security need is the first of the psychological needs

People also want to feel safe from harm. Civilized life and modern technology have all but eliminated the fear of untamed nature. The fears of being assaulted on the street, however, or having an automobile accident can be as potent threats to our sense of safety as the fear of wild animals used to be.

In most adults, the safety needs are expressed by the desire to be stable and secure. To prefer the familiar and the known to the unfamiliar and the unknown reflects the basic need for safety. Organizing one's life around a philosophical or religious system reflects the need to view the world from a stable, secure base.

In the business world, these needs can easily be seen in relation to job security and retirement benefits. The physical and economic safety advantages of these are obvious, especially as we grow older. But they do not tell the whole story. Economic reasons aside, most of us cringe at the possibility of losing our jobs. At such times we feel vulnerable, afraid, and unsure of who we are.

The type of career we choose may reflect our need for security. Such careers might be teaching, accounting, or civil service. Are you thinking of actually working for a large stable company whose growth and future is predictable? Is your choice the changing field of aerospace, electronics, or a more stable area, such as food processing or the fire department? Do you find in job descriptions you look for security phrases like tenure, retirement programs, seniority, promotion from within, and steady growth? If you find the above fits your outlook on a career, then your need for security is very strong. Even more subtle, more sophisticated threats to our security do exist. Consider the billions of words that are invested in discussing air pollution, cancer from smoking, and seat belts. Also, think of millions of dollars spent appealing to man's basic need for security in ads for life insurance and car insurance programs, baby furniture, burglar alarms, and savings programs.

Market research people in the pharmaceutical field sometimes classify physicians into two categories. One is the "innovator." He is the doctor who is among the first to try a new drug, a new surgical technique, or buy a new piece of equipment. The second is the "conservative." He will not try something new until it has been around five years and has been very thoroughly proved. He will tell you that he doesn't want to subject his patients to unnecessary risks, or himself either. Because in this day when legal suits are common, he doesn't want to chance a malpractice charge or hurt his practice and prestige by resorting to what he may consider radical.

We all have a need for security, but some of us have a stronger desire for it than others. Many of our fears are a natural outgrowth of our need for safety. It can motivate us in the purchase of a seat belt, a bottle of vitamin pills, or even marriage.

Another reflection of man's need to feel safe is his preference for the familiar rather than the unknown. "The tendency to have some religion or world philosophy that organized the universe and the men in it into some sort of satisfactorily coherent, meaningful whole is also an example of safety-seeking," according to Dr. Maslow.

Social or Belonging Needs

Generally speaking, once people have satisfied basic physiological and safety needs, they can attend to their needs for group acceptance, affection, and mutual trust. These needs may be filled on the job as well as in private life.

This need reflects itself in a want for someone to love, and someone to love him. It is important to remember that a person needs to *give* as well as *receive* affection.

**Are you a member of
many groups?**

Man's need to satisfy this desire can be seen in the person who is a "joiner." He is the person who joins more than one of the college organizations, such as the Phi Beta Lambda, or the Young Democrats, or Young Republicans. The community "joiner" is a member of the Lion's Club or Rotary Club, as well as an active member of welfare causes. The joiner may use the expression, "Associations like these indirectly help my business," or "I believe in helping my fellow man." Both statements may be true, but they are also helping basic instinctive needs, that of belonging and the need to give as well as receive.

Consequently, the practice of restricting social interactions on the job may curtail the desire to work well. Consider the example of 100 clerks employed to sort and post bills. All 100 worked in one large room, seated in row after row of identical desks. The work was tedious and exacting. The mistakes were many, and heavy absenteeism and fast turnover were the general rule. Then the company changed the layout so that only 10 employees worked together in one room. No other aspects of the job were changed. The result? Mistakes, absenteeism, and turnover decreased. Before the change, employees found it difficult to interact socially and to feel themselves personally important to each other. But, as members of smaller work units, they began to associate socially and developed a sense of group identity and group loyalty. By providing the physical facilities for small groups to develop, the company also made provisions for greater satisfaction of their employees' needs for social interaction.

Other companies that have experimented in this way have also found an improvement in employee attitudes and production. Certainly, such a method should be an important consideration in any management planning.

Esteem Needs

People who value themselves highly develop feelings of confidence, worth, strength, capability, and adequacy. They feel they are useful and important in the world. Lack of self-esteem produces feelings of inferiority, inadequacy, weakness, and helplessness. These feelings of self-dislike lead to discouragement and a sense of failure.

Maslow classifies the needs for esteem into two categories: (1) the desire for a sense of internal worth, and (2) the desire for prestige or reputation that can only be conferred by other people. Perhaps one of the reasons many supervisors work harder than their employees do is that work has special significance for them — it confers self-esteem and the esteem of others. A worker also needs esteem, but may have more difficulty getting it. The more routine a job is, for example, the less status it has. Replacements are easily found for highly routinized jobs. When workers feel dispensable, they are likely to demand more assurances, through wages and fringe benefits, that their futures are secure. There may be a ratio between the need for feeling personal worth and demands for more security.[3] By helping employees feel a greater sense of personal worth, the employer is also helping himself.

Is seeking status important to you?

Vance Packard's book called *The Status Seekers,* dealt strictly with people and the things they care about most, recognition, attention, and prestige. Readers saw comments on almost every page about their friends and themselves. *The Status Seekers* tends to prove that man's need for self-esteem is a fantastically dynamic motivational force.

Management often recognizes that individual needs can be better satisfied with "status" symbols than with money. The executives have their "status" symbols in forms of private dining rooms, carpeted offices, and the key to the executive washroom. Even types of furniture have ratings in the eyes of the employees. The metal desk has the lowest rating. Next up the rung of the ladder of success is the oak desk, and finally the walnut desk. The employee feels he is advancing if he moves from a straight desk to an L-shaped desk, from a desk with his peers to an area fenced off by partitions. The addition of more furniture, such as a filing cabinet, credenza, conference table, all add to the executive status. The smart company recognizes its value and uses it to the best advantage.

The blue-collar worker, while probably sneering at the executive symbols, has many of his own. If he is the shop foreman, or a union boss, he probably rates the end locker or wears some distinctive symbol, such as a jacket or badge, to denote his position. The secretary may gain a feeling of esteem by serving as a private secretary as opposed to a member of the steno pool. Salesmen receive a certain status by driving a company car or by receiving a new car from the company every three years. The gift of a serviceable car by a company for work or family use pays the employee a feeling of recognition and self-esteem. A few police departments have allowed their patrolmen to take the squad car during off-duty hours for family functions, as a hope of satisfying the ego need and satisfying the general public security need.

Sometimes our needs are in conflict. The need to be an integrated accepted member of a group may be in conflict with the need to lead that same group. A good worker may be selected to be a supervisor, but he becomes an ambivalent leader, because his need to be an accepted member of the group has become stronger than the ego drive to be a supervisor.

Self-Actualization Needs

The need for self-fulfillment, the realization of one's potentials to the fullest, is called self-actualization. Needs for self-fulfillment are demonstrated by doing a job well for the sake of doing it well and by striving toward more creative endeavor of all kinds. Maslow distinguishes the needs concerned with physiology, safety, belonging, and esteem as "deficiency" needs—without their satisfaction, people lack the necessary components for developing healthy personalities. Self-actualization is a "growth" need. Healthy people are those who are free to concern themselves mainly with satisfying their needs for continual growth and fulfillment. And, as many businesses are now discovering, these needs cannot simply be relegated to leisure hours.

The Hierarchy of Needs

Maslow explains the five categories of needs in terms of a hierarchy (Figure 4–3), and says that one need must be satisfied before the next need in line can become a driving force. Although this description of a hierarchy of needs is convenient, it is slightly misleading. One need does not require full satisfaction before the next need on the hierarchical ladder makes itself felt.

People are constantly driven by internal forces—they are unceasingly motivated toward new goals. One of the chief reasons the pleasurable feelings accompanying the achievement of a goal are short-lived is that another goal, based on the same or a different need, soon takes its place. *When a need is satisfied, it no longer motivates.* The everchanging nature of needs plays an important role in the theory and practice of incentive systems and job development programs.

HERZBERG'S HYGIENE THEORY

Many managers became thoroughly confused when they tried to apply the need theory to workers. "If individuals all have changing needs," managers said, "how can manage-

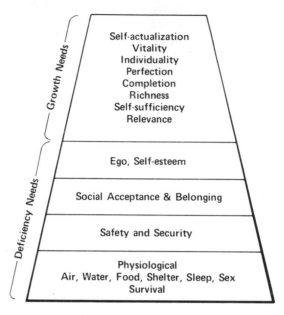

Figure 4–3. Maslow's hierarchy of needs.

ment even attempt to motivate an entire work force?" Proponents of different schools of management theory argue about the best ways to translate basic human needs into sound managerial practices.

Satisfiers and Dissatisfiers

Prior to Herzberg's research, it had been assumed that a positive incentive would increase motivation, while a negative one would decrease it. For instance, according to traditional management theory, offering incentive pay could only increase motivation. Similarly, not offering enough would decrease the incentive to work. The more incentives that were offered, the more satisfied workers would be.

Herzberg, however, found that the factors that make a job satisfying are separate from the factors that make it dissatisfying. For example, offering workers more money can lead to less *dis*satisfaction, but not to true job satisfaction. Employees who hold jobs they consider intrinsically rewarding are satisfied with their jobs: with less rewarding work, they become *less* satisfied. Offering them more money does not *replace* doing fulfilling work.

Workers are often in a neutral position—neither happy nor

unhappy, but simply doing their jobs. Certain negative job factors decrease job satisfaction, and alleviating them brings employees back to a neutral position. Other positive factors can create employee satisfaction on the job. Without them, the employees again drop back to neutral, without turning into dissatisfied employees.

HYGIENE MAINTENANCE THEORY

Satisfying a hygiene factor keeps us from being unhappy

Frederick Herzberg believes that there are certain motivating factors that are used to keep a person from being unhappy (Figure 4–1), much in the same way that food keeps us from being hungry. Having a fine breakfast in the morning does not keep us from being hungry in the afternoon. Such is the case in motivation in industry. For example, a salary raise makes us happy, but not forever. Six months or a year later, we feel we are deserving of a raise again, for one of many reasons. In Herzberg's jargon, money and fringe benefits are known as "negative motivators." Their absence from a job unquestionably will make people unhappy, but their presence doesn't necessarily make them happier or more productive. Satisfying the hygiene maintenance factors only keeps us from being unhappy. Whether man's behavior is motivated by his physical needs, security needs, or social needs, once his "appetites" are satisfied he ceases to be motivated, but he will become "hungry" again. We find that more money in routine amounts, such as the annual raise, is largely taken for granted, anticipated before it arrives

Figure 4–4. Dominance of basic needs; the peak of each level must be passed before the next level can begin to assume a dominate role.

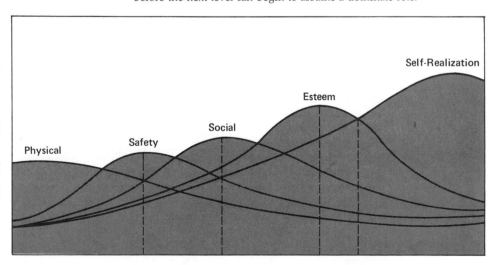

and viewed as a justly deserved reward for past services, not as a stimulus to a new effort.

Another way of viewing Herzberg's theory is that once certain maintenance factors are present, they are adequate and keep a person from being unhappy. Such factors are company policies, supervision, interpersonal relationships, status, money, and security. However, the strong factors that motivate persons to do more on the job are really the opportunities for professional growth, responsibility, work itself, recognition, and achievement.

Table 4–1. Hygiene Factors and Growth Needs

HYGIENE MAINTENANCE FACTORS	MOTIVATORS AND GROWTH NEEDS
Salary, status, & security	Growth and advancement to higher-level tasks
Good factors keep one from being unhappy	Achievement
Company policies and administration	Recognition for achievement
Supervision	Interest in the task
Work environment and interpersonal relations	Responsibility for enlarged task

Source: Frederick Herzberg, *et al.*, *Motivation To Work*. New York: John Wiley & Sons, 1959.

When employees are asked what dissatisfies them about their jobs, they usually complain about things that are not associated with the actual work itself but rather with the work environment. These complaints include such matters as supervision, relations with others, physical conditions, organizational policies, administrative practices, pay, fringe benefits, status, and job security. Such complaints suggest that the context within which the work is done "is unfair or disorganized and as such represents . . . an unhealthy psychological work environment."[4]

Herzberg found that the greatest amount of employee discontent occurs when hygiene maintenance factors are insufficiently met. These needs stem from the desire to avoid pain and to survive in a healthy manner.

When employees are asked what satisfies them about their

work, they will describe aspects of the job itself. Employees are satisfied when the work they do interests them, when they achieve job goals and receive recognition for their achievement, and when they grow or advance in responsibility. The factors that lead to job satisfaction are directly related to the need for self-actualization. People grow psychologically by doing challenging, stimulating work.

Both hygiene and growth needs must be satisfied

Herzberg believes that both hygiene and growth needs must be satisfied. But the relation between motivational and hygiene factors can vary tremendously. Employees with exciting jobs will usually be willing to tolerate unpleasant circumstances, such as low pay or an unfriendly supervisor. However, the fewer possibilities there are for growth and personal fulfillment on a job, the more hygiene factors must be offered in compensation. Workers want something back for what they give. If they can't get personal satisfaction, then they will seek satisfaction in other ways.

INCENTIVES

The Nature of Incentives

An incentive is anything other than the job itself that motivates employees to produce. Incentive systems, which are based on external manipulation, are products of Theory X management philosophy. In this theory, because people are viewed as passive and resistant to business needs, they must be "persuaded, rewarded, punished, controlled—their activities must be directed."[5]

According to Harry Levinson, most executives consider the "carrot-and-stick" philosophy of management the dominant philosophy in management today. Levinson has asked some of these executives to close their eyes and "to form a picture in their mind's eye with a carrot at one end and a stick at the other. When they have done so, I then ask them to describe the central image in that picture. Most frequently they respond that the central figure is a jackass."[6]

What are the characteristics of jackasses? They are stubborn, stupid, willful, and often unwilling to go where drivers want them to go. Is it only coincidental that these are also the characteristics of unmotivated employees? Levinson points out:

> All too often . . . the problem is not that communication is inadequate but, rather, that it is already too explicit in the wrong way. When employees sense that they are being viewed as

jackasses, they will automatically see management's messages as manipulative, and they will resist them, no matter how clear the type or how pretty the pictures.[7]

When Does an Incentive Become a Right?

Today, about the only plan left that can be called a true incentive is the monetary reward offered to workers if they increase their standard output. Most other rewards previously offered as incentives are today considered workers' rights. Rights do not have incentive value; they are taken for granted. Employees who feel underpaid do not work any harder when their wages are raised—their responses are to feel less dissatisfied and to feel that deficiencies have been remedied.

Work standards have changed remarkably in this century. Business owners and managers are more cautious about trying to increase production by manipulating workers' fears of losing their jobs or being demoted. The union movement arose, among other reasons, to struggle against what are now considered inhuman policies—long hours, low wages, job insecurity, unsafe and unhealthy working environments. Many abuses were eventually corrected through legislation or by strong union contracts. Gradually, reward systems have replaced systems of oppression. Business people see the merit of providing high working standards—if only because contented workers are not troublesome ones.

Most managers also want to see rewards as incentives. However, many of these incentive schemes have been a source of frustration, because they have not consistently increased output. One reason for this disappointing state of affairs can be explained by Maslow's principle: a need that is satisfied ceases to motivate. Employees adjust rapidly to changing conditions, particularly when they are for the better.

Many former incentives have become standards of the economy. Wages once raised are rarely lowered. Fringe benefits have little relation to productivity but are instead part of fixed overhead costs. That these hygiene factors do not induce workers to produce more does not mean that they should be cut back. Our complex, technological society continues to struggle with constantly changing values, which affect organizations and employees alike. For instance, no one would think of trying to reinstate the 14-hour day. In fact, some companies are trying out a four-day work week, part-time rather than full-time staffs, staggered working hours, completely arbitrary working hours, and shifts to cover 24-hour working days—all efforts to meet modern organizational and social demands. While such experimentation must be tried, it is not always successful.

Management is thus in the awkward position of offering incentives that are basically irrelevant. Douglas McGregor says:

> But the carrot and stick theory does not work at all once man has reached an adequate subsistance level and is motivated primarily by higher needs. Management cannot provide a man with self-respect, or with the respect of his fellows, or with the satisfaction of needs for self-fulfillment. It can create conditions such that he is encouraged and enabled to seek such satisfaction *for himself*, or it can thwart him by failing to create those conditions.[8]

But to create these conditions the manager must know a great deal about human nature.

Incentives and the Hierarchy of Needs

Frederick Taylor offered incentives

In 1899, Frederick Taylor taught an ironworker named Schmidt to increase by 362 percent the amount of pig iron that could be shoveled in one day. For this stupendous increase in performance, his wages were increased by 61 percent. Industrial engineers have concluded that Schmidt performed well because of the extra wages offered, which may be true. It is also possible that the Dutchman did so well because of the added prestige and self-esteem that such a splendid performance would earn.[9] At face value, therefore, incentives may appear to be only economic gains, but they may also be signals that other needs are being satisfied.

Money incentives can also substitute for *not* satisfying higher-level needs. The Hormel meat-packing plant in Cleveland, Ohio has a wage incentive plan that increases production, but the workers do not appear to be especially interested in their jobs. Frederick Herzberg believes that such an incentive program is not just economic in nature.

> Rather, it provides the means for escape from a job toward which their attitudes are little better than neutral. The sooner they finish the job, the sooner they can get away from it; the more money they can earn, the more effective their escape in pleasant living off the job. It is doubtful that the true production potential of these workers is being tapped; it is undeniable that the incentive system, along with other hygienic factors, serves to make their jobs tolerable.[10]

Many factory supervisors offer incentive pay to get workers to perform beyond their daily quotas, and at the capacity considered possible by time and motion experts. In a study of three heavy-machinery factories, few workers chose to meet more than their minimum quotas; they ignored the incentive systems completely. Management was baffled and irritated because workers would not buy the economic incentive plan.[11]

The study found that, in the first place, workers distrusted management. Although there was no precedent for their belief, they believed that if production increased, management would change the quotas. Also, not exceeding their quotas meant "greater freedom to dispose of their work time as they pleased in the face of a society-wide tendency to routinize and standardize worker activities."[12] The workers perfected ingenious and subtle ways to "beat the system" and to meet their quotas in less time than management allowed for. With their extra time, workers preferred to make devices to reduce production time further, repair damaged factory parts, and make equipment for their own automobiles and homes. In these ways, the workers escaped from routine tasks and gained time to perform more self-fulfilling, creative ones.

The incentive program increased social conflicts. Each factory was split into two distinct social groups: "the office" and the shop. The differences in group standards were marked. The study found that managerial personnel were mainly concerned with economic and status goals. Supervisors competed against each other, looked after individual economic interests, and if necessary pursued their careers, at the expense of the individual and group relations.

Incentive plan cannot always compete with "group pressure"

Shop workers, on the other hand, preferred to restrict output rather than compete against each other. Not cooperating with the incentive plan was a way of expressing resentment toward management's control. In addition, these rank-and-file workers did not expect to advance. As permanent members of their occupational groups, they found it more important to conform to group customs. Their status and belonging need was measured in terms of peer group attitudes rather than management's attitudes.

People have a strong need for group affiliation and support. New factory workers were put into the position of having to choose between the management group and the shop group. Newcomers must depend on shop cooperation for their initial survival. Even though they have received formal training, they must still be taught the tricks of the trade. Often, without "inside" information, it would be impossible to meet the standard daily quota. The standards of coworkers are very compelling—

not meeting them can mean being ostracized from the group. In the three factories studied, exceeding the minimum quota was enough to cause workers to be immediately "frozen out" or ostracized from the group.

INTRINSIC AND EXTRINSIC MOTIVATORS

In the past forty years the growth of fringe benefits has become an important aspect of the American payroll. Companies have provided sick leave, paid vacations, medical plans, and now even dental plans and free legal aid. All of these plans were given by the company in hopes that the employee would show more loyalty and be motivated to do more for the firm. It is rather ironic that the only way an employee can enjoy the fringe benefit, in most cases, is to be off the job. To enjoy a benefit off the job is called an extrinsic motivator. Even today, companies are adding new ideas that can only be appreciated by employees off the company grounds. Intrinsic motivators are plans employees can benefit from on the job. Logically, people work harder on the job when the work is more enjoyable. The use of coffee breaks, cafeterias, clean restrooms, and safe equipment are classically considered as factors that provided employees with the feeling that management cares for them. People are motivated to work because they enjoy the environment and actually the work itself. The University of Michigan's sample of 1,553 workers were asked how important they considered the various aspects of work. The replies related mostly to intrinsic motivators. Of the five top ranked features, only one had to do with tangible economic benefits. And that of good pay ranked fifth.

1. Interesting work,
2. Enough help and equipment to get the job done,
3. Enough information to get the job done,
4. Enough authority to do the job,
5. Good pay.

Accordingly, the self-actualization needs are the strongest motivators in the long run, when other basic needs have been met. Employees will work hard to attain a sense of achievement. To continue to motivate, jobs must be structured to have room for personal growth and development.

111

THE FOREMAN AND HIS SUBORDINATE'S VIEW OF MOTIVATION

What motivates people today are primarily their images of themselves. Opportunities for advancement, greater responsibility, promotion, growth, achievement, and interesting work are consistently identified as factors that make the work situation enjoyable. Further, these factors are primarily associated with the higher order of needs, and are not easily measured. Certainly such factors are more difficult to handle in supervisory strategy.

All too often supervisors think they know what the employees want, but employees claim otherwise. To illustrate this point, the results of a survey is summarized below. The foremen were asked to rank ten job factors in the order they felt their workers would rank them. Independently the workers were asked to rank the same factors in order of importance. By comparison it can be seen that the foremen's perception of what was important to their workers was somewhat out of step with what the employees really felt.

How Foremen and Workers Rated Ten Job Conditions[13]

JOB CONDITIONS	WORKER RATING	FOREMEN RATING
Full appreciation of work done	1st	8th
Feeling "in" on things	2nd	10th
Sympathetic help on personal problems	3rd	9th
Job security	4th	2nd
Good wages	5th	1st
Work that keeps you interested	6th	5th
Promotion and growth in company	7th	3rd
Personal loyalty to workers	8th	6th
Good working conditions	9th	4th
Tactful disciplining	10th	7th

Being appreciated is rated above pay

The most interesting fact of the survey is that supervisors rated wages as the most important factor, while the employees rated the full appreciation of work done as the most important. Perhaps, now, most employees take high wages and excellent benefits plans for granted. For example, most collective bargaining sessions do not start from the question of whether or not there will be a raise in pay; the issue is simply "how much." The key to long-term motivation of employees rests in the higher level needs of people in order to develop a sound, stable economic working environment.

The world is full of boring jobs. Managers must rely on incentives to encourage workers to perform their jobs well because many jobs cannot be made satisfying. But managers can have a great influence on the design of even the dullest jobs. Ideally, jobs should be structured to expand workers' capabilities. Workers can be most effectively motivated when managers allow employees to assume responsibility and participate in a productive way in making decisions. McGregor, however, warns:

> Participation becomes a farce when it is applied as a sales gimmick or a device for kidding people into thinking they are important. Only the management that has confidence in human capacities and is itself directed toward organizational objectives rather than toward the preservation of personal power can grasp the implication of this emerging theory . . .[14]

Participation encourages motivation

Though the following approaches to increasing motivation are not all equally effective, they give a solid foundation for understanding how jobs can be designed to be more interesting.

Horizontal Job Loading

Horizontal job loading assumes that if employees are given more work to do at the *same level* at which they are currently performing they will be motivated to work harder and also be more satisfied with their work. For example, an assembler is told to put together 1,000 parts instead of the 500 previously required.

Vertical Job Loading

Vertical job loading changes jobs to include larger areas of responsibility. Jobs are restructured so that they will become *intrinsically* more interesting. The worker is motivated because the job is more challenging and more meaningful. For instance, the nature of a dishwasher's job would be changed vertically if he or she were also made responsible for keeping track of worn and broken dishes and reporting defects to a supervisor.

More work doesn't motivate; more challenge or responsibility does

Vertical job loading includes the idea of "closure": employees have an understanding of the organization they are a part of. They are no longer just cogs in a wheel but instead can participate in and contribute to the entire work process. To provide

Figure 4–5. Workers can be most effectively motivated when managers allow employees to assume responsibility and to participate in a productive way in making decisions.
(Photo by Robert Curtis)

for closure, tasks that logically belong together are grouped to-gether into one job—steps that one employee can carry through from beginning to end.

Vertical loading implies that employees should be given as much responsibility as possible. Employees should be encour-aged to be accountable for their work, with little supervision. Vertical job accountability applies to managers also. In one com-pany, the vice-presidents became responsible for distinct areas of the company's operations. For instance, the vice-president of production was put in charge of increasing output throughout the company. Previously, each department was concerned with its own production rates. This vice-president now had to deal with the various production problems of each department: how to determine the required numbers of hours for assembly, how to shorten time for paper work, how to eliminate waste motion in shipping, and how to determine the best number of people in each department.[15]

A clerk at a bank remembers her job well. Even a machine would have grown bored with it. "My job was to pull invoices and checks out of envelopes and stack them into three piles: one under $10, another between $10 and $25, and a third over $25. Then I passed the piles onto the next person. After two months of this I was so bored I would have quit within another month." After two more years she was still at the bank, but instead of performing a tiny task in the paper mill, she handled all the processing for 22 corporate accounts. "Handling your own accounts is a lot more interesting, and you feel like you have accomplished something."

Bank employee has control; she is not told what to do

Frederick Herzberg has compiled a checklist of the steps involved in vertical loading, which includes the motivators that can be expected from each step.

Job Rotation

In job rotation, workers learn to do all the different activities necessary in one operation or unit of work. Teams that are used

Table 4–2. Principles of Job Loading

PRINCIPLE	MOTIVATORS INVOLVED
1. Remove some controls while retaining accountability	Responsibility and personal achievement
2. Increase the accountability of individuals for own work	Responsibility and recognition
3. Give a person a complete natural unit of work (module, division, area)	Responsibility, achievement, and recognition
4. Grant additional authority to employee in activities, giving more job freedom	Responsibility, achievement, and recognition
5. Make periodic reports directly available to the worker rather than to the supervisor	Internal recognition
6. Introduce new and more difficult tasks not previously handled	Growth and learning
7. Assign individuals specific or specialized tasks, enabling them to become experts	Responsibility, growth, and advancement

Source: Frederick Herzberg, "One More Time: How Do You Motivate Employees?"
"Harvard Business Review," January–February 1968, p. 59.

to working together adapt well to the rotation method. Job rotation can be easily subjected to horizontal loading. The monotony may be relieved by rotating similarly meaningless tasks, but this does not help to make the job more significant. However, it is quite possible to arrange for vertical job rotation, where both routine and complex tasks are passed around and new skills have to be applied to each job in the operation.

Job Enlargement

Job enlargement, as the term indicates, means that workers are responsible for carrying out a larger number of duties. Workers do not have to perform only simple tasks. They become involved in producing the entire product, or at least distinct portions of it. Job enlargement, though, is also an easy prey to horizontal loading. Asking employees to tighten screws as well as bolts enlarges the job—but meaningless tasks still add up to meaningless tasks.

The classic example of job enlargement is the reorganization of assembly lines into teams that put together entire small products or units of complicated products. For instance, Non-Linear Systems discarded their assembly lines in favor of seven-person teams, who together build complete electronic instruments.[16] The teams pace themselves and maintain their own work rhythms. They decide the sequence of the tasks.

Each team is headed by a technician. Beyond that, team members decide who does the various tasks. Jobs are chosen and allocated according to individual strengths. Members can rotate jobs when they desire it. Skills are perfected and members pass on their knowledge to each other.

The teams are strongly cohesive, and the workers are interested in what they are doing. The company offers continuous, voluntary training programs to encourage employees to use their talents even more. Non-Linear Systems also benefited from the changeover. In three years, productivity increased by 30 percent and complaints about its products decreased by 70 percent.

Job Enrichment

The term "enrichment" gained popularity when job "enlargement" began to be mistaken for horizontal job loading. Job "development" is another term in current use. The terms job enrichment and development try to indicate the fundamental principles of vertical job loading.

DELEGATION OF AUTHORITY WITH RESPONSIBILITY

Delegation must be with
responsibility to carry
out the task

One way to satisfy the need for achievement, recognition, and most of all responsibility is to give employees a task and the authority to carry it out. This is one of the most important positive motivators supervisors can delegate to employees. Many people will be willing to accept additional duties, new challenges, if the supervisor is willing to allow them to have the necessary authority. However, some leaders are often afraid to give employees the authority for fear that they will make a poor decision that would embarrass the supervisor or hurt the department's operation. Supervisors should be looking for new ways to expand rather than to limit the scope of activities of their subordinates. So many supervisors feel the need for more time—it may be because they are not taking the opportunities of spreading their duties to their employees. Such examples of delegation of authority have been seen in Polaroid by letting its scientists pursue their own projects and order their own materials without checking with a supervisor. Film assembly workers are allowed to run their machines at the pace they think best. At another company, female marketing correspondents were allowed to send out letters over their own signatures, rather than that of their executives. American Telephone and Telegraph's "work-itself" program demonstrates the concepts of job enrichment. For example, before the "work-itself" program was introduced in one keypunching department, fourteen women each punched about one-fourteenth of the day's work load. The operators did not identify with the work, and turnover rates were high. The job was redesigned so that:

1. Each employee was made responsible for a specific customer or department. For instance, one operator would keypunch cards for traffic, another for marketing.
2. Each operator set her own verification rates.
3. Operators were allowed to communicate directly with their accounts, instead of going through a supervisor.
4. Operators were more and more given the chance to schedule their own work.

As a result of being given more meaningful responsibility, turnover and absenteeism dropped, and production increased so that only ten employees were needed to handle the same amount of work.[17]

Developing job enrichment programs are not easy nor are they quickly accepted. They must be first accepted at the highest level of management and trickle down to the lowest level. Many may resist the changes that job enrichment brings. Many fear it as a threat to established jobs. When you are talking about productivity, you are really cutting the number of jobs, some say, so workers will look on this with suspicion.

For at least fifty years, industry has strived to break jobs down into their smallest possible components and relying on assembly lines. Managers, assuming that work was inevitably boring, tried to boost morale and productivity by improving benefits and working conditions. We are finding the impact of boredom on productivity outweighs the benefits of extreme specialization.

FLEXIBILITY GIVES SELF-DIRECTION

Such giants as General Foods and Motorola have banished the time clocks years ago. Other companies have staggered the working hours to best fit the parking lot traffic flow. One company has five shifts starting every fifteen minutes. The morning shifts start at 8:00, 8:15, 8:30, 8:45, and 9:00 a.m. The evening shifts end at 4:00, 4:15, 4:30, 4:45, and 5:00 p.m. Each group puts in an eight hour shift. Yet, the most important part of the program is that the employee picks his time schedule.

"Sliding time" or "Flexitime" helps employees decide for themselves

In West Germany, some 3,500 firms have adopted "sliding time." In one form of the plan, company doors are open from 7:00 a.m. until 7:00 p.m., and factory or office workers can come in any time they like, provided that they are around for "core time," from 10:00 a.m. to 3:00 p.m. and they put in a forty hour week. As a result, productivity is up, staff turnover is down, and absenteeism has fallen as much as 20 percent.

One important fact from the point of view of the employee is his feelings about his company's effort to improve self-motivating techniques. If management gives up attempting to motivate, then so does the average worker. To the average employee the world looks rigid and unyielding. Motivation of employees by management must be a constant, continuing program, and ever attuned to new ideas in society that will affect man in the work force.

POSITIVE REINFORCEMENT

The renovated password is positive reinforcement. Employees receive praise and recognition for improved performance. Although this sounds like an obvious elementary principle for any well-managed operation to follow, many companies ignore it. A carefully engineered step-by-step program with frequent feedback of questions and answers lets the salesperson know how he is doing. Psychologist B. F. Skinner contends that to change behavior, to make an employee more productive, one has to manipulate the work situation itself. A fundamental Skinner principle is that behavior can be engineered, shaped, or changed by a carefully controlled system of rewards.

Those who believe Skinner's approach is callous can relate to their own personal experiences. We all appreciate a compliment or a "positive stroke": "You're doing a good job, Alice. I hear many people saying that about you!" The problem with many adult situations is that we are expected to perform a good job and only punished when we don't do an adequate job. My personal belief is that most people don't receive enough sincere, positive statements about their work.

LET WORKERS SEE THE END PRODUCT OF THEIR EFFORTS

Tour of the factory helps workers see the "whole picture"

In today's automated society it is too often that employees work on parts for pieces of equipment they never see. It is common that employees have no idea of the type of equipment that will hold their handiwork. Such a limiting view of the product can more easily develop a more complacent, boring attitude on the job. Some manufacturing firms have sent employees from their supply plants to assembly plants to see where their parts fit into the finished product. Other firms put the assembly line workers on inspection jobs for one-week stints. Said one welder, "I now see metal damage, missing welds, and framing fits that I never would have noticed before." The employee who sees more of the company as a whole can identify with it in more positive terms. There is a great chance of loyalty and motivation under these conditions.

LISTENING SUPERVISORS

A listening supervisor motivates an employee more than a talking supervisor

Studies seem to indicate that employees with listening supervisors have higher morale than those who do not. To be an effective communicator it is necessary to know far more than rules for writing memos or making effective speeches. It is important to develop an insight into human motives and aspirations of employees in order to interact effectively. Xerox and the American Management Society have developed and conducted listening clinics.

As one manager said, "I don't understand why the employees don't perform better." In reply another manager commented: "Perhaps they don't want to be treated better, but want to be used better, and the only way we can find out how to use them better is to listen to them."

SUMMARY

Motivation is the internal need

Motivation refers to any activity that has a goal toward which action is oriented. In business, that motivational action is called work. To want to act is true motivation.

Motivation is an internal state, which may be triggered by

incentives. We all have highly individualized reasons for acting in the ways we do. Therefore, while some generalizations can safely be made about the nature of motivation, it is inadvisable to judge the reasons for motivation on behavior alone.

Because organizations are responsible for job structure and content, they are largely responsible for workers' reponsibilities to satisfy their personal needs—needs which provide the motivating force for their work. Organizations and individuals must constantly reevaluate their mutual satisfactions and dissatisfactions, in an attempt to balance each other's needs.

Maslow's hierarchy of needs

Abraham Maslow widened the scope of motivational theory with his observations on the hierarchy of needs. Maslow found that certain drives were common to all people and with few exceptions operated according to a hierarchy. When the most basic needs were satisfied, the next needs in the hierarchy asked for attention. In order of necessity, the needs are concerned with physical health, personal safety or security, belonging, esteem by self and others, and self-actualization. The first four categories are called deficiency needs because they hamper survival if they are not adequately met. Self-actualization needs have to do with an individual's psychological growth and development. When a need is satisfied, it ceases to be a driving force.

Carrot-and-stick management

Incentives are punishments and rewards that are *ex*trinsic to the job itself. They are used to try to motivate people to work better or harder. The carrot-and-stick management philosophy is a way of describing incentives. Basically, incentives are designed to push or pull employees to perform their jobs even "more." What were once incentives now become rights because the incentives helped to change the accepted working standards. Incentive systems easily can become confused with other motivators. Wage raises can merely indicate levels of achievement and can substitute for the lack of other need satisfactions. Incentives can be ignored if they conflict with the satisfaction of other needs, such as group affiliation and more time to do creative work.

Motivating factors are *in*trinsic to the job. True motivation must come from the job itself—only the job can be satisfying. Part of feeling self-fulfilled is having the sense of utilizing one's energy in a fruitful way. Only when workers feel they are achieving something in *spite* of the routine nature of the work are their jobs satisfying. Managers cannot always change the structures of jobs so that they give more responsibility and decision-making power to employees.

Horizontal job loading

Vertical job loading

Horizontal job loading only increases workers' duties at the same level, without giving workers higher levels of responsibility. Vertical job loading, on the other hand, adds dimension to jobs. Employees are made responsible for entire operations, including many levels of tasks and skills. Job rotation is the con-

Job enrichment

cept of trading jobs, which often relieves monotony and can increase responsibility. Through job enlargement programs, assembly lines have been disbanded, and teams formed that build
entire assemblies together. *Job enrichment* or *job development* are
the terms now commonly used to indicate vertical job loading
methods.

More often, motivated workers are also high producers.
But, when motivated workers do *not* increase production, managers are faced with a dilemma: which is more important in the
long run—workers' satisfaction or higher production rates?

HOW DO YOU MOTIVATE MOTEL MAIDS

Case Study #1

All Western Motels are a franchise operation with six interests in the San Diego area. For the last several years, employee turnover, especially among the lower-salaried workers, has been a major problem. The turnover rate among maids alone reached the level of three employees per month per hotel. This computes to the staggering figure of 45 percent on an annual basis.

The maid is probably the most potent representative of a hotel, even though she is seldom, if ever, seen by the guests. It is the way that she performs her work which will determine, to a large extent, whether a guest will return to the hotel for a second stay; and hotels survive on repeat business. "Repeaters" make a house's reputation—especially through word-of-mouth advertising, which is the best and the cheapest kind! Not only were the hotels faced with the expense of hiring, processing, and bonding employees, but low morale was producing a low-grade, careless approach to the job. In several instances, a complete refund of rent monies had to be made. In addition, maids quit without notice and the cost to train a new applicant was becoming intolerable.

The maids for the Western concerns were being paid the top wages in the area for related employment. These wages were not at all high, however, as no hotel in these days of economic recession can afford to increase its overhead appreciably. The working conditions seemed good. The women were allowed one meal per shift "gratis" at the hotel's coffee shops, and they were allowed to use the pool facilities during their "off-hours" at four of our locations.

The managers tried to interview the girls who had left our employ, but they could get no useful information from them. They spoke in generalities such as "I'm just tired of working here." Finally, the operators approached the franchise's main office in Phoenix, and a general meeting of the concerned managers was called. You were chosen as the franchise representative to the conference.

The meeting was held on the 19th and 20th of September at one of the San Diego locations. Five of the hotels sent representatives. One manager claimed that the whole thing was "just a waste of time and money." After lunch, on the first day, your group sat down to discuss the situation.

It was the general consensus of the group that the fidelity of the employees toward the company should be increased. Personal identity and pride in their jobs seemed to be the ingredients most lacking. But how to induce these feelings into a role such as that of a maid?

1. Put yourself in the role of the motel maid. What physical changes could be made to make your job more enhanced?

2. Personal identity and pride in the job should be given top priority in redesigning the position. Can changes be made in uniform, job functions, reporting times, personal recognition, or "off-duty privileges" to enhance the employees personal identity?

3. What psychological factors can be developed to help the maids' personal images?

HOW DO YOU MOTIVATE A REAL ESTATE AGENT DURING A DEPRESSED ECONOMY

Case Study #2

The real estate firm that you own has a sales staff of thirty people. As any real estate person can tell you, the life blood of any office is its listings. This is the inventory of homes available for sale. The prime job of a salesperson is to find a home to list for sale and to find buyers for those homes. An office of a salesperson will not do well in the realty field without listings.

How does one go about motivating the sales force to bring in new listings into the office? The early part of the year was poor for the sale of real estate. The state of the local economy was a disaster. However, in any kind of economy there will always be some buyers and sellers. In order to encourage the thirty salespersons to bring in more listings, you as the sales broker and owner installed a new motivation technique.

1. Is the technique for this group of people more likely to be physical or psychological? Why?
2. What motivating technique is likely to work the best to bring in more listings?

Terms and Concepts Students Should Know

internal need	intrinsic motivators	ego need
external goal	job loading	self-actualization
fear motivation	job enlargement	growth need
incentive motivation	physiological need	extrinsic motivators
Maslow's basic needs	security need	job rotation
hygiene maintenance need	belonging need	job enrichment

Bibliography

1. ARGYRIS, CHRIS, *Integrating The Individual and the Organization*, New York, John Wiley & Sons, 1964.
2. MASLOW, A. H., *Motivation and Personality*, New York, Harper & Row Publishers Inc., 1954.
3. HERZBERG, FREDERICK, BERNARD MAUSNER, and BARBARA BLOCH SNYDERMAN, *The Motivation to Work*, New York, John Wiley & Sons, 1959.
4. McGREGOR, DOUGLAS, *The Human Side of Enterprise*, New York, McGraw-Hill Book Company, 1960.

Footnotes

[1] Chris Argyris, *Integrating the Individual and the Organization* (New York: John Wiley & Sons, 1964), p. 7.

123

[2] A. H. Maslow, *Motivation and Personality* (New York: Harper & Row Publishers Inc., 1954).

[3] Mason Haire, *Psychology in Management* (New York: McGraw-Hill Book Co., 1956), p. 33.

[4] Frederick Herzberg, Bernard Mausner, and Barbara Bloch Snyderman, *The Motivation to Work* (New York: John Wiley & Sons, 1959), p. 113.

[5] Douglas McGregor, *The Human Side of Enterprise* (New York: McGraw-Hill Book Co., 1960), p. 118.

[6] Harry Levinson, "Asinine Attitudes Toward Motivation," *Harvard Business Review,* January–February, 1973, p. 73.

[7] *Ibid.,* p. 74.

[8] McGregor, *The Human Side of Enterprise*, pp. 121–122.

[9] William F. Dowling, Jr. and Leonard R. Sayles, *How Managers Motivate: The Imperatives of Supervision* (New York: McGraw-Hill Book Co., 1971), p. 5.

[10] Herzberg, *et al., The Motivation to Work*, p. 119.

[11] Orvis Collins, Melville Dalton, and Donald Roy, "Restrictions of Output and Social Cleavage in Industry," in *Management of Human Resources: Readings in Personnel Administration*, edited by Paul Pigors, Charles A. Myers, and F. T. Malm, (New York: McGraw-Hill Book Co., 1964), pp. 371–381.

[12] *Ibid.,* p. 378.

[13] W. C. Menninger and H. Levinson, *Human Understanding in Industry* (Chicago: Science Research Associates, 1956) p. 12.

[14] McGregor, *The Human Side of Enterprise*, p. 124.

[15] Arthur H. Kuriloff, "An Experiment in Management: Putting Theory Y to the Test," *Personnel* 40, November–December 1963, 12.

[16] *Ibid.,* p. 14.

[17] William N. Penzer, *Productivity and Motivation Through Job Engineering: An AMA Management Briefing* (New York: AMACOM, 1973), pp. 23–24.

two

People Seem to Act that Way

Morale and the Environment

"Sometimes I'm Happy" ● ● ● ● ● ● ● ●

OBJECTIVES

After reading this chapter you should be able to:
1. List at least ten questions, the answering of which would be a good guide to your morale on the job.
2. Differentiate between morale, motivation, and feelings in general.
3. List the stages of development of group identity.
4. Describe the four major value shifts in society that have caused corresponding changes in workers' attitudes.
5. Discuss the general attitudes of the following groups toward their jobs in today's society.
   A. Blue-collar workers
   B. White-collar workers
   C. Junior executives
6. Explain how and why employee surveys can be useful in studying morale.
7. Explain how reviewing the company's records can tell us something about the employees' morale.
8. Describe how the physical environment can affect employees' morale.

■ ■

True or False:

Many people do not like their jobs.
Many feel their jobs are too boring.
Most people think they are not paid enough.
The "work ethic" is stronger among older people than among the young.

If you answered "true" to every statement, you agree with most of what is being written on the subject in many popular pulp publications. A study conducted in 1973 found that the "work ethic" is alive and well in America. Over 90 percent of the men and over 80 percent of the women said they like their jobs. Despite the fact that there are always complaints about working hours, repetitious tasks, and mountains of paperwork, by and large most Americans are basically happy with their jobs. Further, 70 percent of the men and women over thirty believed they were being paid a fair day's pay for a day's work.

What is Morale

Morale like health requires attention

Like the word *health, morale* used alone has neither a favorable nor an unfavorable meaning and it is not very specific. In the same way health is important, so is morale. It requires regular attention, diagnosis, and treatment.

Morale has been defined as a state of mind and emotions. It affects our attitude and willingness to work, which in turn affects others. Morale consists of the attitudes of individuals and groups toward life, their environment, and their work. Morale is not a single feeling, but a composite of feelings, sentiments, and attitudes. People may believe that morale is something which can be either present or absent. Actually, morale is always present in some form. It can vary from a positive to a negative form at any given time.

Morale is a composite of feelings

Someone once gave this definition of morale, "Morale is an individual's zest for living or working or the lack of it. A person with high morale has confidence in himself, in his future, and in others. He thinks his work is worth doing well and that he is doing a good job. High morale helps him take minor irritations in stride, and to work under pressure without blowing up."

Maintaining high morale is a continuous task

Raising morale to a high level and maintaining it there is a continuous process, which cannot be achieved simply through short-run devices such as pep talks or contests. High morale usually is slow to develop and difficult to maintain. The level of morale can vary considerably from day to day; it can be as changeable as the weather. Morale is also contagious, both favorable attitudes and unfavorable attitudes can spread among people. Yet, for all its evasiveness, morale is vital.

QUESTIONS TO ASK

Morale is involved in everything that makes a job satisfying. While working on a job, here are some questions you can ask, all of which pertain to morale.

Do you like the people you work with? Do you socialize with them on and off the job? If not, what prevents this exchange? Do you respect their work habits? Whom do you enjoy working with most?

Is your job boring or challenging? If you had your way, how would you change your job to make it more meaningful?

Do you think you and other employees are paid fairly for your jobs? Do you think you have long enough vacations and sufficient medical coverage?

How do you like your supervisor? Does the supervisor allow you to participate in making decisions that affect your job or your department? Are you treated as part of a team or as an employee with only specific duties to perform?

Are you a member of a union? How well does it represent you? Have you ever filed a formal grievance? How was it handled?

Do you feel discriminated against in any way, particularly for reasons of race or sex? Or are you given the same respect as others?

What do you believe your organization thinks of you? Do you feel it evaluates your work correctly? Do you think your talents are being fully utilized? How does the organization indicate that it values your contributions? How do you fit into the organizational structure? Do you feel like a person or a cog in a wheel?

How do you feel about your organization's goals? Do you know what the goals are? Do you think the organization is interested in profits only, or does it have the interests of its employees and society in mind?

Looking at the answers to these questions, you will get an idea of how the total work picture feels. The variables must be weighed *together*. Obviously the more "yes" answers you give to the objective questions the happier you tend to be on the job as compared with others in the class.

Individual Morale

A man with high morale remembers the happy moments rather than the drab

One man described the morale of an individual as a man who is happy and remembers the happy moments rather than the drab moments. He finds interests to fill his spare time, so that his life is a full exciting life. Our general outlook on life depends to a greater extent on how we feel about ourselves. Our self-concept must be in a state of continuous renewal. As we pass through life we accumulate habits and opinions that affect our general feeling for life. A simple explanation of individual morale is knowing one's own expectations and living up to them. If one is clear of his own needs and how to satisfy them most of the time, his morale is high.

Group Morale

Whereas an individual's morale is a single person's attitude toward life, group morale reflects the general tone or *esprit de corps* of a collective group of personalities. Each person either heightens the prospect of the esprit de corps or lowers the concept of a cooperative effort. Group morale is everyone's concern, and it must be practiced continually, for it is never ultimately achieved and is constantly changing. Group morale demands mutual respect for one another.

If a group is composed of five persons, each contributing his own personality to the group, soon a new personality develops, that of the group. Group rapport and trust in each other develops. The growth encouraged by all relates to the height of morale that can be achieved by the group. However, the larger the group the more elusive is the feeling of group morale and the harder it is to determine.

Certainly, good morale is helpful in achieving teamwork, but it is possible that teamwork can be high and group morale can be low. Such a situation might exist in times when jobs are scarce and employees will tolerate close supervision to gain productive teamwork. Those with a strong need to belong often develop the greatest teamwork spirit, with the attitude that "united we stand and divided we fall." It must be remembered that the development of a strong group morale will depend on the task and the individuals involved. Conversely, good teamwork may be absent when individual morale is high; for employees might prefer satisfaction in individual performance rather than group performance and group rewards. High achievement motivated persons usually prefer to work alone and be judged on their individual production.

MORALE AND GROUP IDENTITY

The importance of group identity cannot be underestimated. Without it, there can be no group action. For example, during World War II many American prisoners of war were able to escape from Japanese prison camps because their fellow prisoners were willing to take risks for them. There are reports of one man escaping from ten-man work teams, even though the teams had been warned that the nine others would be shot.[1] These prisoners had created a group identity of such strength that the achievement of the group goal—freedom for even one—was deemed more important than the survival of the many.

In contrast, during the Korean War, *not a single* escape was recorded, even though Chinese prisons were not as heavily guarded as the Japanese camps had been.[2] One explanation for this unprecedented American docility was that group identity, and thus group morale, were completely destroyed by *brainwashing*. The core of the brainwashing technique was to turn prisoners against one another and to convince them that no one was trustworthy. Informers were encouraged by rewards of cigarettes and special privileges. The atmosphere of mistrust prevented all but the most trivial communication. Each prisoner was effectively isolated from the other. Finally, these methods resulted in another kind of "escape"—suicide—the highest rate recorded for American prisoners of war. The sense of a group identity, based on common goals and needs, which is necessary for the morale of prisoners of war, was never allowed to develop. The prisoners experienced themselves as alienated, lonely individuals.[3]

MORALE AND CHANGING SOCIAL VALUES

Individuals and groups operate within larger frameworks. Morale changes when the larger frameworks change. Organizations, and the people in them, reflect the society of which they are a part. Accordingly, workers' expectations change with the changing issues and conditions of the times. As a part of society, an organization is subject to the same value changes experienced by the society as a whole.

Roger D'Aprix has isolated five major value shifts currently affecting workers' attitudes.[4]

Respect for authority is decreasing

1. Workers no longer appear to respect organizational systems and the authorities representing those systems as much as they did in the past. Americans have been presented with scandal after scandal in high places and no longer blindly accept the credibility of leaders and officials. This skepticism has begun to show up in the citizenry's relations with the government. The growing incidence of taxpayers' revolts is an instance of people challenging authority, in this case the government's.[5]

Change becomes more common

Change breeds insecurity

2. Change has become a constant. Consistency, often meaning reliability, is becoming rare, because of our rapidly changing technology. On the one hand, rapid change provides more job opportunities. On the other, it can be terribly threatening to workers whose jobs have become obsolete. In the preface to his book, *Working,* Studs Terkel comments:

> Perhaps it is this specter that most haunts working men and women: the planned obsolescence of people that is of a piece with the planned obsolescence of the things they make. Or sell. It is perhaps this fear of no longer being needed in a world of needless things that most clearly

spells out the unnaturalness, the surreality of much that is called work today.[6]

Change may be "progressive," but it also breeds insecurity.

Economy depends on credit

3. Economic solvency used to be considered socially necessary or else you risked personal disgrace. This was particularly true during and after the Great Depression. Now, our economy depends on credit and the prevailing attitude that denying yourself anything is foolish. Consumerism continues to sell high standards of living, while companies and employees alike groan at the mounting rise in costs. Most Americans must work hard to meet the expenses of living, and they borrow money when they have to.

4. While the spiraling inflation continues, the value of the work ethic is being seriously questioned. Studs Terkel says:

"Work ethic" is challenged

[T]here is a sacrilegious question being asked these days. To earn one's bread by the sweat of one's brow has always been the lot of mankind. At least, ever since Eden's slothful couple was served with an eviction notice. The scriptural precept was never doubted, not out loud. No matter how demeaning the task, no matter how it dulls the senses and breaks the spirit, one *must* work. Or else.

Lately there has been a questioning of this "work ethic," especially by the young. Strangely enough, it has touched off profound grievances in others, hitherto devout, silent, and anonymous. Unexpected precincts are being heard from in a show of discontent. Communiques from the assembly line are frequent and alarming: absenteeism. On the evening bus, the tense, pinched faces of young file clerks and elderly secretaries tell us more than we care to know. On the expressways, middle management men pose without grace behind their wheels as they flee city and job.[7]

More and more people want to find a meaning in their work beyond the reward of the paycheck. This is as true of the white-collar world as of the blue. "I'm a machine," says the assembly line worker; "I'm in a cage," says the bank teller.[8]

The concept of participatory management, the spread of sensitivity training in industries, and the humanistic orientations of some business and union leaders are but a few signs of the changing values of the work ethic.

Social concern vs. company goals

5. Ethical concerns are having a growing effect on the business world. The effects are both external and internal. One example of an external effect is the development of biodegradable products

by detergent manufacturers in response to environmental problems as well as to ecology-minded consumers. Internally, serious morale problems can result when employees in a firm disapprove of the company product. What kinds of action result from ethical conflicts that cannot be resolved? One executive, with years of experience in recruiting MBA trainees, gives this account:

> I noticed a drastic change, starting around 1970. The MBAs we are getting now show a great deal of social concern. We have had a few people who rejected the job because of the type of products we make. We also have had individuals quit or transfer to another division where they would not face any ethical conflict. These people were exit interviewed; and it came down to the fact that they felt some of our products were not truly necessary to the public and they could not in good conscience market them. There are some members of our management who will not speak before management trainee groups because of the violence they have experienced. My interviewing techniques have changed because of all this. I now explore the ethical area [social concern] in detail to see whether we might run into conflicts. When this seems likely, I recommend against hiring.[9]

STUDENT ATTITUDES

In view of the importance to business of changing social values, it is not surprising that student attitudes are being studied in an effort to anticipate morale problems that might appear on the job market in the future. Over the last decade studies have shown trends toward remarkable changes in attitudes.

Getting things done is more important than status

Students at Harvard Business School want to work for smaller organizations and want fewer controls than the students did ten years ago. They are less concerned with status and formal procedures than with "getting things done." They care less about profits then they do about personal and community relations.[10] Students at the University of Connecticut trust one another less. They see themselves as less able to control their own destinies and feel more at the mercy of external forces than their predecessors.[11] University of Toronto students have become suspicious of all authoritarian and dogmatic structures.[12]

One study, conducted on five campuses, polled students for attitudes and motives traditionally considered essential for managerial success. They were: (1) a favorable attitude toward authority; (2) a desire to compete; (3) assertive motivations; (4) a desire to exercise power; (5) a desire to capture the attention of others through distinctive kinds of behavior; and (6) a sense of responsibility. The study shows that these values have declined considerably in popularity.[13] That conclusion seems to correlate with a study done at the University of Washington, which showed that most of the students there felt they could not realize their *major* values in life if they went into management careers.[14] How do you think today's business students feel about achieving their *major life goals*?

EARLY CAREER MORALE

The great majority of young people in America still believe in the work ethic, the idea that hard work and getting ahead are essential for a full and satisfying life. One young man expressed his outlook in these words:

> I think America is the greatest country in the history of the world. One of the reasons? Free enterprise. You can go to your heart's content in life. You can set your goals anywhere you want to set 'em in America. This is all part of the American spirit, to compete, to be better, to be number one. To go as far as you can. If the next man can't go that far, don't stop and wait for him. Life will pass you up.[15]

It is with this spirit of enthusiasm that many young people begin working at their first "real" jobs.

Traditionally, even for college graduates, a first job pays the lowest income and requires the least responsibility. Regardless of these facts, the first year of work has been called the **"Honeymoon year"** "honeymoon year," to indicate the generally high morale most people experience during their first introduction to working life. After the first two or three years, morale often drops considerably. After three to five years of "reality" on a job, morale **Many change jobs after** may be low, which may explain why so many employees **two to five years** change jobs on the average of every three to five years. If employees remain with the same company for five years or more, their morale tends to pick up. Apparently the employee learns to adjust to the company and probably reevaluates his or her job aspirations. Certainly the same routine and plans may not be much different, but things do seem rosier. He learns to adjust to the character of the company and probably his aspirations with the company are far more realistic than his aspirations for himself. We might say at this point, a person's morale is a rough index of how well he can solve his human relations problems in the company. This pattern of high morale in the beginning, followed by low morale and a leveling off, usually occurs when a new career choice is made or a new job is begun.

Although there has been much publicity about disgruntled

blue-collar workers, a six-year study of the Baltimore General Motors plant by three professors at Rutgers University indicates that 95 percent of the workers are basically satisfied with their jobs and that 71 percent do not find any part of their job upsetting or tiring. The researchers say that these percentages don't imply that assembly line work actually "fills people with delight and satisfaction," but at least their jobs are meeting their expectations of a regular paycheck, vacations, and retirement. The researchers found that jobs provided the workers the means to enjoy other pursuits, which were their central interests in life. The Survey Research Center at the University of Michigan, compiling information from fifteen opinion surveys since 1958, recently concluded that job satisfaction for all kinds of workers has not changed in any demonstrable way.[16]

In studies of job satisfaction, black workers under thirty years of age are more dissatisfied with their jobs than any other group. The group with the second highest proportion of dissatisfied workers are males under thirty years of age with some college education, with females under thirty ranking third. Perhaps younger workers are more dissatisfied because they are the "new breed" with higher expectations than their elders.

Younger workers are more dissatisfied because they have higher expectations

For those who are now discovering the various careers, it might be pointed out that higher-level occupations report higher job satisfactions. Several surveys have shown that the proportions of persons who would choose their same occupations again ranged from 82 to 91 percent for professional occupations, while the percentage for skilled to unskilled occupations ranged from 16 to 52 percent. In yet another study there is a greater chance of higher morale in the construction industry or going into business for oneself, based on reactions from those presently employed. The chances of being dissatisfied in these areas were only one in about twenty, while the chances were about one in four for service occupations and the wholesale-retail industry. And if you decide to aspire to the technical, professional, or managerial occupations, your chances of satisfaction with your work is about nine out of ten.

MIDCAREER ADJUSTMENTS

During the decade of the seventies career consultants often help clients by encouraging them to review their background in terms of what they have to offer prospective employers. Three important aspects are experience, education, and breadth of background. A person midway in his career usually has experience to offer, but may find education lacking. Formal education may be a determining factor in the choice between two experienced persons for a position or a promotion. As an employee moves up the ladder of success the competition becomes stiffer,

Higher up the ladder competition becomes greater

and reeducation is one answer. Returning to the classroom may scare the middle-aged person, but more persons of all ages are returning to further their education. The evening college class-room or industrial programs have two features. A way to learn up-to-date methods of handling work problems and to learn a new vantage point to perceive himself in relationship to the world.

The breadth of one's background can show an interviewer that he is willing to accept greater responsibility. Often a com-pany cannot or will not provide more opportunities for an em-ployee. However, one can find challenge in the community. Such experience can prove at a later time to a potential em-ployer that this applicant has accepted responsibility, either in a company or in the community.

The employer who hires workers older than forty years of age usually perceives these qualities:

1. Stability that comes with maturity;
2. A serious attitude toward the job;
3. More reliability, less absenteeism, and proven steady work habits;
4. A sense of responsibility and loyalty;
5. Less of a tendency to be distracted by outside interests or in-fluences.

Noting these advantages, many employers now make a practice of including older workers in every working unit. They find that mature employees have a stabilizing influence on the group as a whole.

As a worker becomes older he becomes more satisfied

Studies have reported a positive correlation between age and general attitude or job satisfaction. As workers become older they tend to become more satisfied with their jobs— regardless of the income.

Morale and the Work Force

EXTERNAL FACTORS

The decline in morale, perhaps indicating senility in the "Amer-ican work ethic," is visible in absenteeism rates on Mondays and Fridays, as they commonly climb to 15 percent above the ab-senteeism rates of the other days of the week. The problem is seen in the white- and blue-collar workers. The decline in workers' morale is traced at least to two factors. One factor is the work itself, which in our highly industrialized society is al-most always very specialized, repetitive, and nondemanding. A common gripe among workers today is, "I do something, day in and day out, yet never see the finished product."

Another is the young worker; 25 percent of the work force is under 25 years of age. Today's young workers simply do not believe that hard work will pay off. Also, fewer of them are willing to submit to authority. A survey conducted in 1972 showed that only 39 percent of the nation's young workers believed that hard work would pay off compared with 69 percent who felt that way four years before. The same survey showed 36 percent would not mind being "bossed around" on the job compared with 56 percent in 1968.

However, it must be pointed out that in another study the young do believe in the work ethic. When people between the ages of 18 and 24 were asked, "If you inherited a million dollars, would you go on working—either at your present job or something you liked better—or would you quit work? Ninety percent of those interviewed said they would go on working. Seventy percent of the same age group said they like their jobs, and almost ninety percent of the 25–29 age group liked their jobs. Perhaps it can be said, in summary, that most young people enjoy work, but do not appreciate the style in which they are supervised.

Most enjoy some work—not the style of supervision

INTERNAL FACTORS

An employee's strong feeling toward his job may be seen by some as caused by how permissive his supervisors are, by others by how clean the plant is and the variety of foods offered by the cafeteria. People's attitudes about a company change constantly, but there are a few things that stand out as constant factors relating to employee morale. The success of a company is reflected in the employee's attitude toward the company. The more successful a company is the more likely the employee will show a loyalty to the company and exhibit a high standing for it. If a company is showing a fine production record and good profits, it is wise to share such information with employees. Several firms send a copy of the annual report to each employee. Second, the employees of today seem to demonstrate a higher morale in small companies than large ones. An employee from a multinational company commented, "Oh, I am only one of a thousand employees, they don't care what my name is as long as I turn out so many parts an hour." Or the statement, "I am lost in this joint, the management only knows me as employee number 456."

The more successful the company, the higher the workers' morale

Small companies enjoy higher morale

It may seem to an employee that the longer he works the higher his salary becomes, but the closer his salary becomes to his supervisor's salary, the more likely his morale will drop. The reason for this is, "Why should I work to become a supervisor

Problems arise when the employee's salary comes close to the supervisor's

when I will only receive three or four cents more an hour for that much more responsibility. It isn't worth it." Likewise, the supervisor may feel he is underpaid, because there is not a wage premium attached to a responsibility factor. As an employer, be sure to make that span of earnings between the employee and the supervisor enough to make it seem worthwhile to both of them. An employee should see a substantial monetary increase in accepting a supervisory role and the supervisor should feel he is being compensated for the task.

By the end of the 1970s, 68 percent of the work force will be under 34 years old.[17] Because the attitudes of young adults are expected to have such an impact on the future course of organizational practices, profiles of young blue-collar workers, white-collar workers, and junior executives are presented in the sections that follow.

Blue-Collar Challenge

There are about 38 million blue-collar workers in the United States today. Of these, 740,000 are hourly-paid workers building cars, and 40 percent of that number are under 35 years old. About one-third of the hourly-paid employees at Chrysler, General Motors, and Ford are under thirty. More than half of Chrysler's hourly workers have been there less than five years. This profile of blue-collar workers is based on automobile plant workers.[18] Judson Gooding, who surveyed the morale of automotive workers, concludes that, "The central fact about the new workers is that they are young and bring into the plants with them the new perspectives of American youth in the 1970s."

Youthful attitudes toward work have already had an impact on some areas of industry and may become influential in the next decade. For example, at General Motors and Ford plants, absenteeism more than doubled from 1960 to 1970. Five percent of GM workers were missing every day, and on Fridays and Mondays, absenteeism could go up to 10 percent. Absenteeism occurred mainly among 10 to 15 percent of the same workers. At the General Motors plant in Detroit, a major company official told one writer that both the total productivity of the plant and the quality of the cars coming off the assembly line had been adversely affected by absenteeism—and that *most of the absences were concentrated among workers under thirty-five years old.* The official also said that absenteeism was becoming a nationwide problem in all heavy industries.[19]

Shortly after talking with the GM official, the same writer got a job in a steel mill and, as a worker, gained the trust and confidence of his fellow workers. He recorded the following

Absenteeism increases from 5% in the middle of the week to 10% or more on Monday and Friday

conversation, which he says typifies a commonly held attitude among the young steel workers.

> "Tommy—you've been out for two days. Don't you miss the bread?"
>
> "I can get by. I'd rather have the time than the money."
>
> "What if they crack down?"
>
> **No one "owns" me**   "They don't own me man! If I want a day off, I take a day off. Nothin's gonna stop that!"
>
> "What if they fire you?"
>
> "Then let them fire me. I ain't seen 'em do it yet."
>
> "Why not?"
>
> "Cause the next guy who comes along is going to do the same thing I am."[20]

Among automotive workers, studies show that both blacks and whites complain of favoritism, although the UAW has made efforts to eliminate bigotry. Blacks (20 percent of hourly workers) and whites are not in open conflict, but black workers prefer to associate with one another rather than with whites. Gooding comments that "it is not uncommon for a black to converse by shouts with a brother twenty feet down the line rather than with the white across from him and only a yard away."

The more serious split is between the young and old. Older workers have begun to air their grievances now that younger men are doing so. One common complaint relates to some of the youthful attitudes: younger workers express alienation and indifference to craftsmanship. Older workers also resent eager efforts at job advancement. Young workers, on the other hand, resent the older workers' seemingly automatic catering to the "company line." Discontentment with the job itself is an issue as much as pay and job security. The ability to install one car fender every minute may be a company goal, but certainly not a goal of every auto fender worker. Job monotony was not even discussed ten years ago, but is now a topic of labor negotiations. Among the new crop of employees, many are better educated and less compliant than their parents. For them pay is not sufficient to compensate for a life spent "on the line." This attitude demonstrated by workers could, in time, result in the decline of the assembly line as we know it today. The results could in time be a major change in manufacturing techniques. One key factor in combating the problem of boredom is work involvement. This ranges from keeping the workers informed as to what is going on, to actual participation and decision making.

Saab–Scania has taken a big step in appeasing the demand of the Swedish trade unions to end dehumanization and dull jobs on the assembly line. The traditional assembly line will be partly replaced by a Swedish-made industrial robot to take over many of the monotonous jobs and allow workers to produce an entire engine themselves, not just part of it. There are teams consisting of four men, each of whom is able to assemble the entire engine himself. A member of the team might work individually on the assembly line or pair up if he chooses. Instead of taking one or two shots with an electric screwdriver, the worker has learned the entire final stage of engine assembly—adding the carburetor, water pump, spark plugs, fly wheel, and other parts to the block. With his teammates the employee decides how they will divide their combined thirty-minute operation. The engines don't arrive inexorably; the team calls for them. If they work quickly, doing three engines in 80 minutes instead of 90 minutes, they can take a supplementary coffee break at the picnic table they have set up in their alcove. "There is a greater feeling of relaxation, not so much stress," said one employee. "We help each other out, you know, when somebody has a problem or gets behind."

Similar experiments are being run in the Volvo plant. The number of workers in such an experiment is small and the program is closely controlled. If the new assembly technique works from the workers' point of view, the union talks of pressing for the assembly "team" concept in other assembly plants. The remaining unanswered question is whether the one-man, one-enterprise concept would work on a high-volume production line. How would it work if there were the necessity of turning out ten times as many automobiles? The prestige gained by the one worker in his accomplishment of the final product may be a goal worth achieving. Ford Motor Company has been experimenting with the team approach to building autos.

The Chrysler plan asked various plants to consult with workers and come up with individual improvements, keeping in mind such principles as:

1. Fix the responsibility as far down the organizational structure as possible.
2. Give enough authority to go with it.
3. Let workers know concrete results of their suggestions and improvements.
4. Create a climate that encourages change.

Procter and Gamble's pet food plants, for example, have broken up their assembly lines into smaller teams of autonomous work groups to perform many different tasks. Because workers participate in the entire canning and packaging process rather than working on isolated jobs, company morale has risen dramatically.[21] The long-term answers to job boredom in United States factories may nevertheless prove to be a mixture of shorter assembly lines, increased automation, and a participative industrial democracy. Maybe technology has driven us to the phoenix of specialization, but human relations may now move us to a new era of generalization.

White-Collar Workers

In a study of white-collar workers, Judson Gooding found that of all groups undergoing transition in America, white-collar workers are changing most rapidly.[22]

There are more white-collar workers today than ever before — thirty-eight million, compared to twenty-eight million blue-collar workers. About half of these have supervisory positions, have investments in business, or are "professionals." The other nineteen million are mainly clerical and sales personnel. They are generally less well educated than supervisors, but better educated than blue-collar workers. In this section we discuss white-collar workers in the lower-level categories.

As higher education has become available to almost all Americans, white-collar status has declined and jobs have become less secure. White-collar workers remain largely non-unionized — little more than three million have union affiliation. Until about 1920, white-collar workers got from 50 to 100 percent more pay than blue-collar workers. By the 1950s, the trend had reversed itself and white-collar workers were receiving 4 percent less than blue-collar; this changing ratio in pay has continued steadily.

White-collar jobs are usually more flexible than blue-collar jobs because they are not as tied to strict production quotas. Working hours are often more flexible, and the correct procedures for doing a job are usually not as rigid. Even so, white-collar workers also often feel dead-ended in their work.

White-collar workers have more opportunity to take different jobs; job hopping is one way of getting ahead. Gooding found that job promotion is the main concern of most white-collar workers because it is seen as the key to more income, more security, and more status.

The traditional affiliations between management and white-collar workers, and the belief that white-collar jobs can be more fulfilling than blue-collar jobs, has sensitized management to white-collar complaints. Job enrichment programs, which try to provide more responsibility in planning and executing work, are more common in white-collar jobs.

Companies that employ white-collar workers generally recognize the necessity for all kinds of training programs, and encourage employees to continue their education. Many people find on-the-job training possibilities one of the great inducements for going into white-collar work.

Many companies have begun to provide their white-collar workers with counseling services and on-the-job medical care as well as the traditional benefits of paid vacations, health services, and company cafeterias. But even so, the evidence of discontent in the white-collar world continues to mount.

In Gooding's study, almost all the people interviewed wished that their work itself was more satisfying. White-collar workers are more involved with their work, dull as it might be, than with other activity. Their jobs are central to their lives.

Tests done by Stanley Seashore and J. Thad Barnowe showed that the blues affect the white-collar worker as well as the blue-collar. The percentage of blue-collar workers who express negative attitudes toward their work is not significantly higher than that for white-collar workers.

The big problem for collar-color seems to occur in the "middle years." At this stage of their lives, nearly twice as many blue-collar as white-collar workers were dissatisfied with

Figure 5-1. White-collar workers are more involved with their work, and their jobs are usually central to their lives.
Courtesy of Chino Valley Bank (Photo by Robert Curtis)

their jobs. One reason for this overall dissatisfaction with work may be that blue-collar workers may experience an "economic squeeze" during their middle years. Blue-collar workers usually achieve their top earnings earlier in life. White-collar workers, however, do not plateau early, but begin to reap the rewards of their greater education in their thirties.

Junior Management Executives

Another study by Judson Gooding found that young managers today, as distinguished from the "organization men" or the "young executives" of the past, are best called the "accelerated generation."[23] Gooding's study was based on interviews with junior managers and executives already earning from $10,000 to $20,000 a year and on their way up. There are about 2,700,000 such positions in United States business today.

Unlike earlier generations of management executives who saw themselves as *successors* to power, younger executives today see themselves as *reformers* who hope to change the style and quality of management theory and practice. They have definite ideas about how to improve the environment and society, and consider their major task the accomplishment of these goals within the corporate framework.

These junior executives are making two kinds of demands on their companies. One is personal: they want to work on projects they believe to be socially useful, either with company support and backing, or at least without endangering their jobs and futures. The other is impersonal: they want the companies and institutions they work for to reappraise corporate goals and, in some cases, change them. These young executives are theorizing that corporations should put back into the economy amounts equal to what they take out of it, in ways that will improve society.

This theory revolves around such crucial areas as pollution control, resource conservation, and minority training and hiring. It holds that profits should be maintained, but not necessarily maximized.

Young managers rate personal values over salary

These younger managers worry less about salary and fringe benefits than personal values. They get the most satisfaction from exercising responsibility. They want the right to make mistakes, viewing this as the only way to learn. The higher the risk, the better the job. Along with this prevailing attitude goes the desire for rapid advancement as a reward for making tough, but correct, decisions. The promotion is desired not so much for the money as for the added authority and opportunity to exercise greater responsibility.

Like white-collar and blue-collar workers, young executives crave more autonomy. They want individual recognition and a sense of belonging. They want to be stimulated by their work and the people they work with. They accept hard work as long as it isn't merely repetitive. They want a free-wheeling, unstructured setting, analogous to a campus environment.

Their most distinguishing characteristic is a dislike of hypocrisy. These executives would rather state their grievances than go along with company policies just to get ahead. They are also intolerant of rules that make no sense to them—such as rigid ideas about dress or hair styles, or inflexible working hours when a looser schedule would work as well. The study concludes that these new managers "are generous and idealistic, anxious to help others, and willing to work hard for valid objectives. Most junior managers combine several of these traits and fall somewhere between the extremes, as people always have."

RELATIONSHIP OF MORALE AND PRODUCTION

When morale and production are used in the same context we are usually referring to morale as an organizational group term, which we can define not only in terms of a person's feelings about attaining his own goals but also in terms of his contributions to the organization's objectives.

High morale doesn't mean high production

The natural tendency is to believe that high morale will produce high production, however, Keith Davis points out that there is not always a positive correlation between the two. A supervisor can push for high productivity by the use of scientific management, time studies, and close supervision. As a result there may be high production, but low morale. It is certainly possible to achieve high production with low morale; nonetheless it is questionable whether such conditions can last very long. The opposite also can be true. The supervisor can work so hard to please his subordinates that they are so happy they don't feel like working. When funds are readily available there may not be a strong goal to achieve high production, but when the economic squeeze comes so do the problems. A relationship between morale and production is illustrated in Figure 5–2.

MAINTAINING AND DIAGNOSING MORALE

How can organizations deal with rapidly changing values? Morale is not static, and because it is constantly changing, it must be assessed continuously. As F. J. Roethlisberger said:

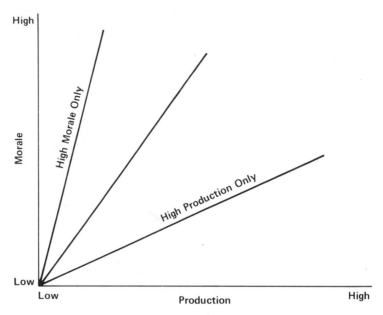

Figure 5–2. Relationship of morale to production

> To expect that human problems can be fixed up once and for all is absurd. No matter how well they are handled, local unbalances will arise. They need to be continuously attended to. To expect loyalty and confidence and willingness to contribute their services from people whose feelings of personal integrity have been damaged—no matter how unwittingly—is to ask for the moon.[24]

Companies, like organisms, are subject to inertia and stasis; that is, they can become resistant to any kind of change or innovation. They easily accumulate practices and policies that can overload their systems. Checking up on morale can be preventive medicine as well as a way to begin a cure for a diseased corporate body. And when treatment is given, further checkups are often useful to reveal whether it has been successful or not.

Maintenance

For proper assessment of a company's morale, good upward and downward communication flow must exist. Messages can be distorted easily and for a variety of motives. For a truthful picture of morale, top management has to understand what employees at all levels are thinking and feeling. Employees have to understand the objectives, economic and otherwise, of top management. Maintaining good morale and diagnosing problems both depend on good communications.

The Importance of Diagnosis

When the problem in morale occurs, it must be correctly diagnosed, which may not be simple. Where are the tensions and strains? What are the issues? Where is the possible source of the problem? Where has communication been blocked? One of the easiest mistakes businesses can make is to provide solutions that don't fit the problem.

Top managements sometimes adopt the latest, most fashionable breakthrough in management theory. Transactional Analysis, job enrichment programs, and participative management, for instance, are all valuable practices. But if they're not appropriate to the problem, they won't be effective. David Sirota and Alan Wolfson have isolated three attitudes that usually result in matching a wrong cure to a morale problem:[25]

Three attitudes of management

1. Management becomes *infatuated* with a particular technique and decides to try it at the next opportunity.
2. Management has a *preconceived* notion of employees' needs, which blocks the ability to see employees and their problems realistically, even when evidence to the contrary is overwhelming.
3. Management is able to perceive the effects of a problem, but does not explore the possible *causes* before making a decision.

Sirota and Wolfson provide some examples of how applying a solution before the problem is properly diagnosed can greatly undermine morale.[26]

METHODS OF COMMUNICATING MORALE

Analysis of Records

How can industry check to see whether their employees have relatively high morale? Actually there are many ways of checking employee morale. The first one is analyzing the company's own records. In reviewing employees' time sheets, a heavy ab-

Check company records first

senteeism would indicate low morale. Excessive tardiness, long lunch hours, quitting early, and poor safety records could all indicate low morale. Low production and a high amount of spoilage may indicate low employee morale. Finally, personnel records can indicate the percentage of employee turnover. Some industries can certainly expect an employee turnover of 10 or even 20 percent. However, an employee turnover of over 20 per year might easily be considered excessive. Some aerospace, technical, research, and chemical companies have experienced employee turnover of over 50 percent in one year. One aerospace firm in the West experienced an 80 percent employee turnover, not only in operative management, but also in top management. By contrast, an electronic data processing company in the Midwest experienced an employee turnover of less than 2 percent every year for over ten years. In such a fast growing industry as data processing, it would not be surprising if the turnover was five times that figure. Obviously, if the employee's morale is quite high he is usually not intrigued by financial offers of competing companies.

Turnover can indicate the status of morale

The personnel department can certainly do much to find out about the company's morale. Every employee who terminated his position should be given an exit interview. In this way the exiting employee can be encouraged to speak freely about his likes and dislikes about the industry.

The personnel department can discover a lot about morale

The reviewing of the following list of records should give some indication of the morale of the employees. These should be reviewed before attempting a company survey.

Records that can indicate the type of morale that prevails

1. Labor turnover
2. Production records
3. Waste and spoilage
4. Absenteeism
5. Tardiness
6. Grievance reports
7. Exit interviews
8. Safety records
9. Medical reports
10. Suggestion boxes

Informal Questions and Answers

Another way to determine morale is to ask employees how they feel and what they want. Employees do not act on the basis of what management thinks, or what management thinks they think; they act on their own opinions. One pitfall is for supervisors and management to assume that morale is high or low. They easily can be mistaken in their understanding of what employees are really thinking and feeling.

Morale is "in the air," and so in many ways it can be talked about informally. The larger the company, the more formal the procedures needed to assure that employees have channels of communication to top management. Two time-honored methods of asking for employee feedback are notes in a suggestion box and letters to management, which can sometimes find an open forum in the employee newspaper. Suggestions and letters do reflect employee satisfaction or discontent, but they do not adequately represent the state of morale of an entire firm.

Personal interviews discover personal feelings

Another method of finding out what employees think is for personnel specialists to hold confidential, informal interviews with employees. The success of this method depends on the impartiality of the interviewer, and the degree of trust the employee feels. Employees with complaints often prefer to remain anonymous for fear of reprisals.

Supervisors close to the working groups can be asked periodically to report on employee morale. As often as not, supervisors may not know what employees are really thinking, and may not be aware, or may not want to reveal, that employees' morale is low *because* of the supervisor. Also, supervisors may be unwilling to reveal low morale because it reflects on their professional competence.

Management executives can be encouraged to tour working areas and chat with employees. They may discover some morale problems in this way, but this kind of survey is spotty at best. Employees may be more concerned with making a good showing than complaining about their work situation.

Exit interviews

Employees who are leaving the company are often more than willing to talk about the negative aspects of their jobs. Some companies conduct "exit interviews" or send letters to elicit such information. Opinions from former employees can be helpful, but companies that wait to ask questions until employees leave may already have serious trouble with morale.

Surveys

Employee surveys are the most comprehensive way to study morale. In a survey, everyone is asked to respond to the same questions so that management can get an accurate view of the general level of morale. Surveys can be conducted by impartial interviewers or by questionnaires. One common way of combining survey approaches is to distribute a questionnaire to pinpoint problem areas and then use the interview technique to find out more details.

EMPLOYEE RESPONSES

Just conducting a morale survey tends to boost morale because it indicates to employees that the company is interested in what they think. Questionnaires that don't require employees to identify themselves add to the validity of the answers. Surveys conducted by mail do not generate as much response as surveys conducted personally on the job. One-page, concise questionnaires draw more response than multiple-page questionnaires.

If the survey is conducted by interviewing employees, the best person for the job is a disinterested third person, such as a consultant. Employees are more likely to be honest with an outside source. Employees experienced in taking surveys, who are outside the direct chain of command, also can be acceptable people to conduct surveys.

OBJECTIVES SURVEY

One reason a survey falls flat is that the management has no clear idea of why it is conducting one. It is always more helpful to know what questions to ask before putting together a survey. It isn't enough to take an employee survey because some company down the road is doing so. Management should be wary of making assumptions about morale before a survey is taken. It is too easy to assume that morale is good or bad. Preconceived notions can prejudice the survey results.

Why conduct a survey?

The basic approach has a great deal to do with how valid a survey is. Indifference, resistance, or fear on the part of management is easily sensed by employees. The approach should always be, "What can be learned from the study?," rather than "Whom can we find to blame?" If management is seriously interested in results, employees will be likely to cooperate.

What questions do you ask?

Once management has determined what questions it should ask, it must know how to ask them. Clear, direct questions elicit the most valid responses. If management wants to know whether employees are content with their working hours, it should ask, "Do you like your working hours? What hours would you prefer?" If it wants to know how many employees are planning to leave the company in a certain period of time, it should ask, "Are you planning to leave the company? When?" An example of a poor question is "How do you like your pay and benefits?" It asks for too much information at once, and the answers cannot be precisely interpreted.

The high correlation possible between direct questions to employees and future probabilities is demonstrated in Table 5–1. Three groups of employees in a company were asked, "If you have your way, will you be working for the company five years from now?" The answers the employees gave correspond directly to actual percentages of employees who left the company within those five years.

Table 5–1.   "If you have your way, will you be working for the company five years from now?"

OCCUPATIONS OF RESPONDENTS	REPLY	PERCENT OF EMPLOYEES LEAVING VOLUNTARILY IN FIVE YEARS
Salesmen	"Certainly"	12
	"Probably"	15
	"Not sure," "No"	31
Technical representatives	"Certainly"	17
	"Probably"	32
	"Not sure," "No"	44
Engineers	"Certainly"	10
	"Probably"	11
	"Not sure," "No"	20

Source: David Sirota and Alan D. Wolfson, "Pragmatic Approach to People Problems," *Harvard Business Review,* January–February 1973, p. 126.

Multiple-choice questions are used on objective surveys

Multiple-choice questions are popular on questionnaires because with standardized responses overall trends can be measured. Survey interviews generally use a direct approach, asking specific questions and categorizing the answers. In this type of survey the respondent reads all the answers to each question and then marks the answer which is nearest to how he feels. The chief advantages to these types of surveys are that they can be administered and analyzed very easily, and they can be scored by a computer, if desired. The results can give statistical data that can be easily measured. The difficulty, however, is that it may not truly reflect the degree of attitudes of employees and certainly not the attitudes of individual employees. *Descriptive surveys* by contrast encourage employees to express their own feelings on a topic in either a direct or indirect manner. Such questions as, "Do you feel your company treats you fairly?" and "In what positive ways could the company improve its employee-employer relationships?" require the employee to express his feelings in a concrete way. Usually, the first questions of a descriptive survey are an attempt to get him to express his

Descriptive surveys ask you to write out how you feel

own attitudes about the company and his work station. The latter part of the survey usually attempts to ask in a participative way how employees would improve the employer-employee relationship if they had an opportunity. Such instruments may be conducted by an interview or in an individual questionnaire. The important thing, however, is that the employee is assured that he will not be identified by management.

COMPETENT ADMINISTRATION

It is extremely important that the person conducting a survey know how to take a good sample, write direct questions, interpret the data once it is collected, and draw up charts to show statistical comparisons. Surveys must fit the facilities of the companies taking them. In determining the scope of the survey, management should also determine how the survey can be handled most efficiently and how much money is to be set aside for it. A survey, after all, is not a conversation between employees and management, but a system for compiling information accurately and presenting it in usable form.

It does no good to administer a survey without management's support and understanding of what the survey is all about. The traditional way of running a survey is to have an independent party conduct the study and make recommendations. This approach often does not contribute to management action and subsequent changes in employee attitudes. Ideally, the investigator and the managers who will be involved in implementing change should work together in determining the questions to be asked. The investigator must be impartial, but management must also be involved and interested in the results.

FOLLOW THROUGH

Morale surveys have a tendency temporarily to raise morale

Morale surveys have a tendency to raise morale, but only as long as employees believe their opinions are contributing to change. Surveys irritate employees when they feel their answers are not given true consideration. Employers who are afraid to publish findings because they do not want to attract attention to problem areas take the chance of actually causing problems by encouraging only negative rumors. Sometimes announcements on bulletin boards or by letter will suffice. At other times, employee discussion groups are useful.

Once the survey results are published, management should be prepared to follow through with remedies for the problem areas the survey indicates. This often means the company must be prepared to spend additional funds to remedy problems in hopes of raising morale. If management cannot effect change, it must be prepared to explain to employees why change is not possible at that time. And it should be prepared to eradicate problems as soon as time and money permit.

The Physical Environment and Morale

Much is said these days about noise pollution and the emotional fatigue that results from a poor working environment. Certainly it is worthwhile to study the effects of the environment on an individual, particularly with the apparent accent on intrinsic motivators in industrial circles. A new focus on the term ergonomics is happening. Once called "human engineering," it means designing a work station that is developed for maximum performance, and in a way that makes the job more suitable to the employee. This means studying not only size and shape of chairs and work benches, but areas of lighting, music, sound, color, and temperature.

NOISE POLLUTION AFFECTS MORALE

Factories are growing increasingly rebellious over noise pollution. It has been suspected for some time that as many as ten million workers may hear poorly due to excessive noise. Now some research links noise to such diverse ills as mental illness and heart disease. A recent study of workers in Germany found that those subject to the most noise for a prolonged period suffered a higher incidence of heart disorders, circulatory problems, and equilibrium disturbances. A number of medical men are certain that job noises are a factor in some neurotic and psychotic illnesses.

Noise can be a source of psychological stress

In a study titled, "Affectiveness of Noise on People," prepared for the Environmental Protection Agency, Dr. James D. Miller of the Center Institute for the Deaf in Saint Louis, wrote, "There is not definite evidence that noise can induce either neurotic or psychotic illness." However his report added, "But all the facts show speech interference, hearing loss, annoyance, and the arousal and distraction clearly support the contention that noises can act as sources of psychological distress." Such distress in turn can contribute to "such unpleasant symptoms as nausea, headaches, instability, argumentativeness, sexual impotence, change in general mood and general anxiety." Another study found that noise contributes to a breakdown in communications and can produce irritable and depressed feelings, as well as a short attention span and hyperactivity.

Noise may affect the physical also

Decibels measure noise

The difficulties in controlling sound are to find acceptable standards and feasible ways to control it. The limits are measured in decibels on a logarithmic scale that runs from the threshold of hearing (one decibel) to the level of hearing impairment (eighty-five decibels, if continuous), to that of acute pain (one hundred and thirty-five). By comparison, a whisper registers at about 20; normal conversation at 50; a vacuum cleaner at 70; continuous noise at 80 grates on the nerves, and a jet taking off at 118 decibels is hardly bearable.

50 decibels for a normal chat

A 20 decibel sound has 10 times as much pressure as a 10 decibel sound, and 80 decibels has, incredibly, a million times as much pressure as 20 decibels. At 120 decibels the sound is deafening—on the threshold of physical pain. You get this sort of sound if you stand too close to an amplified rock band, hear a clap of thunder right overhead, or if you are too near a jet engine.

The important factor that is often forgotten is that many environmental factors cause us to be nervous, irritable, and unable to make simple decisions. Such a problem was evident in a small plant located on a business street. The four-lane boulevard was also an alternate highway used by trucks to a downtown commercial area. Only the two foot parkway, a narrow sidewalk, and six feet separated the company's front door from the 70 decibel traffic noise. Management did not realize the difficulty that the secretaries had in handling their everyday duties. Next to the front door was a large plate glass window; on the floor was linoleum, the desks were far apart, and the ceiling was high. The first solution in the echo chamber was to keep the front door and the door to the plant closed as often as possible. Carpets and drapes were installed. Plants were put outside the window, as well as a decorative cement block wall. Various ceiling treatments were installed and potted plants were placed in the office. It took all of these improvements to drop the sound level down to the point that working conditions were acceptable.

LIGHTING

Lighting is expressed in footcandles

Lighting levels are generally expressed in footcandles. One footcandle is equal to the light of one candle at a distance of one foot, as established by Illuminating Engineering Society. It is an industry group that publishes lighting standards that are widely followed by electrical contractors when lighting is installed. The average level of light nationally in commercial buildings is 125 footcandles. It is estimated that candlepower runs from 10 for a hotel lobby to 150 for proofreading activity.

Incandescent vs. fluorescent fixtures

Supervisors should be aware that incandescent lighting is more economical to install, but more expensive to maintain than fluorescent fixtures. Perhaps the greatest problem is not the lack of candlepower or the illumination of offices as some critics claim, but the misuse of it. The problems of direct glare

Problems of glare

from lighting fixtures or windows, reflected glare from furniture, and contrasting dark shadows usually cause more eye fatigue and low production than lack of lighting.

In considering the adequacy of illumination, it is necessary to take into account the lighting of the total "visual field" rather than the light of the "field of observation." For instance, the light from the outside may be brighter than that at the desk; thus, if a person is facing a window, he must visually adjust to the combined value of the light rather than to that of the work space alone. If one eye receives more light than the other, the adjustment is similarly disturbing. The simple implication is that the whole area should be uniformly illuminated. Another source of fatigue and morale slump arises when the illumination changes too rapidly for the pupil to contract and relax comfortably. Undoubtedly, some of the improvements in production that results from proper lighting is attributable to the favorable attitude created by pleasant surroundings.

COLORS

Color as we know has a definite psychological effect on us, but also it has reflective quality. Such colors as light green and sky blue reflect approximately 40 percent of the light they receive, but dark red only about sixteen percent. The lighting of a factory can be greatly improved by the use of pastel colored paints.

Color and supergraphics are an obvious and important contribution to the environment at International Paper Company, Facelle Division Plant. On one lobby wall, a 40-foot-long mural portrays the papermaking industry. Joining the office to

Figure 5–3. Supergraphics add color, show the way, and help morale.

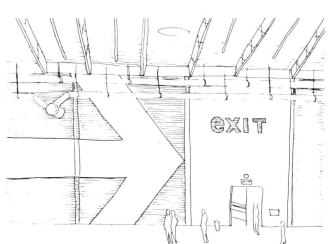

the manufacturing building, a hall, 9 feet high and 12 feet wide, runs nearly 300 feet. Here graphics were needed to relieve the tunnel effect. The design is appropriate; it projects the company image to employees and visitors alike as it spells out the name of the company in letters nine feet high along the entire length of the corridor. Each single letter is different in color, and the spaces between the letters are of different colors. Exit doors are hard to find in large factories, but the exit door in one factory is plainly marked by bright colors high above the door and, as a guide to find the door, a 30-foot-tall arrow reinforces the identification. Such boldness with colors is not used often enough in factories or large industries. The research indicates that proper use of color tones and combinations reduces fatigue, increases efficiency, decreases accidents, and improves housekeeping.

Red encourages movement

Green is best for reflective thinking

In analyzing the color spectrum we find that red increases restlessness, attracts attention, and speeds decisions. As a result bright red is poor for large office areas where people will be working continuously, but is good in areas where many people meet to enter and exit and fast movement is encouraged. Pale blue is the most restful of colors, while green slows muscular responses, steadies the nerves and encourages reflective thinking. Your own business would dictate whether you would use burnt orange and beige, or whether you might use forest green and sky blue.

SUMMARY

Morale, like health, requires attention. It is a composite of feelings, and maintaining high morale is a continuous task for management. It appears that younger workers are more dissatisfied with work, because they have higher expectations. The more successful the company, the higher the workers' morale. Even so, absenteeism increases more on Monday and Friday. One myth is that high morale will lead to high production. Conducting surveys and exit interviews are two ways to check the pulse of employee morale. Objective surveys ask one to answer multiple choice questions, where subjective surveys ask you to write out how you feel. Noise pollution, lighting, and colors all affect the attitudes of employees. The color green seems to be the best for reflective thinking.

THEFT IN THE SERVICE STATION

Case Study #1

Scott Hays is the owner and manager of a service station in the downtown area of a large city. He employs twelve men, four of whom he hired just one month ago when he decided to extend the business hours.

When Scott conducted an inventory this morning of the tires that the station had in stock, he discovered that four tires were unaccountable. His first thought was that someone had broken in when the station was closed, but he could find no evidence of this action. Scott also discounted the idea that someone had managed to sneak into the garage and steal the tires while the station was open. Surely someone would have seen that happen. The only possibility left was employee theft.

Scott had conducted his last inventory just a few days before he had hired the new men. Since that time he had a sales slip for every tire sold, except for the four missing tires. Scott began considering his men. Could one of them have stolen the tires? This had never happened before! Two of his men Scott began to suspect in earnest.

Pete, who is the station mechanic, has worked for Scott for a number of years. Until recently Pete's performance has been good. But a few weeks ago, Scott caught Pete in the process of overbilling a customer for work done on his car. Scott corrected Pete's error without much thought until later, when he found that Pete had written two bills. There was a higher amount listed for the customer and the lower one for the station, thus enabling him to pocket the difference. When Scott confronted Pete, he apologized. Pete said he had never done it before and would never do it again. His reason was that temptation was too strong.

The other man Scott suspected was Dave. Dave has had to be corrected on more than one occasion for not giving the proper change back to customers. Were these shortchanges honest mistakes? They only seemed to happen when Scott would be away from the station. Dave is apparently in financial trouble, because last week he requested an advance on his next paycheck. Yesterday he found out that Dave had been asking some of the men if he could borrow money. Scott wonders if Dave stole the tires for the money he would get for them?

If you were Scott, what steps would you now take?

1. Would you fire Dave and Pete?
2. Would you release all four new men?
3. Would you call a meeting of all the employees and discuss the matter?
4. Would you tell them that you felt one of them was a thief?
5. Would you demand that they all take a polygraph test?
6. Would you tell them that if it didn't happen again you would forget it?

DON'T KNOCK IT IF YOU HAVEN'T TRIED IT

Case Study #2

You are the manager of a plant that manufactures sewing machines. For the past several weeks there has been hostility in the air due to an increased amount of work required of the men. In the past, the men were required to produce forty-five machines an hour. But several weeks ago, the assembly line was speeded up and this amount was increased to sixty-seven machines per hour. When the company decided to increase production the employees' union was notified. The union was favorable toward the increase.

However, many of the workers do not feel the increase was reasonable. They feel that they are being overworked without due cause and see this as a way for the company to take advantage of the employees.

One day while you and one of your plant supervisors, Ralph Fox, are touring the plant you both happen to see a worker push one of the sewing machines off the assembly line belt. The machine fell onto the auxiliary belt and caused the entire assembly line to come to a screeching halt. The worker who did this began to walk back toward his work station amidst a loud roar of approval from his fellow workers.

As you begin to step forward. Ralph grabs you by the arm and says, "Wait, if you say or do anything now, matters may become even worse than they are now." What should you do?

1. Immediately discipline the disgruntled worker?
2. Call the worker into your office immediately?
3. Do nothing that day, but contact the worker the next day?
4. Pretend it never happened?
5. What kind of discipline would you invoke if you felt a punishment was necessary?
6. As a manager, how would you handle the basic issue of poor morale?

MORALE POLLUTION

Case Study #3

Have you ever experienced an increasing foul odor from your refrigerator and on inspection been unable to locate the source? In such cases it becomes necessary to investigate, in order to find the curdled milk or spoiled fruit. There is sometimes a parallel in organizations—in a person who over the years has soured in attitude to the point where the radiation from him pollutes the system's morale.

In one such case, the member was an original employee in a large and successful organization. He had been a central figure in the top management groups and had the prerequisites that go with the status. But he had not, in his own eyes, kept pace with the upward mobility of his peers. So far as position was concerned, James Whitmore, 55, had been put in charge of an essential, but to him peripheral, component of the business. He sulks unhappily. His subordinates knew that they had a discontented, demoralized boss and they did not feel properly represented to the rest of the company.

1. What are the options available to solve this morale problem that has affected Whitmore's whole division?
2. What do you believe is the best option, considering the company? Considering the employee?

Terms and Concepts Students Should Know

group morale	noise pollution	diagnosing morale
early career morale	decibels	exit interviews
mid-career morale	individual morale	objective surveys
blue-collar challenge	morale vs. production	descriptive surveys
white-collar morale	larceny and employee theft	

Bibliography

1. D'APRIX, ROGER, *Struggle for Identity: The Silent Revolution Against Corporate Conformity,* Homewood, Ill., Dow-Jones-Irwin, 1972.
2. ARGYLE, MICHAEL, *The Social Psychology of Work,* New York, Taplinger Publishing Co., 1972.
3. HAIRE, MASON, *Psychology in Management,* New York, McGraw-Hill Book Company, 1956.
4. ROETHLISBERGER, F. J., *Management and Morale,* Cambridge, Mass., Harvard University Press, 1941.
5. TERKEL, STUDS, *Working,* New York, Pantheon Books, 1974.

Footnotes

[1] Roger M. D'Aprix, *Struggle for Identity: The Silent Revolution Against Corporate Conformity* (Homewood, Ill.: Dow Jones-Irwin, 1972), p. 7.

[2] *Ibid.*

[3] *Ibid.,* pp. 39–40.

[4] D'Aprix, *Struggle for Identity,* pp. 5–8.

[5] "Millions in Lost Taxes—and IRS Can't Cope," *San Francisco Chronicle & Examiner,* 14 April 1974, sec. A, pp. 15–17.

[6] Studs Terkel, *Working* (New York: Pantheon Books, 1974), p. xvii.

[7] *Ibid.,* p. xii.

[8] *Ibid.,* p. vi.

[9] John B. Miner, "The Real Crunch in Managerial Manpower," *Harvard Business Review,* November–December 1973, p. 154.

[10] Lewis B. Ward and Anthony G. Athos, *Student Expectations of Corporate Life:*

Implications for Management Recruiting (Boston: Division of Research, Harvard Business School, 1972), p. 81.

[11] Julian B. Rotter, "Generalized Expectancies for Interpersonal Trust," *American Psychologist*, May 1971, p. 443.

[12] Daniel A. Ondrack, "Attitudes Toward Authority," *Personnel Administration*, May–June 1971, p. 9.

[13] Miner, "Crunch in Manpower," pp. 146–158.

[14] Terence R. Mitchell and Barrett W. Knudsen, "Emerging Occupational Values: A Review and Some Findings," *Academy of Management Journal*, September 1973, p. 423.

[15] Terkel, *Working*, p. 456.

[16] "Blue-Collar Blues?" *Newsweek*, 29 April 1974, p. 90.

[17] Bennet Kremer, "No Pride in This Dust," in *The World of the Blue-Collar Worker*, edited by Irving Howe (New York: Quadrangle Books, 1972), p. 12.

[18] Judson Gooding, "It Pays to Wake Up the Blue-Collar Worker," *Fortune*, September 1970, pp. 133 ff.

[19] Kremer, "No Pride in Dust," p. 17.

[20] *Ibid.*, p. 19.

[21] Richard E. Walton, "How to Counter Alienation in the Plant," *Harvard Business Review*, November–December 1972, p. 74.

[22] Judson Gooding, "The Fraying White Collar," *Fortune*, December 1970 pp. 78 ff.

[23] Judson Gooding, "The Accelerated Generation Moves into Management," *Fortune*, March 1971, pp. 101 ff.

[24] F. J. Roethlisberger, *Management and Morale* (Cambridge, Mass.: Harvard University Press, 1941), p. 194.

[25] David Sirota and Alan D. Wolfson, "Pragmatic Approach to People Problems," *Harvard Business Review*, January–February 1973, p. 121.

[26] *Ibid.*, pp. 121–123.

Personal Problems at Work
" We all Have Hang-ups, Don't We?" ■ ■ ■

■ ■ ■ ■ ■ ■ ■ ■ ■ ■ ■ ■ ■ ■ ■ ■ ■ ■ ■ ■

OBJECTIVES

After reading this chapter you should be able to:

1. Discuss the pros and cons of supervisors being trained to act as counselors on the job.

2. Clearly formulate Levinson's four rules of behavior for solving personality clashes at work.

3. Compare the differences between directive and nondirective counseling in relation to their
   A. Objectives,
   B. Assumptions,
   C. Attitudes,
   D. Methods,
   E. Results.

4. Discuss the growing problems of alcoholism and drug addiction in business, as well as be able to
   A. Recognize some symptoms of alcoholics and drug abusers,
   B. Recognize some "slang" terms used by drug abusers,
   C. Develop some background in how to deal with alcoholics and drug abusers in the work scene.

Again here are some questions to start you thinking about topics in the chapter. You know the answers to some already, and you will find answers to the others in the chapter.

Who would you go to with a personal problem at work? To a friend, your supervisor, or a counselor?

Do you think people should express their feelings or try to keep themselves under control?

Which is better, to get rid of problem employees or rehabilitate them?

What can you do for the alcoholic employee or drug abuser?

Do you think you could recognize the point at which the alcoholic or drug abuser was performing his job ineffectively?

Can you recognize an employee under the influence of marijuana, heroin, or LSD?

TYPES OF PERSONAL PROBLEMS

> To regard all behavior as the meaningful attempt of the organism
> to adjust itself to the environment . . . appears [to be] more fruitful
> than to categorize some behavior as abnormal.
>
> Carl Rogers[1]

10% of the employees have problems

Although most dealings with people do not involve unpleasant experiences or misunderstandings, things do happen that are significantly disturbing to cause management to become interested in some of the basic concepts of counseling employees. Among supervisors, there is a general acceptance that about 10 percent of the employees have problems.[2] Such adjustment problems found in industry include a whole spectrum of behavior that could be found in a clinic. Such problem employees are known up and down the hierarchy of management, and the discussion of them takes much of their valuable time. Important skills in handling emotionally disturbed people have been developed in laboratory situations that are now being applied in industry.

The main purpose of counseling is to discover an employee's principal problem and find a way of decreasing it. First, one must find a way to understand the employee, to help him recognize his concern and deal with it objectively. An empathetic supervisor may condemn the problem, but not the employee. Perhaps the hardest part of counseling is for the employee to accept it and the counselor be willing to give it.

It is impossible for us all to be in optimal emotional balance all the time. We all occasionally "blow up" so we depend on others to help us overcome our moments of stress, and management depends on supervisors to see that it is done.

Just as there are many kinds of personal problems that find expression at work, so too there is great variation in the kinds of help available to troubled people. In some work situations, help may be forthcoming because of the friendships and loyalties that develop naturally among people who work well together. In other situations, management provides assistance with various kinds of counseling programs, which range in scope from psychiatric care for executives, to vocational guidance for younger employees, to drug and alcohol rehabilitation programs for the personnel needing such aid.

How to Identify Someone with a Problem

Sudden behavior changes may signal signs of stress

People who are coping with personal problems at work frequently show signs of emotional distress. Harry Levinson has identified three behavioral changes that signal coworkers and friends that "emotional first aid" is needed.[3] They are:

EXAGGERATED BEHAVIOR

An emotionally disturbed person's behavior patterns may become highly exaggerated. For example, an orderly person will become excessively meticulous. Or a quiet person will become extremely withdrawn. Or a friendly person will appear to be in a perpetual life-of-the-party mood.

When ordinary behavior is exaggerated in this fashion, it is often a sign of stress. The troubled person tries to hide stress symptoms by *acting* as if everything were normal. In fact, everything is *not* normal; and because such behavior *is* an *act*, it will be discernible as such to those who are familiar with the person's normal behavior.

DISTRESS SYMPTOMS

There are a number of distress symptoms that are apparent even to nonprofessional eyes. Disturbed persons are seldom able to concentrate, and may be highly agitated. If they are worried and fearful, they may be jittery and perspire freely. They may be excessively startled by loud noises, or by the sudden appearance of the boss. If they are depressed or grieving, they may speak in dejected, exhausted tones. They may lose weight or seem to be suffering from lack of sleep. Some are likely to be constantly irritable, others will cry at the slightest reason.

RADICAL CHANGE SYMPTOMS

When someone's behavior at work changes radically, it may indicate severe stress. In such cases, irrational thoughts and actions will become apparent. For example, a quiet unassuming clerk with no official authority to do so, might begin to issue orders to coworkers in an authoritarian manner. Or an ordinarily controlled and sober person might return drunk from lunch for several days in a row. Or an executive noted for forceful decision making might become incapable of deciding even the most trivial matters.

WHO CAN HELP?

FRIEND

Friends, supervisors, or specialists can help those under stress

Perhaps the closest confidant an employee can find to discuss a situation is his friend at the plant or office. A friend will tend to be receptive, open, and willing to listen without passing judgment. These qualities can be found in some, but not all superiors. In the informal setting the "counselor-friend" can give empathy and friendly advice. Usually there is little pressure for the employee to follow his friend's advice and the problem does not become public knowledge.

When some people recognize that a coworker is upset, they may be reluctant to speak to the person about their perceptions. They may feel that it is a private affair and that discussing it will only add to the distress. But there are two sets of circumstances in which it is permissible to intrude on another person's privacy at work. The first is when help is requested, which is certainly not an intrusion. The second is when two people have worked well together and one has strong evidence that the other person's job performance is falling down. Calling attention to work-related problems often enables disturbed people to open up and talk about their personal problems.

SUPERVISORS

Supervisors agree that at least 10 percent of the total labor force has emotional adjustment problems that affect job performance.[4]

The most logical choice on the part of an employee is to go to a listening supervisor with his minor problems. The good supervisor will soon discover whether he is capable of handling a particular situation. If the supervisor is inexperienced, he should consult with his superior or an expert in the field before having an interview with the disturbed employee. It is wise to call in an expert's opinion early in a case involving drugs, alcohol, or legal entanglements. But, according to I. L. Heckmann, Jr. and S. G. Huneryager:

> The current status of counseling as a managerial tool, at least as far as industry is concerned, is somewhat hazy. Among supervisors and managers the consensus would probably be that in theory it is fine, but in reality it is not very practical. They would likely respond that they do not have the time or the skills to act as counselors and that it should be the part of some college-trained specialist.[5]

Nevertheless, many companies do not provide professional counseling services, and the job automatically falls on the shoulders of supervisory and managerial staff. Since situations that call for counseling must arise between supervisors and subordinates when no specialized counseling services are available, current training programs for most managerial positions usually include some training in counseling techniques.

Beginning supervisors are often reluctant to discuss subordinates' personal problems with them because they feel poorly equipped to deal with such matters. Additionally, most supervisors are job oriented rather than person oriented, and counseling takes time, which is a valuable commodity. Nevertheless, the longer they work in supervisory positions, the more practice they get in dealing with personal problems because, inevitably, some employees will need to talk about disturbing aspects of their lives and jobs, or personality clashes will occur among employees which demand supervisory intervention.

In addition to the purely human satisfaction of helping someone get through a painful period, the supervisor-counselor also experiences the satisfaction of knowing that he has kept a valuable employee, and that he does not have to expend time and energy finding and training a replacement.

Experienced supervisors know that well-conducted counseling is hard and tiring work, especially when they have to deal with hostile and critical subordinates. They learn how to avoid being pushed into defensive postures and how to remain calm. But no matter how good they get at it, such encounters always use up a lot of energy. Himmler says that the problem of *mutual* feeling in a counseling session is a very delicate matter, and the degree to which the counselor must also experience strong emotions is a very difficult subject to assess. In terms of his own experience he says that:

> sometimes I've felt that the amount of feeling you get out of it is in reverse proportion to the reluctance you have to start with . . . and that means that it is work. After a day of it you can be as tired as if you had dug a six-foot ditch.[6]

The major limitation most supervisors experience in counseling is time. Follow-up is often essential for effective counseling and that can consume a great deal of time. In the long run, if insufficient time is set aside for counseling, more problems may result with an even greater loss of time.

Suppose a supervisor never took the time to counsel an employee with problems, but that person's inefficiencies resulted in the loss of an hour's worth of work every day for three weeks. Wouldn't three or four hours of counseling be a better investment of time?

SPECIALISTS

Counselors, attorneys, physicians, personnel directors, and ministers can act as specialists

The personnel counselor, the attorney, the medical physician, all become counselors under one condition or another. Personnel directors by their very role can act as uninvolved third parties in labor disputes, salary placement, and job transfers. The advantage company physicians or attorneys have is that they are not labeled by the stigma of "counselor" and find they can perform the role of a counselor very effectively on problems of abortion, adoption, and marital strife. Perhaps the specialist needs to spend considerable time with managers to help them cope with the constant stress of daily activities. Some company psychologists are giving yearly emotional check-ups, much as a person

Calling in specialists is often advisable in cases of abortion, adoption, and marital strife

would have a yearly physical. An emotional check-up might discover undue tension and nervousness that need attention in the same way a physical would detect the danger of high blood pressure.

In order to help such employees, some companies have instituted various kinds of counseling programs to deal with the specific kinds of personal needs.

Some large companies, like Eastman Kodak and Dupont, employ full-time staff psychiatrists. Others, like Hughes Aircraft and Raytheon, maintain full-time social workers to advise employees on marital, financial, and personal problems.[7]

COMPARISONS OF SUPERVISORS AND TRAINED COUNSELORS

The relative advantages of training supervisory staff as counselors or hiring expert personnel to handle the task are shown in Table 6–1.

Table 6–1.   Comparisons of Trained Supervisors and Specialists as Counselors

ADVANTAGES OF TRAINED SUPERVISORS	ADVANTAGES OF USING EXPERTS: PERSONNEL DIRECTORS, PSYCHOLOGISTS, MEDICAL SPECIALISTS
1. More available to employees	1. Usually more skillful
2. More natural relationship	2. Less bias and more confidential
3. Know job performance of the employee	3. Less conflict with other employee roles
4. No need to introduce the outside person to conflict	4. Less emotional involvement

It is clear from Table 6–1 that both approaches have distinct advantages. One *dis*advantage of hiring experts is that programs using experts have had great difficulties winning the acceptance of supervisory personnel. Apparently, many supervisors feel threatened by such programs because they fear that employees will criticize them unjustly. Two companies, Western Electric and Ohio Bell Telephone, abandoned their pioneering counseling programs, not because the programs failed, but because top management refused to support them after the initial supporters had retired.[8]

HOW TO COUNSEL

Levinson has formulated four rules of behavior that are extremely helpful for solving personality clashes at work.[9] They are:

Don't procrastinate

1. Don't procrastinate about doing something about the clashes. Procrastination may make them worse.

Evaluate the scope

2. Evaluate the scope and extent of the conflict. Is it with one person or many? Is it chronic and repetitive? If there are many persons involved and it has become a chronic problem, you may need professional help.

Talk to someone you can trust

3. Talk to a third party whose judgment you trust. If the third party agrees to mediate between you and the person with whom you are having difficulties, try to arrange for a three-way conference.

You may have to accept and live with a problem

4. Remember—not all problems can be solved. Sometimes you have to learn to accept a situation and live with it.

Self-Counseling

1. Don't fight tension—use it. Built-up tensions can cause grave trouble, and telling ourselves not to be tense rarely works. There are not always times when we can remove the source of our tensions. However, when you are tense, you are temporarily more energetic, alert, and aggressive. Start doing a job you have been putting off for a long time or one that seems to be a tremendous task. It is amazing how much can be done at a time like this. You will enjoy the feeling of accomplishment such a drive can give. Gradually your tension will ease, and perhaps even disappear.

2. Tackle one thing at a time. Anxiety gives us a restless dissatisfaction with ourselves when we attempt to do too many things at once. For example, you find that you are not as successful at work as you would like so you decide to go to night school to work on your degree. You barely get started and you are asked to join the civic club. You decide that it would provide some good contacts. You wish you had more money to buy better clothes, you think of moonlighting to buy a new wardrobe. If you suffer persistent anxiety by starting things, dropping them, and becoming hopelessly distracted, then tackle one thing at a time. Stick with it until you have done all you can do about it.

3. Often we worry about the question rather than the consequences of the answer. We worry about indecisiveness rather than trying to answer the problem, and, as a consequence, use a lot of excess energy. The key is to make a decision and live with it. We never make a better decision by worrying about it.

Make a decision and live with it

Laugh at yourself

4. Laugh at yourself on occasion. The way to tell whether you are leaning too heavily toward role-playing or pretense is to ask yourself: When was the last time you had a good belly laugh at your own expense?

Directive Method

The traditional method of counseling is called directive because the counselor *directs* and controls the form, flow, and content of the exchange between counselor and counselee.

Even though it may be impossible for one person to understand exactly the attitudes of another, there are times when a person in a confused state wants concrete advice that can be given by such guidance. The employee with an inferiority complex may find that reassurance from a manager may give him the courage to face a problem or the confidence to pursue a given task. Asking questions, making a diagnosis, giving advice are characteristic of the direct counseling approach. Such counseling is often expected in an organization with a strong formal chain of command.

Directive is the easiest counseling method

The direct counseling technique tries to establish what the employee is thinking in order to clarify facts and set the chain of events into logical order.

Directive methods usually appeal to novice supervisors, because they often seem to be the easiest paths to follow in troubled situations. They are fast, seem to require little skill, and are relied on much too heavily.

Directive method gives advice

1. ADVICE.   This is the most common, garden-variety, type of counseling available. It is easy to give advice—if you know what is suitable.

This doesn't mean the counselor should not answer direct questions requiring factual answers. Factual answers, and opinions clearly labeled as opinions, are often both necessary and helpful. But when emotional problems are under consideration, direct advice seldom is helpful unless solicited.

2. REASSURANCE.   There is nothing wrong with reassurance—in the right place and at the right time. It especially encourages new and timid workers.

Nondirective Method

Nondirective method requires active listening

Nondirective counseling, also known as "client-centered therapy," is the method that often lends itself to current human relations practices in industry. In large measure, it is the way in which professionally trained people practice active listening as a counseling technique. Nondirected counseling is so called "because the counselor does not direct the client with advice at any stage. The client, not the counselor, determines what will be discussed, and the interest centers on the client's feelings rather than a diagnosis."[10]

THE THEORY

Catharsis is talking out one's feeling

The basic theory of nondirective counseling holds that by skillful, active listening a counselor can help a client to release pent-up emotions. The process of obtaining relief from psychic and emotional tensions by talking about deeply felt emotions is called *catharsis*. Only after the client experiences catharsis and feels free of the weight of locked-in emotions, can he or she then identify and solve personal problems in a rational frame of mind, and with minimum direction or advice from the counselor.

The ultimate goal of nondirective counseling is to stimulate the growth of self-recognition and self-knowledge. The theory and the goal are based on the belief that the client is responsible for his own behavior, and that he will solve his own problems once they are fully recognized. It holds further that self-recognition can develop only when the counselor establishes what professionals call a "permissive atmosphere," one in which the counselor remains neutral and accepts all statements and actions without passing judgments.

According to Norman Maier, counselors must hold six sets of values, beliefs, and attitudes if they are to practice nondirective counseling skillfully.[11]

1. A fundamental belief that the client is responsible and the desire to strengthen that sense of responsibility.

A person can solve his own problems

2. A belief that the client can solve personal problems if given the opportunity to do so, and that every person basically is interested in doing the right thing.

3. An understanding that the solutions to problems must fit the client's value system, and that clients understand their own feelings better than anyone else does.

4. An understanding that only in a permissive atmosphere will a client feel accepted and not judged, and that only when clients feel accepted will they feel free to express such feelings as confusion, guilt, rage, or hatred.

5. An acceptance of the client as a worthy person whose problems merit attention, and an acceptance that what the client says is important and interesting.

6. A deep respect for the reality and validity of all feelings, no matter how vehemently they are expressed or how irrational they might appear to be.

THE PRACTICE

There are four basic practices nondirective counselors follow when conducting counseling interviews. They are:

1. READINESS.   They know that when they have appointments to see clients, it pays to learn as much about the person as possible beforehand. In most companies, personnel files will be open for counselors' inspection.

2. ACTIVE LISTENING.   Nondirective counselors listen for all positive and negative feelings. They don't interrupt. Often they repeat statements they don't understand to the client until both understand the intended meaning.

A nondirective counselor does not give advice

3. NO ADVICE.   They can answer questions about company policies and procedures, but if the client asks, "What should I do?" about a personal problem, they will not answer it. They believe that if the client expresses everything he or she thinks and feels about the problem, sooner or later the client will come up with self-generated advice. Further, they believe the best advice is always self-generated.

4. CLARIFICATION.   When the client does begin to arrive at solutions, they encourage the exploration of the ideas through to their logical consequences. They may offer occasional questions and suggestions at this stage. They help to clarify alternative courses of action as clearly as possible, but require the client to make the decisions.

The spirit of the questions asked in a nondirective interview is important. Some inquiries that work well are: "Would you like to tell me about it?" Do not pursue lines of inquiry that can be answered with "yes" or "no." If the employee contradicts him or herself occasionally, such changes usually indicate confusion, which is often a preliminary step in the clarification process.

ACTIVE LISTENING

Active listening is probably the most overworked phrase in the whole field of human relations. Everybody talks about it, but few practice it. If people are really listening actively, they are not judging, they are not faking attention, they are not anticipating what is going to be said—*they are trying to understand.* Active listening is much more than just not speaking. An active listener's behavior shows acceptance of the person as well as the words being spoken. Active listeners put energy into understanding—not into judging, not into criticizing, not into disagreeing, or even into agreeing—they concentrate on understanding.

To listen actively to a disturbed person, it is essential to recognize and accept the fact that the person has not made a conscious choice to be distressed. If anyone *could* feel better simply by choosing to, no one would ever feel distressed. If someone says to another person, "Pull yourself together! You don't have to feel that way," all that is communicated is lack of understanding. No one *wants* to feel bad. No one *chooses* to be depressed, or jittery, or anxiety ridden, but it is sometimes easier to shake a cold or recover from the flu than it is to get over a depression—and no one would think of telling someone with the flu to "pull himself together." Emotional problems are as real as physical illnesses, and require time to heal, just as physical illnesses do.

Emotional problems are frequently caused by unsatisfactory or demoralizing relationships with others. People often find new strength to deal with their problems more effectively if they can experience sympathetic and constructive relations with others. If personal problems appear to be extremely serious, help should be obtained from professional, medical, or legal advisors.

Cooperative Counseling

Cooperative counseling blends direct and nondirect counseling

Somewhere between directive and nondirective counseling lies the style called cooperative. It is a blend of the direct guidance and authority typical of directive counseling and the nonjudgmental, active listening behavior typical of nondirective techniques. This form of counseling is especially effective during appraisal and evaluation interviews, but it also has been used to good effect for counseling employees with personal problems. When using this method the counselor's role is neither a judge nor a sympathetic listener, but a complex mixture of the two.

In cooperative counseling the counselor tries to stimulate the client's thinking by asking specific, *nonthreatening* questions at the beginning of the interview. These questions are directive in that they determine the subject of the interview, but they are also nondirective in that the client is encouraged to express emotions as well as thoughts and attitudes. If the expression of

Figure 6–1. In cooperative counseling the counselor stimulates the client's thinking by asking *nonthreatening* questions at the beginning of the interview.
Santa Barbara City College Photo (Picture by Rob Reilly)

these emotions brings tears or anger, the counselor should remain sympathetic and patient until the outburst is over. When nonthreatening questioning works, it stimulates honest, deeply felt communication very quickly.

"Mirroring"   This style also uses the nondirective device called "mirroring," that is, restating a client's own words not only to reflect and clarify the client's feelings but as material from which to form nonthreatening questions. Silences and pauses for thought are also customary in cooperative counseling, but they are not as long-lasting, or as frequent as in nondirective practice. The counselor will indicate by words or gestures that the time of the interview is limited. When the client *does* speak the counselor will not interrupt, but wait for the thought to be completed, no matter how long the client takes.

An example of a case that was not likely to expose itself under direct interviewing but lent itself to a cooperative style is the case of the stubborn repairman.

A stubborn repairman
may be hiding his
epilepsy

Dennis appeared unusually stubborn when asked to cooperate in a company wide "share the ride program" using the company's trucks. After all kinds of excuses he revealed that he was an epileptic and had mild attacks or black-outs. When he felt an attack coming on he would drive to the curb and put his head on the steering wheel, blackout for a minute, rest, then drive on. During counseling the personnel director decided he should visit his doctor, who prescribed dilantin, which was a good remedy for his particular condition. After a few months he had his case of epilepsy under control and no longer had blackouts.

Because of the combination of directive and nondirective features, cooperative counseling is particularly effective in dealing with alcoholics and drug addicts. Its nondirective aspects encourage and stimulate honest communication quickly. Its directive features allow the counselor to set realistic behavior limits for troublesome employees.

USES OF COOPERATIVE COUNSELING

Cooperative counseling is effectively used during times of *evaluation and appraisal.* The spirit of the interview is to evaluate past job performance and not the person, with emphasis on improving future job performance. Cooperatively, the manager and the employee establish what the employee can effectively perform in the next six months by mapping out his "management by objectives" (MBO).

Cooperative counseling is necessary for *lateral transfers.* It is important that foremen understand the employee's feelings and make the best use of the person's ability. Hopefully, there are ways to capitalize on the employee's strong interests and also to discover his aspirations for advancement.

Finally, the *exit interview* can best employ the cooperative method to find out the real cause for an employee's leaving the company and determine whether the decision should or can be reversed.

Comparisons of Counseling Methods

Table 6–2 summarizes the different features of directive, nondirective, and cooperative counseling.

STRESS AND TENSION

To do our best work, we all need to generate some tension, some stress. We need to get the adrenaline flowing in

Table 6-2. Comparisons of Various Counseling Techniques

METHOD	DIRECT COUNSELING	COOPERATIVE	NONDIRECTIVE
	Judge	*Judge-Helper*	*Helper*
Objective	To communicate To evaluate To persuade the employee	To communicate To evaluate To stimulate self-help	To stimulate growth and self-help
Assumptions	Employee desires to correct known weaknesses	People will change if defensive feelings are removed	Growth can occur without correcting faults
Attitude	People profit from criticism, appreciate help	One can respect the feelings of others if one understands them	Discussion develops new and mutual trust
Motivation	Use of positive or negative incentives	Help overcome resistance to change Use of positive incentives	Increase freedom Increase responsibility
Risk	Loss of loyalty Inhibition of independence Face-saving problems created	Need for change may not develop	Employee may lack ideas Change may be other than what the superior had in mind
Gains	Success is most probable when employee respects interviewer	Develops favorable attitude toward superior which increases probability of success	Almost assured of improvement in some respects

order to "stay on our toes." And so we cannot hope to, nor would we want to, eliminate all excitement and accompanying stress from our jobs.

Many causes of stress, however, originate off the job and only disrupt it. They result in lower and poorer production, difficult relationships with other workers, inadequate attention and concentration, memory lapses, tardiness, and absenteeism. About 80 percent of the emotional problems of employees are of this nature; yet the good supervisor must be prepared to help with problems no matter what their cause.

Responsibility for the executive, it seems, is healthy. In most cases the man — not the job — creates the tension. The age-old adage, "the road to success consists of sleepless nights, skipped meals, poor family life, and poor health," doesn't hold as true any more. Eighty-seven percent of all executives today cope well with their jobs, according to a survey conducted by the Life Extension Institute of New York.[12] They like their jobs, get along well with their associates and families, and their families cooperate with their responsibilities.

However, there are things bothering the businessman of today. In recent years, one of the biggest changes in attitudes of businessmen is the problem of worry. In 1971, those who worried over decision making had risen to 32%, up from 13% in 1968. "Tension is clearly identified with the personality of the person and comes from within the man, rather than from the outside forces of his living and working environment," contends the Life Extension Institute.

A promotion frequently will create added stress that can ruin a man's work and spill over into his home life. Some persons welcome and thrive on heavy stress and pressure at work. Some recognize when they have had enough and refuse an advancement — which often confounds people in management. Most people want the promotion, but don't want the added headaches, stresses, and responsibilities that accompany it.

> For 15 years Frank had worked as a cable splicer for a telephone company. Because he was known as the best cable man in the company, he was rewarded by a promotion to the ranks of management. For the first 3 months he performed as well as could be expected from a person who was a boss for the first time in his life. But then everything began to fall apart for him, on and off the job.
>
> It was almost impossible for him to say "no" to requests for favored assignments from his former co-workers. Soon he lost all control of his men, of his desk work and of his good relations with his peers and superiors.
>
> According to his wife, "Frank would just sit around all day and stare into space, had no appetite, couldn't sleep and felt there was nothing left in life." She believed there was a connection between his promotion and the change in his behavior. Later Frank said, "I didn't really want to be a supervisor, but how could I turn it down?" Perhaps he should have refused the promotion for his own good. Or management should have helped Frank make the adjustment from "one of the workers" to "one of the bosses."

This kind of preparation for enlightened management

You hire the "whole man," not just his hands

works two ways to decrease stress in both the manager and worker. To feel at ease in his job the supervisor must remember the old saying, "You hire the whole man, not just his hands." Every employee brings his assets to the job—his skills, experience, and personality. But he also brings with him his home problems, his frustration, and perhaps his bad temper.

How Change Can Make Us Ill

We rarely think of a car accident or a suicide attempt as an illness. Surgical operations are not illnesses. But all of them involve a certain disruption of the state of health and functioning.

Psychiatric disorders such as depression and schizophrenia involve more than emotional imbalance. Depressed people, for example, almost always experience marked decreases in appetite and sex drive, along with weight loss, insomnia, fatigue, and constipation.

Watch for "overloading the human system"

"Life charts"

Alvin Toffler popularized in *Future Shock* the term of "overloading the human system." He defines it as "the distress, both physical and psychological, that arises from the overload of the human organism's physical adaptive systems and its decision-making processes." This idea has been around for many years. Adolf Meyer, professor of psychiatry at Johns Hopkins, recognized this idea around the turn of the century and began keeping "life charts" of his patients. In 1949 Dr. Thomas Holmes began to apply Dr. Meyer's life chart to case histories of more than 5,000 patients.[13] The items listed in Table 6–3 show some of the changes in life styles that are socially desirable and some that are undesirable. We are all aware of the drain on energy and resources associated with such "stressful" events as divorce, troubles with the boss, and death of a spouse.

The numbers in the right-hand column of the figure represent the amount, duration, and severity of change required to cope with each item, averaged from the responses of hundreds of people. Marriage was arbitrarily assigned the magnitude of 50 points, and the subject then rated the other items by number as to how much more or how much less change each requires in comparison with marriage. For instance, the scale implies that losing a spouse by death (100) requires, in the long run, twice as much readjustment as getting married (50), four times as much as a change in living conditions (25), and nearly 10 times as much as minor violations of the law (11).

The more changes you undergo in a given period of time, the more points you accumulate. The higher the score, the more likely you are to have a health change of one kind or another, for example, a serious illness, possible physical injuries, sur-

Table 6-3. The Social Readjustment Rating Scale

LIFE EVENT	MEAN VALUE
Death of a spouse	100
Divorce	73
Jail term	63
Death of close family member	63
Personal injury or illness	53
Marriage	50
Fired at work	47
Retirement	45
Pregnancy	40
Sex difficulties	39
Gain of new family member	39
Son or daughter leaving home	29
Wife begin or stop work	26
Change in living conditions	25
Change in sleeping habits	16
Vacation	13
Christmas	12
Minor violation of the law	11

(Partial list only—See T. H. Holmes, and R. H. Rahe, "The Social Readjustment Rating Scale," *Journal of Psychosomatic Research* 1967, 11:213–218.)

gical operations, psychiatric disorders. And the higher your score, the more serious the health change will likely be.

Leonard Himmler described a moving example of one such serious life adjustment for one of his employees. A young woman who had been married for only a year was widowed suddenly when her husband was killed in the Korean War. She took a few days off from her job and returned to work sad and subdued, but quite capable of working. As the weeks went by, the letters she had sent to her husband before his death were returned to her, one by one, unopened and unread.

The day she received the purple heart she broke down, and marched into Himmler's office and announced that she was unhappy in her job and wanted to quit. As Himmler put it:

> What should (a supervisor) do in such an instance? Take the distraught girl's word for it and release her? Offer her an opportunity to transfer to another department as a willingness to help? Refer her to a psychiatrist? Obviously none of these possibilities will entirely take care of the situation that has flared up in an acute emotional episode.[14]

What he did was to sit and listen to her outpourings of grief: he allowed her to cry at length without trying to stop her. Eventually, it became clear to the woman and to him that her pain resulted as much from her need for sympathy as from her loss. And even though he had no ready-made solutions for her problems, he did have deeply felt sympathy to give her—and he refused to accept her resignation. In a matter of time her job performance was up to par.

Type A and Type B Behavior

Type A is impatient, goal oriented

Different types of people are predisposed to different medical problems when under stress. Their different behavior can to some degree be catalogued. The Type A person is highly competitive, feels the pressure for time, and may react to frustration with hostility. For example, the Type A person is likely to set deadlines or quotas for himself at work or at home at least once a week. The Type A person brings his work home frequently. Such a person is highly achievement-oriented and pushes himself to near capacity. Hard-driving type A students earn more academic honors than their peers. Some behaviorists say that the Type A person earns the rewards he seeks, but perhaps at the cost of his health. Those with Type A behavior are at greater risk to heart attack when under heavy stress than Type B. Research has also found that such personality types are more likely to experience migraine and tension headaches, asthma, colitis, and some types of backaches.[15]

Type B enjoys leisure activities

The Type B person puts his time in at work and seldom brings his work home. He is more inclined to have interests in sports or leisure time activities. Time is not his master, and proving his worth to himself or others is not a strong requirement of his personality. He can be as intelligent as Type A, but doesn't work hard to prove it. The Type B person is less likely to demand strong control of his life and environment. He flows with the river of life, he doesn't fight upstream like a salmon.

How to Cope with Stress

The driver of a truck carrying high explosives drives more carefully than the driver carrying bricks; and the driver of a high explosives truck who does not believe in a life after death drives more carefully than one who does. The story illustrates an important point: The potential stress in any activity—whether driving a high-explosive truck or being an executive in a turbulent world—depends partly on the ideas that are in the person's head.

One thing we know about stress is that it is usually accompanied by feelings of arousal or agitation. A person under-going stress feels "keyed up." The problem is that when such arousal occurs, thoughts and action become more primitive. As a person becomes more and more agitated, his thoughts become more simplistic, he notices less in his environment, he reverts to his oldest habits, and all complicated responses in his repertoire disappear.

When people say that a piece of metal is "stressed," they mean that the metal is stationary and that something is done to it. Strain is the result of this stress. Notice that stress occurs when something external has been applied. The implication for us is that if an individual sees himself as passive and his fate controlled by others, he is more susceptible to stress in the form of unplanned external events. On the other hand, a man whose self-concept is of a more active nature is less susceptible to stress. If we could persuade people to think of themselves in dynamic rather than static terms, they might be more resistant to stress.

Situations are not inherently stressful

We put labels of stress there, not nature

We have to get away from the assumption that a situation is inherently stressful or nonstressful. We put the labels there, not nature, and we can also remove them. The feeling is often that stress will go on forever. It is not the stress itself that is painful and disabling, but rather the impression that it will never end.

Suppose an executive finds himself or herself faced with the question of whether or not to take a promotion that involves relocating his or her family. This classic executive problem is one of the more stressful decisions executives face. No one denies that moving decisions can be painful and disruptive, but it's easy to get wrapped into thinking that the momentary pain won't let up and that the stress will go on forever. It is this erroneous projection of a feeling, rather than the pain itself, that reduces the executive's ability to cope.

"Writer's block"

Suppose that you're trying to write a five-year plan for your department and you get stalled. You experience what some people would call a "writer's block." One way to handle that block is to imagine that it is now six years later. Then write yourself a letter from your boss, congratulating you in great detail on how well your five-year plan worked. Be as specific as possible in the congratulatory letter. Although you are writing a letter for a set of activities that have not yet occurred, in doing so you may clarify things you want to accomplish in those five years.

People like to control their own fate

People like to see themselves as able to control their own fate. And one of the main things that precipitates stress is the feeling that "I am losing control." The painfulness of the subsequent stress may result not from the actual fact of losing control, but from the individual's unwillingness to admit that he is capable of losing control. If he were to accept both his strengths and his weaknesses, and regard himself as a person who is capable of controlling events, even while recognizing that there are occasions when he cannot, then he will be in a much better position to manage stress.

While I was writing this text I suffered a heart attack. It was a frightening experience, and the period of recovery was marked with the customary feelings of anxiety and depression. As a Type A person I wished to have control of myself and my environment, yet I had let myself down. I was not overweight and had maintained a low cholesterol diet. As a nonsmoker and nondiabetic, I therefore wondered how it could happen to me. But as I overcame self-pity, I realized that periods of illness, stress, or crises are times to reevaluate one's life style. I learned that these can be times of profound personal growth. Such events can offer a real chance for a major new life cycle. In a sense, a physical or mental breakdown can be seen as a breakthrough.

The cycle of illness and healing can be potentially regenerative rather than inherently destructive. A thought to consider is that medical symptoms may be a useful signal for a change.

ALCOHOLISM

It is almost a cliche that the increased complexities of modern life have added to nearly everyone's share of tensions, guilts, anxieties, and inhibitions. Perhaps the most important function alcohol serves in human life is precisely that it reduces and relaxes tension, guilt, anxiety, and inhibition. But excessive alcohol consumption also reduces efficiency, sensitivity, and caution—three essential qualities for good job performance. Regular, predictable behavior is also essential to working well, and excessive alcohol can wreck regularity of behavior.

How Many Alcoholics Are There?

Dr. Harry Johnson, medical director of the Life Extension Institute of New York, has called alcoholism the major health problem in the United States. In a 1971 study of the drinking habits of 8,000 executives, he found that 27 percent of them drank more than six ounces of alcohol every day.[16] The figures on the number of chronic alcoholics in the United States vary according to who has conducted the study. Estimates run from eight to nine million alcoholics or from five to six percent of the work force.[17]

Dr. Harrison Trice, who has specialized in studies of alcoholism in industry, says that the percentage of alcoholics found among professional and white-collar employees is roughly similar to the percentage of alcoholics found in the blue-collar world.[18] And although there may have been some rise in female alcoholism, the ratio in the United States in 1970 was five male alcoholics to every female alcoholic.[18]

Problem Drinkers and Industry

Dr. Trice has summarized what constitutes alcoholism in a work environment as follows:

> Numerous companies have discovered that the popular stereotype of the problem drinker as a chronic "Lost-Weekender" is not accurate. They have found that they are employing early- and middle-stage alcoholics who are not yet chronic, but whose work has been substantially impaired by their developing alcoholism. As a consequence of this common experience a definition of alcoholism from the job standpoint has emerged: *any employee whose repeated overindulgence in alcoholic beverages sharply reduces his or her effectiveness and dependability in carrying out a work assignment is an alcoholic.* [Italics added.][19]

Although alcoholism, or problem drinking, is a problem with medical, social, and economic ramifications, experts view it as a disease with identifiable causes and a cure. It ranks fourth among the major threats to health after heart disease, cancer, and mental illness.[20]

The disease generally progresses from a mild social or psychological dependence, to a physiological dependence, and finally to a true addictive state. The entire process can take from ten to twenty years, and, consequently, most early- and middle-stage alcoholics in business and industry are between 45 and 55 years old.[21] Relatively few full-blown, late-stage alcoholics are employed because the symptoms at this stage are completely unsupportable in a work environment.

Problem drinking in industry has been called "the billion dollar hangover," and with good reason. Various surveys have indicated that problem drinkers cost three or more times as much as other employees in terms of absenteeism, accidents, inefficiency, and sickness benefits.[22]

Supervisors should keep records of absenteeism and investigate causes of on-the-job accidents. They should be suspicious if there is a decline in the quality or amount of work produced by a usually competent individual. There are many signs that will indicate if the problem is due to excessive drinking. Figure 6–2 outlines several signs that may be visible to the supervisor. No single sign is any indication of problem drinking, but a combination of several of them should be a definite signal to an alert supervisor that he or she may be dealing with an alcoholic.

Stages of the Alcoholic

STAGE A.   Stage A symptoms often show up on the job in the early stages of chemical dependency. They are not absolute

Figure 6–2. Stages that the alcoholic passes through from inconsistent performance to the time he is fired.

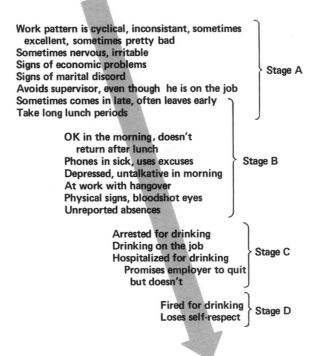

proof that the employee is developing a dependency problem—they could be symptomatic of some other problem. You will naturally exercise caution when interpreting them.

One thing is certain, the employee who is exhibiting Stage A type symptoms is sending out signals that *something is wrong*. These early warning signals indicate that the employee is having serious personal problems. The nature of the symptoms is such that the possibility of chemical dependency should be seriously considered.

At this point the disease may not be affecting the company directly, but it is already affecting the employee a great deal. The person who helps him recognize the disease at this early stage performs a real service. *You* may help him arrest the disease *before* he suffers many of its consequences, for example, the loss of family, friends, and health.

STAGE B.   Stage B symptoms are pretty consistently related to chemical dependency. By now, the problem with alcohol or drugs is affecting both the person's home life and his work. It affects co-workers, department morale, and production. The worker is in trouble and he knows it. It is possible, however, that he does not yet recognize the chemical as the source of the trouble.

Usually the worker's actions have become serious enough at stage B that the supervisor *must* take some sort of action. At stage A, intervention was desirable. At stage B it is unavoidable. The only question left is "what kind of intervention?" To try to find some way other than facing the dependency problem would be a disservice to the worker.

STAGE C.   Stage C symptoms leave no room for doubt that the problem is being caused by alcohol or other drugs. The symptoms are so serious that the company is forced to an either-or position—"either you quit drinking, NOW, or you're fired!" The worker can still be helped at this stage, but his chances for successful recovery are not as good. The range of options open to the company is much narrower. The worker has already done a lot of damage to himself and to the company.

STAGE D.   By this time he has been fired for drinking on the job and his performance is too low to be considered adequate.

The Supervisory See-Saw

Supervisors can be willfully blind if they choose to, because problem drinkers are often in the early or middle stage of the disease, and their symptoms are far less noticeable than the strange behavior of skid-row alcoholics, which is the popular stereotype many people think of when the term alcoholic is used. Many supervisors have mixed feelings about their alcoholic employees. On the one hand, the immediate boss of a problem drinker is often very disturbed about having to work closely with him. The supervisors in one firm were asked to rate who among neurotics, psychotics, and alcoholics were the most troublesome—and the alcoholics won—hands down.[23]

On the other hand, while supervisors tend to view alcoholics as their most difficult personnel problem, the way they generally handle their alcoholic employees all too often reflects the ambivalence about drinking typical of American cultural attitudes. The supervisor may have come up through the ranks with the problem drinker and may know his family. He may even have spent some nights "out on the town" drinking with the offending employee.

Early- and middle-stage problem drinkers often have "dry periods," when they are on the wagon and work very hard and very well. The sympathetic supervisor will continue to hope that the employee will snap out of what might just be a bad phase.

Occasionally, supervisors prefer to handle such problems alone rather than seek medical or counseling help, because they believe that they will receive no support and be forced to fire an old and trusted employee. Even though this employee is no longer worthy of such trust, the supervisor may feel compelled to remain loyal to the past.

The manager becomes concerned when employee's drinking interferes with doing a good job

It cannot be stated too strongly that it is only when the use of alcohol *interferes* with work that the supervisor is obligated to recognize the problem and come to grips with it. When an employee's drinking habits create no problems at work, they are *not* any concern of the supervisor. The sensible managerial view is the one that says, "What my employees do during their leisure time is no business of mine. It becomes my business when drinking prevents them from doing their jobs properly."

Dealing with Alcoholics

Early identification of alcoholism is important, and the earliest cause for action is a poor work performance. Supervisors who suspect that an employee's work difficulties may be due to problem drinking should discuss the matter with the employee. The matter should be treated *confidentially*, and discussed with no one else except counseling or medical personnel.

Once the problem has been identified and admitted by the employee, neither the supervisor nor the employee should entertain any notions that the problem will cure itself. If there is no company program, it will be necessary to work out some kind of personal rehabilitation plan. Advice on how to do this can be obtained from doctors, counseling personnel, psychiatrists, governmental agencies, or Alcoholics Anonymous. There is no one "best" way to handle an employee with a drinking problem. The approach will vary according to the individual. But there are some general rules worth observing.

Exact no promises

1. The supervisor should not exact or demand any promise the employee might make to stop drinking. Alcoholics are often incapable of keeping promises of that nature.

Don't moralize

2. Supervisors should not moralize or lecture. It's a waste of time.

Shape-up or ship-out

3. It is not a waste of time to threaten dismissal if the threat is sincere. "Shape-up or ship-out!" is the best threat. Often a problem drinker's job is the last thing of value left to him. He will try to keep it. Very few alcoholics conform to the skid-row stereotype. They must continue to work in order to survive.

Keep it confidential

4. The problem should be kept confidential. There is nothing to gain and much to lose when someone's personal problems are broadcast to the world at large. Also, it makes good sense to try to assist someone in whom the company has made a substantial investment of time and money by training.

Company Programs

Programs are best developed quietly without "fanfare." And witch-hunts should be avoided. Since alcoholism is a medical-personnel matter, all the confidential safeguards should be observed. However, when employees continue to refuse diagnosis and help and their work performance remains unsatisfactory, the normal procedures for handling poor work performance should apply: firm, corrective disciplinary action. The essential point is for employers to believe sincerely in the policy and be consistent in the administration of it.

When the alcoholic person is not playing the game of adulthood fairly, we get angry and decide to give him the "good-old-kick-in-the-pants" treatment. This may be an overt and conscious wish to help the patient and a covert and unconscious wish to punish him.

In the last decade, a few of America's largest corporations instituted company programs that offered comprehensive medical and psychiatric programs to their problem drinkers. These programs were available only to managerial and supervisory staff who represented enormous investments that would have otherwise been wasted.

Today, several hundred companies offer their employees alcohol rehabilitation programs of varying excellence. Some are given in conjunction with local chapters of Alcoholics Anonymous; others are conducted exclusively within the corporation. Some of the more successful of these programs claim a recovery rate of 70 percent.[24] All the programs depend on communicating to alcoholics the idea that the company and supervisors care about what happens to them, but cannot permit them to continue on their self-destructive paths. The company method is to support the alcoholic by forcing a confrontation with reality and by realistically limiting the alternatives.

Employee assistance programs claim a recovery rate of 70%

A typical company program will require the orientation and indoctrination of company doctors, nurses, and training personnel as a first step. Then a training program is instituted for supervisors, who learn to work with the medical staff and to refer their problem drinkers to them.

When employees are referred by their supervisors, or come on their own, they are given a series of physical and psychological tests and are then referred to various agencies, such as Alcoholics Anonymous or the local chapter of the National Council on Alcohol. Employees select a rehabilitation agency of their own choice, and weekly consultations with the company's medical staff are held thereafter.

Of course, many approaches to rehabilitation are possible. What is important to remember, however, is that alcoholism is usually a symptom of other, deeper social and psychological problems—and that for rehabilitation to actually work, these problems must be taken into account.

THE DRUG ABUSES

Companies find bent spoons in the washrooms, hypodermic needles and rubber tubing in the factory parking lot and even in the stairwell of the executive office building. Evidence is mounting that drug abuse is every company's problem. The American Management Association has been surveying a large number of firms for several years, asking: "Do you have a drug problem in your company?" Seven percent said "Yes" in 1967. In 1968, 13 percent replied affirmatively. The figure leaped to 23 percent in 1969 and skyrocketed to 41 percent in 1970. Thirty-four thousand heroin users were found in conventional jobs in New York.[25] Today, companies are accepting their respon-

Over 40% of companies surveyed have a drug problem

sibility to inform the public, to press for greater financing of rehabilitation, and to treat addiction as a medical problem rather than a criminal offense—and, most important, to provide jobs for "clean" addicts. A large insurance company now pays for the hospitalization of addicts. The company promised all working addicts an opportunity for rehabilitation while they retained their jobs. One plant at General Motors began a similar program in 1970 and promised complete anonymity and job security for any addict who volunteered for treatment at the local center. Such companies, however, are exceptions and most would rather fire drug abusers. "There's just too much fear and mystery and stigma attached to the drug problem for corporate management to want to get involved with. Yet, firms may be forced to look into the problem." It is estimated that $2-billion worth of stolen merchandise is "peddled" to support the drug habit. By one estimate addicts account for 80 percent of the shoplifting in New York.

Billions of dollars are stolen to support the drug habit

One West Coast representative for a rehabilitation program stated that half the people in the program between the ages of 20 and 35 are polydrug users. Such a term means that the employee is taking more than one drug. Therefore it is not uncommon to have people in the program who are alcoholics and drug addicts. Those people responsible for rehabilitation programs often use the word "drug" to mean either alcohol or hard drugs, because the treatment is often similar.

Many people are polydrug users

Permissive Drugs

Since so many drugs are legitimate or permissive because of medical reasons, many are available. Amphetamines, barbiturates, cocaine, codein, methamphetamine, and morphine are essential to the practice of medicine and are legally manufactured. The difficulty is the misuse of such drugs by the public. Dr. Robert Wiencek, medical director for the GM program, believes that if a company can find the drug user early, before he becomes a hard-core addict who resorts to crime to support his habit, he has a good chance for rehabilitation.

Medical and psychological reports vary widely

A major problem of drugs is that only a few people are aware of the complexity of the issue. Medical reports, state laws, and psychological opinions differ widely from state to state. Despite the federal statute controlling drugs under the "Comprehensive Drug Abuse Prevention and Control Act of 1970" the increase in drug abuse is startling. One difficulty that companies face is that supervisors and management alike cannot understand the "lingo", what the drugs look like, or even the symptoms exhibited by the user.

The growing popularity of marijuana has been documented in innumerable newspapers and magazines and in at least a dozen movies made during the early 1970s. In 1973, the city of Ann Arbor, Michigan, reduced the penalty for smoking or selling small quantities of marijuana to a misdemeanor. Several other cities have similar legislation pending. The state of California reduced the penalty for the possession of a small amount of marijuana to a misdemeanor.

"Pot" is more socially accepted now than a decade ago

A secretary in New York reports that at "ad agencies, people stand around and smoke pot in the corridors and no one thinks a thing of it." Steel mill workers light up on the job without fear of reprisal whenever they feel like it.[27] And, at a company dinner party, held by a major publications firm, a group of young executives sitting at one table smoked marijuana as openly as if it were tobacco.

Marijuana and other much stronger, more dangerous drugs are hawked openly and competitively at rock concerts and at other gatherings of young people, and the vendors are not hassled by the police.

There are many social and political ambiguities related to drug laws

Today a high percentage of arrests throughout the nation are for drugs or drug-related charges. Thus the ambiguities of the political and social situation have not made drugs any less illegal. Maybe it is time for new assessments and considerations. Certainly, when members of the "White House" family have tried "pot" and the public has not been tremendously upset, it is time to reevaluate the laws. Do you agree?

Dangerous Drugs

In New York during the mid-1970s it was estimated that the number of deaths due to heroin overdose averaged at least 500 a year, with the toll rising steadily. At about the same time, the phrase "Speed Kills!" was coined. This is a very precise description of what heavy abuse of amphetamines can do. It is common knowledge that some interstate truckers pop stimulants such as Benzedrine almost as if they were candy. It is also common knowledge, though the facts are hard to come by, that many horrendous highway accidents have been caused by the heavy speed user's habit of "blacking out" while driving.

It has been speculated that one of the reasons so many cars have been recalled by Detroit as "unsafe at any speed" may be that the assembly lines are manned by scores, and possibly hundreds, of veterans who returned from Vietnam with king-size heroin habits. Many heroin users, or "junkies," tend to get drowsy when they are on the drug. Certainly, a heroin addict's ability to focus and concentrate is sharply curtailed by the drug.

STIMULANTS

"Pep pills" help users to go for long periods without sleep

Stimulants act directly on the central nervous system, producing a feeling of excitation, energy, and the ability to go without sleep for prolonged periods. There is often a loss of appetite, and during such periods the user's body expends its reserve of energy, thus resulting in a "blackout." *Amphetamine* or methamphetamine are stimulants that are known as "speed, dexies, pep pills, uppers, bennies, or drivers." Highway accidents are caused as a result of blackouts or reckless behavior that has been provoked by stimulants.

The abuser may exhibit nervousness, tremors of the hands, dilated pupils, dryness of the mouth, and heavy perspiration. In short, the person abusing stimulants may exhibit dangerous, aggressive behavior that may resemble paranoid schizophrenia.

DEPRESSANTS

The downers, redbirds, yellow jackets, goofballs, or blue heavens, are pentobarbital, secobarbital, or other forms of barbiturates that are taken to excess. The *barbiturates* and tranquilizers depress the central nervous system to relieve tension or to induce sleep. The abuser will exhibit common symptoms of drunkenness, but there is no odor of alcohol unless both have been taken. A small dose will make him believe he is relaxed and sociable. Increased doses cause sluggishness, depression, and, in some, a quarrelsome disposition. The tongue thickens and speech is slurred. There is a loss of physical coordination that may be accompanied by mental or emotional instability.

Symptoms to look for include confusion, difficulty in thinking, impairment of judgment, and marked swings in mood between elation and depression. There may be increased irritability and inability to control fighting or weeping.

Hard Drugs

Heroin and opium are the hard drugs

Heroin and opium belong to that class of drugs known as narcotics, or "hard drugs." Hard drugs cause physical addiction in the user. Physical addiction means that the body develops a tolerance for the chemical, and alters its activities to correspond to the amount of the drug used. As a result, the user has to use more and more of the drug to get any kicks, or the pleasure of what addicts call "the rush."

The more of the drug that is consumed, the greater the physical dependency that develops. The greater the dependency, the harder it becomes to stop usage. Once the body adapts to the chemical, withdrawal pains begin if it is not administered at regular intervals. Withdrawal can involve stomach cramps, twitching nerves and muscles, diarrhea, and vomiting. However, many people report that the pain of withdrawal is nowhere near as hard to handle as the psychological need, or craving, that accompanies the physiological desire.

Soft Drugs

All other kinds of dangerous drugs are called soft drugs, but not because they are any mellower than the hard ones. Barbiturates (sleeping pills) are physically addicting, and the body develops a tolerance similar to narcotics tolerance. Some doctors believe that it is more difficult to cure a barbiturate addiction than it is to cure heroin addiction. The sudden cessation of barbiturates can cause convulsions, and has been known to cause death, particularly when alcohol has been consumed. Large doses of barbiturates and alcohol, taken together, can kill.

"Crashing down" can cause psychological depression

Amphetamines, besides causing the blackouts described earlier, can also cause withdrawal problems. When someone has become addicted to amphetamines and is suddenly cut off from them, withdrawal will result in severe psychological depression, laced with bouts of paranoia. "Crashing" or coming down from an amphetamine high may cause weeks of psychological distress.

Hallucinogens

LSD can alter time and space perception

Of this class of drugs, marijuana is the least intense, but even marijuana can cause time and space distortion, which are exceedingly dangerous when driving. Mescaline and LSD cause hallucinations as well as altering time and space perceptions. Some people have reported very unpleasant hallucinations, while others have described their "trips" as very pleasant. In the early days of LSD experimentation, great success was reported concerning its use with terminal cancer patients. It apparently eases the fear of dying for some people. However, it is not legal in the United States for many legal and medical reasons.

Use Drugs! Don't Abuse Them!

Nearly all of us have the occasion to take drugs at one time or another during our lifetimes. The ordinary use of insulin for diabetics, digitalis for heart patients, or antibiotics for staph infections is one of the miracles of modern medicine and also one of the major reasons our population is as healthy and as vigorous as it is. A great many people get started on heavy drug trips because they want to make their lives a little bit easier. Morphine, from which heroin is derived, is a justly famous pain killer that has a long and honorable record as an anesthetic. However, numbers of morphine addictions have been reported which began in the hospital when the patient was administered morphine too liberally. It is a very powerful drug and should never be treated lightly, even when severe pain warrants its use.

Tranquilizers can be addicting

Tranquilizers, although neither as potent nor as dangerous as morphine, can be equally addicting. They should be used very sparingly, even though a physician may have prescribed them. Some people find it more rewarding in the long run to suffer the anxieties and tensions that the tranquilizers were prescribed for than to go through the difficult psychological weaning process that has to be accomplished to break the addiction, after such medication has been taken over a period of time. A good rule of thumb regarding tranquilizers, even if they have been prescribed, is first to try deep breathing, gymnastics, or meditation to cope with tension.

SUMMARY

Personal problems cannot always be left at home. Sometimes they travel to work. At work there are two kinds of personal problems: (1) those that result from contradictions between work and nonwork elements of one's life; and (2) those that result from contradictions and imbalances among individuals in the work environment.

A person distressed by personal problems can be recognized by: (1) exaggerated behavior problems; (2) specific distress symptoms; and (3) radically changed symptoms. Once distress is recognized, friends and co-workers can often help each other through rough times. Their main counseling tool is the practice of active listening. Effective self-counseling is also a technique that can be learned to good advantage.

Both professionally trained counselors and supervisory staff perform counseling functions, which are very tiring and time consuming but necessary, and sometimes rewarding. The three major counseling styles are: (1) the traditional directive; (2) the newer nondirective; and (3) the cooperative—a combination of the first two. In directive counseling, the counselor directs the subject matter; in nondirective counseling, the subject is allowed to develop spontaneously. Cooperative counseling combines features of both and is particularly useful when dealing with alcoholics and drug addicts.

Alcoholism is a major disease that does great damage to our national productivity and results in great waste of human resources. Drug addiction, although perhaps not as prevalent, is increasing throughout the entire population, and some companies have instituted counseling programs to help their afflicted employees lick these disabling illnesses.

When a case of alcoholism or drug abuse is encountered, company policy often recognizes the problem as an illness that can be cured and offers the problem employee an opportunity to cure himself. If, after many trials, the employee refuses help and his job performance does not improve, two choices are left to him—leave the company or cure himself!

THE SWEET SMELL OF GRASS

Case study #1

Tom Nowak walked to his office on Monday morning to find Dan Porter waiting for him at his door. "Tom, I would like to see you right away in my office." Tom was surprised at the sudden approach that his boss had used and the first thing on a Monday morning. It must be serious, he thought, as they walked down the hall together. He thought that they had always had a stable, amicable relationship.

"What's up?" asked Tom trying to keep from sounding too apprehensive as they arrived at Dan's office.

"Sit down, Tom, it's important. It involves some of the men in your department." Dan was obviously disturbed. You have been responsible for the shipping room for several years, and I haven't had any serious reason to doubt how you handle your men or the decisions you make in that department. But this new development upsets me."

Dan continued, "I've heard, and occasionally seen, a group of your boys, a clique, seem to take their breaks surreptitiously in out-of-the-way places, the restroom, and behind the loading dock. I've heard the reason is because they're smoking marijuana. Is that true, Tom?"

"You might be right, Dan, I really don't know, but I suspect it."

"Have you ever confronted them with the idea? Have you asked them outright?"

"No," said Tom quietly, "and I am not sure it is a good idea."

"Why not," replied Dan quickly and rather irately, "do you have a better idea?"

"The first reason is that they would probably lie if I asked them outright if they were smoking pot. They would lie for fear of losing their jobs. Another is I am not their mother or guardian of their morals. Their break time is strictly their own. Oh, I know it is illegal, and the company could get into trouble even though we don't control their breaks. However, we might be opening 'Pandora's Box' if we approach it head on."

"What do you mean by a crack like that, Tom?" inquired Dan.

"You know as well as I do," said Tom, "that there are some guys under you that have openly discussed the effects of pot, and who have admitted trying it. I don't have to name them, you know them."

Dan looked perplexed, "You're right, but they haven't stepped out of line at work to my knowledge. If we condone its use at work we have a problem. It is illegal, you know. We just can't take the risk that it is being done on company time."

1. What would be your approach to solve the immediate problem?
2. If you were to counsel any of the employees which counseling approach would you use?
3. Should Tom and Dan try to solve the problem between themselves or should they confer with others?
4. There is not a company policy on the matter; should they develop one?

JUST A LITTLE LARCENY—I'LL DRINK TO THAT

Case Study #2

In the opinion of Bob Ruppert, hospital administrator, the theft of various items ranging in value from $1 to $10 has become a major problem at the Bisbee Memorial Hospital. And it is increasing. At the recent monthly supervisors' meeting, Ruppert stated: "All the evidence we have been able to gather seems to indicate that the problem is serious and the loss is quite large. We must take steps to stop our loss. Hopefully we can take care of it on an individual basis. I hope so. I have no idea whether it is the problem of a few or many."

A few days later you are in the home of a long-time friend who works at the hospital with you, but not under your supervision. Darryl Gossage has been with the company as a maintenance man for more than 15 years and has been considered one of the company's most competent men in his field. You also knew his drinking habits were getting worse, and some of your friends say that he has become an alcoholic. This particular Saturday Darryl has imbibed rather heavily and as you chat with him in the garage you notice a microscope in his garage with the initials BMH marked on the side. You mention to him, "Isn't that one of our microscopes, Darryl?" "Yah," Darryl replies hesitantly, "it needs fixing." Subconsciously, you go over to the microscope and check it out. It appears in good order. You say, "_____."

1. What would you say? Do you make an accusation or let it pass?

2. Do you ignore it and ask Darryl for suggestions on what can be done about theft of hospital property?

3. What is the best way to handle Darryl's possible "light finger" problem?

4. If you think Darryl's drinking is now a serious problem, how would you handle it?

Terms and Concepts Students Should Know

self-counseling	depressants	polydrug user
nondirective counseling	LSD	stimulants
type A behavior	directive counseling	hard drugs
life charts of stress	cooperative counseling	hallucinogens
rehabilitation programs	type B behavior	
marijuana	alcoholism	

Bibliography

1. FARBER, SEYMOUR, ed., *Man Under Stress,* San Francisco, University of California Medical Center, 1964.

2. LEVINSON, HARRY, *Emotional Health in the World of Work,* New York, Harper & Row, 1964.

3. MAIER, NORMAN, *Psychology in Industry,*
4th ed., Boston, Houghton Mifflin Co.,
1970.
4. STRESS, A Report from Blue Cross of

Northern California, 1974.
5. WHITNEY, ELIZABETH D., editor, *World Dialogue on Alcohol and Drug Dependence,*
Boston, Beacon Press, 1970.

Footnotes

[1] Quoted in "Stress: an Overview," by William O. Reinhardt, in *Man Under Stress,* edited by Seymour Farber (San Francisco: University of California Medical Center, 1964), p. 13.

[2] "Mental Health Realities in Work Situations, *American Journal of Ortho-psychiatrists,* 1963, 33: 562–565.

[3] Harry Levinson, *Emotional Health in the World of Work* (New York: Harper & Row, 1964), p. 222.

[4] Norman R. F. Maier, *Psychology in Industry,* 3rd ed. (Boston: Houghton Mifflin Co., 1965), p. 653.

[5] J. I. L. Heckmann and S. G. Huneryager, eds., *Human Relations in Management,* (Cincinnati: South-Western Publishing Co., 1960) p. 503.

[6] Leonard E. Himmler, "The Counseling Interview," in *Human Relations in Management,* edited by I. L. Heckman, Jr. and S. G. Huneryager (Cincinnati: South-Western Publishing Co., 1960), p. 452.

[7] Daniel Bell, *Work and Its Discontents* (Boston: Beacon Press, 1956), p. 27.

[8] Maier, *Psychology in Industry,* p. 672.

[9] Levinson, *Emotional Health,* pp. 265–266.

[10] Maier, *Psychology in Industry,* p. 277.

[11] *Ibid.*

[12] "The Busy Boss—How Tense is He?", *U.S. News and World Report,* 12 March 1972, p. 69.

[13] *Stress,* A report from Blue Cross of Northern California, 1974, pp. 66–75.

[14] Himmler, *Human Relations in Management,* p. 542.

[15] David C. Glass, "Stress, Competition and Heart Attacks," *Psychology Today,* December 1976, pp. 54–57.

[16] "Business Drinking: A Health Hazard," *U.S. News and World Report,* 13 March 1972, pp. 70–71.

[17] Warren Boroson, "How Your Career Can Affect Your Drinking," *Money,* January 1976, pp. 46–50.

[18] Harrison Trice, "Alcoholism and the Work World: Prevention in a New Light," in *World Dialogue on Alcohol and Drug Dependence,* edited by Elizabeth D. Whitney (Boston: Beacon Press, 1970), p. 223.

[19] Harrison Trice, "The Job Behavior of Problem Drinkers," in *Society Culture and Drinking Patterns,* edited by David J. Pittman and Charles R. Synder, (Carbondale, Ill.: Southern Illinois University Press, 1962), p. 494.

[20] Robert Clyne, "Detection and Rehabilitation of the Problem Drinker in Industry," *Journal of Occupational Medicine* Vol. 7, No. 6, 1965, p. 265.

[21] *Ibid.*

[22] Trice, "Job Behavior of Drinkers," p. 493.

[23] Levinson, *Emotional Health,* p. 142.

[24] Clyne, "Detection of the Drinker," pp. 265–268.

[25] "A Drug on the Market," *Newsweek,* 27 March 1972, p. 90.

[26] "Drug Addicts are Aided at a GM Plant, *Nation's Business,* March 1972, p. 20.

[27] Harry Klonoff, "Marijuana and Driving in Real-Life Situations," *Science,* Vol. 186, 25 October 1974, pp. 317–323.

Creativity
"The Idea Just Came To Me!" ▪ ▪ ▪ ▪ ▪ ▪ ▪

■ ■

OBJECTIVES

After reading the chapter you should be able to:

1. Show how the following qualities relate or do not relate to the meaning of creativity:
   A. Timeliness,
   B. Usefulness,
   C. Originality.

2. Describe Riesman's view of the transition from individualism to conformity in American society.

3. Discuss the relationship of creativity to the following human factors:
   A. Intelligence,
   B. Education,
   C. Age,
   D. Behavior.

4. List the four "P's" of Creativity and various theories behind those ideas.

5. Discuss the importance of accommodation and rewards in promoting creativity.

6. Describe the following four stages of the creative process:
   A. Perception,
   B. Incubation,
   C. Inspiration,
   D. Verification.

7. Describe the basic uses, rules, and variations of brainstorming.

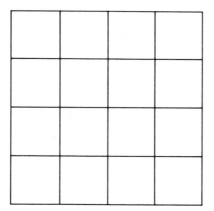

How many squares are in the box?
Now, count again.
Only sixteen?
Take away your *pre*conception of how many squares there are.
Now, how many do you find?[1] You should find thirty!

WHAT IS CREATIVITY?

How Is It Defined?

Mark Twain said, "The man with a new idea is a crank until the idea succeeds."

Like justice, democracy, and liberty, creativity is a word with many different meanings for many different people. It is also a very fashionable word. The New York Telephone Directory lists about one hundred businesses whose names begin with the word "creative." The one factor common to all creativity is that it always "involves a new association of existing elements, *as far as the creator himself is concerned.*"[2] The existing elements are the sum total of our cultural heritage. What is new is *the combination of these elements into new patterns of association.* Einstein could never have postulated the theory of relativity if the patterns of Newtonian physics had not been so firmly established. In this regard Henri Le Chatelier commented:

> Pasteur did not invent the contagion of diseases, which was known by all doctors, or create the life of the infinitely small organism, which had been studied since Spallanzani; *he only brought those two classes of phenomena together and recognized the relation which joined them to each other.* Without knowing these facts he would not have been able to make discoveries. [Italics added.][3]

Who Has It?

Creativity can be a universal trait

Have you ever met a child who didn't enjoy building castles in the sand? Have you ever marveled at a child's drawing or eavesdropped on a "conversation" between a child and an imaginary playmate? Like the use of language, creativity appears to be a universal human trait.[4]

If creativity is defined as the ability to combine already existing elements in new ways, we can see clearly that a child's creative energies do not disappear with the onset of adulthood. They are simply expressed in different ways in many aspects of daily life: in homes, schools, offices, and factories. A secretary who designs a new, more efficient filing system, a factory worker who uses an unconventional tool to perform a familiar task more easily, a needy student who uses cement cinder blocks to build a bookcase—all are acting creatively.

Timeliness relates to the recognition of an idea

Three criteria have been suggested for recognizing a creative idea. They are timeliness, usefulness, and originality.[5] A moment's reflection on these qualities, however, reveals certain inconsistencies in their application to creativity. If an idea is ahead of its time, that idea is not useful at *that* time. Are we to say, then, that Leonardo da Vinci was not creative when he drew elaborate designs for a flying machine hundreds of years before technology could build it? Gregor Mendel discovered the laws governing the behavior of recessive and dominant genes thirty-five years before they were applied to the selective breeding of plants and animals. Does that time lag invalidate his creativity in discovering those laws?

No one would wish to deny Edward Teller his right to the title "Father of the Hydrogen Bomb," but what is the usefulness of that bomb to most of the world's population? How useful does an idea have to be, to be called creative?

And what about originality? Consider the case of the telephone:

> On February 16, 1876, two descriptions of an invention for "transmitting vocal sounds telegraphically" were filed in the U.S. Patent Office. Alexander Graham Bell, of Salem, Mass., and Elisha Gray, of Chicago, Ill., were the applicants. It was necessary to determine the precise hour that each was filed. Bell, of course, was finally awarded the patent.[6]

Was Gray less original than Bell?

When the spirit of the times is right for an idea to bloom, it often occurs to more than one person simultaneously. If identical concepts occur to people living thousands of miles apart, the separate elements are still put together individually, and thus the idea is still original.

Do these inconsistencies make the criteria of timeliness, usefulness, and originality meaningless? As often as not, the criteria *do* apply, at least to the current *recognition* of a creative idea. The discovery of the molecular structure of DNA and RNA is a case in point. In the early 1950s the search for the "building blocks of life" was a full-time occupation of scores of scientists. The laboratory investigations of James Watson and Francis Crick were conducted with the secrecy of a spy operation because so many investigators were hot on the trail. As Watson and Crick are the first to admit, they got there "the firstest with the mostest" purely by chance and luck.[7]

202

PRESSURE OF SOCIETY ON CREATIVE PEOPLE

Social Direction

Our culture can lead us to be creative artists or creative mechanics

All children everywhere are born with some degree of innate creative energy, but the channels into which that energy will flow are determined by the values of a particular culture. In some parts of the world, such as the island of Bali, artistic ability is very highly valued and almost every child grows up to be skilled in at least one art form. In our part of the world it often seems as if the training we give to our children may damage the innate, creative, "artistic" energy we are born with. Most of us, if asked, would say, "I'm not a creative person: I don't paint or write poetry." But this is a very narrow view of the scope of the creative force.

In America, technological change is very highly valued, and in every new generation many children grow up to be skilled practitioners of at least one technological innovation. In the 1920s, if you wanted to own and drive a Model-T Ford, and hundreds of thousands did, the odds were that you had to learn to repair it yourself. There were very few skilled auto mechanics to be found outside the largest cities, and thousands of patents for automobile improvements were granted in those years to self-taught, *creative* auto mechanics.

Today, because of the highly specialized division of labor typical of modern industry, it is sometimes very difficult to determine the exact moment creation occurs — or even who the creator is. Who should take the credit for creativity? — the person who first conceives the idea, the one who first makes a model that functions properly, or the one who first designs it for actual on-the-line production?

Social Pressure

Society can pressure us to find solutions to today's problems

Society often puts a great deal of pressure on creative people to channel their energies into specific areas to solve specific problems. The old adage, "necessity is the mother of invention" holds true at all times. Pollution, clean and abundant sources of fuel, and mass transportation, to name but three of the most pressing of today's social problems, require solutions as quickly as possible. The necessities of the society as a whole generally govern what the inventions of creative people will be.

Or society can create a "rebel spirit" to force the society to see new creative ways

The more pressing the problem is on society, the more effort is made to find solutions. Today, in the research departments of many major industries, experimental work is underway to find a cleaner fuel than gasoline, and many chemists of a creative bent are drawn to such departments because the need is obvious and the pay is good.

Artists, who are supposedly the most "free" of all highly creative types, also respond to the pressures of society, if only to describe them. A good rock station is an outlet for popular artists' commentary in the form of songs about drug addiction, the horrors of war, the women's liberation movement, and the decline of the cities. Even abstract paintings have been interpreted by some critics as expressions of alienation in modern life.

Social Values

What effects do social values have on creativity? For one, society helps to condition our ideas of individual potential. William H. Whyte noted in *The Organization Man* that the American belief in the Protestant ethic, which glorifies individualism and self-reliance, has given way to a new "social ethic," which values teamwork and group decisions. It was Whyte's view that teamwork and group decisions tend to promote those "skeletons in the American closet," mediocrity and conformity.[8]

In *The Lonely Crowd,* David Riesman described the transition from valuing individualism toward valuing conformity in terms of two personality traits: "inner-directedness" and "other-directedness."[9] The inner-directed person looks mainly to his or her conscience for guidance. There is little need for the approval of others, and behavior is determined by that person's internal concepts of right and wrong. Writing in the 1950s, Riesman contended that Americans were once primarily inner-directed, as the images of the pioneer and the rugged individual suggest.

As the American population became concentrated in cities, the pioneer values of rugged individualism and self-reliance lost their strength, according to Riesman. Individuals adopted values that were determined primarily by others. The other-directed person requires the approval of other people. The individual conscience was no longer sufficient as a guide, and its loss created a great deal of insecurity for many people.

Inoffensive opinions are safe

Insecurity in their personal lives led Americans to seek values that were safe. Opinions were respected if they were inoffensive and noncontroversial. What resulted was the safety of thinking in numbers, which eventually led to the classification of the United States as a "nation of sheep" and to the description of Americans as mediocre and conformist.[10] Riesman concluded that in seeking the safety of the masses, Americans sold out their most basic freedom — their right to be themselves and to be independent.

Mass thinking and the average American

Mass thinking is deeply entrenched in the American way of life. The idea of majority rule, for example, is the basis of our national philosophy. However, the bland image of the "average American" is currently being countered by a renewed insistence on individual and collective rights. Everywhere today we see attempts at new life styles and new ways of solving old problems.

Americans are still group oriented. The early 1960s saw the beginnings of new combinations of the elements of individualism and social conformity. People with creative "new" ideas found others with similar ideas and banded together into "movements," often challenging traditional social values. These groups usually encourage the expression of individual needs and desires.

For several decades, American businesses have concentrated on developing and using skills calculated to increase the potential and efficiency of groups, and members of social movements have adopted many of those techniques. Groups have inherent strengths — the abilities to wield power, to get things done efficiently, to provide support for the ideas and actions of members — and social movements rely on those strengths. This kind of group action is both inner- and other-directed. People are becoming increasingly aware of the need to tap and use the creative energy that has been stifled by conformity.

Human history has been greatly affected, positively and adversely, by just such attitudes. Groups, functioning to combine existing elements into new solutions for old problems, can sometimes effect change. The problem, in a social milieu, is sustaining the faith and energy necessary to carry out group goals, often despite the disbelief or disapproval of others.

THE CREATIVE PERSON

Although all people have a creative spark, that potential is not always fully utilized. How does one recognize those who are developing their creative energies to the fullest? Mad painters and tormented poets are only comic stereotypes of the creative personality. The essential traits of creativity are found among a wide variety of less conspicuous creators: scientists, carpenters, social reformers, teachers, gardeners, business people, politicians, doctors, parents — people in all walks of life. The potential for creativity resides within us all. Unfortunately, the structure of our social and educational environment does not always promote its growth.

Perception

We all see the world slightly differently

Because of differences in temperament and environment, everyone sees the world in a slightly different way. Some people perceive the world as orderly and just, while others see only disorder and injustice. In the same way, some people perceive their environment as just so many disorderly specific details against a blurry background, while others try to focus on the orderly relations of parts to wholes. Generally speaking, creative people tend to view nature as fundamentally orderly. That is, they perceive a universe that is capable of order because they tend to perceive the interrelatedness of all things. They often believe their purpose in life is to discover and implement that relatedness, to make order out of disorder, to bring together isolated ideas and materials, and to fuse them into a unified whole.

A creative person brings together isolated ideas into a fused whole

The creative person often sees problems where others see none and questions the validity of even the most widely accepted answers. Creative personalities are compulsive problem seekers, not so much because they thrive on problems, but because their senses are attuned to a world that demands to be put together, like a jigsaw puzzle scattered on a table.

Approach

Several tests now in use reveal that highly creative people are much more open and receptive to the complexities of experience than are less creative people.[11] Highly creative people are apt to make "leaps of reasoning" from one fact to a seemingly unrelated fact and construct a bridge of logic across the chasm. The

A creative person distrusts "pat" answers

creative temperament distrusts pat answers and implicit assumptions. It has a tendency to break problems down into their most basic elements and then reconstruct them into whole new problems, thereby discovering new relationships and new solutions.

The curiosity of a child

Highly creative people aren't afraid to ask what may seem to be naive or silly questions. They ask questions like, "Why don't spiders get tangled up in their own webs?" And, "Why do dogs turn in circles before lying down?" Such questions may seem childlike, and in a way they are. Children have not yet had their innate creative energies channeled into culturally acceptable directions and can give full rein to their curiosity—the absolute prerequisite for full creative functioning, in both children and adults.

Unlike children, creative people appear to have vast stores of patience to draw upon. Months, years, even decades can be devoted to a single problem. Charles Darwin spent a lifetime developing the theory of evolution, and Einstein—the boy who flunked grade school math—spent the better part of his life devising and revising the theory of relativity.

Intelligence

One of the most common misconceptions about the highly creative personality is that there is a positive correlation between creativity and intelligence. The problem here is that *intelligence* is another word that means many different things to different people. If we mean by intelligence simply the ability to learn a lot of facts and relationships by rote memory, and to put that knowledge into useful service, then there appears to be little correlation between intelligence and creativity. On the other hand, if we mean by intelligence the ability to solve complex and unusual problems, then there is a high correlation. Lewis Thurstone studied the "Quiz Kids" of radio fame and noted:

There is little correlation between I.Q. and the creative quotient

> To be extremely intelligent is not the same as to be gifted in creative work. The Quiz Kids are often referred to as geniuses. They would undoubtedly score high in memory functions. . . . But it is doubtful whether they are also fluent in producing ideas.[12]

In a study of highly successful architects, the relation between creativity and intelligence was found to be zero.[13]

Education

Formal education does not necessarily develop creativity

Apparently education is not a factor in creativity either. People who have had no formal education at all have exhibited outstanding creative talents, while many highly educated persons are creatively sterile.[14]

Creativity probably has even less direct relation to genetic inheritance than intelligence does. The creative personality is nurtured not in the mother's womb, but in the social and educational environment. The home that encourages inquisitiveness contributes to creative development. The teacher who stresses questions rather than answers and rewards curiosity rather than restricting it is "teaching" a child to be creative.

Age

Age does not seem to decrease creativity

Contrary to popular myths that glorify youth, more creative achievements are likely to occur when people grow older. One researcher made a list of 1,000 ideas that have been important to the world and found that the average age of the innovators when they actually had those ideas was 74![15] Genius may flare early and die young, but imagination generally grows by being used. Another researcher has found that mental ability grows until about age 60, then decreases—but so slowly that at age 80, it is as if you are 30.[16] While memory may falter with age, creativity is ageless.

Sex

Neither males nor females are more creative

Dr. E. Paul Torrance has found no significant relationship between creativity and gender.[17] It does appear that less rigid male and female role identification increases the chances for creativity. For instance, the group of architects who were studied for intelligence were also given the Minnesota Multiphasic Personality Inventory (MMPI) to inquire into their psychological natures. The most striking aspect of the MMPI profiles was the tendency for creative males to score high on the femininity ratings. One writer has commented on the meaning of these scores:

> The evidence is clear: The more creative a person is, the more he reveals an openness to his own feelings and emotions, a sensitive intellect and understanding self-awareness, and wide-ranging interests including many which in the American culture are thought of as feminine. In the realm of sexual identification and interests, our creative subjects appear to give more expression to the feminine side of their nature than do less creative persons.[18]

Behavior

Creative people are sometimes more interested in ideas rather than people

Creative people are more concerned with the world of ideas and images than the world of society. As a result, they tend to be somewhat antisocial. In their personal lives they may appear to be highly sensitive and self-centered. Their life styles may seem chaotic, but inner-directed as they are, it doesn't matter to them what their lives look like to others. Their rewards are the joys of discovery, not the approval of society.

Abraham Maslow, a psychologist who worked with many gifted persons in the course of his career, said:

> They tend to be unconventional; they tend to be a little bit queer, unrealistic; they are often called undisciplined, sometimes inexact, "unscientific," that is, by a specific definition of science.

They tend to be called childish by their more compulsive colleagues, irresponsible, wild, crazy, speculative, uncritical, irregular, emotional, and so on.[19]

Table 7–1 compiles research on personality traits that often appear in creative personalities. Not all of these traits *must* be present, however, for a person to be creative. All of them rarely appear together and their presence does not always indicate creativity. The value of the table is to familiarize you with possible indicators of creative ability.

Table 7–1. Possible Personality Traits of a Creative Person

IN RELATION TO OTHERS	JOB ATTITUDES	ATTITUDES TO SELF
Not a joiner	Preference for things and ideas to people	Introspective
Few close friends	High regard for intellectual interests	Open to new experiences
Unconventional morality	Less emphasis on job security	Inner maturity
Independence of judgment, especially under pressure	Less enjoyment in detail work and routine	Less emotionally stable
	High level of resourcefulness Skeptical High tolerance for ambiguity Persistence, capacity to be puzzled	Spontaneous Adventurous Compulsive Anxious

Source: Adapted from John W. Haefele, *Creativity and Innovation* (New York: Reinhold Publishing Corp., 1962).

Inhibitors

Early training and environmental influences can discourage natural curiosity and stifle impulses to explore and experiment. Schools still stress acquiring information rather than learning how to think. In many ways, the educational system tends to foster imitative rather than creative behavior.

Creativity may be inhibited by factors that we may not be aware of. By becoming more conscious of inhibiting behavior and learning to change it, we can release much of our creative energy. One of the most common reasons for lack of creativity is simply *poor health*. Not having a healthy body can lead to anxiety, illness, tension, pain, and worry. These states inhibit to some extent the ability to concentrate.

Mental laziness is a way of conserving energy. To be creative, you have to be willing to think, which often takes a great deal of focused energy. A lazy person can still be curious, however. *Lack of curiosity* means an inability to wonder, an unresponsiveness to various stimuli. *Faulty observation* is the problem of being oblivious to the obvious, which may include the obvious existence of a problem. Another related block to creativity is *superficiality* of thought. Creativity requires delving below the apparent features of things. Incomplete, hasty, or shallow conclusions do not usually produce truly creative ideas.

Some states of mind are less conducive to creativity than others. *Emotion-mindedness* is the habit of allowing feelings to distort reasoning and block objectivity. *Judicial-mindedness* is the tendency to find fault immediately with a new and different thought, thereby inhibiting further thoughts in that vein. *Label-mindedness* filters thought by finding the names for things rather than evaluating the facts about them.

The habit of *not* being creative may be encouraged by any one or combination of these attitudes. The important thing to remember is that these behavior patterns can be changed. Striving toward creativity will tend to make psychological blocks more evident and speed a freer flow of ideas. With the appropriate effort, most people can increase their creative abilities in these specific areas: being more sensitive to problems, having more self-confidence, being more fluent with ideas, being more flexible in thinking, having more original ideas, and being motivated to elaborate on and follow through on ideas.[20] We have discussed the pressure of society and the attributes of the person. See figure 7–1 for a more complete breakdown. Now it is time to discuss the process of creativity.

THE CREATIVE PROCESS

Stages

The unfolding of the creative process is still mysterious. Many attempts have been made to analyze it, but it remains little understood. However, there are certain obvious *stages* to the process that can be identified. They are called perception, incubation, inspiration, and verification.[21]

Here are nine dots to test your creative quotient, or C.Q. (Figure 7–2). Can you draw four straight connecting lines through all nine dots without lifting your pencil? It is possible.

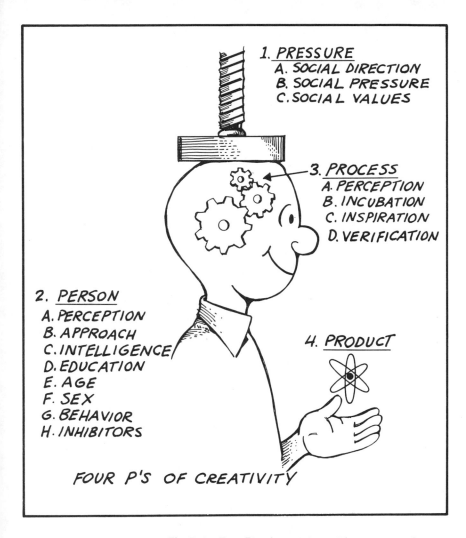

Fig. 7–1. Four P's of creativity: 1. The pressure of society, 2. Person who is creative, 3. The process of creativity, 4. The product.

Once you have done it you may refer to the end of the chapter for the answer.

PERCEPTION

The person with originality tends to view society from a different perspective than the custodial person. An analogy might be that the creative person sees the forest, while the custodial person sees the trees (see Table 7–3). A creative person is able to see

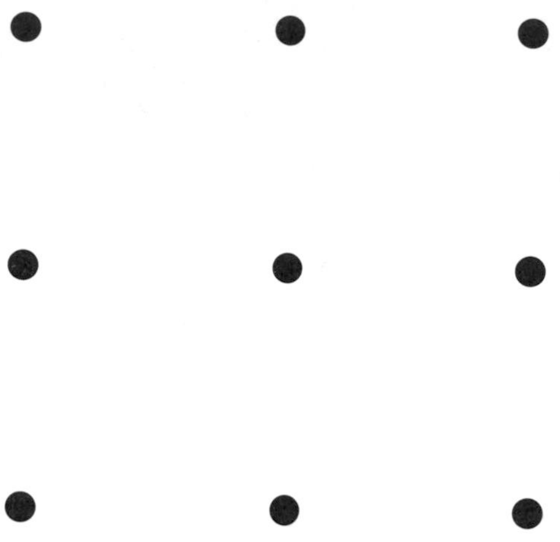

Figure 7–2. Practice your creativity ability. Can you draw four straight lines through all nine dots without lifting your pencil?

problems that others are not able to see, or don't want to see. He has an asymmetrical way of thought. He finds an original kind of order in disorder; it is as if he stared at the reflection of nature in a distorted mirror, where custodial people are able only to see the image in a plain mirror. Most highly intelligent people, as measured by tests, have symmetrical way of thought, and everything balances out in some logical way.

As the first step toward solving a problem, both pertinent and seemingly impertinent information is gathered. This may be through research, experimentation, or an experience. This analytical process is a way of "making the strange seem familiar." In search for originality he may poke at the material, shuffle it around, turn it upside down, look at it sideways. He may seek metaphors just as poets seek them, or in inventions, he may compare the flow of electricity to the flow of water inside a pipe.

He is always *borrowing ideas* from other sources outside the

Table 7–2.   Differences between the Custodial and the Creative Person.

CUSTODIAL	CREATIVE
Enjoys routine and details	Enjoys variety
Works for simplification and streamlining	Speculates, guesses
Predictable personality	Unpredictable personality
Enjoys the status quo	Cannot understand people who are reluctant to try something new
Firm, fair, friendly	Enthusiastic
Microorientation (details)	Macroorientation (the whole)

212

confines of the problem. His broad outlook on situations and his desire to have many *different experiences* may classify him as somewhat of a *"cosmopolitan."*

Some change is a desire of a creative person and sometimes his viewpoint is seen as radical. But as Ralph Waldo Emerson said, *"'Every reform was once a private opinion." A creator is willing to dare to be different. He is more likely to be a "Jonathan Livingston Seagull" than just another member of the flock.*

INCUBATION

The mysterious part of the creative process that takes place subconsciously is called incubation. It is rather like a hen sitting quietly for days on end to hatch an egg. There appears to be no activity whatsoever occurring, when, in fact, the creative action is astonishing. In the hen's egg the embryo of a chick is developing, and in the innovator's mind a massive amount of data is being sorted, filed, classified, discarded, combined—in short, developed into a meaningful whole. During this stage the highly creative person may appear to be absent-minded or a daydreamer. The process continues, even in dreams. The second law of thermodynamics came to Johannes Kepler in a dream—after twenty years of conscious searching. This stage can last anywhere from a few hours to many years, depending on the complexity of the problem.

The creative person will work on it for some time, leave it, but continue to think about it throughout the day. The problem is not forgotten, but lies smoldering, waiting for more fuel. Some doodling or absent-minded thinking is part of the incubation period. The problem will not be left unsolved, but the feeling will remain unpressed. Persistence and self-confidence allows the creative person to work on the complex problem until he arrives at a solution he is satisfied with.

INSPIRATION

The payoff for all this conscious and subconscious mental activity is usually experienced as a flash, an instant insight, a slap on the forehead and an astonished "Aha!" or, "Eureka, I found it!," as the answer comes bursting through to consciousness. After days of patient, silent sitting, the hen's egg cracks and a live chirping chick emerges. This stage is called *inspiration* or illumination. It is the moment representing the culmination of hours, days, or years of thought, although the actual time it lasts may be just a few moments. It is a release of psychic tensions that have been building up all through the incubation period.

There is no way to predict when this moment of illumination will occur. Often it comes when least expected—say, in the middle of a conversation about a seemingly unrelated subject. A particular phrase or image or idea will ring a bell, providing the final link in the puzzle, and bringing the parts together to a new whole. It is the moment that cartoonists represent by a light bulb suddenly flashing on over the head of a character.

VERIFICATION

In one sense illumination represents only the end of the beginning of the creative process. As Thomas Edison said, "Creation is 1 percent inspiration and 99 percent perspiration." Now the innovator must elaborate on the idea. It must be tested, evaluated, reworked, retested, and reevaluated. The idea must be stacked up against the real, practical world—and it must be foolproof—no leaks, loopholes, or weaknesses. If such problems do arise, then the idea must be transformed and the solution mended.

It is during this stage that the innovator should, and often must, work closely with others of a more practical nature. Scientific discoveries must be thoroughly tested in the laboratory, and innovative ideas in business must be tested against all aspects of the enterprise, from production costs to marketability. For these evaluations, the people directly responsible for the specific divisions of the business are those best able to determine the practicality of the idea. At this point, what we call the "custodial person" should offer encouragement and financing for the sometimes tedious and often expensive process of evaluation. Many a great idea has languished simply because the innovator lacked the resources to transform his or her idea into reality. (See Figure 7–3 for a representation of the four stages of the creative process.)

Verification is when the creative person needs the help of the custodial person

Often an innovation will require many years of analysis and evaluation before it becomes practically useful. A genuinely new idea, however, whether in business, science, or human relations, can shake the foundations of all prior understanding and lead to completely new ways of being in and perceiving the world. Einstein's theory of relativity continues to generate research, although he first published it in 1905.

Those who are in a position to support innovative ideas, either with time, money or interest, must understand the stages involved so that research is not brought to a premature end.

Brainstorming

Various techniques that encourage creativity can and should be used in almost any business situation. One of the most successful and well known of these is called "brainstorming." Developed by Alex Osborn in 1938,[22] brainstorming means to use the *brain* to *storm* a problem. Brainstorming sessions are designed to generate ideas to solve specific problems. The key to brain-storming is that it is devoted solely to creative thinking. All criticism and discussion of suggested ideas are deferred until a later time. Brainstorming is only one step in the problem-

Figure 7–3.   Four steps of the process of creativity.

Figure 7–4. There is no way to predict when the moment of inspiration will occur. Often it comes when it is least expected.

David W. Johnson and Frank P. Johnson, Joining Together: Group Theory and Group Skills,

© *1975, p. 256. Reprinted by permission of Prentice-Hall, Inc.*

solving process—a way of finding ideas that might be applicable to the solution of a problem.

The following four rules provide the basis for a good brainstorming session.

1. *Criticism is ruled out.* Comments like "That's stupid" are not allowed.

2. *"Freewheeling" is welcomed.* The more outlandish the idea, the better. It's always easier to tame down an idea than think it up.

3. *Quantity and variety are welcomed.* The greater the number of ideas expressed, the greater the likelihood of there being a winner.

4. *Combinations and improvements are welcomed.* Modifying, elaborating, and combining ideas is very productive, and combinations often generate totally new ideas. Hitchhiking on another person's idea is encouraged.

Brainstorming can be done individually, but sessions seem to work best with about five to seven participants. Tests have demonstrated that free associations of ideas are from 65 to 93 percent more numerous when working in a group than when working alone.[23] The problem should be as specific as possible, even if it means breaking it down into parts. The backgrounds of the people in the group, and their acquaintance with the details of the problem, do not seem to matter.

Early judgment stifles brainstorming

One of the difficulties in keeping a session creative is the desire to think judicially. Dr. Olson tells of the vice-president

216

of a large corporation who had been attending a number of brainstorming sessions on civic matters. The vice-president said:

> It was hard to get through my head what you were trying to do with us. My 15 years of conference after conference in my company have conditioned me against shooting wild. Almost all of us officers rate each other on the basis of *judgment*—we are far more apt to look up to the other fellow if he makes no mistakes than if he suggests lots of ideas. So I've always kept myself from spouting any suggestions which could be sneered at. I wish our people would feel free to shoot ideas the way we have been doing in these brainstorm sessions.[24]

Group brainstorming has the advantage of producing many ideas quickly. For instance, Fred C. Finsterbach conducted a brainstorming session at American Cyanamid that produced ninety-two ideas in fifteen minutes. That's more than six ideas a minute, and an average of eight ideas from each of the dozen people attending.[25]

"Hitchhiking" is fun and productive

When ideas are shared in a group, they stimulate more ideas, just by the power of association. Pooling thoughts has a chain-reaction effect. Ideas that are triggered by the suggestions of others are called *hitchhikes*. One organization found that out of 4,356 ideas produced in 38 brainstorming conferences, 1,400 of them were hitchhikes.[26] Just the atmosphere of acceptance and friendly rivalry has a way of reinforcing the desire to make suggestions.

Initial sessions may be as short as five minutes, later ones as long as an hour or more. Because ideas usually come so fast that many are lost, be sure to keep a record of all ideas, no matter how zany or impractical they seem. A tape recorder is a valuable tool for maintaining a record of the meeting. Never stop the spontaneous actions of the group so information can be written down by a secretary. The chairman enforces the no criticism rule by using a bell to signify an infraction of the rule. Keep the meeting in a light humorous spirit. The leader can repeat phrases and add to them as ways to stimulate action and motivation and close the session when fatigue comes or long periods of silence continue.

Once all the ideas are accumulated, then comes the time of judgment. The secretary or tape recorder can review the information and the panel can evaluate the material with hopes that one or two excellent ideas are available out of more than twenty or thirty. The appraisal session can even come a day or two after the brainstorming session rather than immediately following. At this meeting, *all* the ideas should be reviewed in expectation that several usable ideas can be derived from them.

BRAINSTORMING VARIATIONS

Brainstorming sessions set up an environment that is intentionally uninhibited. The basic aim is to challenge established assumptions and to let go all expectations. Here are some variations on the basic brainstorming approach.

1. THE "HOW CAN WE USE IT?" METHOD. The group is shown an industrial waste object, such as a discarded packing box, and asked to list the various uses that might be made of it.

2. THE "WHAT ELSE IS IT GOOD FOR?" METHOD. A suggestion is offered, and each participant, in turn, must come up with an added use for the original idea. For instance, "Let's install a teletype to communicate with our branch offices." "Yes, we can also use it for receiving the stock market quotations."

3. THE "WHAT'S WRONG WITH IT?" METHOD. This is like brainstorming, only in reverse. The object is to enumerate all the limitations and weaknesses of the product or idea under discussion. The same rules apply, except for "no criticism." Afterwards, the list of weaknesses is analyzed with a view toward improving the product or idea.

4. THE "TURN IT INSIDE OUT" METHOD. Turn the problem on its head. Get as many different perspectives on the subject as possible. For instance, if a pen will write on a desk, will it write on the ceiling, under water, or at zero gravity?

Participants in creative brainstorming meetings should be encouraged to look for that element of the problem that seems to be the most unchangeable, and then find a way to change it. For example, an RCA Victor manager in Montreal once confronted the problem of bulging files. Most people assume that when it comes to filing correspondence, the minimum is reached with two items: the original letter and the carbon reply. That assumption seemed unshakable. But this manager dared to challenge it. He reasoned, "Let the back of the original be used for the carbon copy of the reply. Then you only have to file one item."

THE PRODUCT

The end result of the creative process is called the product. As a rule, it is easy to identify the end product of artistic creative energy, although as modern life grows more complex, so do works of art. Certainly the advent of mixed media has made the identification of works of art more difficult than it used to be. Still, as a general rule, poems, plays, musical compositions, and sculpture leave little room for confusion as to *what* they are. Identifying the products of scientific or industrial creativity is not always as easy. Fortunately, the United States Supreme Court has helped to settle the issue. An *invention,* says the Court, is an *idea.* Inventions are not poems, or symphonies, or machines, but the ideas behind things.

An invention is an idea, not an object

The creative product is anything that results from bringing previously unrelated elements into new patterns of associations. Abraham Maslow observed: "From one man I learned that constructing a business organization could be a creative activity. From a young athlete, I learned that a perfect tackle could be as esthetic a product as a sonnet and could be approached in the same creative spirit."[27]

The attitudes that organizations have toward innovative ideas greatly determine the creative outcome. Witness the international competition to develop a nonpolluting automobile engine. Detroit's auto manufacturers, limited by their attitudes toward the existing technology, have encouraged their research and development personnel to stay within the design limits of the internal-combustion engine, which has served Detroit well for a long time. For them to attempt any radical change in engine design would be extremely costly. A successful radical change would, especially at first, be disruptive and would require many changes in other divisions of automobile manufacture.

"Innovation" in Detroit

In contrast, manufacturers in other parts of the world, notably Germany and Japan, have not been confined by such limitations, since their experience with automobile manufacturing has been relatively brief, and, consequently, their thinking is more flexible. As a result, researchers in those countries have developed a truly revolutionary new engine, called the rotary, which could replace the internal-combustion engine in the near future.

Product development is not the only way in which the innovator contributes to business success. Some businesses, for instance, don't deal with products at all. A management consulting firm would have little use for an inventor, but would value the creative person who could devise a bold reorganization plan for a failing business.

One of the areas in which creativity makes a big difference is advertising. Anyone can see the difference in effectiveness between a competent but dull, run-of-the-mill TV ad and one that excites comment and interest. Behind every successful advertisement there is at least one creator, someone who sensed that there was a new and better way of presenting a product. Creative personnel can contribute to better business office management or business systems analysis. An innovative office manager, for example, may discover new methods of operating the office for maximum efficiency. New, unusual incentives may encourage the office staff to increase productivity, and new ways may be tried to improve staff morale. A creative systems analyst can take a fresh look at the accounting system used by a business for fifty years, and in one swoop eliminate 75 percent of the busy work. Computer programming is popular among creative people, as witnessed by the many unofficial clubs of "computer freaks" who find countless ingenious ways to use mechanical brains for fun and profit.

In fact, there is virtually no aspect of business that can't be improved by a creative worker. However, having too many innovators in too many departments can be like having too many cooks standing over the same pot of soup: the result is apt to be disastrous. Balance, as in all things, is the key to success. Management itself must become more creative in order to see what is needed and where.

MANAGEMENT AND THE CREATIVE EMPLOYEE

Management Attitudes

While the creative temperament has much to offer to business and industry, it has special needs and does not always fit smoothly into an organization. Because of their sometimes unorthodox ways of doing things, creative people can create serious problems for organizations that aren't designed to accommodate them.

A satirical ad that has appeared in a number of different magazines presents a humorous, but all too accurate, view of the ambiguous attitudes held by many American business people toward their creative employees:

Creative person wanted, but not encouraged

WANTED: TOP EXECUTIVE — Unusual opportunity for an imaginative (but not unconventional) planner who thinks quickly (but isn't impatient), acts aggressively (but ruffles no fur), and can get things done (through channels without stepping on toes). Should have an A.B. in Business Administration (preferably from an Eastern University), but the equivalent in experience will be considered (for blood relatives of management). Applicant should have varied and broad background (yet be a specialist) and have a work record demonstrating job stability (without being a "job-hopper," he must nevertheless have acquired a varied and broad background). The man chosen will be a member of an executive committee (team) jointly responsible (he'd better fit in) for company policy.

This parody of how American business deals with creativity highlights a basic contradiction: An organization may encourage creative behavior while at the same time establishing policies that prevent the use of independent judgment, discretion, and innovation.[28]

Management often prefers efficiency to unproven ideas

Management tends to prefer the efficiency that results from using proven methods. It fears that the innovator will cause unrest in the organization, challenge the status quo, and generally disrupt what has been a successful company policy. At the same time, most managers give at least token recognition to the need for the creative employee.

This basic contradiction is often a reason why some small companies never quite get off the ground and some large companies stagnate and stop growing. Creativity, although acknowledged to be necessary, is continually stifled, and the company goes its merry way toward mediocrity, led by the boss and followed by legions of "Yes Men."

Strategies for Independence

Leonard Sayles, an authority in the field of management training, believes that sometimes organizations "tend to stimulate creative responses in direct proportion to the extent to which they limit creativity," and that organizational repression serves only to challenge the ingenuity and resourcefulness of the workers being repressed.[29] Sayles argues that certain kinds of malingering and job sabotage, particularly on assembly lines, are, in fact, creative behavior. He refers to such behavior as "strategies for independence."

> In one plant, studied by Cornell investigators, there was a chap named Sam, who was able to burn up drills every time the time-study man reached a speed Sam thought would constitute too high an incentive rate. The investigators were able to discover that Sam had found a method of grinding his drill whereby it would overheat at much lower speeds than when ground correctly. This example may not gratify those who equate creativity only with company-serving bursts of inventiveness. Sam's behavior is incredibly creative—from Sam's point of view. [This was] his strategy of independence (which, incidentally, kept his work load within bounds that would earn him a comfortable

bonus without great exertion, gave him prestige among his peers, and satisfied his instinct of craftsmanship as no mass-produced product could.[30]

Countless shortcuts are invented by workers, on even the most simplified tasks, often for no other reason than to create a break in the routine.

Relation to Decision-Making Process

Decisions usually involve choosing one of several alternate solutions to a problem. Creativity also involves problems and finding solutions for them. If both creativity and making decisions are based on solving problems, then what are the differences between them and how are they similar?

Chapter 9 discusses the steps in making decisions: defining and analyzing the problem; developing and evaluating alternatives; selecting and implementing a solution; and reevaluating and modifying the solution if needed. These steps can include the creative process at any point. Research on creativity has found, for instance, that increasing the time between formulating and articulating the problem and subjecting it to creative thinking results in a more flexible solution.[31] This time period between defining the problem and arriving at the solution is when the creative process occurs.

The more a problem can be solved by past experience or by applying a specific method, the less reason there is to approach it creatively. Creativity is required when there *is* no best answer, at least according to your own research and experience, or when there is no known solution!

Creative problem solving involves formulating new ideas or alternatives rather than relying on old ones for making decisions. Creative problems require more "divergent" than "convergent" thinking. In divergent thinking, the mind is encouraged to travel in many different directions, searching for answers, and trying a variety of approaches. Convergent thinking includes the more logical, fact-finding, judgmental side of problem solving. Eventually, both types of thinking go into solving problems. The unstructured, intuitive process that is used to come up with the ideas will at some point give way to making a logical choice between them—using analysis, reason, and experience.

"Divergent thinking" is side-track thinking

"Convergent thinking" is logical, quick solutions

We may need more "divergent thinking"

Often, creative problem solving is stifled by well-meaning managers or leaders who do not realize that divergent thinking, however superfluous it may seem, must be encouraged if a solution is to appear.

Rewards

A serious problem in dealing with creative personnel is finding adequate ways to reward successful effort. Monetary rewards alone are not the answer. Creative people are often satisfied to receive a merely comfortable salary as long as the job offers the freedom and time they feel they need to work well.

Perhaps the greatest possible reward that can be bestowed for a creative effort is enthusiastic recognition and immediate application of the idea. Witnessing the application of an idea is often the highest form of reward. Other avenues may be explored, such as granting greater degrees of freedom, or equipping the scientific researcher with his own private laboratory. More money is seldom frowned upon. But what the true innovator responds to most is neither money nor status, but the enthusiastic "Hurrah" for the difficult problem that has been solved.

Perhaps the best reward for a good idea is recognition and immediate use

Possibly the major contribution that management can make to creative effort is to bring creative people together and provide them with the materials they require for their work. The ability to do this demands an unusually deep understanding of creative personalities and a degree of creativity in the manager. Introducing one innovator to another creates a new pattern of association of existing elements—in this case, people—and is thus itself a creative act. Howard Gossage, a highly successful advertising executive, gained his reputation for innovative advertising by bringing together unlikely combinations of creative talent who found inspiration in one another's ideas and methods. By acting as the connecting link, Gossage was himself acting in a creative way.

Managers should not only seek out innovative talent, they should also institute training programs to develop and enhance the latent creative talents in their staffs.

SUMMARY

The creative act combines old elements in new ways. Current concepts are the building blocks for new ideas. All people are born with the ability to create. This ability does not disappear with adulthood, but takes many different forms. Although timeliness, usefulness, and originality are not always applicable criteria for recognizing a creative idea, they are frequently reliable indications.

The channels into which creative energy will flow are largely determined by cultural norms. In America, technological innovation is highly valued and the American creative genius is linked with it. Industrial structures have also perpetuated anonymous and group-oriented creativity. Social needs often dictate how people channel their creative energies. (The values of society at large become more and more common.)

People who constantly use their creative energies tend to develop certain personality traits. They perceive and approach life in particular ways, although they may not be more intelligent than others, or have more education. Highly creative people are often very unconventional in their behavior

While creative people are necessary to successful organizations, creative behavior can definitely conflict with the smooth running of a business. The ambiguous feelings that many managers have toward creative people can be stated as the reasonable desire for a balance between creativity and practicality.

The creative person is valuable to employers because it is through creativity that companies come up with new products. Products may be tangible, or they may be ideas. An employee may not want status or more money as a result of a creative idea, as much as he or she wants recognition for it. The most direct rewards are acknowledgment of the creative act itself, and encouragement for further creativity.

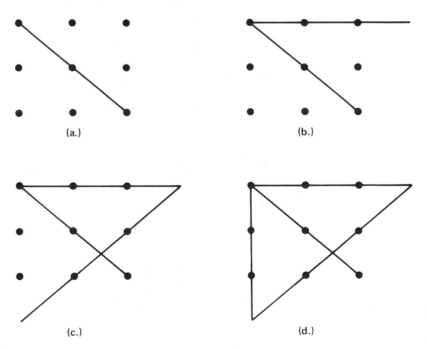

Figure 7–5. Solution to problem: "Practice your creative ability."

The creative process is still a mysterious one. Four stages have been recognized: perception, incubation, inspiration, and verification. While making decisions implies a problem demanding a solution, creativity also focuses on solving problems. However, creativity requires an unstructured, illogical approach, while decision making uses structured, logical thinking. Both are necessary to solve problems, and can be used together, alternating between the two kinds of thinking. Brainstorming, and the variations on that activity, provide a good method for free associations of ideas to occur in a group setting.

Figure 7–5 holds the solution to the nine-dot problem. We find that our education and culture causes us to accept certain limits or boundaries that have not been stated or even implied. Such self-imposed limitations stop us from exploring and discovering new experiences. In learning to be more creative, we must learn to question the rules or facts implied or stated when attempting to solve a problem, and we must also learn to stay with the problem as long as necessary to solve it.

DO CREATIVE PEOPLE BELIEVE IN THE SUPERNATURAL?

Case Study #1

(Case studies for this chapter are somewhat different from others in the text simply because of the nature of the topic—*creativity*.)

E.S.P., precognition, clairvoyance, psychokinesis—the more creative you are the more likely you are to believe in these psychic phenomena. This hypothesis is discussed in an article called "Attitudes, Motivation, Sensation Seeking and Belief in ESP as Predictors of Real Creative Behavior," published in the *Journal of Creative Behavior* the first quarter 1974 issue. The authors of this article feel that the following excerpts from creative literature seem to support this idea.

Some research showing a correlation between measures of belief in E.S.P. and scores received on creative rating tests was unearthed and published by Paul Torrance in 1972. In an earlier publication Torrance also listed "attraction to the mysterious" as a trait of creative individuals.

In 1971 Donald Mackinon, who is noted in the field of creative research, published an article dealing with the realm of the unconscious mind. In the article he describes a highly creative Berkeley student whose unconscious activity would surface in the form of automatic writing. Automatic writing is a psychical phenomenon in which the pen appears to write without any apparent conscious control by the person holding it. This phenomenon is often called psychokinesis (PK) or parapsychology.

Another source cited by the authors is Gardner Murphy, past president of the American Psychological Association. Murphy has written two articles relating creativity to parapsychology, in which he reports that exceedingly creative people, such as Mark Twain, Robert Schuman, and Goethe have reported supernatural happenings. He proposes that creativity and paranormal capability would be expected to occur, because both are rooted in the unconscious, and creative people are more in touch with their unconscious selves.

From the literature that has been cited, does a relationship between creativity and psychic phenomena seem to exist? The authors state that some of the characteristics of the creative person, such as tending to be more open-minded, flexible, receptive, and imaginative than the average person, may provide the basis for any such correlation.

1. Do you believe in psychic phenomena?
2. Give reasons for your feelings to support your belief. Can you?
3. Do you feel creative persons would tend to be more in tune with psychic phenomena than the average person? Why do you feel this way?
4. Do the believers in psychic phenomena more often accept the theory presented here? Why?

ACHIEVEMENT—ACCOMPLISHED BY INDIVIDUAL CREATIVITY OR BY "GROUP-THINK" TEAM EFFORT

Case Study #2

In the United States today, individual achievement is highly valued. In our business setting, success or failure depends largely upon individual capability, and the road toward success is an individual effort. This is pretty much the way it has been for the first 200 years of our country's existence. But according to a recent poll of top corporate executives across the country, this characteristically American ideology is being replaced by an emphasis on group achievement rather than individual effort.

Ideology 2, our ideology of the future, will stress the use of teamwork in achieving goals. An effective team will be a group of people who work together noncompetitively to complete certain tasks. Idealistically, the members of the team will support one another, be receptive to new ideas coming from both within and outside the team, and be able to communicate well among themselves. Individuals within the effective team will be recognized for individual efforts and achievements, but the success will be credited to the group as a whole.

The use of teamwork in our business world, according to the poll, will be dominant by the year 1985. Today, the use of teamwork is stressed in many areas, and is considered more effective than individual effort in that cooperative action leads to a total effect greater than independent contributions.

When considering the creative individual, which ideology—our ideology of today or our ideology of the future—will best aid creative potential?

Terms and Concepts Students Should Know

creative traits	verification	inhibitors
inner-directedness	brainstorming	perception
mass thinking	rewarding creative people	inspiration
age and creativity	organization man	cosmopolitan
pressure of society	outer-directedness	"hitchhiking"
incubation	I.Q. vs. C.Q.	

Bibliography

1. Osborn, Alex, *Applied Imagination,* New York, Charles Scribners and Sons, 1963.

2. Whyte, William H., *The Organization Man,* New York, Simon and Schuster, 1956.

3. Riesman, David, *The Lonely Crowd,* New Haven, Conn., Yale University Press, 1950.

4. Lederer, William, *A Nation of Sheep,* New York, W. W. Norton & Co., 1961.

5. Maslow, Abraham H., *Toward a Psychol-*

ogy of Being, New York, Van Nostrand Reinhold Co., 1968.

6. "Creative People, Creative Times, *Journal of Creative Behavior,* First Quarter, 1975.

7. HALLMAN, RALPH J. M., "HUMAN RELATIONS and Creativity," *Journal of Creative Behavior,* Vol. 8., No. 3, 1974.

Footnotes

[1] M. O. Edwards, "Solving Problems Creatively," *Systems and Procedures Journal,* January–February 1966, p. 17.

[2] Eugene K. Von Fange, *Professional Creativity* (Englewood Cliffs, N.J.: Prentice-Hall, 1959), p. 8.

[3] *Ibid.,* pp. 9–10.

[4] Alex F. Osborn, *Applied Imagination* (New York: Charles Scribners & Sons, 1963), pp. 15–16.

[5] Von Fange, *Professional Creativity,* pp. 5–6.

[6] *Ibid.,* p. 7.

[7] James D. Watson, *The Double Helix* (New York: Atheneum, 1968).

[8] William H. White, *The Organization Man* (New York: Simon and Schuster, 1956).

[9] David Riesman, *The Lonely Crowd* (New Haven, Conn.: Yale University Press, 1950).

[10] William J. Lederer, *A Nation of Sheep* (New York: W. W. Norton & Co., 1961).

[11] Donald W. MacKinnon, "The Nature and Nurture of Creative Talent," in *Readings in Managerial Psychology,* edited by Harold J. Leavitt and Louis R. Pondy (Chicago: University of Chicago Press, 1964), p. 96.

[12] Osborn, *Applied Imagination,* p. 22.

[13] MacKinnon, "Nature of Creative Talent," p. 96.

[14] Osborn, *Applied Imagination,* p. 22.

[15] *Ibid.,* p. 18.

[16] *Ibid.*

[17] *Ibid.,* p. 22.

[18] MacKinnon, "Nature of Creative Talent," p. 96.

[19] Abraham H. Maslow, "The Scientific Study of Inventive Talent," in *A Source Book for Creative Thinking,* edited by S. J. Parnes and H. F. Harding (New York: Charles Scribners & Sons, 1962), p. 102.

[20] Edwards, "Solving Problems Creatively," p. 16.

[21] Osborn, *Applied Imagination,* p. 315.

[22] *Ibid.,* pp. 151–165.

[23] *Ibid.,* p. 154.

[24] *Ibid.,* p. 160.

[25] *Ibid.,* p. 152.

[26] *Ibid.,* p. 154.

[27] Abraham H. Maslow, *Toward A Psychology of Being* (New York: Van Nostrand Reinhold Co., 1968), p. 136.

[28] Leonard Sayles, *Individualism and Big Business* (New York: McGraw-Hill Book Co., 1963), p. 44.

[29] *Ibid.,* pp. 44–45.

[30] *Ibid.,* p. 37.

[31] Osborn, *Applied Imagination,* p. 315.

Resistance to Change
"I'll Be Damned If I'll Do It!" ▪ ▪ ▪ ▪ ▪ ▪

8

OBJECTIVES

When you finish reading this chapter, you should be able to:
1. Discuss psychological resistance to change from the point of view of
   A. Occupational identity,
   B. Free-floating insecurity,
   C. Status considerations.
2. List and understand the four basic economic reasons for fearing change.
3. Explain in your own words why the idea of homeostasis is necessary in understanding how change takes place in groups.
4. Discuss the advantages and disadvantages of change through mandate and change through participation.
5. Explain in your own terms how change can be brought about by a pragmatist and by a manipulator. Can you identify which you are and give reasons for your selection?
6. Describe the seven principles related to the group dynamics of change. Give examples of each.
7. Discuss the importance of communication in overcoming resistance to change.

Look at these questions before reading the chapter. Such questions may start a discussion after studying the chapter.

Is your first reaction "No!" when you are asked to change a procedure you are used to doing a certain way?

Do certain kinds of change frighten you or threaten you?

When it is clear that change must take place, do you try to hinder it or help it? Do you have any ideas about how to implement change?

What is the value of change?

PATTERNS OF RESISTANCE TO CHANGE

The cliche that our technological society is rapidly changing expresses a truth that affects everyone. In the past, the progress of technology was measured by millenia, or at least by centuries.

Six thousand years elapsed between the first appearance of the hand plow in ancient Egypt and Cyrus McCormick's reaper in 1832. Today, we find it difficult to imagine the changes the next twenty years will bring.

Today's technology has already outstripped the imaginations of the science fiction writers of a generation ago. Steel plants mass produce steel plates with the kind of minute precision only computers can achieve. Freight trains are dispatched and rail-car inventories are handled by computer banks. Instant credit checks are run in less than twenty seconds. Our increasingly sophisticated communication systems will soon give us picture telephones, and microminiaturization holds the promise of wireless telephones to carry in our pockets.

Technological change has always been equated with progress, and who is against progress? Yet when we examine the dynamics of change we find that although nearly everyone says he is in favor of change, actual behavior patterns reveal contradictory and ambivalent feelings concerning its value. Dr. Donald Schon says that if the unspoken, but deeply felt, attitude many people have about technological change were to be expressed, it would go like this:

Study change, praise it, but don't do it: we may resist

Technical innovation is dangerous, disruptive and uncertain. It is the enemy of orderly, planned activity. It changes everything about the business we are in. It hurts. Let us talk about it, study it, praise it, espouse it—anything but do it![1]

The phrase "resistance to change" has been borrowed from psychotherapy. A therapist attempting to help a patient change his or her behavior learns to expect resistance. Even though certain behaviors may cause the patient unhappiness, they have also been a means to achieve some satisfaction too. Therapists learn to expect resistance—especially when the therapeutic process begins to effect genuine change. Patients resist change in all kinds of ways. Some of the most common are breaking appointments, becoming angry with the therapist, falling silent during session, or even telling lies.

Initiating changes in the work environment may cause the development of similar patterns of resistance. Hostility may be openly expressed or only implied. It may be directed against supervisors or against the work activities. The manner in which it is expressed depends on how much hostility can be expressed safely without endangering job security. It may take the form of sloppy efforts, slowdowns, lots of lip-service but no actual change in behavior, or a subtle combination of apathy and apple-polishing.

Lip service doesn't mean acceptance

When to Expect Resistance

If the nature of a proposed change is not made clear to the people who are going to be affected or influenced by it, resistance can be expected. People who dislike their jobs are particularly resistant to ambiguous or unclear orders to change. They want to know exactly what they have to do in order to minimize the unpleasant aspects of their jobs.

The amount of resistance can be related to the amount of participation people have in the timing and direction of the innovation. Resistance will be least evident when workers *have the most to say about procedural matters, and most evident when they have the least to say.*

If change is the expected result of personal persuasion, then resistance can be expected. In one firm, a supervisor posted the notice:

> I have always felt that promptness is an indicator of an
> employee's interest in his job. I will feel much better if you are at
> your desks at the proper time.[2]

In response to the supervisor's personal plea the workers formed a committee to obtain information to justify their tardiness, so that the supervisor need not feel bad about it!

Some resistance can be expected to occur when there are changes in: (1) machinery, tools, and equipment; (2) procedures and methods; (3) personnel; (4) formal organizational structures; and (5) informal organizational structures.

Most people at all job levels in business and industry resist change for either psychological, economic, or social reasons.

PSYCHOLOGICAL RESISTANCE

Occupational Identity

Any environmental change that affects an individual always involves some loss of security. Change, by its very nature, forces confrontation with uncertainty. Familiar, predictable routines produce a sense of security that is psychologically both necessary and satisfying. When there is a *strong sense of occupational*

The stronger the occupational identity, the greater the security

identity, there is also a *strong sense of psychological security.* When these feelings of security are threatened, there is resistance to change.[3]

Consider the case of skilled factory workers who have had to relearn their jobs using automated machinery. Work that used to require skilled hand, eye, and brain coordination is now done by automated methods. Unless those workers have learned new skills, their sense of occupational identity has probably been severely damaged.

The greater the security and expertise, the more likely resistance

Some workers feel that management's desire for change implies that they have not been doing their jobs properly. Pride in craftsmanship is often a cause of resistance to change. Professor Elting Morison cited an interesting example of such prideful resistance in the introduction of the steel industry to Pennsylvania in the late nineteenth century. In the years between 1864 and 1871, ten Pennsylvania steel companies imported British workers to introduce and oversee its development. By 1880, Cambria had become the leading manufacturer of steel in the state. Why did this happen?

During that decade the refining process underwent many changes, but the British workers, who felt secure in their mastery of the original techniques and took pride in their craftsmanship, stuck with their "tried and true" experience while "[t]he Pennsylvania farm boys, untrammeled by the rituals and traditions of the craft, happily and rapidly adapted themselves to the constantly changing process."[4]

Workers often oppose change because they fear that greater specialization may result in boredom and monotony, or that more and harder work will be required as a result of a proposed change. They may also be used to following stable, predictable work patterns. When these stable patterns are disturbed, the feelings of pressure and dissatisfaction that result may take the form of either direct opposition or subtle resistance to change.

Free-floating Insecurity

Factory workers have no monopoly on resistance based on feelings of insecurity. In *Technology and Change,* Dr. Donald Schon describes a number of examples of opposition to technological innovation among members of top management staffs whose actual behavior proved that they *unconsciously* resisted change although they outwardly endorsed and even championed it.

Dr. Schon visited a small company that had been making foundry products since the turn of the century. It had established a good reputation built on old technology, but it was under severe competitive pressure from larger companies. For two years the company's managers had explored the possibilities of manufacturing various new products. What could they make in order to diversify? Their product director showed Dr. Schon a file drawer that contained twenty-five examples of new products. He was also shown a sheet of paper listing the criteria a new product had to meet. Any new product had to: (1) promise a gross of $3,000,000 within five years, (2) show a large profit margin, (3) be able to utilize present production facilities, and, (4) be marketed and sold through the present sales force.

Not one idea in two years had been able to pass those tests! Clearly the criteria had been set up to make product innovation impossible, but from the company president on down, it was stated and believed that finding new products was both necessary and desirable.[5]

The insecurity demonstrated here is not as simple a matter as occupational identity, encompassing as it does complex financial, production, and sales aspects of the business. There can be no doubt, however, that fear of an uncertain future and possible failure played a large role in establishing rigid, impossible-to-meet criteria for change. The fear of the unknown is as potent a force in business as in any other realm of life.

Fear of the unknown is potent

Status Considerations

Another psychological factor leading to resistance to change is the feeling many people have, often justified, that change threatens their status within the organization. Consider the changes in banking in the past decade. Traditionally, the bank personnel who dealt with customers in the front offices were the employees who enjoyed the highest status. The back offices were for the clerks and calculators of low status. When computers, run by highly skilled and highly paid systems personnel and programmers, were moved into the back offices, the status balances were profoundly shaken. Front office personnel found themselves competing for deference and other signs of power with "backroom" employees.

Front office status versus back office pay

Status always involves comparison, and major organizational changes usually bring in their wake the unintended side effect of lowering and raising the status of one or more individuals or work units. Naturally, the people who will be downgraded resist any such organizational change.

For example, in many automated factories, new technology has eliminated the supervisors' old function of giving out job assignments. Yet, in some cases, supervisors continue to give such directions—even though they are superfluous. These supervisors have been allowed to maintain their status because top management has understood the importance of sticking to ego-saving routines. Even though these routines are irrelevant to the technology, they sometimes help to create a more hospitable atmosphere for major innovations.

CHANGING THE INDIVIDUAL

A supervisor who seeks to change an individual in some way faces the fact that an individual may resist the change. When we want to change an individual, we are seeking to modify one or more of the forces that make him behave the way he does. If we want a model of an individual, we might consider one that is shown in Figure 8–1. If we want to change Richard Hodges we can try to do this by adding or subtracting from one or more of the forces affecting his behavior. For example, one could add something new to his experience in order to move him into another direction. If this succeeds we may produce a fundamental change in the way he behaves.

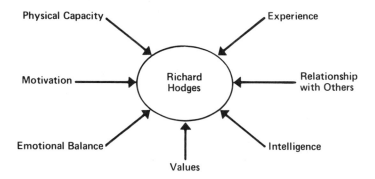

Figure 8–1. Various influences on an individual.

The more pressures are in harmony, the more predictable the outcome

Naturally, pressure can invoke change, but the outcome cannot always be predicted. There are many forces on an individual and the outcome of the various pressures can produce unexpected outbursts as a pinprick into a balloon. The more forces working in harmony with each other, the more likely a predictable outcome can be generated. For example, teachers, neighbors, and parents working in harmony can more effectively develop a desired change in an emotionally disturbed child.

Social adjustment to a new work environment can be difficult for those who belong to a tightly knit group. The process of breaking social ties with those at the old work station and making new acquaintances can be threatening.

Conflict between individual and group loyalties

Studies have also shown that resistance to change often results from a conflict of individual and group loyalties (Figure 8–2). An individual may want to "please the boss," but he may be restrained by group pressure to protect the slower members of the group who would be hurt most by a change. Group pressure may force him to resist change even if he believes in the innovation, because group acceptance is more important. Mason Haire believes that for every force of change there is a counter pressure. As shown by Figure 8–3, the group may pressure from above against the desires of the individual below.

The employee who would like to make a bonus by producing more parts consistently will be buttonholed by the other workers.

> Hey Charlie, we don't want a "rate-buster" in our shop. Sure, we can all produce more parts than is required, but why bust our asses? If we all did that, the guys in the head office would raise the standard and then where would we be? No bonuses, and we

Figure 8–2. Various counter forces can produce an unpredictable change.

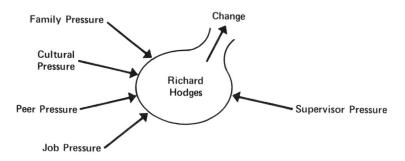

Figure 8–3. Group pressures versus individual beliefs.

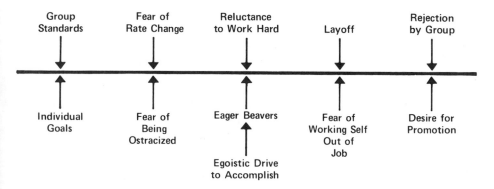

would have to produce more. Now, be a nice guy, Charlie, don't make waves. If you come in late, we will cover for you, so relax. Don't be an "eager beaver."

One of the important effects of this example is that the level of production can be raised either by increasing the forces below the line or reducing the forces above the line. The greater the opportunity for a promotion for Charlie, the more likely he will become a "rate-buster." Likewise the more turnover within the department, the less likely group pressure will be strong enough to influence Charlie's production.

ECONOMIC RESISTANCE

Economic reasons for resistance to change are much easier to isolate than psychological ones. How many blacksmiths are there in your town? Any chimney-sweeps, stone cutters, or whale-bone corset manufacturers? In the past century, perhaps as many time-honored occupations have disappeared from the economic sector as new ones have been born. Since the Industrial Revolution, technological change has always meant the destruction of old industries as well as the creation of new ones.

Frank Cousins, a leader of the British Trade Union movement, expressed a common sentiment when he spoke approvingly of the Luddites, who rose up 150 years ago and smashed the "new" machine looms. He said, "The machine looms destroyed the jobs of thousands of hand loom weavers. They were introduced without consultation, without regard to human values, and they had a dire consequence for the men directly concerned."[6] The Luddites were faced with certain starvation as a result of technological change. In our century there are many more options open to the labor force, but unemployment and economic dislocation are always very unpleasant— even when cushioned by regular unemployment compensation checks.

Economic reasons to fear change usually focus on one or more of the following: (1) fear of technological unemployment; (2) fear of reduced work hours (and thus less pay); (3) fear of demotion, and thus reduced wages; and (4) fear of speed-up and reduced incentive wages.

Today many workers are justifiably afraid of being phased out of their jobs by automation. They see changes in the incentive system and speed-ups as moves toward pushing them out. Of course they resist change, and their resistance can be quite effective.

Consider the case of a hypodermic syringe manufacturer. The company's research and development staff introduced a ma-

Unions can resist change

chine that increased the production rate from 400 to 1,500 syringes an hour. At least, that was the machine's performance at the test site. Union representatives examined the machine and predicted that it would increase production to no more than 700 syringes per hour. They were right. Production rose to 700 an hour, leveled off, and stayed put. Of crucial importance to this story is the fact that the company's history of management–union relations was extremely bad, characterized for years by mutual distrust and hostility. No assurances from management would have been believed—so the workers took their job security in their own hands and kept production safely down.

SOCIAL RESISTANCE

The Theory of Homeostasis

A clock is more than a collection of hands, cogs, and wheels because when it is assembled something new results: the registering and measuring of time. Similarly, a work group is more than a collection of individuals because when it is assembled something new results: important functions relating to establishing common standards, attitudes, goals, and leadership.

Homeostasis theory helps to maintain a balance or stability

The psychologist Kurt Lewin has proposed a model of the dynamics of group behavior to support his theory that groups tend to maintain an equilibrium that allows the group to behave pretty much the same way from day to day.[7] Whenever change threatens a group, the group acts to oppose it and to maintain the kind of balance it is used to. This balance-maintaining characteristic of groups is called *homeostasis*, which means a state of stability or equilibrium.

For example, if management imposes new controls on a work group, the group may react with increased adherence to its own standards of group loyalty, as the workers at the syringe factory did. Outside pressure did produce some changes in behavior, but it also caused a reaction that simultaneously resisted change, and the group moved in the direction of homeostasis, or the maintenance of familiar routines.

Driving Forces and Restraining Forces

In Lewin's model, the forces that "up" production (new machinery and specific instructions and supervision in its use) are called *driving forces*. The forces that keep production down to a level deemed safe for job security are called *restraining forces*. Other driving forces to increase production in a work group might be the desire of some members to win promotions or higher salaries. These forces would be balanced by the group's fear of layoff—restraining forces that would make themselves known in the form of hostility to "eager beavers" or even ostracism of the offending group members.

Lewin's studies show that change occurs when an imbalance develops between the restraining and driving forces. Such imbalance "unfreezes" the pattern, and the group struggles to achieve a new balance of equilibrium. Once found, the new pattern will be made up of different components. That is to say, the group refreezes at a new and different equilibrium level. These studies also show that when efforts are made to change a work group by increasing the driving forces, the most common response of the group is to increase restraining forces, in order to maintain the same balance. When a restraining force is weakened, the patterns are more easily unfrozen and the group experiences little difficulty moving on to new and different patterns of balance.

Balancing the Forces

There is a good reason why it is difficult to bring about change through the increase of driving forces. When driving forces are increased, the tensions in the total system are likely to increase also. More tensions mean greater instability and more likelihood of irrational behavior on the part of group members.

The equilibrium of any group at any time is a balance of forces that work for and against change within the group. All groups are working simultaneously both for and against their ways of life. *Resistance to change is a normal part of the total process of change.*[8] People have always objected to change when it threatens their accustomed ways of living. This applies to all groups: employees who resist change invoked by supervisors, companies opposing governmental regulations, and management objecting to union demands.

The Changing Value of Change

The following quotations express an attitude typical of thousands of speeches and articles made by American business people since the end of World War II.

New products, *new* industries and markets, *new* methods of making current products . . . *new* is a way of life with us today.

Take the chemical field, for instance. In any given year, 30 or 40 per cent of sales are of products that didn't exist ten years ago.

Bell and Howell estimates that more than 80 percent of its current sales are from products that were not in existence even five years ago.

Du Pont estimates that more than half its current sales are from products developed during the past 20 years or so.[9]

While it is true that technological innovation paved the way for the standard of living we enjoy in the United States today, it is also true that the quality of our life has not always been enhanced by those changes. The environmental and ecology movements that have sprung up in the past decade are but one indication that growing numbers of people no longer believe that unchecked technological growth is the wisest course to follow.

It may be that in the near future we will see the entire direction of change focus less on technological innovation and more on technological "containment," and on interpersonal, intergroup changes in human behavior. Today, ideas to preserve the environment are being aired that call for changing our notions of the value of technological growth. Progressive social change may come to mean greater emphasis on the quality of life of the total population, and less on the kinds and quantities of the goods we produce.

If this occurs, there will be resistance to these ideas, too, for resistance is an integral part of the change process and must always be reckoned with when planning for change.

THE CHANGE AGENTS

The Pragmatist

Intervention, directed change, and planned change are all synonyms for a situation in which someone interferes actively with the social behavior of others. The ideological issue ultimately resolves itself in the argument about means versus ends and which is more important. We can refer to one end of the continuum as the pragmatic strategy.[10] This strategy is concerned mainly with creating a climate conducive to gaining the acceptance of an innovation. Tactics from this approach are based on a large body of literature supporting the notion that people are more ready to accept changes that (1) they can understand and perceive as relevant; and (2) they have had a hand in planning. The pragmatic interventionist or humanist is one who sees tac-

Pragmatist is interested in means rather than the end

A pragmatist is a humanist—people help in planning

One big change is better than several small changes

tics and strategies that are geared mainly to the means rather than the end. A pragmatist knows individuals can tolerate only so much change, and if they are bombarded with many small changes, they are less apt to accept a big change. Likewise, the pragmatist takes his definition of the problem from those who seek assistance, and works from there.

The Manipulator

Do things to people rather than with them

The other type of strategy is utopic. In this case the interventionist's role is mainly one of manipulation to gain the acceptance of change. His basic premise is that results are best achieved by doing things to people rather than with them. Tactics are designed to gain acceptance of an innovation by means of positive and negative sanctions to insure compliance. As we indicated earlier, this strategy is apt to be used when the manipulator presumes that his expertise will not be questioned. The utopic maneuverist is one whose tactics are geared to the end rather than the means.

Some people feel that it may be unethical to manipulate personalities. The practice of "playing god"—but getting the job done—is the role of the leader. It must be pointed out that the role of the supervisor is to maintain a balance among personalities for the comfort of all, which may require a utopic approach. Then, too, the profit of the company is dependent on keeping pace with a dynamic society.

Figure 8–4. Diagram of the pragmatist and manipulator line of continuum.

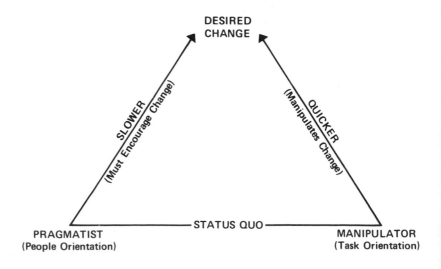

The major advantage of the manipulator's model is that change can be effected quickly whereas the pragmatic strategy requires more time. The question is one of manipulating change or encouraging change. Do you believe those are the only choices?

Parkinson's law of the "will of the people" states that there is no majority feeling on any subject and that the attitudes of most are influenced by a strong-willed minority. At an annual meeting the determined group does not stick together, but disperses into the audience to sit next to the undecided. There the manipulator begins to influence the ambivalent person to vote for his cause. The outcome is predictable. Not by accident, but by design, the strong-willed minority has influenced enough "sheep" to vote for its cause.

Although there are points to be made for and against each model of intervention, the manipulator is for the conservation of time, energy, and money. However, the pragmatic model seems to insure a greater opportunity for genuine, lasting cultural change.

Figure 8–5. Groups everywhere tend to cooperate rather than resist when presented with the opportunity to participate in planning for the change. *Courtesy of Santa Barbara City College (Photo by Rob Reilly)*

OVERCOMING RESISTANCE

Participation

There is greater chance for success when all involved participate

Management theorists such as Kurt Lewin, Peter Drucker, and Leonard Sayles have created an impressive body of evidence indicating that when all the parties to be affected by change participate in the planning of that change it has a real chance of succeeding. Groups everywhere tend to cooperate rather than resist when presented with the opportunity to evaluate a situation and participate in planning for change. Social psychology theory has established that the least effective way to motivate for change is through discipline or the threat of punishment. In the past few decades, behavioral scientists have stressed the fact that force in human affairs, just as in physics, breeds counterforce.

Lester Coch and John R. P. French designed an experiment that demonstrated conclusively the effectiveness of employee participation in promoting change in productive output.[11] Their experiment used four groups. The first group followed traditional business custom in introducing change. Workers were told when and how to change, received training in the new methods, and were then switched from old to new. The second group was instructed to choose delegates from among its members to study the new methods, and to report back to the group on their studies. All of the members of the third and fourth groups took an active part in planning for the proposed changes.

When the productive output of the four groups was compared after the change was installed, group one barely averaged 75 percent of its previous production rate. Also, there were many signs of internal conflict within the group. Some of its members quit the company during the changeover. The second group achieved 15 percent higher than before, while the third and fourth groups averaged 125 percent more productivity.

Participation in the process of change motivates the individual by: (1) fulfilling the developmental needs of a healthy personality; (2) promoting security through knowledge of the environment and exercising control over it; and (3) reducing basic fears of the unknown that cause resistance to change.

There is a large gap, however, between social psychology theory and practice in the business world. A good example of this gap is the following account of the recent experience of a company that wished to convert to electronic data processing systems (EDP) from their old manual tabulating methods.

244

Company Y, a financial institution . . . [made] a major methods change from manual tabulating systems to EDP. [The change] *was conducted in such a way as to discourage all participation below the level of top management.* Management in this case took the position that soliciting ideas from people who had been doing the clerical work was a waste of time. Rather, they relied completely on the systems planners. Predictably, considerable ill will arose between the systems group and the operations supervisors. The end results were employee animosity, thinly veiled sabotage of the new system, and continuing high costs. The initial effort at EDP installation was a complete failure. A second attempt, bolstered by a management edict, got the system working but at a high cost and with a residue of resentment against top management and the computer systems group.[12]

Compare Company Y's method of introducing change with Company Z's methods as outlined in Table 8–1. Company Z performed *four* separate steps before arriving at the first step used by Company Y.

Company Z's top management understood the value of participatory planning and did everything they could to stimulate and encourage it. In order to guarantee effective participation, they arranged for early involvement. However, such foresight is still unusual. Most companies currently switching to

Table 8–1

COMPANY Y	COMPANY Z
1. Define problem	1. Stimulate thinking regarding change possibility
2. Gather data	
3. Analyze data	2. Define areas of investigation
4. Develop alternatives	3. Educate personnel in concepts needed to investigate anatomy of change
5. Choose best alternative	
6. Recommend	
7. Get management acceptance	4. Develop mechanisms of participation
8. Inform those affected by change	5. Define problem in specific terms
9. Make change	6. Gather data
	7. Analyze data
	8. Develop alternatives
	9. Choose best alternative
	10. Recommend
	11. Make change

Source: George S. McIsaac, "How to Practice What We Preach in Making Business Changes," in *The Nature and Scope of Management,* edited by Maneck S. Wadia (Glenview, Ill.: Scott, Foresman and Co., 1966), p. 201.

EDP installation look upon employee participation as extravagant and time consuming.

Reducing resistance to change through participation is important, but another good reason for encouraging employees to take part in planning for change is that they usually have a great deal of useful information to contribute to the planning. Assembly-line operators frequently see important details that industrial designers miss, but they seldom volunteer information because they feel it will not be wanted or accepted.

In some cases, it is actually better to introduce changes without preliminary discussions with those to be affected. Often the effects of change cannot be assessed properly until well after the change has been installed. For example, it was not until department stores were forced, by federal mandate, to hire blacks as sales clerks that top management realized that customers and store personnel would accept the change as a matter of course.

Mandated change is fast
The main advantage of mandating change from above is that *change can take place fast and efficiently.* It took less than a decade for the white populations of southern cities to become thoroughly accustomed to black sales clerks, a phenomenon that reversed 200 years of tradition. And, during World War II, the heads of industries ordered their plant managers to operate the plants on 24-hour-a-day work schedules. Within two or three months, most major industries were producing around the clock.[13]

In government, the right to issue mandates for change is firmly held in check by the democratic electoral process. The government's own mandate to rule is subject to the will of the electorate. If the government issues orders or institutes changes that the population does not wish to comply with, the government will eventually forfeit its power. In the business world, profit is the major check on those who hold power. Only if profits fail to meet the desired expectation will those in power be dislodged. Government is more vulnerable to social pressure as a force for change than are business and industry.

Mandating change is a strictly authoritarian approach. The authoritarian is entirely responsible for major decisions. Resistance can be taken care of simply by firing or transferring employees who are unruly. Resistance can be minimized because the authoritarian assumes the burden of risk—in fact, the authoritarian will often go to great lengths to protect employees from doubts or worries, fearing the resulting confusion. Authoritarian style has the image of being "strong" leadership because it appears always to be able to overcome resistance. However, resistance is to be expected when employees are pressured without a chance to contribute their own input. Therefore, authoritarian leadership may appear to be strong only because it counteracts the resistance it breeds.[14]

Nevertheless, it is possible to lessen resistance to the mandate through good downward communication explaining the reasons why the change is taking place. The role of the supervisor is thus quite important. By taking the time to meet personally, both formally and informally, with key employees, the supervisor can and should create an atmosphere in which employees do not need to vent their frustrations through morale-lowering gossip and speculation.

Management Attitudes

Participatory change and mandated change have been described in their most extreme forms, but rarely are they used so purely. Leaders have a wide range of styles to choose from between the two extremes.

Regardless of how change is introduced, the feelings people have about those making the change have as much influence as the method chosen. Even if change is well conceived, *employees will resist change if they do not trust those attempting to introduce it.* If leadership is not effective in planning for change, probably the change will not succeed. If employees believe in management's goals and in its attempts to be fair, resistance is likely to be less than if they feel management is unyielding and hostile.[15]

Employees resist change by those they cannot trust

Whether or not management believes in participatory or authoritarian leadership methods, introducing and implementing change requires whole-hearted commitment, energy, and communication from top management levels. No matter how committed lower levels of employees might be, the organization will not be able to move in the direction of change without leverage from the top. For example, suppose a conflict were to break out between the research department and the sales force of an old company built on traditional products, whose sales had recently taken a sharp drop. Research personnel would view the problem exclusively in terms of the need for new product development, while sales personnel would see it as indicating the need for new marketing techniques and more advertising. Only top management would be able to assess accurately the overall picture and institute change based on all the relevant data.

But again, much time, money, and emotion can be saved if management spends a little extra energy in communicating the overall picture to the different departments. While this may not necessarily insure commitment to the change, it will insure a much smoother transition.

Time Allowance

Even if there is no resistance to change itself, it takes *time* to put the change into successful production use. Assembly-line operators, clerical workers, salespersons, and supervisors all need time to iron out the bugs from a new system or process. If the supervisor loses patience with the amount of time a subordinate needs to learn how to handle a procedural change, then the subordinate will begin to feel pushed. That sense of feeling pushed can itself create change in customary working relationships and breed resistance where there was none before.

Although most top management personnel are extremely concerned with time structuring, they usually tend to underestimate the time needed to effect change efficiently. Because they don't recognize that most jobs demand synchronized, interlocking patterns of relationships between workers and supervisors that sometimes take months to develop, management frequently fails to calculate realistically the time factor involved in change.

For example, the United States Navy can train destroyer crews to operate new electronic gear in one or two weeks, if the crews are taught in regular Navy schools on shore. But, because of the intricate complexities of human relationships, it takes Navy personnel six months to learn how to operate the equipment properly if they are trained at sea, where they are spending *all* their time together, rather than just training time.[16]

Managers and supervisors need to become much more aware of how human relationships affect the rate at which change can take place. Often, in the name of speed and efficiency, and without understanding the rhythms involved in creating the necessary atmosphere for change, management simply creates obstacles which later take much time and labor to overcome.

Implementing Change

Goodwin Watson and Edward M. Glaser of the Human Interaction Research Institute have outlined a flow chart of what they believe to be the most important stages in creating a positive climate for change.

Table 8–2. Steps in Planning Change

1. Make clear the *needs* for change, or provide a climate in which group members feel free to identify such needs.

2. Permit and encourage relevant group participation in clarifying the needed changes.

3. State the *objectives* to be achieved by the proposed changes.

4. Establish broad *guidelines* for achieving the objectives.

5. Leave the *details* for implementing the proposed changes to the group in the organization or to the personnel who will be affected by the change.

6. Indicate the *benefits* or rewards to the individuals or groups expected to accrue from the change.

7. Materialize the benefits or rewards: i.e., keep the promises made to those who made the change.

Source: Watson, Goodwin, and Edward M. Glaser, ''What We Have Learned About Planning for Change,'' *Management Review*, American Management Association, November 1965, pp. 34–46.

Group Dynamics of Change

The process of implementing change in individuals requires subtle guidance, as fine as the tuning of a radio. A slight change in words can cause certain actions to be interpreted as ''enforced change.'' The influence of groups in bringing about change often yield equally amazing consequences. The term *group dynamics of change* refers to those forces operating in groups. Since change is an integral part of group life, it becomes necessary to study the group as a medium of change. Therefore, those properties of groups are worth noting.[17]

1. A STRONG SENSE OF BELONGING. The chances for reeducation seem to be increased whenever a strong ''we-feeling'' is created. If the group is to be used effectively as a change agent, those people who are to be changed and those who are to exert influence for change must have a strong sense of belonging to the same group. The implications are far-reaching in areas of teaching and of supervision, whether it be in the factory, army, or hospital.

2. GROUP PRESTIGE. The more attractive the group is to the members the greater the influence the group can exert on its members. The more desirable the group the more cohesive the group becomes and the more ready the members are to in-

fluence and be influenced. Suffice it to say that the more attractive the group, the more it satisfies the needs of its members. One question that arises, of course, is how to raise the importance of the group. Some practitioners of group dynamics have increased group cohesiveness and prestige by increasing the liking of members for each other as persons and by increasing the perceived importance of the group goal.

Group pride often creates a dynamic quality of give-and-take within the group itself—a deep sense of what each member has to offer and a willingness of each member to adapt to the needs of the whole.

3. ATTITUDES, VALUES, AND BEHAVIOR. The group is most successful in changing its members' attitudes, values, and behavior in areas closely related to the group's purpose. This is why labor leaders can exert so much influence over rank-and-file union membership in relation to management and strikes, but hardly any at all in relation to politics. If someone joins a union primarily to keep his or her job, or to improve working conditions, the union will probably not have much influence in other areas of the union member's life.

The greater the status, the greater the influence

4. INDIVIDUAL PRESTIGE. The more prestige or status a group member has in the eyes of the other members, the greater *influence he or she can exert. Prestige is not so much being popular as being respected.* Nor does it always accompany authority. This is why the official leader and the actual leader of a group are often quite different personalities.

Both in effecting change and in responding to it, it is important to recognize the influence of the actual leaders of the group. For they can reinforce the sense of group identity and purpose that needs to be shared for effective change to occur.

5. DEVIATION FROM GROUP NORMS. Efforts to change individual members or subparts of a group so that they will deviate from the established group norms will encounter strong resistance and should not be used. If such efforts are made, resistance will usually take the form of rejecting or expelling the offending member from the group. In practical terms, this means that for one member of a group to be changed in a new direction, the whole group must be changed. In group interaction the idea of homeostasis must always be taken into account.

6. SHARED PERCEPTION. Strong pressure for change can be established in a group when members share a perception that change is needed. The source of pressure for change lies within the group. For instance, a group will resist a set of facts brought in by experts that would be accepted if discovered by the members themselves. Here is an example of this principle:

A manufacturing concern had a policy against hiring women over thirty because it was believed that they were slower, more difficult to train, and more likely to be absent. The staff psychologist was able to present to management evidence that this belief was clearly unwarranted, at least within their own company. The psychologist's facts, however, were rejected and ignored as a basis for action because they violated accepted beliefs. It was claimed that they went against the direct experience of the foremen. Then the psychologist hit upon a plan for achieving change which differed drastically from the usual one of argument, persuasion and pressure. He proposed that management conduct its own analysis of the situation. With his help management collected all the facts which they believed were relevant to the situation. When the results were in, they were now their own facts rather than those of some "outside" expert. Policy was immediately changed without further resistance.[18]

Shared information brings shared perception

7. SHARED INFORMATION. Information that relates to the need for change, the plans for change, and the consequences of change must be shared by all people in the group. This principle has been stated in a variety of ways in this chapter. Another way of saying it is that any efforts to change require frank and open communication in order to succeed without arousing undue amounts of resistance. Shared information not only brings shared perception in its wake, but a feeling among all members that they play an important part in the plans. When this occurs, each member is bound to act with more responsibility.

The Importance of Communication

If a program instituting major change is to gain acceptance and use, it is essential that each manager should be well aware of the various principles just mentioned and should be willing to discuss any problems with the members of his group or subgroup. Even under the best of conditions some people will be disturbed by change. The existence of readily available personnel and facilities to "talk it out," will greatly ease their resistance.

Regular informal meetings between small groups of employees and a representative of top management should also be used. Resistance which is brought out into the open relieves the unhappy worker before group morale can be seriously affected. Such meetings are also a good way to test the value of new procedures or methods in an informal, ongoing way. Sometimes the need for further changes will become apparent at these meetings.[19]

Resistance is often caused by the use of highly technical language to describe a change:

A staff specialist was temporarily successful in "selling" a change based on a complicated mathematical formula to a foreman who really did not understand it. The whole thing backfired, however, when the foreman tried to sell it to his operating people. They asked him a couple of sharp questions that he could not answer. His embarrassment about this led him to resent and resist the change so much that eventually the whole proposition fell through.[20]

To minimize resistance, understandable language should always be used. Straightforward explanations and sufficient time for questions and answers must be provided if the proposed change is to succeed.

The expectation of resistance may create it. The most productive attitude an innovator can hold is that resistance is *not* something to be overcome. Rather, it is a signal that something is going wrong. Resistance serves the same function in a social organization that pain does in the physical organism. It doesn't tell you *what* is wrong—only that something *is* wrong. When resistance becomes apparent, the most useful action to take is to find out what its causes are.[21]

MURPHY'S LAW

Perhaps in concluding this chapter it is worthwhile to mention Murphy's law. It has been written in a humorous fashion with several parts, yet there is a thread of real truth in each of its sections.

In Murphy's law— nothing is easy

1. Nothing is as simple as it looks.
2. Everything takes longer than it should.
3. If anything can go wrong, it will.

As an example, the changing of the date of the monthly paycheck from the first of the month to the end of the month seemed like a simple problem to solve. Instead of receiving your check on the first of the next month you would receive it at the end of the present month. Certainly everyone would like to be paid one day early. Surely there would not be any resistance to such an administrative change. The county schools found out differently after informing the school employees of their plan.

Things will go wrong

Immediately, the county school office was informed of the income tax problem. Instead of receiving twelve paychecks the first year, each employee would receive thirteen, thereby having to pay income tax on a larger income. Finally, it was solved. The teachers would be paid the first day of January and the last day of February. Every month after that they would be paid on the last day of the month, except for December at which time they would be paid on January first. Yes, everything takes longer than it should. This plan took two-and-a-half years to put into effect, and a few things did go wrong.

It takes longer than planned

SUMMARY

In our rapidly changing technological society, resistance to change is a normal result of psychological, economic, or social factors, or a combination of the three. Underlying all of these is the basic human fear of the unknown. Occupational identity, pride of craft, and status considerations can all lead to resisting change as much as the fear of job obsolescence does. All groups interact in a manner that attempts to maintain a steady-state equilibrium between the forces working for a change and the forces working to maintain the status quo.

Resistance to change is a normal part of the process of change. Because of the desire of a group to maintain equilibrium, a group will resist change. Imbalances that occur between driving forces and restraining forces create a need for change to occur to find a new pattern of balance. This theory of finding and maintaining balance is called homeostasis and is the basis of all patterns of change.

Today, the value of unchecked technological growth is being seriously questioned by many groups of citizens. Environmental problems have given rise to a growing dissatisfaction with the idea of change itself. We may be moving toward a time when the future changes we will experience will be in the interpersonal and intercultural realm rather than the material and technological sphere.

Participatory techniques that allow all parties to the change to take part in its implementation are very effective in overcoming resistance. Change by mandate, when it is acceptable to the population, can quickly and efficiently overcome traditional forms of resistance.

The nature of the relationships among the members of a group to be affected by change should be carefully considered when planning for change. The group members should be consulted and kept up to date on all proposed changes. In some cases, management may wish to make provisions such as regular informal meetings with disgruntled employees to facilitate change and reduce resistance. Clear, straightforward language should always be used when describing change procedures and methods. However, managers must be careful not to create resistance just because they expect it.

HOW CAN WE ACCEPT THE NEW COMPUTER?

Case Study #1

Fred Lambert is the supervisor of 25 persons in the business office of Channel Electronics. The company is a fast-growing corporation, and employs a total of 500 people from the local community. Due to the rapid and continual growth rate that the corporation is experiencing, Fred has been informed by higher management that the accounting and payroll functions of the office will be computerized.

Fred has been told by the president of the corporation that it is his responsibility to inform the business office of the plans to computerize accounting and payroll and that he will also be in charge of working with the employees who will be directly affected by the change. Of the 25 employees in the office 12 will be required to adjust their job responsibilities and seven will require training in the use of the computer. Fred has been informed that when the computer has been installed and is ready for use two of the office employees may no longer be needed;

however, that point in time could be two months away.

Fred has contemplated the best method of handling this situation. He was thinking of a similar situation which occurred six months ago, when the corporation decided to lease computer time to handle the production inventory. Many members in the production voiced concern at the time over the corporation's desire to begin using computers. They felt that the use of computers would eventually place all of them out of work. Now it is necessary that he inform his staff that a permanent computer will be placed in their office and that many of their jobs will be affected by it.

If you were Fred how would you go about informing the office employees of the change-over to the use of the computer, and how would you go about encouraging them to accept the change.

1. Would you inform the entire department of the situation, or just the 12 persons directly affected, or the 7 people who will be retrained?
2. Would you inform people by a written memo or at a group meeting?
3. Would you inform the employees that 2 people may have to be let go? Would you tell them initially about possible layoffs or tell them later?
4. Should you decide initially who will be retrained and laid off or should these decisions be left to the employees?

GROUP PRESSURE—"RATE BUSTING"

Case Study #2

Engineer Frank Gonzales came to set up a new piece of equipment in the plant. According to Mr. Krieger, the plant manager, the new machine would improve the production rate of the assembly crew.

Leon Robbins, the informal group leader, doesn't like the idea of the new fancy machine. "What they're really after is a way to get more out of us without paying us any more than they have to. When they are done, you and I will be without a job. Just wait and see, one day this company won't need skilled people anymore, all they will need is a few button pushers."

When Frank completed the installation of the new machine he asked for a volunteer to operate it. With the approval of the supervisor of the assembly department, John O'Neil began operating the machine under Frank's supervision. At the end of the day the machine and the operator far exceeded Frank's anticipated increase in production.

"What effect will these new machines really have on our jobs?" asked one worker.

"According to the plant manager, if the system works out well, we'll all be either running the machines or we'll have some other related task," replied O'Neil.

"Well, we know we don't have to worry about losing our jobs, that's one of the first things we were told," said another worker.

"I've been around a long time, friend—you haven't. Let's wait and see what happens," retorted Leon Robbins in a disgusted way.

During the second day of testing, Frank chose another person to operate the new machine. After giving the operator instructions on how to run the machine, Frank began to supervise the employee's performance. Throughout the day Frank felt that the man was performing at less than an appropriate speed. In fact, Frank got the feeling that the man was stalling. At the end of the day, the operator's rate was only marginally higher than the average production rate using the old machine. Playing the role of Frank, you are convinced that the machine is superior to those already in the plant. You also feel that some people do not want to learn the operation of a new machine and are quietly sabotaging any possibility of a really successful run on the machine. What would you do?

1. Go to the employee's supervisor?
2. Go to management and complain about your suspicions?
3. Spend more time with the employees through informal chats?
4. Call for a general meeting with the employees to explain the merits of the machine.
5. Keep trying in the same manner, but be sure that you are picking those employees to work on the machine who are willing to bust the group pressure.

occupational identity	group dynamics	Parkinson's law of the
free-floating insecurity	Murphy's law	"will of the people"
conflict and pressure	homeostasis	mandated change
"rate-buster"	pragmatist	
unions and resistance	manipulator	

Bibliography

1. DOWLING, WILLIAM F., JR. and LEONARD SAYLES, *How Managers Motivate: The Imperatives of Supervision*, New York, McGraw-Hill Book Co., 1971.
2. SCHON, DONALD, *Technology and Change*, New York, Delta Books, Dell Publishing Co., 1967.
3. BERKMAN, HAROLD, *The Human Relations of Management*, Encino, California, Dickenson Publishing Company, Inc., 1974, Chapters 11, 12, and 13.
4. DAVIS, KEITH, *Organizational Behavior, A Book of Readings*, New York, McGraw-Hill Book Company, 1977, Chapter 10.

Footnotes

[1] Donald Schon, *Technology and Change* (New York: Delta Books, Dell Publishing Co., 1967), p. 43.

[2] Alvin Zander, "Resistance to Change—Its Analysis and Prevention," in *Human Relations in Management,* edited by I. L. Heckmann, Jr. and S. G. Huneryager, (Cincinnati: South-Western Publishing Co., 1960), p. 436.

[3] William F. Dowling, Jr. and Leonard Sayles, *How Managers Motivate: The Imperatives of Supervision* (New York: McGraw-Hill Book Co., 1971), p. 370.

[4] *Ibid.*

[5] Schon, *Technology and Change*, pp. 46–47.

[6] Dowling and Sayles, *How Managers Motivate*, p. 372.

[7] Kurt Lewin, "Frontiers in Group Dynamics," in *Field Theory in Social Science* (New York: Harper & Brothers, 1951), pp. 188–237.

[8] Edward Spicer, *Human Problems in Technological Change* (New York: Russell Sage Foundation, 1952), p. 18.

[9] Schon, op. cit., p. 43.

[10] Art Gallaher, Jr., "The Role of the Advocate and Directed Change," *Media and Educational Innovations*, University of Nebraska Press, 1964, pp. 30–40.

[11] George S. McIsaac, "How to Practice What We Preach in Making Business Changes," in *The Nature and Scope of Management*, edited by Maneck S. Wadia (Glenview, Ill.: Scott, Foresman and Co., 1966), pp. 199–200.

[12] *Ibid.*, p. 200.

[13] Paul R. Lawrence, "How to Deal with Resistance to Change," in *Human Relations in Management,* edited by I. L. Heckmann, Jr. and S. G. Huneryager (Cincinnati: South-Western Publishing Co., 1960), p. 444.

[14] Chris Argyris, *Integrating the Individual and the Organization* (New York: John Wiley & Sons, 1964), pp. 118–119.

[15] *Ibid.*, pp. 219–220.

[16] Dowling and Sayles, *How Managers Motivate,* p. 375.

[17] Dorwin Cartwright, "Achieving Change in People: Some Applications of Group Dynamics Theory, in *Human Relations in Management,* edited by I. L. Heckmann, Jr. and S. G. Huneryager (Cincinnati: South-Western Publishing Co., 1960), pp. 464–467.

[18] *Ibid.,* p. 467.

[19] Robert N. McMurray, "The Problem of Resistance to Change in Industry," in *Human Relations in Management,* edited by I. L. Heckmann, Jr. and S. G. Huneryager (Cincinnati: South-Western Publishing Co., 1960), p. 431.

[20] Lawrence, "How to Deal with Resistance," p. 451.

[21] *Ibid.,* p. 452.

three

Someone Must Do the Job

Making Decisions
" Suppose It Doesn't Work? " ∎ ∎ ∎ ∎ ∎ ∎

■ ■

OBJECTIVES

After reading this chapter you should be able to:

1. Explain the differences between short-term and long-term decisions in relation to risk and uncertainty.
2. Describe the differences between humanistic and environmental approaches to decision making.
3. Define and give examples of the four fundamental steps in decision making.
4. Discuss the various ways in which the following personality traits influence decision making:
   A. Ability to take risks,
   B. Fear of failure,
   C. Biased thinking,
   D. Decisiveness,
   E. Deciding on the basis of experience,
   F. Deciding on the basis of intuition,
   G. Always seeking advice.
5. Discuss the advantages and/or disadvantages of the three main ways that centralized decision making takes place:
   A. One-person decisions,
   B. Decisions by the few,
   C. Decisions by the many.
6. List the general personality characteristics of key people in decision making.
7. Explain the process of polarization during conflict and ways of overcoming it.

■ ■ ■ ■ ■ ■ ■ ■ ■ ■ ■ ■ ■ ■ ■ ■ ■ ■ ■ ■

How would you react to the following ad if you ran across it in your daily newspaper?

FOR SALE OR RENT
DECISION-MAKING COMPUTER
Guarantees Good Decisions
No Hassles — No Worries
Easy to Operate — Good Terms
Call 843-7000

You would probably be more than a little skeptical and pass the ad off as a joke or a racket, and you would be right. There is no such infallible computer yet, nor is there likely to be one in the near future, although computers do play an increasingly important role in some aspects of decision making. Decisions are made by people alone and in groups. And, decisions are made all the time.

STYLES OF DECISION MAKING

Defining a Decision

A decision is a kind of commitment—*a resolution to do or stop doing an act, or to adopt or reject an attitude.* It could probably be shown that if the manager of a telephone company ordered ten telephone poles moved from one location to another, carrying out that order could involve 10,000 decisions made by 100 workers located at fifteen points. The decision to move the poles would probably also require some consideration of the social, legal, economic, and physical facts of the environment, as well as the problems of telephone-pole transportation. An inquiry would probably show, however, that not more than a dozen "decisions" would be remembered as worthy of the name. Can you calculate the number of decisions you've made in the past day?

Decisions involve attitudes

Decisions also involve attitudes. Because attitudes often develop unconsciously, they are hard to see as part of the decision-making process until decisions are actually made. For example, many men in the business world today resist the idea that women should hold managerial or executive positions. Social and legal pressures currently being brought to bear on such resistance have had something to do with changes in business attitudes and policy. If the attitudes continue to change, we can expect to see many more women in top managerial positions by the end of the 1970s.

Personal and Group Decisions

There are two main classes of decisions: personal and group. The distinguishing feature of a personal decision is that it is made by one person alone. The person may seek advice, but the responsibility for making the decision cannot be delegated to anyone else. Only you can decide whether you are going to see your friend tomorrow, or buy a car, or continue to go to school.

Group decisions, on the other hand, involve transactions among people. Group decisions are usually, although not necessarily, arrived at by more than one person. A decision made as part of a group process always affects the whole group. In moving telephone poles, for example, specific decisions are made by many people, each decision affecting the possible decisions that could be made by others.

In formal groups, such as business organizations, job responsibility is determined by the decisions that are delegated to each person. In the telephone pole example, the manager is responsible for deciding to move the poles in the first place. The foremen in each of the fifteen districts are responsible for determining where to move the poles. The men on the routes have to decide how best to move the poles.

In informal groups, decisions depend on such considerations as who the leader is, who has status, or who has experience. In deciding whether to move a telephone pole from Maple Street to either Walnut Street or Cherry Street, a foreman may consult with his crew about the best location. The crew may decide unanimously that Walnut Street is best. If the foreman adopts the crew's decision as his own, both informal and formal decisions will have been made.

Short-Range Decisions

Short-range decisions involve little risk

Short-range decisions are usually routine decisions that involve *little risk or uncertainty.* Many industries and business organizations try to create work environments in which as many decision-making functions as possible are standardized for greater production efficiency. The assembly line is the classic example of decisions made into a set of routinized behaviors.

Perhaps you who are supervisors are more concerned with short-range decisions and the effectiveness of those decisions. A common way to unite with others is to have a common purpose. There is one basic precept which will make you a better manager. Learn to persuade others to do willingly what you want them to do. There are eight basic principles of persuasion for short-range effects.

1. Make crystal clear where you stand and why you take that position.
2. Emotions persuade more effectively than facts, particularly in the short run. An emotional catalyst helps leaven the facts.
3. Take your time. Even intelligent people have trouble with new ideas.
4. Repeat your message in as many different ways as possible.
5. Expect resistance.
6. Strive for positive personal involvement. Seek allies.
7. Show that the desired action is possible.
8. State your motives frankly, as self-interest is normal.[1]

Long-Range Decisions

Long-range decisions involve risk and are made by top management

Long-range decisions require a different process from routine decisions. Long-range decisions require planning, and planning always involves the *future*. Whenever you plan for the future, you are automatically involved with a certain amount of *risk and uncertainty*. In a short-range decision, the outcome can be seen readily, if not immediately. A long-range decision involves *predictability*. Routine decisions need to be made in drawing up a life-insurance policy. But both the customer and the insurance broker are involved in predicting the long-range usefulness of the policy—the customer predicts a need for the policy, while the broker predicts that the customer won't need it.

Peter Drucker says that it's easier to define long-range decision making by what it is *not* than by what it is. First of all, it is not forecasting. People neither predict nor control the future. Long-range decisions do not deal with future decisions, but with the probable results of present decisions. The long-range planner does not ask, "What should we do tomorrow?," but instead asks, "What do we do today to be ready for an uncertain tomorrow?"[2] Organizations engaged in training programs for minorities and for women are preparing for the desirable working relationships of tomorrow.

Good planning minimizes risk

Long-range decisions cannot eliminate risk and uncertainty. However, good planning pivots on whether the *right* risks are taken. Sometimes, a company cannot afford not to take a risk. For example, consider some of the implications of the risks incurred by General Electric in the case below:

> The best General Electric scientists advised their management in 1945 that it would be at least forty years before nuclear energy could be used to produce electric power commercially. Yet General Electric—rightly—decided that it had to go into the atomic energy field. It could not afford not to take the risk as long as there was the remotest possibility that atomic energy would, after all, become a feasible source of energy.[3]

Humanistic and Environmental Approaches Compared

Some years ago, during a severe electrical shortage in New York City, two methods were used to reduce the heavy use of electricity. One was to put a card on the wall above the light switch stating, "Save a Watt," to influence people to turn off the lights when they were not being used. The second was to take out some of the light bulbs in the corridors. This method assumed that people would not voluntarily turn off the lights; the environment was changed instead.

In the humanistic approach people make the change

The humanistic approach to making decisions places emphasis on the changes that *people* can make. Environmental decisions affect the environment without any interaction with the people concerned. For example, the workers in a clothing factory might be dissatisfied because they believed their antiquated sewing machines were not as efficient as modern ones. One approach to alleviating the discontent and the resultant low morale would be for management to discuss the relative merits of the old and new machines with the employees, in an effort to change their attitudes; that would be the humanistic method. Another approach would be for management to replace the machines without consulting with the employees; that would be the environmental approach.

It is sometimes difficult to separate decisions that affect people from those that affect the environment. Nevertheless, approaches to problems can be seen in *terms* of either humans or the environment, and both are appropriate depending on the decisions to be made. Most often, one approach follows or is mixed with another. In the clothing factory, the workers might be told that the old machines are still serviceable and that factory policy will be to continue to use them. This decision might be followed by an attempt to educate the employees about the reasons for the decision. Or, in the same factory, the workers might be encouraged to find out everything possible about the available sewing machines, and after acquiring the necessary information, they might decide to keep the old machines before management reaches a final policy decision.

What Kind of Decision Maker Are You?

Answer the following questions. Based on the answers you may be able to see how you attempt to influence outcomes.

1. When compared with most parents I am or would tend to be soft or easy on my children.
   Yes _____ No _____ ? _____
2. There is nothing wrong in making a profit.
   Yes _____ No _____ ? _____
3. Training programs really are good at changing attitudes.
   Yes _____ No _____ ? _____
4. I enjoy arguments and would prefer to solve problems as they arise.
   Yes _____ No _____ ? _____
5. Enjoying your work is more important than how much you make.
   Yes _____ No _____ ? _____
6. Citizen groups have effected changes in our society as related to discrimination against race, sex, social status, unions, and ecology.
   Yes _____ No _____ ? _____

7. I believe taking a psychology or sociology course is more important to me than taking a political science course.
Yes _____ No _____ ? _____

8. Profit is more important than employees' morale.
Yes _____ No _____ ? _____

9. It is more important to worry about individual employees' morale rather than the company's morale.
Yes _____ No _____ ? _____

10. Employees should be docked (lose a portion of their pay) if they return more than 5 minutes late from their coffee break.
Yes _____ No _____? _____

SCORING: Disregard all questions that were answered with a question mark. A humanist would tend to answer "YES" to all of the odd-numbered questions and "NO" to all of the even-numbered questions. Likewise the environmentalist would tend to answer the questions in the opposite fashion: "YES" to all of the even-numbered questions and "NO" to all of the odd-numbered questions. What are you? Read on to find out more about these two types—how they try to influence decisions and influence people.

J. Victor Baldridge of Stanford University summarizes the main difference between the two styles, as shown in Table 9–1.

Table 9–1. Comparative Approaches to Problem Solving.

	HUMANISTIC APPROACH	ENVIRONMENTAL APPROACH
Intellectual heritage	Small group research Social psychology	Sociology of organization Political theory Systems theory
Level of analysis	Individual attitudes Interpersonal relations	Administrative systems External relations Political processes
Goals	Emphasis on improving means (competence in dealing with fellow members of the organization)	Emphasis on attaining goals
External environment	Largely ignored	A major focus
Image of leaders	Small groups expert Interpersonal relations expert	Political statesman
Leadership training techniques	T-groups Sensitivity training Training in social psychology	Negotiation and bargaining Rational planning Computer simulation Training in sociology and political theory

Source: J. Victor Baldridge, "Organizational Change: The Human Relations Perspective," *Economic Record,* February 1972.

HUMANISTIC DECISIONS

When employees working under similar conditions consistently perform similar tasks differently, it can reasonably be assumed that the environment needs less change than the employees. Training is a common way to change job-related behavior. An inefficient or slow employee may need only a little more education about his job or a little more skill development to be able to perform tasks as well as other employees. An environmental approach in this case would be to replace one employee with another in the hope that the change would resolve the problem.

Humanist tries training programs

Environmentalist changes people

Humanists are interested in affecting decisions by modifying attitudes. A humanist would be more concerned about whether a personnel manager felt racial prejudice, whereas an environmentalist would want to make sure company policy adequately eliminated prejudicial treatment.

Humanists are concerned that people express their points of view before decisions are made that affect them. For instance, if production is low, a foreman can arbitrarily decide to speed up the assembly line—an environmental decision. *Another* approach would be to find out why production is low, and give employees the opportunity to weigh their attitudes and to raise production on their own accord. The humanistic approach to decision making, as might be expected from its greater emphasis on interpersonal relations, focuses on participatory methods.

Scores of training programs for the unemployed and to-be-unemployed, supported by the Department of Labor, operate on the principle that people can be fundamentally changed. The 1968 Manpower Report suggests "the necessity of direct effort to modify the attitudes of the disadvantaged before introducing them to job situations."[4] One major training program is aimed at teaching communications skills, grooming and personal hygiene, and the standards of behavior expected by many employers. Training of any kind assumes that employees can change. For instance, sensitivity groups have been developed to sensitize and deepen awareness both of one's self and others so that the desired internal, psychological changes will result.

In his concern for the human situation, at least one researcher has taken a different stance by contending that people's rights and needs should be respected whether or not they *want* to change. Dr. Amitai Etzioni, Director of the Center for Policy Research at Columbia University, believes that it is unethical to try to change people in ways that would affect deep-seated job preferences. For instance, someone who shows creative talent should be encouraged to use it on the job, rather than be trained for routine work. Dr. Etzioni feels we should be matching jobs to people rather than the other way around. Perhaps we should be matching jobs to persons and not persons to jobs.[5]

No matter what their theories are, humanists are likely to be concerned with such matters as the emotional problems of employees, whether job satisfaction and morale are high, whether employees are aware of potential job accidents, whether complaints have a meaningful forum for airing, whether employees maintain good personal and social relationships—in short, people-related concerns.

ENVIRONMENTAL DECISIONS

The environmentalist focuses attention on the external forces that determine a situation. In dealing with employees who perform the same job at different levels of competence, the environmentalist would check to make sure the conditions really were appreciably similar. For instance, environmental thinking would be responsible for the introduction of safety devices, adequate lighting, and improved methods of maintaining equipment.

Management must take into account the environment that exists within the organization. It must also examine the organization's relation to the outside environment, since much of the change within an organization comes about in response to larger social issues. For example, universities are finding it increasingly difficult to remain insulated from the pressures of

Figure 9–1. The environmental approach recognizes that conflict is natural and that bargaining is a major factor that leads to viable compromises.
Courtesy of Santa Barbara City College (Photo by Rob Reilly)

various segments of society. Both hostile and friendly groups outside the university try to influence crucial decisions concerning internal academic affairs. A similar process is happening in all kinds of organizations. Business now must cope with such social challenges as urban unrest, equal opportunity hiring, and air, noise, and water pollution. New social issues are more and more affecting management's ability to make long-term decisions. In the automobile industry, for instance, pressures concerning customers' rights, driving safety, pollution from exhaust fumes, gasoline shortages, and prices are affecting the industry in ways that have never been experienced before.

The environmental approach studies decision making from the point of view of long-range goals, with the best interest of the company in mind. Very little emphasis is placed on the psychological relationships among people, and a great deal is placed on authority, structure, and evaluation of performance. In other words, policy is more important than keeping people happy.

Dr. Baldridge lists five assumptions that are essential to making decisions from an environmental approach.[6]

Conflict is natural

1. *Conflict is natural.* It is to be expected in any dynamic company. Conflict is not abnormal, nor is it always a result of a breakdown in communication.

2. *An organization is pluralist.* The organization is fragmented into many power blocks. Various groups will attempt to influence plans so that their values will be given primary consideration.

A few make the major decisions

3. *Small groups of political elite make most major decisions.* This does not mean that one elite group governs everything; the decisions may be divided up, with different elite groups controlling different decisions.

4. *Bargaining is a major factor.* The formal authority defined by the bureaucratic system is limited by the political pressure and bargaining tactics that groups can exert against authorities. Decisions are not simply bureaucratic orders, but are instead negotiated compromises among competing groups. Officials are not free simply to order decisions, instead they have to jockey between interest groups, hoping to build viable compromises among powerful blocs.

Outside groups can influence inside decisions

5. *External groups can influence decisions.* Outside interest groups have a great deal of influence over the organization, and internal groups do not have the power to make policies in a vacuum.

The adherents of the environmental approach study organizational change in terms of the best interest of the company and from the point of view of long-range goals. The psychological approach is largely abandoned in favor of a sociological-organi-

"HOW MANY WANT TO STAND UP FOR THEIR PRINCIPLES AND HOW MANY WANT TO BACK UP?"

zational system. The policy strategist in business is more interested in making the company responsible to its primary interest, and only secondarily with keeping his staff satisfied. The humanist would work to keep his staff happy and conflicts defused. Which type are you?

In terms of organizational hierarchy, decisions can originate in three distinct ways. Decisions that *result from executive mandate* involve the interpretation and carrying out of instructions, and can sometimes be delegated further down the hierarchical chain. This can create a chain of nondecisions common in bureaucracies, called "passing the buck."

Cases *referred by subordinates* for decision usually arise from conflict of orders, or jurisdiction, or uncertainty of instruction. These decisions usually require judicial decision making.

Other decisions are made on a *person's own initiative*. Decisions of this type test the ability to make decisions most clearly. A good decision maker knows when to decide and when not to; often *no* decision is the best decision for the moment.[7] The executive who succeeds in business while really trying often turns out to be the one who has the knack of saying NO. The wrong way of saying NO may leave the No-sayer with a life-long legacy of ill will, but choosing the right words can save time and heartache. The highest form of the art of saying No is convincing the other person that your decision is in his best interests. But deciding not to decide is also a decision.[8]

STEPS IN DECISION MAKING

What are the steps that must be taken to yield the highest probability of successful decisions? Here are four fundamental ones: (1) define and analyze the problem; (2) develop and evaluate alternative solutions; (3) select and implement a solution; and (4) reevaluate and modify the solution.

Defining and Analyzing the Problem

Problems can be defined as the *obstacles* that prevent the achievement of goals or purposes. Often, the surface problem is only a symptom of a more important problem. For example, having a fever is a symptom of something more serious—perhaps a cold, the flu, or even pneumonia. Similarly, in a company with rapid employee turnover, the turnover itself is not the real problem; it is a symptom of more serious trouble. The question that needs to be asked is: "Why is there so much employee turnover?" Attempting to cure a symptom usually does not cure the cause. An aspirin may bring down the fever, but it will not cure the illness. Similarly, a retirement program may encourage some employees to stay on the job, but it will not cure their desire to leave.

It is often necessary to delve deeply into a situation in order to locate the real problem and define it. For example, a supervisor may believe that he is confronted with a problem of conflicting personalities in his department. The symptom is that two employees are continually bickering. After checking into the situation, the supervisor may find that the problem is not one of personalities at all; rather, the work functions and specific re-

sponsibilities of each employee have never been clearly outlined.

When you think you have defined the real problem, it is
useful to try to state it clearly and concisely to someone else.
This may sound easy, but often it is not. Care must be taken not
to make subjective judgments.

Once the problem is defined, it must be analyzed in order
to be solved. Collecting information for use in analysis is sometimes recommended as the first step in good decision making,
but until the problem has at least been identified and defined,
you won't know what to look for. What sometimes happens is
that the problem has to be *re*defined and *re*analyzed as more information is found, because the new information casts so much
light on the nature of the original problem that its original
boundaries are no longer accurate.

Intangible factors may play a significant role in a problem,
especially when people are involved. It is difficult to gather specific information about such factors as reputation, morale, discipline, and personal bias, but these factors must be considered
in analyzing a problem that requires a decision.

Collecting accurate information for decision making is crucial. Using wrong or irrelevant data as the basis for a solution to
a problem can be more detrimental than not solving the problem at all. Often the ability to collect useful information depends
on how good the communication is within the firm. People
sometimes hold back information to play it safe or to look good.
Also, all information is filtered through individual perceptions,
which are, by definition, subjective. Facts don't speak for themselves; people speak them. Conflict situations especially do not
stimulate dispassionate accounts of events.

The hidden assumptions to be found in most so-called factual statements also must be taken into consideration. As Edward Hodnet put it:

> The trouble often lies with our hidden assumptions—the ones
> we accept without conscious awareness of their existence . . . .
> Over and over you will see that a vast amount of your effort as a
> problem solver will go toward changing assumptions—your own
> as well as other people's. . . . The skilled problem solver starts
> with an ingrained, automatic skepticism. He is not cynical. He
> simply starts with the premise that the assumptions on which
> any problem rests may be challenged, just as the alleged facts
> may be. He is particularly skeptical about dubious answers and
> rigid dogmas—the things that "everybody knows are true."[9]

Another important point to keep in mind when gathering
information is that organizing the information properly is usually as important as understanding it. Peter Drucker describes a

pharmaceutical company that organized the research findings on a problem so well that the company was able to play some very lucrative hunches based on them, even though the research personnel never did solve the original problem or fully understand all of its implications.[10] In any case, without the proper organization of information it is most often impossible to understand, let alone to solve, a problem.

Information related to a problem's solution is not always easy to acquire. A problem in real life is unlike a classroom case study in which all the facts relevant to the case are available. In real life it is necessary to search thoroughly for the various facts that may illuminate a problem. Some of the ways of collecting these facts are: (1) personal interviews; (2) reviewing records; (3) flow charting; (4) organizational charting; (5) consulting previous studies and outside information. Each method provides a specific kind of information. Often a balanced combination of the appropriate methods will yield a fairly objective and broad spectrum of data to use in assessing a problem.

Developing and Evaluating Alternative Solutions

Decision makers need to learn to stretch their minds in order to develop all the possible alternatives, even in the most discouraging situations. Even when one of the available alternatives is desirable, it is better to have choices than to be left with no choice at all. Doing nothing is also a decision—and can be worthwhile or fatal. Brainstorming is one of the best known methods for developing alternatives to problems. The freewheeling, receptive atmosphere of a brainstorming session often produces workable solutions.

Take the case of a business concern that is in financial straits. The creditors have offered three possibilities: forcing the company into bankruptcy; agreeing to a moratorium of one year in which to pay bills; or compromising on a small percentage of the outstanding debts and clearing out the indebtedness. The smart decision maker might see an additional possibility: having the company purchased by another firm. Such a merger would be the best of the alternative solutions in terms of good will and public image, certainly preferable to letting the indebted company go into bankruptcy.

When more than one person is involved in making a decision, it is often a challenge to arrive at a solution with a minimum of conflict. For example, suppose the sales personnel of a cosmetics firm insist on a particular kind of packaging for a new product because of its eye-catching appeal. The production department, however, is firmly opposed to it on grounds of expense and difficulty of manufacture. Both groups are right, at least within the respective areas of their specific concerns. This is the kind of situation that calls for developing and evaluating alternatives. Solutions to this kind of conflict are usually plentiful as soon as the parties involved agree to explore alternative choices together.

The question of *timing* will often make one alternative preferable to another. It is important to gauge how much time is available to implement a decision. Factors such as resources, facilities, records, and tools must also be considered. Different alternatives should also be judged in terms of the economy of the effort: which action will give the greatest results for the least amount of time? In business (as the saying goes), time is money. Value must be placed on abstract qualities so that reasonable decisions can be made. For instance, a manufacturer is faced with annual losses from one of his factories located in a small town. Weighed against this tangible loss is the fact that if he closes or moves the factory, the town will cease to exist. How does the factory owner assess the intangible value of a town? The tangible and intangible values must be compared to arrive at a decision: Is keeping the town functioning worth a loss of $10 million, $100,000, or $10,000?

Selecting and Implementing a Solution

After the alternative solutions have been developed, the probable desirable and undesirable consequences of each should be mentally tested by the decision maker. The selection must be the best solution from the point of view of time and energy as well as money. The decision maker's selection will probably be based on a combination of factors, such as experience, intuition, advice, experimentation, and computer forecasts.

Alternatives can lead to experimentation

In the scientific world, many decisions are based on experimentation. When experimentation is not too costly, it is worth following. Even on a small scale, experimentation is almost always justified by good results. Moving machinery around in a factory to change the work flow, or changing the location of desks in a department to see if production rises or falls, are examples of small-scale experimentation, which can sometimes yield surprising results. Another experiment that companies have tried and liked is staggering the work shifts of different departments by fifteen minutes so that the parking lot will be less crowded at 9 a.m. and 5 p.m.

When experimentation is not possible, the decision maker must select an alternative based on the most objective forecasting possible—the premise of strategic analysis, for example, that decisions are different because the initial objectives, assumptions, and expectations are different. In an effort to eliminate arbitrary factors, strategic analysis proceeds by clarifying goals, examining assumptions, and determining expectations. The best analysis leaves the least room for doubt that a decision is a good one. For example, a paper mill may have a serious problem in being able to secure trees. The problem may extend strategic planning decades into the future, which would include proper analysis of the amount of reforestation needed, what logging roads will be required, and how to preserve the ecology of a logging region.

**We seek out positive alternatives;
choosing among negative choices
seems like no choice at all**

NEGATIVE: The pipe under your kitchen sink springs a leak and you call in a plumber. A few days later you get a bill for forty dollars. At the bottom is a note saying that if you do not pay within 30 days, then there will be a 10% service charge of $4. You feel trapped with no desirable alternatives. You pay $40 now or $44 later.

POSITIVE: The same case as above, but with two changes. The plumber sends you a bill for $44, but the note says that if you pay within 30 days you will get a special $4 discount. The difference is that you will save $4.

Good solutions must be backed up by good plans. Workable plans have four features in common: *unity, continuity, flexibility,* and *precision.* A plan may be divided into several parts, but those parts should be linked. The action of the plan should be continuous. Starting and stopping a new plan in the middle of the testing period can be disastrous for morale, but the plan should be flexible enough to bend to new pressures when necessary. A good plan exhibits as much accuracy as is compatible with the amount of risk attendant on all new plans.

Once a plan has been accepted, it must be put into action carefully and watched closely to ensure that it will work. In planning for implementation, *Murphy's law* must be remembered: Everything always takes more time, money, and energy than anyone had imagined.

General Foods Corporation provided a good example of planning for implementation when it decided to close down four plants in four states and combine operations in one new, larger plant in yet another state. About 1,800 employees were notified of the move by letter a year before it was scheduled to take place. A few months later, a policy statement on transfer and termination was circulated to all employees, indicating the company's intention to transfer those employees who wished to move. Transferring employees were given job preferences over newly hired people. General Foods assisted those who did not wish to transfer in finding other employment. Such a carefully implemented long-term approach not only eliminates many last-minute problems, but it keeps employee motivation and morale at their maximum. A system that is frequently used in market-

PERT ing, advertising, and research and development is PERT. The *Program Evaluation Review Technique* is a system that evaluates each project at each step along the line in terms of each new input and how it may affect the final result. The cost of the program up to that step is determined both financially and in terms of human adjustment. This valuable technique has forced management to alter products, expend more time and dollars on a project, or sometimes to abandon a project completely.

Reevaluating and Modifying the Solution

The best solutions, and the most careful planning for implementation, will not insure against later flaws that almost always arise. When a particular solution is put into action, unthought-of difficulties will occur. A good decision maker must always be ready to consider new information and readjust a plan to satisfy new needs. If the solution is a good one, reevaluations and modifications will be concerned with details, and will not affect the intention and general nature of the solution. How many times have you made a decision to go to the library to read a reserve book, only to find when you arrived that the book you wanted would be out for another two hours? You may have had to change certain details of your day so that you could return in two hours to read the book, but the essential plan remains unchanged.

TRAITS THAT INFLUENCE DECISIONS

Decisions may be helped or hindered by the basic philosophies decision makers have about life, and how they interrelate with the people around them. People react to problems in many different ways; the solutions chosen by a person reflect some of the assumptions he or she makes. Some of the personality traits that are particularly influential in the decision-making process are discussed below.

Taking Risks

50–50 chance gambles

There is no such thing as a riskless decision, but the degrees of risk vary. Many decision makers have an aversion to risk taking. Most people, when offered a 50–50 chance that a gamble will succeed, would choose not to gamble, even if winning would bring in many times what the risk is worth. Most people do not want to jeopardize the gains they have made.

A graphic way to illustrate the degree of risk would be to offer a decision maker a high payoff on an even-chance gamble. A majority would turn down such a proposition even if the pay-off were ten times as high as the sum at risk. Practically none would be interested in quadrupling their money. If the sum at risk involved all or most of the corporate resources, this attitude would be entirely rational. Mature corporations are not in the business to gamble their corporate existences on a 50 percent chance of high returns. Most decisions, however, involve only a small fraction of total corporate resources. And the opportunities for them occur dozens of times every year. Taking several 50-percent chances every month to risk a small percent of total resources for a tenfold return would appear to be very good business practice indeed and should pay off handsomely in the long run. Nevertheless, each decision maker tends to behave as though the fate of the company or his own were in balance with each decision.

Businesses, like people, want to make the least risky choices. They are in the habit of taking monetary risks with relatively small amounts of capital; but no matter whether the risk is low or high, decision makers often act as if their fate, or their company's hangs in the balance. Many decisions that should be made are often suppressed because of the fear of failure.

Success and Failure Attitudes

Fear of failure gives little chance for great success

Fear of failure can stalemate the decision-making process. Worry about the unknown results of a decision can be paralyzing. As long as no decision is made, no judgment can be reached as to whether the decision is a good one or not. By not making decisions people lose the opportunity to learn either from their failures or their successes. Only by making decisions can one learn how to make successful decisions.

To make a decision might be the first step to failure, so decisions may be delayed. Until a decision is made judgments on individuals are often deferred. For the lack of decisions little growth or experience can be obtained concerning success or failure. As Americans, we have little open association with failure. There are few models to follow to help us cope with failure, so many people shy away from decision making for fear of failure.

Personal Biases

It is impossible to appeal to neutral principles to determine the rationality of competing systems. It is in the name of one kind of logic that another kind of logic is rejected. Each system of thought, whether it is religious, political, economic, scientific, or poetic, has its own rationale.

Systems of reason are influenced by habits, reflexes, prejudices, appetites, and emotions. All logic is biased by personal feelings and affinities. Sometimes these feelings are appropriate to the situation and sometimes they are not. When making decisions, it helps to know what your personal biases are. Often the very price that has to be paid in making a decision is the sacrifice of a particular set of biases. In many instances, it is only in this way that one can be aware of the various alternatives.

Decisiveness

A Zen master continuously stresses to his disciples the art of living spontaneously. In fencing, for example, movements must be made without slow logic or hesitant reasoning. The fencer learns to take all of the human and environmental variables into account, translating them into immediate action.

Another expression of spontaneous decision making can be seen in the Cumiye school of Zen painting. This form of painting is executed on paper so thin that the slightest hesitance will cause it to tear. The strokes have to be swift and accurate; their positions are irrevocable.

Think of these examples the next time you have trouble making up your mind. Some people are indecisive because they don't have adequate information, so that their decision is really guesswork. Others just don't like to take the responsibility; the moment they see a problem they become hopelessly confused.

Experience

Knowledge gained by experience is a helpful guide to decision making, and its importance should not be underestimated. On the other hand, it is dangerous to follow experience blindly. It is too easy for the person with "many years of experience" to fail to listen to innovative ideas from others. His biases insulate him from anything new.

Experience must be put into perspective according to the demands of new situations. Past experience is not always useful in evaluating the circumstances of the present and the future. And even when it is, it will seldom apply in a direct way. In order for experience to be useful, a person must be flexible enough to see that it is just one of the many ingredients that goes into the decision-making process.

Intuition

Intuitive feelings and hunches also help determine decisions. Hunches are based on information or experience recorded in the subconscious. The predisposition to make a certain decision comes to the conscious mind, but without articulated reasons. Often, intuition can provide the essential direction for solving a problem in a certain way, while the justification comes later.

Decisions based on intuition or bias

Decisions based on intuition gain much more credibility when they are also supported by logic and experience. Unfortunately, it is often difficult to tell the difference between intuition and bias.

Seeking Advice

It is one thing to be aware that you are the only one who can make a decision. It is quite another to seek opinions about what action should be taken. Listening with an open mind to what other people have to say can greatly enlarge the potential of making a good decision. Other people can also act as sounding boards—providing a chance to hear how ideas sound. The person who makes a practice of not consulting others takes greater risks in making decisions because he isolates himself from feedback. By going to the other extreme, by seeking too much advice too much of the time, not only can a person appear to be incapable of making a decision on his own, but he can undermine his own confidence in his powers to do so.

WHO MAKES THE DECISIONS?

Most people can learn to make decisions but to make good ones they must have proper decision-making channels.

Decision making involves a process, and "if the process is well organized, average people will produce superior decisions. If the process is poorly organized, then only geniuses can save the company from disaster."[11]

The connection between individual decisions and organizational policy isn't always simple. A person who tries to shape an organization entirely to his or her thinking can expect to meet resistance. A strongly motivated person will form factions and cliques to work for the desired change. Those opposed will also band together. Many people today still think for themselves—even in large corporations, the sabotaging of top management's decisions with other lower-level decisions is quite common. Adopting a policy is by no means the same thing as putting it into effect.

A successful organization is built on setting realistic goals and meeting them. Meeting organizational goals requires well-defined administrative relationships, including the assignment of authority and the responsibility for making rational decisions. Even so, the question of who should make the decisions has never been adequately answered. In most businesses, responsibility for decision making is measured by the significance of the decision: how much money and how many people will be affected. Thus, decision making follows the organizational hierarchy, with those at the top responsible for the most important decisions.

Many large corporations have separate divisions whose sole function is to do research for long-term planning. However, final decisions must be agreed on by the division heads whose units are to be affected by the proposed changes. In recent years, General Electric and Ford Motor Company, to name but two firms, have considered the techniques of decision making important and complex enough to devote special training programs to the subject. Hundreds of their middle and senior managers have been taught decision-theory analysis, which is a highly developed statistical theory using computer programs.[12]

Major decision making tends to be highly centralized in most large companies, especially when the decisions concern financial, legal, and industrial-relations problems. There are three main ways in which this centralized control operates.

One-Person Decisions

First, there are the one-person businesses, which Chester Barnard believes are more widespread than most people think.[13] The owner-manager may have difficulty delegating decision-making power to subordinates because of a belief that power and prestige are lost when authority is delegated. However, in actuality, more work can be gained by delegation and more experience can be learned by the subordinate.

The supervisor who believes in more independent delegation spends less time checking up on the employee and thus has more time for more important work. Ideally, the employee gets a chance to develop himself by correcting his own errors. A climate of confidence results when the employee is allowed to check up on himself, without the boss looking over his shoulder.

Decisions By a Few

Oligarchic decisions are made by a powerful few

In decisions made by the few, or oligarchic decision making, major decisions are made by a small group, usually at least three but no more than seven. In addition to participating in joint decisions, each person usually has an area in which he or she has the final say, such as in sales or production matters. Oligarchic control can create delay, or even bring action to a standstill, if there is a deadlock and no one has the final power to decide. In one large corporation, three executives with equal power were deadlocked over several important labor matters. The production specialist wanted to settle with the union to keep the plant operating. The other two opposed agreement for various reasons. The deadlock was broken only when a competing firm signed with the union, thus forcing the two executives who opposed settlement to capitulate. Since that time the corporation has steadily been moving toward one-person control.

Ernest Dale says that oligarchic control is often "a passing phenomenon that may either regress to one-person control or progress toward greater participation by an increasing number of executives."[14]

Decisions By Many

Decisions made by many people have been called integrative or participative decisions. These terms are preferable to democratic decision making because "democratic" implies an equality that does not exist in this context—certainly not for income, or status, and usually not for the power to influence major decisions. Participatory action normally takes the form of friendly, informal consultation among top management and sometimes their subordinates. The real test of participation is the extent to which disagreement is tolerated, especially by those who are superior in rank.

Many firms use consultative decision making to bring

those employees with technical background and know-how to the conference table. The technical staff is more likely to participate in making decisions when specific skills are involved than in those areas requiring long-range planning.

Group decision making can be an exceedingly complex affair, but two facts hold true. First, majority decisions usually represent something less than total group commitment. Few groups, outside of a few religious orders, operate with total group consensus.

Second, the more abstract the matter being considered, the greater the chances of agreement are. Put another way, the more concrete the matter, the less the chances are for full agreement. For example, at one company, contract negotiations come to a halt over a clause about hiring "part-time employees." The term needed definition. One proposed was, "a part-time employee is one who works less than forty hours a week, on irregular schedules, and is not subject to the benefits of regular employees." Another was, "anyone who works less than forty hours a week." Clearly, the second definition covered many more people than the first did, and offered a wider range of interpretation. The company wanted the broad definition so that it could choose who would be entitled to regular benefits. The union wanted the narrow definition so that it could then claim all employees as dues payers. An agreement was reached only by structuring a definition more abstract than either party wanted: "Part-time employees are all those employees who are not regular employees." While this more abstract definition did not solve any concrete problems, it did allow negotiations to continue.[15]

Few decisions have total group consensus

The more abstract the matter, the greater the chance for agreement

Key People in Decision Making

The people between the innovators and the major policy decision makers are often the key link in bringing about effective results. Several hundred scientists in a division of a NASA laboratory were asked to name the colleagues who had been most helpful to them in problem solving.[16] Those who were named most often were interviewed to identify character similarities and differences. They were found to share the following characteristics:

1. They derived a greater feeling of accomplishment from helping people grow and develop than did nonkey personnel.
2. They enjoyed working with others. They communicated more often with more people, in their own labs and outside their own units. They worked under greater time pressure than did their

fellows, and, as a result, spent a smaller proportion of their time on their own projects than did nonkey personnel.

3. They placed less importance on working with congenial workers and more emphasis on working with a competent work force.

4. They used the environmental approach more than the humanistic, preferring to work with others on technical rather than social grounds, and emphasizing the "big picture" in all of its innovative aspects.

5. They enjoyed a greater feeling of accomplishment from doing creative work, rather than exceeding expected standards of job performance. Practical problems and top management were the main sources of stimulation. This may suggest that managers who want to increase the supply of such personnel should think about extending their interest further down the business hierarchy than they might presently be doing.

6. They scored no better and no worse than their colleagues on a test of creative ability, but had more formal education. Taken as a whole—supervisors and nonsupervisors together—the key people averaged roughly $6,000 more a year than their colleagues.

Key people would rather work with competent than congenial people

Key people are not more creative, but more educated

To summarize, key people in decision making can be predicted with reasonable accuracy. They are apt to be concerned with the broad features of problems and with the innovative aspects of their work. They may even be troublemakers, since meeting organizational standards is relatively unimportant to them. Key people prefer to interact with other workers, but on a professional rather than a social basis. Their past-performance record is usually good, and they probably have been influential in shaping their job goals.

MAKING DECISIONS DURING CONFLICT

Polarizations

Making decisions always involves people—they either participate in the process of problem solving or are affected by the decisions made. Decisions often involve disagreements, which sometimes can be resolved through discussing and understanding the different points of view. But deep-seated conflicts are not easily resolved. When such terms as "confrontation" and "nonnegotiable" are used in describing a situation, the resistance to argument may be so firm that effective decision making seems impossible. The biggest problem in making decisions is when deadlocks occur as a result of conflict. Effective action is blocked until a way out of the dilemma is discovered.

Hard lines result in conflict

Hard lines that develop around an issue may indicate more than simple differences in taste. In conflict, one side is right and the other is wrong; one is good and the other is evil. In other words, deep conflict almost always implies that an issue has been moralized. War is an example of men and women fighting for what their side believes to be right, making the other side "dead wrong." A typical symptom of conflict is that both sides will reject solutions that are profitable to both. The game is that a price must be paid—by the other side.

There is no neutral ground in a hard line stand

Unfortunately, when one group develops hard lines around an issue, the other group usually assumes an equally rigid stance. For instance, during a showdown between management and a union, management might say, "There are no neutrals. Since you're on strike, you're against us." The striking union members might reply, "We won't back down. We demand our just rights."

Conflict over issues can easily degenerate into personal conflict, often called mudslinging. Adversaries often employ irrelevant personal information about one another to strengthen their arguments. Personal attacks can usually be reduced to two phrases: "I don't like you," and "You don't like me." Personal attacks can increase animosity so much that the other side may justly feel that it cannot even talk about the suggested terms, much less meet them. When one side accuses the other of personal animosity, defensiveness or guilt can result. Naturally, charges against an opponent derive much power from the vehement manner in which they are cast. Another tactic adversaries employ is to make negative statements based on matters difficult to prove, such as values and beliefs.

Nonperson status

One typical pattern in polarized conflict is called *nonexistence*. This occurs when one side refuses to listen to the arguments of the other side. Nonrecognition is often a ploy to force the antagonist to quiet down or to go away. You may be able to recognize this tactic in such circumstances as the "freeze out" in a lovers' quarrel, or the temporary banishment of a "difficult" child from the family. Russia has institutionalized the practice of treating people as nonexistent by creating a specific "nonperson" status.

Universal plot theories can be used to explain just about anything. "It's a Communist plot" is a famous example of a conspiracy theory that can gain immediate support in some circles. It is a very human response to treat behavior we dislike as the work of our adversaries. Universal plot theories gain strength from their supporters' convictions.

Win-lose approach

The *win-lose* approach to conflicts implies a "go-for-broke" attitude where something is at stake. It assumes that a person's contributions to group effort will result in a *personal* gain or loss in esteem, prestige, or responsibility. This win-lose method of interaction requires some degree of personal involvement. It also discourages the possibility of free expression and exchange of ideas. Consciously or unconsciously the person feels that he is personally being tested, rather than his ideas.

The idea of winning or losing is so ingrained in the American character that some management personnel accept it as a natural part of the human condition. This assumption rules out the easy use of such methods as group brainstorming and group decision making. Some advocates of competitive games such as win-lose maintain that without such games employees may become more content, but they also become less productive, and the quality of their work suffers.

Methods of Noncommunication

What can be done when two or more sides are locked in combat? How can a decision be arrived at that will prove effective and advantageous to all parties? As long as the hostile attitudes that frequently accompany conflict exist, it is difficult to arrive at meaningful decisions. Without *real* listening and a *real* desire to understand the other side's point of view, conflict cannot be resolved.

In a conflict situation, it is important to be able to recognize sincere efforts to communicate and agree, as opposed to partial or superficial efforts. True communication is sometimes feared because of the changes that may follow in its wake. Frequently, insincere efforts can be recognized by the *manner* in which the problem is stated. For example, an opening like this does not indicate a sincere desire to reach accord: "We are ready to participate in reasonable discussions, but we will not submit to blackmail."

People who are insincere in their efforts to communicate often take the position that their decisions are made solely in *reaction* to the other side's actions. "We regret this decision, but it has been forced upon us. We have no choice." The advantage of this posture is that whatever happens as a result of a decision can be blamed on the other side.

You forced a decision on us

When one party to a conflict says to the opponent, "What you *really* mean is . . . ," and refuses to listen to the opponent's own description of the problem, that is an insincere attempt at communication. It is only when you can state your opponent's position in a manner that is *satisfactory to the opponent* that true communication occurs.

Another way to continue hostility is to *deny* that a decision has been made as a result of pressure from the other side. A typical remark from this position would be, "We were going to do it anyway; it was on our timetable." Refusal to acknowledge an opponent's influence can be carried to the extent of accusing the opponent of delaying the action by wasting time in bringing the matter up!

Finally, and most important, is that the bargainer place himself in the shoes of his adversary so that the final outcome does not publicly disgrace himself or his opponent. For, to humiliate the opponent may only give him a temporary victory. To allow his opponent to "save face" may be in the best interest of the company, the union, or the nation.

There is, of course, no simple solution to confrontation. Nevertheless, it is possible, through listening and the other communication techniques described in earlier chapters, to create an atmosphere in which, while there may still be disagreement as to details, the total process of decision making can continue. When this happens, solutions often emerge that neither side had envisaged.

SUMMARY

A decision is a commitment to take or not to take an action or to accept or reject an attitude. Decisions are made by individuals and by groups. In an individual decision, only one person can be responsible for the outcome. In a group decision, various individuals can make decisions, although other group members may be responsible for carrying them out. Jobs are often defined in terms of the kinds of decisions that are expected to be made.

Short-range decisions require little risk. Some industries attempt to routinize short-range decisions to speed up efficiency. No matter how routine decisions are, their importance is often incalculable because they are all links in a larger process.

Long-range decisions require planning for contingencies, which automatically means that risk is involved. The future can only be predicted, whereas decisions are always based in the present. Decisions are often made as insurance against future events.

Two basic approaches are used in making decisions: one considers problems from the human point of view, and is called humanistic. The other sees problems in terms of the environment, and is called the environmental approach. Their appropriateness depends on the situation, but most people tend to rely more on one than the other.

Decisions can be categorized according to the problems they are meant to solve. Problems require executive, judicial, or legislative thinking. Often, the way a problem is introduced indicates the appropriate nature of the response.

There are four steps to decision making: defining and

EVERY BIG
DECISION INVOLVES
A BIG RISK

analyzing the problem at hand; developing and evaluating different solutions; figuring out the best solution and implementing it; and examining the solution as it is being implemented to see if it needs modification. The smaller the decision, the less distinguishable these steps will be.

Personality traits can influence the way problems are handled. Alternative solutions reflect which philosophies are acceptable to the decision maker. Attitudes about taking risks, success and failure, and prejudice greatly affect the quality of decisions. The ability to be decisive as well as to seek advice, and to use experience as well as intuition, contribute to the decision-making process.

Decisions affecting groups are made by one person, by a few, or by many; and each method has its own rewards and drawbacks. No matter who has the final word, key people are always involved. Key people are go-betweens—they help to get an idea proposed by one party to be decided upon by another.

Conflict situations have certain characteristics that indicate degrees of polarization. The only way to solve a polarized issue is through careful communication.

We make decisions all the time. Decisions, whether good ones or bad ones, determine all action that is taken. The process of decision making, the clarity of communicating decisions, and the steps for implementing them have a continuing and powerful effect on the daily quality of our lives and interactions with other people.

MISSING COMPANY PROPERTY

Case Study #1

One of the most difficult problems the personnel department can face is how to track down company property which it suspects was "lifted" by light-fingered employees. No matter how careful the management might be in searching for the culprits, its activities are likely to step on someone's toes.

Applied Computers was missing several things, from office supplies to small special hand tools. The office manager, Bob Miller, was convinced that the pilferage was done by company employees.

"Our clients don't have access to our supplies, but many of our employees do. One problem may be our checkout system in our warehouse and tool room," said Miller one day. Finally he was convinced that he should take a bold tack. He asked a representative of the local union, a shop steward, to meet him at the employees' locker room. You have overheard the conversation. As the company's personnel director you are torn between telling Miller, your superior, something about his possible action, and reporting to his superior, Jim Sanford, the vice-president of the firm. You know that there is nothing in the company policies about such action.

1. What will you do? If you talk to Bob Miller, what will you say? If you talk to Jim Sanford what will you recommend?

2. Does the employer have the right to invade its employees' private lockers, where personal belongings are kept without the employees' permission?

3. If the company takes items from the lockers that belong to the company, is this an unwarranted invasion of privacy and an illegal search and seizure?

4. If the company had requested permission of the employees, then would the company still have the same opportunity to find the missing property?

DAYLIGHT MOONLIGHTING — OR HOW TO MAKE AN EXTRA BUCK ON THE SIDE

Case Study #2

As employees receive more and more fringe benefits and more self-determination, employers tend to twinge as employees take advantage of company time and expenses.

Such is the case of a man hired by the John Hopkins and Co. Pharmaceutical Company. Robert Paderewski was a sales representative and his job required him to follow up on many leads that the company gave him. Robert was a capable man who worked faithfully and followed up his leads well. His sales were above average and better than his predecessor. For his efforts he was paid about $12,000 a year, plus expenses.

After a year of success with John Hopkins, the division manager, Oliver Newberry, was walking by his desk and overheard a conversation on the phone. Oliver listened unobtrusively and discovered that Robert had just received an order over the phone for a sizable purchase of office supplies.

When the call was over, Newberry furiously confronted Robert Paderewski: "Who ever gave you permission to run a sideline on company time?" "Nobody ever said I couldn't," replied Robert.

"I don't care what you do on your own time, but you don't solicit business for others on our time."

Paderewski calmly replied, "Why should you care? You don't sell office supplies, and I am doing a satisfactory job for you."

1. Oliver Newberry contends that Paderewski should devote his time pushing John Hopkins' products not his own. Further, Paderewski was disloyal and dishonest, and he has every right to fire him. Is Oliver's viewpoint correct?

2. Paderewski claims that if the company was against daytime moonlighting, it should have told him when it hired him. Because nothing was said on the subject, he thought it would be all right for him to solicit an occasional order from an office supply house. Is Robert's viewpoint correct?

3. What are the alternatives to you, as their superior, to solve the problem?
   a.
   b.
   c.

4. What solution would you select and why?

Terms and Concepts Students Should Know

short-range decisions	group decisions	alternatives for decisions
humanistic approach	polarizations	risk taking
conflict is natural	win-lose approach	decisiveness
Murphy's law	long-range decisions	key people
success and failure attitudes	environmental approach	universal plot

Bibliography

1. DRUCKER, PETER, "Long-Range Planning: Challenge to Management Science," in *Information for Decision Making*, edited by Alfred Rappaport, Englewood Cliffs, New Jersey, Prentice-Hall, 1970.

2. MORGAN, JOHN, "The Nine Principles of Persuasion," *Nation's Business*, March 1975.

3. SEARS, WILLIAM R., "The Art of Saying 'No'," *Nation's Business*, October 1974.

4. BITTEL, LESTER, *What Every Supervisor Should Know*, 3rd ed., New York, McGraw-Hill Book Company, 1977.

CHAPTER 9

Footnotes

[1] John Morgan, "The Nine Principles of Persuasion," *Nation's Business*, March 1975.

[2] Peter Drucker, "Long-Range Planning: Challenge to Management Science," in *Information for Decision Making*, edited by Alfred Rappaport (Englewood Cliffs, N.J.: Prentice-Hall, 1970), p. 110.

[3] *Ibid.*, p. 116.

[4] U.S. Department of Labor, *Manpower Report to the President* (Washington, D.C.: Government Printing Office, March 1968).

[5] Amitai Etzioni, "Human Beings Are Not Very Easy to Change After All," *Saturday Review*, 3 June 1972, pp. 45–47.

[6] J. Victor Baldridge, "Organizational Change: The Human Relations Perspective versus the Political Systems Perspective," *Economic Record*, February 1972.

[7] William R. Sears, "The Art of Saying 'No'," *Nation's Business*, October 1974.

[8] Chester I. Barnard, "The Environment of Decision," in *The Nature and Scope of Management*, edited by Maneck S. Wadia (Glenview, Ill.: Scott, Foresman and Co., 1966), p. 81.

[9] Edward Hodnet, *The Art of Problem Solving* (New York: Harper and Row, 1955), pp. 54–55.

[10] Drucker, "Long-Range Planning," p. 113.

[11] William F. Whyte, *Organizational Behavior: Theory and Application* (Homewood, Ill.: Richard D. Irwin and Dorsey Press, 1969), p. 699.

[12] Rex V. Brown, "Do Managers Find Decision Theory Useful?" *Harvard Business Review*, May 1972, p. 78.

[13] Barnard, "Environment of Decision," p. 88.

[14] Ernest Dale, "New Perspectives in Managerial Decision Making," in *The Nature and Scope of Management*, edited by Maneck S. Wadia (Glenview, Ill.: Scott, Foresman and Co., 1966), p. 89.

[15] John W. Keltner, *Interpersonal Speech Communication* (Belmont, Calif.: Wadsworth, 1970), p. 153.

[16] Robert Swain and George Farris, study reported in *Innovation*, no. 25 (October 1971): p. 26.

Leadership
" Will Someone Follow Me?" ■ ■ ■ ■ ■ ■

■ ■ ■ ■ ■ ■ ■ ■ ■ ■ ■ ■ ■ ■ ■ ■ ■ ■ ■

OBJECTIVES

After reading this chapter you should be able to:

1. Discuss the role that leadership plays in the functioning of groups.
2. Discuss the relevance of charisma and popularity as essential ingredients of leadership.
3. Explain each of the following functional roles that leaders play in order to keep a group unified:
   A. Providing symbols,
   B. Providing behavior models,
   C. Attaining goals,
   D. Making decisions,
   E. Resolving differences.
4. Define the formidable leadership tasks that Bennis believes are applicable to today's problems.
5. Explain the advantages and disadvantages of the following styles of leadership behavior and how they relate to McGregor's theories of leadership:
   A. Autocratic,
   B. Participative,
   C. Free rein.
6. Discuss how communication patterns are related to group structure.

Look at these questions before reading the chapter. Some answers may be found in the chapter and some can only be answered by personal opinion.

Is there an ideal type of leader for all situations?

What do leaders look like?

And what are their personalities?

What kind of leader is needed for a crisis?

Do leaders have more intelligence than their followers?

What is the function of a leader in a group?

Could you pick one out in a crowd?

What is the best type of leader in classroom or group discussion?

Free-rein leadership means almost no control by the leader, therefore should not be used by supervisors. Do you agree?

WHAT IS LEADERSHIP?

Breaking Through the Myths

Boards of directors of business organizations complain, "What we need are more leaders!" Whole nations cry, "If only we had a great leader, we would be on the way to solving our major problems." But, what *is* a leader? Chester Barnard, a telephone company executive and business theoretician, said about leaders:

> Leaders as functioning elements of organizations are not formally nominated, selected, elected, or appointed, nor are they born to leadership; they are accepted and followed; and are sometimes pressed or (rarely) coerced into leading. Indeed, I have never observed any leader who was able to state adequately or intelligibly why he was able to be a leader, nor any statement of followers that acceptably expressed why they followed.[1]

Leadership is such an elusive concept partly because people do not define themselves in leadership terms. Someone coming home from a community meeting might say, "I sure got them to come around to my point of view." Or, "I was surprised at how carefully they listened to what I had to say." But if asked, "Did you *lead* the group?," that person would be apt to answer, "Well, not really." Furthermore, followers are unclear about their reasons for choosing leaders.

Leadership is not so mysterious
Researchers who are interested in what leadership is are continually coming up with new ideas about it. One safe generalization, based on studies that have been made in the past 40 years, is that leadership is not nearly as mysterious as has been commonly thought.

Defining It

Inspiraton, salesmanship, and persuasion cannot have any impact unless there is some measure of *influence* over the audience or group. A person may be good at making dramatic speeches, but not inspire anyone to become a follower. The best propaganda in the world may not convince anybody. The most persuasive arguments may fall on deaf ears. Only if a group *wishes* to be influenced can a leader function. Leadership can be defined as the *ability to cause others to follow willingly, usually in initiating change.*[2] The ability to cause others to follow for a common goal is one sure way of recognizing leadership.

296

Following Leaders

There is nearly always an element of uncertainty or confusion that prompts people to choose and follow a leader. Sometimes followers are attracted to a leader who represents their values. They are willing to place themselves under the leadership of someone who can help them refine and act on values that are new to the followers, but that are so attractive that followers will adopt them and be willingly molded and educated by the leader to put those values into practice.[3]

Groups need leaders to reduce confusion and uncertainty

Groups need leadership to reduce uncertainty and confusion. If a group is functioning smoothly, very little leadership may be required. Leadership can have an important effect on a group's morale, especially since one of its chief functions is to keep the group focused on its goals. When it becomes necessary to stabilize unstable situations, aggressive leadership is required.

Leaders initiate change

Leaders initiate change, either by making decisions or by encouraging others to make them. A group's trust in its leader is affected by the quality of his decisions. Whether or not the decisions are good ones, people who follow leaders must accept the decisions made and the process used in making them.

Being a Leader

Well-functioning groups never remain leaderless, but a group doesn't necessarily have only one leader. A group *can* have one leader, but *every* member of a group can also be a leader. Some leaders prefer to monopolize power, while other leaders rely on all or several members of the group to individually display leadership. Group members who trust one another can mutually influence group decision making. People may hold back their abilities to lead for many reasons—perhaps because they lack confidence in themselves, perhaps because the situation does not allow leadership. However, *all people are potential leaders.* And, given the desire and the opportunity, people can develop into effective ones.

All people are potential leaders

Robert Dubin says:

> A group abhors confusion, including the confusion resulting from being leaderless. Every organization has more people in it who can exercise leadership, at least temporarily, than there are positions of leadership to be filled. It is often in situations of crisis, where an individual, not previously known to possess such qualities, becomes a leader, that officials of an organization learn where the potential leadership skills are to be found.[4]

As group goals and tasks change, new leaders and shifts in power occur. As work is delegated, authority roles change. Leadership in a group depends on the group standards and what leadership rules are acceptable.

Situational Theory

A leader in one situation is not necessarily a leader in all situations, even in the same group. Various situations call for various leadership responses. The same leader can display different personality traits to deal with different problems.[5] Of this concept of leadership, Ross and Hendry stated:

> leadership is not something that can be imported from the outside. Leadership is something that emerges, that grows, and that is achieved. It is not enough to have certain qualities of personality and performance that one associates with leadership. Nor is it enough to have experienced leadership acceptance in one or more groups in the past. Leadership is a *function of the situation,* the culture, context, and customs of a group or organization, quite as much as it is a function of personal attributes and group requirements.[6]

Leaders must assess the situation, personal needs, and anxieties

Effective leaders must be able to understand a situation from the points of view of all those involved, including their own. Further, leaders must be aware of their impact on others, and the impact others have on them. A low degree of defensiveness makes it possible to measure many relevant factors that must otherwise be ignored. Leaders must be able to assess all relevant factors in a situation, including personal needs and anxieties.[7]

POWER RELATIONSHIPS

Leaders obtain authority from groups

People who have authority are not necessarily leaders. All leaders have authority; but all authoritarians are not leaders. Leaders derive their authority *from* the group.

Supervisors and Leaders

Supervisors have a legitimate *right* to act authoritatively because they have an official position in an organization that carries with it specific kinds of authority over others.[8] For example,

Coercion is not leadership many supervisors have the authority to hire and fire. They may also abuse their authority and make the work environment miserable for their subordinates, and they may constantly harass the employees and lower morale by doing so. However, such supervisors are not displaying leadership; they are only displaying their authority. Coercion is *not* leadership.

Leaders, on the other hand, do not necessarily have legitimacy in their roles as leaders. They act and exercise power regardless of the formal structure within the organization. A revolutionary is an extreme example of a leader who acts with power, but without the legitimate right or formal authority to do so.[9]

Supervision and leadership can occur together, and, naturally, that is the most desirable situation. Supervisors with true leadership qualities can change and motivate the group to act. For example, managers who have high regard for their staff are often leaders. They have definite ideas about what they want done, but they make sure to communicate their goals *carefully*. They are usually sure of their decisions, but are interested in hearing what their subordinates think, particularly concerning the best way to carry out the group's goals. Such supervisors have authority, but they are able leaders as well, because their employees follow their directions.

Rensis Likert has shown that when a supervisor gives up leadership, or is not capable of it, informal leadership will automatically develop in its place. Groups tend to create group loyalty and team spirit—which encourages leadership roles. However, informal leadership is more likely than not to establish goals that run counter to organizational goals.[10]

Where External Power is Derived

Authority, or externally derived power, usually stems from *position* or rank. Heads of small firms, and managers of departments, have authority because of their job positions. The director of a corporation will influence numbers of people, because of the considerable authority he has in the organization. Because of the power vested in the position of the presidency of the United States, a President's policies influence the destinies of the nation and all its people.

External power may also come from *knowledge* or *expertise*. For example, a group applying for a grant may turn for leadership to someone who has applied for grants successfully in the past. A company interested in building a nuclear power plant will look to the most educated and experienced experts in the field of nuclear physics for leadership.

Leaders are given power by group consensus

It is common practice to grant leadership power to people who already have some authority. But leaders are given their power *only* by *group consensus*, without necessarily having any special status, such as position, skill, or education, to recommend them. Leaders gain power within a group gradually, by establishing trust and recognition. Consider the group concerned with getting a grant. Suppose they are discussing ways and means to achieve their goal with a person experienced in getting grants. Suppose further, that one of the members of the group, who has no prior information about grants, keeps coming up with one logical suggestion after another. By accepting the merit of this person's ideas, the group becomes willingly influenced, and thus grants that person leadership.

Authority is conferred; leadership is earned

The distinguishing difference between a leader and an authority figure is that the group *chooses* the leaders. "It is well accepted in management thinking today that leadership has to be earned, it cannot be conferred."[11]

Role Conflicts

Traditionally in business, it is customary to think of leaders as those with high positions—the ones at the helm making sweeping policy decisions. This may well be true, but it is also true that various kinds of leadership occur at any organizational level.[12] It cannot be too strongly stressed that a person in authority—and who makes decisions using that authority—does not necessarily have the knack of being followed willingly, in initiating change.

It is extremely convenient when people with responsibility turn out to be effective leaders. A supervisor who is a leader is welcomed by management and employees alike. But supervisors may be perfectly competent in task roles *without* having much skill at leading others. There are even times when authority conferred by status or rank can work against natural leadership ability. A group may distrust someone precisely because he or she has been granted so much power that it may not wish to confer more by allowing that person to assume leadership—even though he or she may have great leadership talent.

Power and leadership can be related in many ways. Although opportunities for leadership may be the result of having a position of authority, effective leadership itself is the result of using the authority with the willing cooperation of those who do not have that power.

Figure 10–1. Groups need leaders to reduce confusion and uncertainty, but it must be remembered that authority is conferred and leadership must be earned. *Courtesy of Santa Barbara City College (Photo by Bob Reilly)*

LEADERSHIP TRAITS

For many years, social scientists tried to isolate and analyze the personal characteristics necessary for people to be effective leaders. Most of these attempts were found to be unsound because the research conclusions were based on predetermined models of leadership. Many of these lists of traits have been helpful only in clarifying what people *think* leadership *should* be like.[13]

Today, researchers have examined more aspects of the human personality than was conceivable twenty years ago. And, remarkably few consistent leadership traits have been isolated.

Murray Ross and Charles Hendry designed a personality profile of a leader from the many tests given to identify leadership traits.[14] In general, effective leaders

1. are self-confident, well-integrated, and emotionally stable;
2. want to take leadership responsibility and are competent in handling new situations;
3. identify with the goals and values of the groups they lead;

4. are warm, sensitive, and sympathetic toward other people, and give practical, helpful suggestions;
5. are intelligent in relation to the other group members;
6. can be relied on to perform leadership functions continuously;
7. in elected or public positions usually possess more enthusiasm and capacity for expression than other types of leaders do.

Perhaps surprisingly, such traits as height, weight, appearance, self-control, dominance, alertness, cheerfulness, and geniality have little relation to leadership.

Leader's I.Q. is usually higher than the average of the group

Intelligence, you will notice from the profile, has only a relative relationship. The leaders usually have a higher intelligence than the average of those they lead, regardless of the group, whether it is a group of manual laborers or professional technicians. Intelligence as we know it is partly based on environmental factors such as formal education and past experience. The intelligence of a leader may not be much greater than that of his peers, but he is able to see the relationship between the task at hand and the personalities of those who must perform it. His perception of his followers is such that he is able to motivate them into action, and he also tends to have more abstract reasoning ability than his peers.

Psychologist Ghiselli found that an individual's intelligence level is an accurate indication of how successful he will be up to a certain level, but those with higher intelligence scores were less likely to be successful leaders. He believes that those individuals with superior intelligence and ability to deal with abstract concepts may not find managerial activities to be an intellectual challenge.[15] Do you agree?

The leadership personality does not depend in any way on reputation, position, wealth, acquaintances, or morals. Philosophical standards have not even proved applicable to measuring leadership characteristics. Alex Bavelas believes that "it may be a significant commentary on our society that there appears to be no particular correlation between a man's ethics and morals and his power to attract followers."[16] What do you think?

The leader reflects the group's values

A leader's personality traits tell just as much about the group as they do about the leader because the leader always reflects the group's standards and values. For example, the members of a chamber of commerce might choose to be influenced by the president of a large bank, while the members of a group studying crime in the cities might accept the leadership of a person living in a ghetto.

In spite of their role in groups, leaders are often still thought of only in terms of their personal abilities. They are still admired as extraordinary beings who do not have much in common with nonleaders. However, if you look again at the personality profile of a leader, you will see, as Alex Bavelas stresses, that "the abilities in question are the same as those possessed by all normal persons: individuals who become leaders are merely presumed to have them to a greater degree."[17]

Popularity

Popularity and leadership are not the same things. A socially popular person is (1) sought after in a social context within and outside of the group, and (2) "liked" during the decision-making activities of the group.

A popular leader is (1) effective in influencing the group's decisions and (2) sought after in the performance of other leadership functions, such as representing the group to others outside it.

SOCIAL POPULARITY

Being popular implies a desire for friendly personal interaction. A leader can be very decisive and even unpleasant during a group discussion, and very amiable among friends in a social setting.[18]

However, the desire to be well liked may inhibit certain leadership abilities. For instance, at a two-week training session at the National Training Laboratory in Bethel, Maine, one observer noticed that out of the 20 people in a group, the most popular person did not contribute very much at all to formulating group goals. "The individual in question was, in everybody's opinion, a 'nice guy.' He was pleasant to everyone. But he never suggested what the group should do, nor did he give strong support to any position stated by any other member of the group.[19]

Group members concerned with social relations often act as leaders in attempting to keep the group unified. One study reported that the best-liked people rate higher than average in releasing tension — mainly by smiling and laughing — and in indicating agreement rather than disagreement.[20]

LEADERSHIP POPULARITY

Helen Hall Jennings comments that, "No leader is invariably a 'pleasant' person . . . instead each is definite in her stand and will fight for what she considers 'right.' "[21] Assuming leadership by presenting new ideas and helping to make decisions may make a person admired but not liked. Part of "taking the risk" of leadership is that "taking a stand" does not always make a person popular with all group members.

The group leader is not the most popular

Robert Bales found that it is difficult for people ranked as leaders in ideas to also be ranked as well liked. In one set of experiments, the leader in ideas had an even chance of being best liked at the first meeting. By the end of the fourth meeting, the chances were about one in ten. Bales found that in most groups the best-liked person is second or third in the hierarchy of group participation.[22]

Philip Applewhite reports that the amount of group cohesiveness determines whether a leader is also sought after. When the group is unified, and group members are attractive to each other and to outsiders, the group's representative will be highly attractive also. When the group is falling apart, its leaders also lose social favor.[23]

GROUP RELATIONSHIPS

The best-liked person often supports the best-idea person

The best-liked person in a group and the best-idea person often rely on and support each other even when they don't agree with each other's point of view. The idea person, for instance, may be more outspoken about advancing group goals if he or she can depend on the socially oriented person to soothe the group's feelings. The well-liked person depends on conflict to perform the social leadership task. His leadership role is concerned with maintaining a positive atmosphere in which to make decisions; therefore, this person will be more tolerant of the expression of opposing views.[24]

The "social leader" and the "task leader"

This gives rise to the fact that a group might develop two types of leaders, the "social leader" and the "task leader," each one having their own function and each complementing the other in achieving the goal with a minimum of conflict.

The social leader maintains group unity

The task leader contributes most to the achievement of the task, but difficulty may arise, because in playing this role, the task leader may irritate people and injure the unity of the group. It is the social leader's role to restore and maintain group unity and satisfaction. Seldom can one person fill both roles, so it is important for the task leader to recognize the social leader and to achieve a coalition with him.[25]

FUNCTIONAL ROLES

What is a Leadership Function?

What, after all, do leaders do? How do leaders function in a business setting? The concept of functional leadership "stems from the underlying idea that leadership acts are those which help the group achieve its objectives ... to satisfy its 'needs'.... That person who can assist or facilitate the group most in reaching a satisfactory state is most likely to be re-garded as the leader . . ."[26]

Within one organization, there may be many leadership roles: Who does the long-range planning? Who is responsible for giving out information, for producing, evaluating, reward-ing? The list of leadership roles could go on and on. The func-tional approach tries to match personalities and styles with the kinds of leadership that must be exercised. First, an organiza-tion must decide what leadership functions are needed, then de-termine how these functions can be distributed most effectively.

Work groups have different leaders who perform different functions. For example, suppose a group's collective job is ad-justing the small parts that go into telephone equipment. One leader deals with all outsiders, including supervisors and union representatives. Another enforces the group's work standards and monitors on-the-job behavior. One leader handles external affairs, while another deals with internal matters—a system sim-ilar to the division of domestic and international problems in the President's cabinet. Divisions of leadership responsibility reflect group recognition of the strengths and weaknesses of the people involved. Occasionally, leadership responsibility is di-vided to maintain group cohesion.[27]

Two Types of Functions

Almost any member of a group may become a leader when cir-cumstances enable him or her to perform the required lead-ership functions. The function may be relatively straightforward, such as choosing the group goal, supervising performances, making decisions, or completing plans. Or the function may be much more complex, such as serving as the group's ego. When the leader in some way integrates the group's needs with *outside* realities, he or she is serving the same function that the individ-ual ego does for the individual person. Just as with an individ-ual ego, the group ego develops by (1) integrating the group's needs and goals with the reality outside the group; (2) satisfying interpersonal needs within the group; and (3) creating an atmo-sphere free of conflict for group members.[28]

Functional Behaviors

A leader's actions are determined by his or her role in the group. These actions reflect different kinds of *functional* roles the leader plays to keep the group unified and acting effectively. *None* of the functional roles discussed below necessarily applies to any single leader, and rarely do they all apply to one leader at the same time. Rather, they are roles that a leader at the time has, depending on the needs and demands of the group.

IDENTIFYING WITH GOALS

Group goals create group bonds. The more firmly leaders are identified with the group's goals, the more followers are likely to identify with the leaders. Additional trust and loyalty result when the leader is at least partially responsible for articulating group goals. Nonleaders may want their leader to take the major responsibility for determining group goals. However, setting goals is not a requisite for leadership. Some groups have long-established goals, and choose a leader whom they feel sure will help to attain them. Whether or not a leader has helped to formulate goals, he or she must always help the group attain them.[29]

MAKING DECISIONS

When a decision cannot be reached easily, some leaders simply make the decision, for better or worse, with group compliance.[30] The leader's wishes certainly have weight in making choices— how much depends on the distribution of power within the group. Leaders can help clarify possible alternatives of action, and a leader can prevent a group from stalemating or turning into a debating society.

RESOLVING DIFFERENCES

When groups experience internal differences, whether based on emotional or intellectual clashes, a leader often can resolve the differences.[31] In this function, the leader does not usually participate directly in the group process, as when group decisions are being made, but tries to stay uninvolved and neutral. In this arbitration role, the leader listens to all sides of the argument and helps group members arrive at a solution, or, ultimately, takes action to decide the issue alone. A leader is often put in the position of arbitrator to *prevent* serious group splintering. To be effective, a leader must be aware of and in agreement with group goals, the standards by which the group operates, and the sensitivities of its members.

A leader can act as an arbitrator for the group

New Organizational Functions

Warren G. Bennis maintains that the roles and functions of organizational leaders must become more flexible. The time is past when a leader can play an exclusive role, or serve an exclusive function to provide successful leadership. Bennis believes that leaders must become adaptable to rapidly changing situations, and learn to view their roles as temporary accommodations, at best.

Bennis lists four major reasons why such leadership flexibility is now necessary:[32]

1. We are experiencing rapid and unexpected change in society, and therefore, in organizations.
2. Organizations are growing by leaps and bounds, but the volume of an organization's traditional product is not enough to sustain growth.
3. Modern technology grows more and more complex, and integration between activities and persons of very diverse, highly specialized competence is required.
4. There is a psychological threat to leaders and others stemming from the movement toward more humanistic, democratic practices in managerial behavior.

Bennis feels that organizational leadership will become a more and more powerful social force as our environment becomes more unpredictable and turbulent. Organizations are faced with complex and diverse problems that will require at least as much skill at interpersonal communication as technical competence. Organizations are moving so fast that they are encountering problems they have never before had to solve. Table 10–1 lists what Bennis believes to be the formidable leadership tasks of the present.

By *developing rewarding human systems,* Bennis means that we must come to grips with the fact that economic rewards are not enough to motivate employees. Employees want to develop their talents and utilize their training, to continue to learn and to develop their full human potential.

No one leader can any longer comprehend or control the complexities of the modern organization. The concept of developing *executive constellations* simply recognizes those limits and indicates that leaders at the top must begin to collaborate by building cabinets or teams.

A *collaborative climate* is one in which the organizational structure is flexible, talents are utilized, and the organization's members are in agreement with organizational goals. Furthermore, there is an atmosphere of openness, trust, and cooperation. A balance is achieved between a high degee of autonomy and group participation in making decisions.

Organizations resist change while at the same time seeking it. Modern organizations are extremely dependent on new discoveries, but our society has not adapted *emotionally* to the process of change. Tensions due to the speed of change must be reduced, and an environment created with increased tolerance for human diversity.

Table 10-1. New Organizational Leadership Functions

PROBLEM	TASKS OF THE LEADER
Integration The problem of integrating individual needs and organizational goals	Developing rewarding human systems
Social Influence The problem of distributing power	Developing executive constellations
Collaboration The problem of producing mechanisms for the control of conflict	Building a collaborative climate
Adaptation The problem of responding to a turbulent, uncertain environment	Identification with the adaptive process
Identity The problem of clarity, commitment, and consensus to organizational goals	Developing supraorganizational goals
Revitalization The problem of growth and decay	Organizational "self-renewal"

Source: Warren G. Bennis, "New Patterns of Leadership for Tomorrow's Organizations," in *Readings in Industrial and Organizational Psychology*, edited by Edward L. Deci, B. von Haller Gilmer, and Harry W. Karn (New York: McGraw-Hill Book Co., 1972), p. 319.

Organizations also experience fragmentation, intergroup conflict, power plays, and rigid compartmentalization. Leaders are needed who can transcend special interests and bring people together. To do this, commitments that transcend the organization—supraorganizational goals—must be found.

Organizations must take responsibility for their own *self-renewal*—they must either grow or decay. Leaders must be found who can participate in the organization's social evolution, against unknown odds. Leaders must gather what information they can. Then they must set the future in motion by gambling reasonably but fearlessly.[33]

BEHAVIOR STYLES

Along with different leadership traits and functions, the *styles* in which leaders perform can also be described. The various styles are based on types of *control* leaders exercise in a group and their behavior toward group members.

Theorists of behavior styles did not dismiss the force of leaders' personalities, but they found that leaders use leadership styles consistent with their personalities. For example, someone who has trouble trusting other people's judgment will tend toward an authoritarian leadership style. Someone else will choose to be authoritarian simply as a way to save time. One person's lack of trust and the other's desire for efficiency are both consistent with the authoritarian leadership style. As this example indicates, leaders' personalities derive from so many different factors that many different kinds of behavior are chosen to satisfy a wide spectrum of needs and desires.

Given the wide variety of personality differences, some researchers decided that it would be more productive to examine the *structure* of the interactions between leaders and their followers than to study the personal reasoning behind the adoption of particular styles. The examination of leadership behavior indicates that people are not "born leaders," but can be trained in leadership techniques. Some researchers believe that concentrating on learning specific leadership skills and ignoring the significance of personality traits will create mechanical leadership behavior—a robot-like version of true leadership. Others believe that knowing how to analyze leadership structures helps to dispel some of the mystery associated with leadership. They also believe that learning how to perform leadership skills instills confidence in people so that they will more readily assume leadership roles.

Leadership Quiz

Take the following quiz and find out something about yourself and your leadership capabilities.
1. People work mostly for money and status rewards.
   a. I agree
   b. I disagree
   c. I feel it is sometimes true, sometimes not.
2. People need to be "inspired" (pep talks) or pushed or driven.
   a. I agree.
   b. I disagree.
   c. I feel the statement is sometimes true, sometimes not.
3. People are naturally compartmentalized; work demands are entirely different from leisure activities.
   a. I agree.
   b. I disagree.
   c. I feel the statement is sometimes true, sometimes not.
4. People naturally resist change; they prefer to stay in the old ruts.
   a. I agree.
   b. I disagree.
   c. I feel the statement is sometimes true, sometimes not.
5. Jobs are primary and must be done; people are selected, trained, and fitted to predefined jobs.
   a. I agree.
   b. I disagree.
   c. I feel the statement is sometimes true, sometimes not.

6. The main force keeping people productive in their work is the desire to achieve their personal and social goals.
   a. I agree.
   b. I disagree.
   c. I feel the statement is sometimes true, sometimes not.
7. People are naturally integrated; when work and play are too sharply separated, both deteriorate.
   a. I agree.
   b. I disagree.
   c. I feel the statement is sometimes true, sometimes not.
8. People naturally tire of monotonous routine and enjoy new experiences; in some degree everyone is creative.
   a. I agree.
   b. I disagree.
   c. I feel the statement is sometimes true, sometimes not.
9. People are primary and seek self-realization; jobs must be designed, modified, and fitted to people.
   a. I agree.
   b. I disagree.
   c. I feel the statement is sometimes true, sometimes not.
10. People constantly grow; it is never too late to learn; they enjoy learning and increasing their understanding and capability.
   a. I agree.
   b. I disagree.
   c. I feel the statement is sometimes true, sometimes not.

Now is the time to score your quiz.
SCORING

1.	a. X	5.	a. X	8.	a. Y
	b. Y		b. Y		b. X
	c. neither		c. neither		c. neither
2.	a. X	6.	a. Y	9.	a. Y
	b. Y		b. X		b. X
	c. neither		c. neither		c. neither
3.	a. X	7.	a. Y	10.	a. Y
	b. Y		b. X		b. X
	c. neither		c. neither		c. neither
4.	a. X				
	b. Y				
	c. neither				

If you answered more than five questions with the letter C, it is probably because you have not given too much consideration to leadership. Perhaps this chapter will give you more ideas to think about concerning leadership. Some people might think they are playing it safe by answering C, but they are not really giving leadership in terms of direction and solution. If you answered A for the first five questions and B for the second five questions you would be considered an X leader. By contrast, if you answered B for the first five questions and A for the second five questions you could be considered a strong Y leader. Questions 1–5 identify with the X leader and questions 6–10 identify with the Y leader. Are you more of an X leader or a Y leader? Read on to find out more about this theory of leadership and yourself.

Behavior theorists developed a scale of leadership qualities based on: (1) the forces at work within a leader; (2) the forces at work within followers; and (3) the arena in which the leader and followers interact.

McGregor's X and Y theory
Such a theory, developed by Douglas McGregor, has been popularly known as the X and Y theory of leadership.[34] During the "sweat shops" of the early twentieth century the leadership style demonstrated by the supervisors was primarily autocratic or "X" in nature. Today it is still in operation, and many believe that people work mostly for money and status rewards. However, McGregor believed that leaders can have a feeling for the employee as well as for the accomplishment of the company goal. The participative leader, or "Y" leader, believes that many people naturally aspire for independent responsibility and self-fulfillment. Further, that people need to feel respected as capable of assuming responsibility and correcting mistakes on their own. In brief, the X leader is interested in production and the Y leader is interested in employees.

Autocratic Leaders

Autocratic leaders or X leaders leave no doubt about who is in charge. They use the power they have acquired by their rank, knowledge, or skills to reward and punish as they see fit. Their ability to command is the major or only method by which things get done. This posture does not imply hostility or negativity, but rather sureness of will. Authoritarian leaders give orders and assume that people will respond obediently. This style can be "soft-sell", but is usually perceived as "hard-sell"—in either case, subordinates are permitted little freedom.

The autocratic style is efficient. Little time is needed to consult with others during the decision-making process. The style works particularly well in developed situations when decisions must be made and acted on quickly and without question. The style of leadership in the military during time of war is an excellent example.

Some employees adapt well to an autocratic system—instructions are clear and often detailed. Any ambiguity can be straightened out easily. These employees would feel unfair demands were being made on them if they were given more freedom to make their own decisions.

McDonald's success with the X theory
The strong dominant X theory can be seen in the McDonald hamburger chain. Their success is founded on following strictly the company policy of Q, S, and C, or *quality, service,* and *cleanliness*. The rigid training programs of potential

managers, the uniform structure of each franchise, the production line method of serving, and the automatic program of inventory all point to the success of the X theory in progress.[35]

Other employees resent and resist leadership that excludes them from any involvement. Since autocratic communication is essentially one-way, the resulting lack of feedback can lead to misunderstandings and subsequent errors. The lack of feedback also means that the leader does not always know what subordinates are thinking. Making decisions without first listening to the advice of others can result in poor decisions.

Participative Leaders

Participative leaders or Y leaders invite decision sharing. Their style calls for subordinates to exercise high degrees of both responsibility and freedom. They use as little authoritarian control as possible, and are concerned with group interrelationships as well as getting the job done.

There are two types of participative leaders. *Democratic* leaders who confer final authority to the group; they abide by whatever the group decides, with no exceptions. *Consultive* leaders who require a high degree of involvement from employees, but make it clear that they alone have the authority to make final decisions.

Participative leaders do not try to disguise their power to make the final decision, particularly when faced with crises. But they also encourage employees to contribute opinions and information, and to participate in the decision-making process as much as possible.

Participative leaders request and expect constant feedback, a practice that provides them with the best available information, ideas, suggestions, talent, and experience. When people participate in making the decisions that affect their lives, they support those decisions more enthusiastically and try hard to make them work. Most people demonstrate high productivity when they are given a fair amount of freedom. They maximize their potential in creative and productive ways and experience personal satisfaction and accomplishment in their work tasks. Further, when most people are given a little leeway, they develop and grow, personally and in job competence. Often they will take on more responsibility than their job descriptions call for because of the pleasure they take in their work.

Participative leadership can be very time consuming and requires a great deal of energy. Participation can sometimes mean that little or no planning gets done at all, which can result in situations getting out of control. Although the participative style can be terribly inefficient in some circumstances, in others, the relaxed atmosphere that accompanies the style may give only the appearance of inefficiency—while, in fact, the work is being accomplished very effectively.

There are certainly ambiguities attached to participative leadership. For it certainly does not mean that one considers the employee first and the company second. The employee-centered supervisor who gets the best results tends to recognize that high production is also among his responsibilities. Texas Instruments, Inc. has followed the Y theory of leadership through its P + A or *People plus Assets* effectiveness program. The company president feels the success of the firm is the human element. He feels that there has been increased production through motivation by management's willingness to try new approaches to any given problem. An example of this is retiring employees at age 55 and rehiring them for different positions. The benefit to the person is a pension, plus a productive life with additional income. The company benefits too by allowing necessary changes in management and putting an experienced person on the payroll who needs little training. Texas Instruments has found little worker turnover with the installation of P + A, because the company has concern for the individual.[36]

Texas Instrument's success with the Y theory (margin note)

Participation can be used by people with authority as a guise for shirking their own responsibilities and as a way to pass the buck to others. Participative leaders must take care that *real* participation occurs, when they call for it. People resent acts of bad faith—if asked for recommendations, they do not like to see them ignored or rejected without further discussion.

In studying the task of leading employees while maintaining a satisfactory level of production, we come to the problem of deciding which is more viable, the autocratic leader who is task oriented or the participative leader who is employee oriented. In actual practice, however, it must be pointed out that each leadership role has its place depending upon the group of followers, the time span, the problem, and the environment.

In Table 10–2, a comparison of leadership styles is presented. Which one is the most comfortable for you?

Free-rein Leaders

Free-rein leaders are also referred to as *laissez-faire* leaders or *group-centered* leaders. Free-rein leaders are almost completely nondirective. They communicate goals and guidelines, and then allow employees to meet them without issuing further directions, unless specifically requested. One goal is to involve all nonleaders in participating as equally as possible in a project.

Table 10–2. Traits of X and Y Leaders

AUTOCRATIC STYLE X THEORY TRAITS	PARTICIPATIVE STYLE Y THEORY TRAITS
task oriented	employee oriented
interested in details	interested in generalizing
efficiency minded	democratic to very permissive
time and motion studies	sensitive to individual's needs
knows the product	knows the people
	aware of morale
interested in promoting himself	trains his replacement
fast in arriving at decisions	slow in decisions
tends to be an extrovert	tends more to be an introvert
self-appointed or company appointed	group appointed
employee knows where he stands 　with the supervisor	employee is not always sure 　where he stands with 　the supervisor
close supervision	general supervision
task specialist	maintenance specialist
paternalistic	democratic

Although free-rein leaders have ultimate decision-making authority, they often choose not to use it, in accord with the stated group goal of solving problems together.

This leadership system offers the greatest use of time and resources. The highest possible degree of authority is vested in the group—it is almost as if the group were leaderless. This laissez faire atmosphere can motivate people to initiate and carry out complex work plans efficiently and responsibly.

Free-rein leaders give leadership roles to group members. The theory of participation can extend so far that some groups seem leaderless or led by the group rather than by an individual. Even when a group has an appointed leader, that leader may not use the authority at his disposal. Such leaders are known as free-rein leaders.

Guidelines are established by a good free-rein leader but a day-to-day direction is seldom used. Route salesmen typically cannot have close supervision. To some degree free-rein leadership can be found among certain professional workers, such as engineers, scientists, and teachers, as there is a limited amount of supervision on people in these areas. In some research organizations a supervisor may develop a pattern of leadership that may appear laissez faire to the outsider.

DEGREES OF LEADERSHIP

In every organization a different style of leadership will be demonstrated, from the strong autocratic to the liberal free rein. In studies done by Tannenbaum, Weschler, and Massarik,[37] leadership is viewed along a continuum as shown in Figure 10–2. At the left the autocratic leader makes and announces the decision. The benevolent autocratic or X leader presents the decision subject to changes, seeks ideas, and sells the decision. The participative leader, Y leader or consultive supervisor, seeks ideas before he decides. The democratic leader decides with the group, on a "one-man, one-vote" basis. The free-rein leader asks the group to decide on their own.

Self-fulfilling Prophecy

Pygmalion management

Do you believe in self-fulfilling prophecy? What you expect of others determines the reactions of others. If you expect low achievement they will produce little. People in some organizational settings become X-minded. If treated as inferior, lazy, materialistic, dependent, irresponsible, etc., they become so. People in different organizational settings become Y-minded. If treated as responsible, independent, understanding, goal-achieving, growing, and creative people, they tend to become so. The term "Pygmalion management" comes from this concept. Manage-

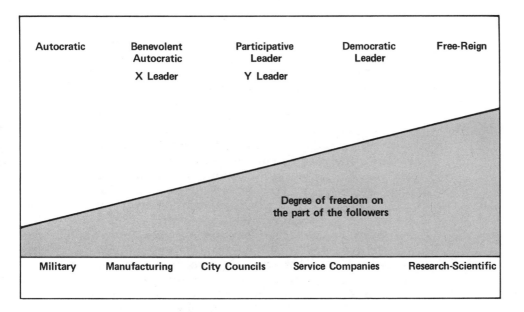

Figure 10–2. Comparisons of leadership styles and societal groups. Based on studies done by Tannenbaum, Weschler, and Massarik.

Source: Robert Tannenbaum and Warren Schmidt, "How to Choose a Leadership Pattern." Harvard Business Review, *March–April 1958, p. 97.*

ment can expect elegant performance from an ignorant employee if the training is good, and, most important, if the expectations and responsibilities are high enough. Do you feel there is some truth in this theory that is expressed by leaders through their actions and attitudes?

LEADERSHIP COMMUNICATIONS

Speech Patterns

Leaders tend to speak more

Some researchers began to wonder if they could detect or predict group leaders by communication skills alone. In one experiment, speech behavior was studied. Twenty-two groups made up of three people discussed a human relations case study for twenty minutes, and then chose a representative (leader) from each group to continue to discuss the same problem with other representatives. Members chosen talked on the average of 44.8 percent of the meeting time, while nonrepresentatives talked an average of 27.6 percent of the time. Those chosen to be leaders made a significantly high number of suggestions, asked for suggestions from the two others, and gave background information to the case study.[38]

One who speaks first builds a reputation

Robert Bales tried to determine how leaders gain influence through their speech behaviors by examining communication patterns among group members. He found that unequal participation affects how groups organize. The person who consistently speaks first builds a reputation. Someone who proves successful at solving problems will attempt to solve more problems, and in this way, assumes a leadership position.[39]

Another researcher found that the communication patterns leaders use serve different purposes. If the purpose is to influence attitudes, the content of the communication will be highly redundant, stressing a few points over and over again, but it will be expressed in slightly different ways. In this strategy, the form varies, but the message stays the same. If the purpose is to achieve action, the communication will offer much more content in a single style. The strategy here is that the form stays constant, but the message keeps changing.[40] For example, someone running for public office has essentially *one* message: "Vote for me"; the message may be delivered in many different ways and backed up by many different reasons, but it is always the same message. The same person, having been in office for two years and now required to make a speech about why the budget isn't adequate to pay municipal employees, will deliver a very different sort of speech. His tone will stay constant, probably sweetly reasonable, but the message will vary enormously in content as reasons and rationalizations pile up.

Group Structure Patterns

In another experiment, communication patterns were related to group structures and studied over a period of time. Groups of five journalism students were assigned a project in which they were to simulate the work on an actual newspaper staff. All group communication was recorded. Groups were structured in three ways: (1) work assignments were completely unstructured, and no roles were assigned; (2) a leader was appointed to help determine assignments; and (3) no leader was appointed, and everyone was assigned a specific job. Some leadership always appeared in these groups, sometimes in spite of assigned leadership. At the end of the experiment, participants were asked to summarize their perceptions of leadership, and this is the pattern that emerged:

1. When group members perceived an increase in leadership, the uncertainty and disorganization of their communication decreased. It could more easily be predicted which members would talk to which other members.

2. As the group became more accomplished in arriving at its goals, the communication decreased, and the total time required to do the job also decreased.

3. Similar communication patterns occurred when groups were assigned a leader or specific roles. As expected, the perceptual and organizational differences changed most in the unstructured group because leadership or job roles had to emerge. The performance level of each group differed vastly and could not be correlated to the group structures, indicating that it made a difference who was appointed or chosen to lead.[41]

It has also been found that as group size changes, leadership roles change. As groups become larger, leaders must concentrate on attaining group goals and maintaining group solidarity. Leaders must be more "firm and impartial" in enforcing the policies they feel will move the group toward its goals. The larger the group, the more a leader is required to communicate to maintain group unity. At the same time, there are fewer personal interactions, and impersonal direction is displayed to a much greater degree than before.[42]

THE QUADIKA OF LEADERSHIP

The Russians have a word for their political leadership program—Troika, which means three leaders of equal power. A coined word, "Quadika" means four equal parts to leadership: the leader, the group, the problem, and the solution (Figure 10–3). Each will influence the other and its effectiveness. The structure of the group may somewhat determine which leadership style would best encourage action and change. The problem itself may determine whether quick action is required or if slow positive action would be best. All three forces will cause interdependent action on the solution, and the solution will in turn react on the group, the initial problem, and the effectiveness of the leader. The solution can change the group, the leader, and even the nature of the problem.

As we have seen, the personality traits of leaders, the functional role of leaders, and the group to be led, as well as the problem that must be solved by the leader and the environment in which it exists, all contribute to which leadership style would be most effective. It may be academic as to which is more important, the complexities of the task or the nature of human relations. However, the leader, the group, and the problem are all dynamic and with each passing day they effect the best possible goal or solution.

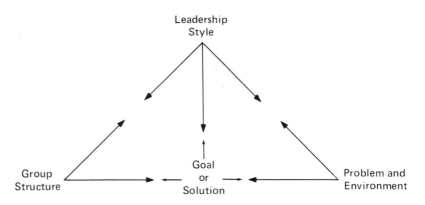

Figure 10–3. The Quadika of leadership.

SUMMARY

Many people admire or fear leadership and do not recognize the leadership potential in themselves. Leaders initiate and facilitate change by interacting with members of groups to make decisions about matters having a high risk or uncertainty factor. Followers follow because they already agree with the changes the leader is initiating, or because they want to be changed. Leadership is not always aggressive or autocratic; often the best test of effective leadership is how smoothly a group functions. Groups *always* have leaders, and new leaders emerge as group shifts occur. In fact, every situation calls for different leadership responses. Because of the many functional variables inherent in each situation, there are plenty of opportunities to demonstrate different leadership traits and styles.

Authority, derived from position, knowledge, expertise, or status, may be very advantageous to leaders, but is no measure of leadership skill. Leaders gain their authority over a group by group consensus alone.

Much research into the personality traits of leaders has led to the conclusion that leadership is directly attributable to relatively few traits, such as self-confidence, responsibility, sensitivity, relative intelligence, reliability, and enthusiasm. In fact, a leader's traits are not out of the ordinary, although they are highly developed. Being well liked socially and being a well-liked leader are two different things; they sometimes go together and sometimes do not. Often, social leaders and idea leaders are mutually supportive. Both inner-directed and other-directed leaders have successful records, again depending to a great extent on their social milieu.

The main function of leaders is to help groups achieve their objectives. To do this, leaders must also perform many different roles in their groups. Leaders often unify groups by becoming symbols, or behavior models, or by being identified with group goals. Practically, they initiate changes, help make decisions, and resolve differences. Because of vast and rapid technological and social changes, modern organizations must find new ways for leaders to function more flexibly in organizational structures.

Leaders should choose leadership behavior patterns that are most consistent with their personalities, the function to be performed, and the situation at hand. The most common behavioral types are autocratic, participative, and free-rein leaders. On a continuum scale, these types fall somewhere between strict authoritarianism and completely open group participation.

Leaders communicate differently from nonleaders. They talk more, and their speech is laden with suggestions, information, and encouragement for others to participate. Leaders are quick to utilize different speech patterns to achieve their purposes. Effective leadership unifies group goals, evidenced by less group discussion and an increase in efficiency.

The effectiveness of a leader is not always determined by the person's personality traits, but by the composite relationship of the group to the problem, the environment, the feasible solution, and the leader. All situations do not require the same type of leader.

WHICH LEADER WOULD YOU PICK?

Case Study #1

Mr. Lockwood is the president of the Preston Plastics Corporation. Recently, it was decided by the Board of Directors that it would be profitable for the corporation to open its own Marketing Department. Mr. Lockwood has been directed to pick a person who he feels is capable of heading the department, and then putting this person in charge of getting the department on its feet. After considering a number of good men, Mr. Lockwood has narrowed the field down to two possible choices, Ted Edmonds and Pete Hernandez.

Ted Edmonds has a good track record with the company. He was hired eight years ago, and through the years he has shown a good deal of drive and initiative in all of his endeavors. Ted is an aggressive young man, and he has received the nickname of go-getter in his department. Although Ted seems to be more concerned at times with ends rather than means, he is very efficient and he is considered a good leader by those who work under him. As one worker stated, "Although he can get rough with you at times, you always know where you stand with him, and when you've done a good job, he lets you know it." Ted is also credited with accepting full responsibility, in all cases, and making quick decisions when action is called for.

Pete Hernandez has been with the company for eleven years. He is well liked by all in his department, and his work is first rate. Pete's leadership style differs from Ted's in that Pete is not as aggressive and quick to act as Ted. Before Pete makes a decision, he generally consults others who he feels can contribute further information on a given subject. This oftentimes includes those who work under him. Those who work under Pete consider him a good leader, and state that the atmosphere of participation produced by Pete really encourages their utmost individual output while on the job. This can be seen by the production increase which soon occurred when Pete became the head of his work force.

Which man should Mr. Lockwood choose to head the new department? Why?

Terms and Concepts Students Should Know

authority	autocratic leaders	task leader
power	free-rein leaders	X and Y theories of leadership
social popularity	group structure patterns	participative leaders
social leader	formal authority	leadership communications
arbitrator	leadership popularity	quadika of leadership

Bibliography

1. McGREGOR, DOUGLAS, *The Human Side of Enterprise,* New York, McGraw-Hill Book Company, 1960.

2. TANNENBAUM, ROBERT, IRVING WESCHLER, and FRED MASSARIK, *Leadership and Organizations, A Behavioral Science Approach,* McGraw-Hill Book Company, 1961.

3. SANFORD, AUBREY C., *Human Relations, The Theory and Practice of Organizational Behavior,* 2nd ed., Columbus, Charles Merrill Publishing Co., 1977. Chapter 7.

4. LUTHANS, FRED, *Organizational Behavior,* 2nd ed., New York, McGraw-Hill Book Company, Inc. 1977, Chapter 18.

Footnotes

[1] Chester I. Barnard, "Dilemmas of Leadership in the Democratic Process," *Human Relations in Administration*, 3rd ed., edited by Robert Dubin (Englewood Cliffs, N.J.: Prentice-Hall, 1968), p. 390.

[2] Robert Dubin, *The World of Work: Industrial Society and Human Relations* (Englewood Cliffs, N.J.: Prentice-Hall, 1958), p. 389.

[3] William F. Dowling, Jr. and Leonard R. Sayles, *How Managers Motivate: The Imperatives of Supervision* (New York: McGraw-Hill Book Co., 1971), p. 93.

[4] Dubin, *World of Work*, p. 393.

[5] Alex Bavelas, "Leadership: Man and Function," in *The Nature and Scope of Management*, edited by Maneck S. Wadia (Glenview, Ill.: Scott, Foresman and Co., 1966), p. 152.

[6] Murray G. Ross and Charles E. Hendry, *New Understandings of Leadership* (New York: Association Press, 1957), p. 28.

[7] Chris Argyris, *Integrating the Individual and the Organization* New York: John Wiley and Sons, 1964), pp. 215–216.

[8] Philip B. Applewhite, *Organizational Behavior* (Englewood Cliffs, N.J.: Prentice-Hall, 1965), p. 111.

[9] *Ibid.*

[10] Rensis Likert, "Motivation: The Core of Management," in *The Nature and Scope of Management*, edited by Maneck S. Wadia (Glenview, Ill.: Scott, Foresman and Co., 1966), p. 146.

[11] Malcolm P. McNair, "Thinking Ahead: What Price Human Relations?" in *The Nature and Scope of Management*, edited Maneck S. Wadia (Glenview, Ill.: Scott, Foresman and Co., 1966), p. 161.

[12] Robert Dubin, ed., *Human Relations in Administration*, 3rd ed. (Englewood Cliffs, N.J.: Prentice-Hall, 1968), p. 387.

[13] Bavelas, "Leadership," p. 151.

[14] Ross and Hendry, *Understandings of Leadership*, pp. 59–60.

[15] Edwin Gheselli, "Managerial Talent," *American Psychologist*, Vol. 18, October 1963, p. 631.

[16] Bavelas, "Leadership," p. 152.

[17] *Ibid.*, p. 151.

[18] William Foote Whyte, *Organizational Behavior: Theory and Application* (Homewood, Ill.: Richard D. Irwin and Co., 1969), pp. 176–77.

[19] *Ibid.*, p. 177.

[20] Robert F. Bales, "How People Interact in Conferences," in *Communication and Culture*, edited by Alfred G. Smith, (New York: Holt, Rinehart and Winston, 1966), p. 101.

[21] Ross and Hendry, *Understandings of Leadership*, p. 30.

[22] Bales, "How People Interact," p. 101.

[23] Warren G. Bennis, "New Patterns of Leadership for Tomorrow's Organizations," in *Readings in Industrial and Organizational Psychology*, edited by Edward L. Deci, B. von Haller Gilmer, and Harry W. Karn (New York: McGraw-Hill Book Co., 1972), p. 322.

[24] Bales, "How People Interact," p. 101.

[25] Amitai Etzioni, "Dual Leadership in Complex Organizations," *American Sociological Review*, October 1965, pp. 688–698.

[26] Bavelas, "Leadership," p. 153.

[27] Dowling and Sayles, *How Managers Motivate*, p. 92.

[28] Applewhite, *Organizational Behavior*, p. 123.

[29] *Ibid.*, p. 387.

[30] *Ibid.*, p. 388.

[31] *Ibid.*

[32] Bennis, "New Patterns of Leadership," pp. 317–318.

[33] *Ibid.*, pp. 318–321.

[34] Douglas McGregor, *The Human Side of Enterprise* (New York: McGraw-Hill Book Co., 1960).

[35] "The Hamburger that Conquered the Country," *Time*, 17 September 1973.

[36] "How T.I. Turns its People On," *Business Week*, 29 September 1973.

[37] Robert Tannenbaum, Irving Weschler, and Fred Massarik, *Leadership and Organizations, A Behavioral Science Approach* (New York: McGraw-Hill Book Co., 1961), pp. 88–100.

[38] Applewhite, *Organizational Behavior*, p. 116.

[39] Bales, "How People Interact," p. 101.

[40] Applewhite, *Organizational Behavior*, pp. 128–129.

[41] Wilbur Schramm, "Information Theory and Mass Communication," in *Communication and Culture*, edited by Alfred G. Smith (New York: Holt, Rinehart and Winston, 1966), pp. 532–533.

[42] Applewhite, *Organizational Behavior*, p. 129.

Training
and Human Behavior
" You Make It Seem So Easy!" ▪ ▪ ▪ ▪ ▪

■ ■ ■ ■ ■ ■ ■ ■ ■ ■ ■ ■ ■ ■ ■ ■ ■ ■ ■ ■

OBJECTIVES

After reading this chapter you should be able to:

1. Discuss the two major approaches to training:
   A. Traditional method,
   B. Human relations method.

2. Discuss training from the point of view of
   A. Learning and attitudes,
   B. Goals and methods,
   C. Effectiveness.

3. Relate the need for employee orientation on a new job in relation to
   A. Induction,
   B. Policies and practices.

4. Describe the advantages and disadvantages of the following instructional methods of training:
   A. Written material,
   B. Lectures,
   C. Programmed instruction,
   D. Audio-visual aids.

5. Describe the "simulation techniques" used in training. Also discuss your personal reaction to each method.
   A. In-basket method,
   B. Case method,
   C. Incident process,
   D. Management games,
   E. Role-playing.

6. Discuss the following "experiential" methods of training. Develop ideas that are "pro" and "con" for each experiential method.
   A. Sensitivity training,
   B. Transactional analysis,
   C. Assertiveness training,
   D. Transcendental meditation.

7. Discuss the reasoning behind planned organizational development methods of company training. Why must the employer change the employee to change the attitude of the company?

Take a look at these questions and check your reactions to them. Do you have some attitudes toward training programs already that may influence your review of the chapter?

What is the difference between job training and general education?

Why do you think some training programs are worthwhile, while others are not?

Do you know what transactional analysis means? Or such terms as transcendental meditation, assertiveness training, or organizational development?

Are you aware of how much a company's orientation can affect job attitudes?

What are the differences between instructional, simulation, experiential, and organizational training methods?

TRAINING ASPECTS

Misunderstood orders are costly, they waste time and often material. These are times when supervisors must train and direct employees in areas in which they have no experience on materials that are expensive and on procedures that are complex. Therefore, the likelihood of errors because of communication problems becomes more common in our technical world. It is wise then to consider training programs.

What is Training?

Before attending a conference, salespeople are "briefed" on how to represent their firm. A lawyer has just seen a client who wants to file suit against a factory for unnecessarily polluting the environment. The lawyer has never handled a case like this one, and consults with another lawyer on what steps to take. A pharmacy assistant attends a class about the uses and effects of some of the latest drugs. An ice-cream parlor attendant learns how to scoop ice cream to minimize muscle strain. The supervisor of a construction crew attends role-playing classes in an attempt to learn how to relate to subordinates more effectively.

All these people are engaged in formal or informal training. Many kinds of training are vital to today's working world. Without it, misunderstandings are likely to occur, which often result in costly wastes of time, money, and human energy and emotion. Nowadays, employees are rarely expected to work at tasks for which receive no training. Managers who do not know how to work with people are at as severe a disadvantage as drill press operators who do not know how to run a drill press. In the complicated, technical world in which we live, even a job that appears simple may have many complex aspects to it. Without job training, employees are put in the position of having to "muddle through" as best they can.

Training is the *process of transmitting and receiving information related to problem solving.* Educational programs transmit information for its own sake, with no expectation of how and when the information will be used—if ever. The specific purpose of training is to communicate information that is applicable to practical situations. After training, trainees should be able to demonstrate changes in behavior or performance that contribute to their abilities to deal skillfully with specific problems. People learn all the time. The accumulation of what is learned during the process of working at a job is called "job experience." Training, however, implies a formal commitment of time—be it ten minutes or six months—set aside to learn specific, directly applicable information.

Training can change behavior

Training implies formal commitment of time

Traditional vs. human relations

Training can be separated into two major categories: traditional and human relations. *Traditional* training is concerned with learning skills and theoretical concepts that can be applied to performing the mechanics of a job. Traditional skills are oriented to the "how to" aspects of work. *Human relations* training passes on skills dealing with the ability to interact with others: co-workers with co-workers and supervisors with subordinates. Human relations training is concerned with the attitudes and assumptions that people have about their jobs, about themselves, and about other people.

What Is Learning?

Learning means change

To learn is to change. To demonstrate change, a person's capabilities must change. Learning has taken place when students: (1) *know* more than they knew before; (2) *understand* what they have not understood before; (3) develop a *skill* that was not developed before; (4) *feel* differently about a subject than they have felt before; or (5) *appreciate* a subject that they have not appreciated before.[1]

Robert Mager, a learning specialist, comments further on the intentions of training:

> We talk about developing skills, or competencies, or attitudes, or enthusiasm. We talk about encouraging growth or self-actualization, about helping the student to develop, or about assisting him to develop to his fullest potential. Regardless of the words we use to describe our teaching goals, and regardless of the goals, *no teaching goal can be reached unless the student is influenced to become different in some way than he was before the instruction was undertaken.* [Italics added.][2]

Attitudes about Learning

Some learning techniques have been traditionally employed for transmitting task-oriented data, skills, and concepts, whereas others have been developed to encourage better human relations. The training process itself, however, always involves human relations because the purpose of training is to produce change. The attitudes about the training greatly affect the ability to learn and thus to change. Consider these questions, all of which affect the success of a training program: What is the attitude of the trainee before and after training? What is the company policy about training? Do managers follow an extensive training policy grudgingly or with enthusiasm? What attitudes do supervisors have toward newly trained personnel? Do they encourage employees to use their new training or to continue in the old methods? How does the trainer feel about the subject being taught — excited or bored?

Positive attitudes from everyone concerned with training and its spheres of potential influence help to make the learning process a worthwhile experience.

Goals and Methods

Whether an employee comes to a job with previous experience or is trained by the company after being hired, job training of some kind, formal or informal, must go on. Often the most difficult problem in job training is recognizing the *need* for it. Managers must be convinced to allow time and money for training endeavors. Once the need has been demonstrated, there are the major headaches of finding appropriate training programs, or setting them up, or working out how to implement training and still have time on the job to get work done.

The training director or a committee on training may select areas that need training programs and prepare a priority list of those areas selected. Such a list might look like this:

AREAS NEEDING TRAINING PROGRAMS

1. New employee orientation
2. Stock room
3. Reservation desk
4. Evaluation of programs

First select the goals — then the methods

A distinction must be made between training goals and the methods by which the goals are undertaken. Training methods are appropriate only according to the training goals. Methods can be compared only in terms of objectives. For instance, role-playing does not help employees learn more about running a drill, although it may help people learn how to become better managers. Therefore, training goals must be clearly defined before a specific program is undertaken. Once the goals are well formed, the methods fall into place. The content of a training program may not be learned adequately if the appropriate methods are not used.

In looking at the list that has been developed for training needs and the goals to be accomplished during the sessions, the methods in accomplishing them become more evident. A look at the list and the method used helps to see that different methods do better at achieving different goals.

AREAS OF TRAINING	METHOD OF TRAINING
1. New employee orientation	1. Classroom technique daily from 8–10 a.m. or 1–2 p.m.
2. Stock room training	2. Closed circuit TV
3. Reservation desk training	3. Programmed manuals
4. Evaluation of program	4. Survey of participants and management

Human relations is learned by doing

It is, for instance, inadequate to teach human relations without actually "doing" them. Instead of a lecture, some method involving interaction with other people must be employed.

Effectiveness

Suppose a manager goes on a retreat as part of a sensitivity training group and returns enthusiastic about what he or she has learned. An immediate conclusion might be that the sensitivity training has been successful. It is true that the participant was excited about his or her personal experience, but whether the training was successful is usually defined in terms of company rather than personal goals. Companies usually choose to train their employees to increase production rates. One of the reasons production may not be as high as it could be may be that morale is low and/or communication is poor. The effectiveness of training is usually determined by measuring production rates before and after training has occurred. This tangible measurement is not always easy to make because training results usually do not make themselves felt for some time. Companies may settle for more intangible results to find out if training is worthwhile. Even when a program is considered a failure there are so many factors involved that it is difficult to know what went wrong. Norman R. F. Maier comments:

> Failure of a program to produce results might mean any of the following: (a) the training was a waste of time; (b) the method used was ineffective; (c) the training objective was not a basic one; (d) supervisors and trainers did not agree on how the job should be done; (e) the measuring procedure was ineffective; or (f) the training was discontinued before measurable gains were made.[3]

Training is hard to measure

Not only is the effectiveness of training difficult to measure, but there is no guarantee that a training program will enable an employee to successfully perform a job. However, the risk is as great in the other direction: without it, mistakes in skill and judgment are more possible. Often, training is a small risk when compared with the potential errors that result from no training.

TRAINING NEW EMPLOYEES

General Orientation

When new employees decide to take a job, they already have some impressions about the companies they plan to work for. The job interview will have given them a sense of the company's environment and of a few of its employees. They may have heard reports from friends about what it is like to work there, and may have formed ideas about the company's policies through newspaper and magazine stories and other literature.

However, the on-the-job impressions of the first few days greatly influence and solidify attitudes toward their jobs and the companies they work for. Orientation is the formal means by which employees learn about their new employer. New employees have a trial period with employers, but the company and department are on trial for new employees as well. Orientation can have a powerful effect on employees' attitudes and morale.

Orientation is a form of job training. It is distinguished from on-the-job training in that it orients employees to all those matters that do not pertain to performing the job itself. Orientation is concerned with accomplishing two major tasks: (1) informing employees of company policies and benefits; and (2) making employees aware of locations and procedures that affect their abilities to do their jobs. Formally, the first point is called *orientation*, and the second *induction*. Loosely, both tasks fall under the general concept of orientation—acquainting new employees with their job environment and co-workers, and with company policies and procedures.

New employees must learn an amazing amount of detail in a short time, not to mention performing the actual job itself. Without some kind of general orientation, new employees can easily feel "lost" or "alienated." New employees do not usually like to be overwhelmed with constant talking and a great deal of complicated information. However, they have certain needs that someone should be responsible for providing, according to company procedure.

INDUCTION

New employees must learn where things are that are pertinent to their jobs: parking spaces, employee entrance and exit, time clock, locker, bathrooms, bulletin boards, cafeteria, coffee and smoking areas, and work-related departments. It is a sad comment on a company's orientation program to encounter a new employee wandering the halls in search of the bathroom or the cafeteria. Further induction should include company procedures: uniforms, safety equipment, rest breaks, and the details of pay.

Employees must also meet their co-workers and other people they will need to know in the course of their occupations. Some managers consider it good management practice for an established co-worker to sponsor a new employee, at least during the first few days. In this way, a new employee can establish immediate rapport with a person in the same department, which helps the newcomer overcome feelings of shyness and strangeness. The co-worker is available to answer questions and to introduce the new employee to others. This procedure does not mean that managers and supervisors should not show concern for the new employee, but this can be done sporadically by "dropping by" the work station or by having occasional follow-up interviews. In general co-worker orientation is a good method for easing the new employee into the company environment. But the manager must be careful whom he chooses for this responsibility.

POLICY ORIENTATION

Another general area that new employees must become acquainted with is department and company policies and practices. These orientation subjects usually include absentee policies, vacation times and amount, holidays, disciplinary procedures, and filling out certain company forms. Employees will need to study the possibilities of medical and other fringe benefits, use of the credit union, stock purchase plans, employee purchases and discounts, retirement and insurance plans. Some companies find that detailed information should not be presented for about a week, or until after new employees have time to feel comfortable with more immediate concerns, such as the job, co-workers, and the work environment.

Large organizations may have specific orientation programs. Lectures and films may be relied on to help employees understand the company's purposes, production processes, and the parts employees play to create company products. Some orientation programs include training in company attitudes: for example, a movie may be shown stressing workers' feelings of job satisfaction and security.

Orientation is approached in two ways: moving from part

Important details—pay and restrooms

Employee sponsors the new recruit

Inductive vs. deductive

to whole (*inductive*), or moving from whole to part (*deductive*) (Figure 11-1). The inductive method favors expansion of orientation. Employees are first instructed in the details of their jobs and necessary locations and procedures. Gradually, employees are exposed to more information. They learn the details of company benefits, the overall company objectives, how people and departments interrelate, and how the company relates to the community. Many new employees like to begin by learning their jobs and making themselves useful, and then gradually widen their scope. One disadvantage is that employees may form incorrect opinions about the company, opinions which are difficult to alter later on in orientation.

The deductive method   In the deductive method, employees are first introduced to the company as a whole. The company is treated as a family that employees must get to know before beginning their job duties. The deductive method is exemplified by the way in which two foreign firms orient their employees. It is a pleasure to work for Coats and Clark, a British buttons and fabric firm, or Mitsibuishi, a large Japanese conglomerate, said several of their employees of their strong paternal companies.

From the whole to the   The deductive method is learning from the whole to the
part   part. During the first week, a film on the company is often

Figure 11–1.   Illustration of the inductive and deductive methods of learning.

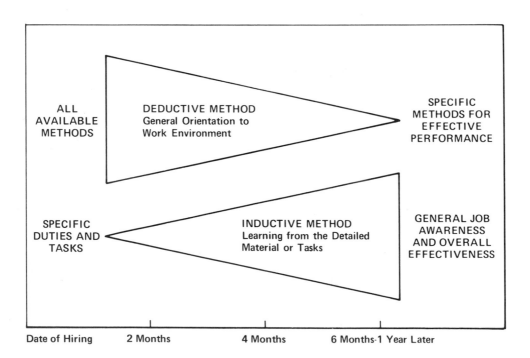

shown, which emphasizes the products, but interwoven in the scenario are words about employee security and company success. Early in the employee orientation a new recruit is aware of the steps in production and what part he will play in the process. A disadvantage is that he may become anxious to get to his job and learn his duties while he is being indoctrinated. However, he is learning to identify, associate, and feel comfortable with his firm. This approach may be more successful in cutting down employee turnover. This method is a large part of the philosophy of Coats and Clark. It is better to train a good, productive, loyal employee to become a statistician, a computer operator, or a labor relation specialist than to hire a highly trained outsider.

On-the-Job Training

Good OJT means a good trainer

No matter what skill training is necessary to acquire a job, some on-the-job training is helpful. Without it, new employees learn only through trial and error. On-the-job training, or OJT, can include informal comments and suggestions from others, but supervised OJT is the most effective.

In OJT, the burden is on the trainer: it is generally assumed that when a worker does not learn the job thoroughly, the teacher hasn't correctly taught. For an instructor to present material consistently, OJT should be preplanned. Information should be presented in manageable sections and in a logical sequence. To facilitate this process, the trainer should break down the job to be learned *on paper*. All the steps don't have to be covered in the written outline — the idea is to make sure all the principal steps or actions are named.

A person new to a job is nervous, which makes it difficult to concentrate. The trainee must be put at ease and not feel rushed. For training to be most effective, a rapport must be established between trainer and trainee. The trainee must feel receptive to the trainer's remarks and must feel that the trainer desires to be of real assistance. Impatience, irritation, or criticism almost completely stops learning. The learner's accomplishments and efforts must be praised, helping to build self-confidence. A trainer should not interrupt when a trainee is performing correctly, because it will break the concentration. However, when a trainer sees that an error is going to be made, the trainer should interrupt, thereby preventing the error from occurring. A bad habit can be formed by incorrectly doing something just once. To correct an error, the trainer should return to the step immediately preceding the error.

When the employee is sufficiently trained to do the job alone, the trainer should be available to answer questions. The trainer should continue to observe the employee frequently, but without breathing down the trainee's back.

INSTRUCTIONAL METHODS

To instruct means to impart information, ideas, or skills so that they may be learned by others. On-the-job training is an example of applied instruction. Instruction can be made available not only through human teachers, but also through literature, films, and teaching machines—in fact, with any aid that provides students with materials to learn. The students' participation in this process is to learn what is presented to them.

Written Material

Probably the most popular way to disseminate general information is through the written word. Businesses like to keep employees and the interested public informed of fundamental company background and policy. Consumption of this information is encouraged by providing well-designed memoranda or pamphlets, which are made easily available. Reading material is often essential to keep employees informed about job-related matters. Job manuals collect specific job data and often contain information that helps employees do their jobs more effectively.

Written material is good for details and easy access

One advantage of relying on reading matter is that anything written down can be referred to over and over again. Repetition is a sound learning technique. Also, job-relevant information can be accumulated so that maximum accessibility is assured. The mind is freed of learning many details when sources of information are available. Written communications can be disseminated widely, assuring a consistency in the opportunity to read certain material.

Written material, however, is often *not* read, or superficially read and soon forgotten. Writing is suitable for transmitting intellectual or technical data, but it is not always useful for training that deals with emotions or attitudes. For instance, human relations training is based on experiential methods, although background reading is sometimes helpful.

Lectures

Lectures can present a considerable amount of material to a considerable number of people. Like written material, the lecture method is best employed to convey ideas. It is used in company training programs as the most reliable way to pass on informa-

One of the most reliable
ways to give
information

tion. Narrowly defined, a lecture transmits information delivered orally by a lecturer. However, such visuals as blackboards and demonstration charts are common aids. Lectures do not cater to individual needs and they provide for little feedback. A question-and-answer period, interspersed throughout or following a lecture, allows for some individual participation to occur and should be used whenever possible.

Whether or not lectures are interesting depends on two factors: the material presented and the presentation. Lectures can be presented by anyone familiar with the information, but the listening rate often depends on the lecturer's speaking style. The most accomplished lecturers are able to sense the overall moods of the crowd, to which they respond spontaneously and appropriately. Some industries use a "teacher-of-the-day" approach. This procedure forces employees to become authorities, to identify and organize issues, and to learn by helping others to learn. One disadvantage of lectures, however, is that, unless people know how to take good notes, much of the material is usually forgotten.

Programmed Instruction

PI is self-teaching

Programmed instruction (PI), also called programmed learning, is a self-teaching method particularly useful for transmitting information or skills that need to be learned and placed in logical order. The "instructor" is replaced by an instruction booklet, or a "teaching machine," or both. It is possible to present programmed instruction entirely in written form. Automated teaching machines, of which there are a great variety, are sometimes preferred.

PI courses can be developed to suit the particular learning problem, or they can be bought ready made. The American Management Association, for example, has developed a series of "shelf" courses called "PRIME"—Programmed Instruction of Management Education.[4] PI has provided learning tools for many businesses and industries. Du Pont Corporation has a library of about 50 courses on how to solve problems occurring in their plants. First National City Bank of New York uses PI to train tellers and clerks. Humble Oil & Refining Company once bought 2,500 training machines and other devices to teach their salespeople techniques for selling their products.[5] Like other training programs, programmed instruction is not always easy to assess. National Cash Register Company, however, has favorably reported that its class in computer techniques now takes one week to complete, instead of an instructor's time over two weeks.

Programmed instruction presents what is to be learned in

brief, logical sequence, one step at a time. Two main approaches have been developed based on this concept: linear programming and intrinsic or branching programming. Of the two the linear is the most common.

LINEAR PROGRAMMING

The author will never forget the experience of hiring Benkins to move all of his family's possessions. He had heard of the Benkins' "certified packers" and was confident they could do a good job. The shock came when the "certified packer" opened his mouth and spoke with an "Irish brogue."

"Are you from Ireland?" I asked.

"Oh, yes I have been here for about a week."

"Then how did you become a "certified packer?"

"Simple, I took their programmed book. They said, when I finished it to come back, take a test, demonstrate my skill and if I passed, the job was mine. Sure and be gory, I passed with flying colors."

Incidentally, he did a fine job packing.

Simple steps called frames

Immediate feedback

Self-pacing

Programmed learning can be carried out by the use of either machines or booklets, depending upon the need. The method is to present a small amount of information called a "frame", followed by a simple question that requires an answer on the part of the learner. The answer may be written or said silently, but in any case there is immediate feedback for each response as the learner finds the answer on the next page or elsewhere. The learner knows whether he is right or wrong immediately. Since it is designed to have a low error-rate, he is further motivated. The best advantage to such an individualized problem is that it is self-pacing. The more motivated the employee is the more he will work on it, but likewise since it is strictly individual, motivation can drop very fast. A long programmed course for the equivalent of an 18-week college course may not be very effective, but for remedial instruction, enrichment material, or short segments this method works well. Programmed booklets have been developed for how to read new instrument dials in cockpits, how to do business mathematics, and how to play bridge.

INTRINSIC OR BRANCHING PROGRAMMING

An intrinsic program, or branching program, relies on specially written textual material. After the instruction is presented, a multiple-choice question appears, with a page number listed by each alternative answer. The student picks the answer thought to be correct, then turns to the designated page number. If the answer is correct, the student continues with new material. If the answer is incorrect, the page turned to gives an additional explanation. Then the student is asked to read material that builds a better background, and finally he is asked a simpler question on the material he has just read. For each multiple-choice question, the student has the possibility of "branching" out to a number of possible answers. Sometimes the corrective instruction alternatives have other branches of their own. Obviously, this system can become quite complex.

The intrinsic programming method, developed by Norman L. Crowder, is geared closely to the individual's needs. The difficulty with writing intrinsic programs is that the most commonly chosen alternatives must be correctly anticipated in order for the branches to be useful. The system demands the greatest cleverness in constructing meaningful questions and answers. If they are too easy, students will pick the correct answers without fully comprehending the material.

ADVANTAGES AND DISADVANTAGES

Whether you use B. F. Skinner's linear programming or Norman Crowder's branching programming, here are some points to remember:

Programmed instruction has these advantages:

1. Students can proceed at their own pace, without being held back by slower students or pushed ahead by faster students.
2. Students are given constant feedback so that they know how they are doing and what they need to know to progress further.
3. Students are rewarded, immediately or eventually, by picking correct responses, which encourages them to learn further.
4. Students can become involved actively with the material, rather than passively reading or listening.[6]

Programmed instruction has these disadvantages:

1. It can be costly and time consuming to prepare.
2. It is possible for the learner to become bored if the program is not well written or if it is too simple.
3. There is the possibility that the programmed instruction will contain erroneous information or end up being a series of unrelated sentences with blanks to be filled in.

Audio and Visual Aids

Audio aids are radios and tape recorders. Visual aids are items such as charts, blackboards, and slide films. Audio-visual aids include motion pictures and television. Audio, visual, and audio-visual aids are being increasingly used as training devices.

CLOSED-CIRCUIT TELEVISION OR VIDEO TAPE

TV is good on assembly lines

This method is used to instruct new employees how to perform their jobs. An assembly line can be filmed from several positions by a TV camera, and the finished TV cassette can be installed in a TV monitor or screen above the work station. A well-timed tape recording describing a multistepped job can supply more job understanding than supervised on-the-job training. The new employee can watch the process on the screen several times before he tries the project. He can start or stop the filming at any point he wishes; in fact, he is learning at his own rate. Nervousness is minimized, because he is not under the watchful eyes of an impatient supervisor. Likewise, the supervisor can use his valuable time to attend to other duties, with only spot checks on the recruit to reassure him. Video tape has several special advantages over motion pictures, in that there is no need to process the film and it can be used immediately after "shooting" the training sequence. Lastly, it can be made "in house" with only a limited staff.

Such audio-visual aids can be effective teaching aids because they are repetitive. They can be watched or heard many times by the same or other individuals. They assure that the same material is presented, and they usually require less personalized teaching time.

SIMULATION METHODS

The major goal of simulation techniques is to solve problems, particularly management problems. Real work situations are duplicated for the purpose of arriving at decisions. The simulation process can take place with the use of written materials, individual study, group discussion, and dramatization. Simulation tries to build up problem-solving skills in anticipation of solving "real" problems.

In-Basket Method

Problem solving under a time limit

As the name indicates, in-basket training is structured around the familiar receptacle used for collecting incoming mail, memos, forms, and reports. Materials that require problem solving are put into an in-basket, and the student plays the role of a manager responsible for solving the problems found in the in-basket. The students are given background information on the personalities and situations involved. Then, using their experience as a guide, students are asked to take the appropriate action within a short time period. Individual or group discussion follows the written part of the exercise. Even students who are satisfied with their methods of handling problems usually find that discussions broaden their knowledge of the various possible ways to approach the same problem.

The in-basket method teaches planning and delegating

So far, the in-basket method has been used mostly to learn about effective management and supervision. It has dealt with the concepts of organizing, delegating, and planning work. The technique attempts to simulate real-life situations. Using a time

"THE 'IN-BASKET' METHOD IS REALLY A GAME TO FORCE PEOPLE TO MAKE DECISIONS."

limit helps to create the tension inherent in workaday problem solving. The problems are organized to approximate work experience as closely as possible.

One typical in-basket approach is to ask students to pretend they are a manager who has just returned from a business trip and must leave again shortly on another trip. The student managers have twenty minutes to make decisions on materials that have accumulated in the in-basket. How well can the manager list priorities? What assumptions are made, and are they warranted? Is the work distribution planned adequately? Is the work delegated appropriately? Figure 11–2 gives two examples of in-basket exercises.

MEMO:

TO: JOHN ENWRIGHT, MANAGER

FROM: STEVE RIDER, PERSONNEL DIRECTOR

John, the approval came through for a Facilities Foreman. Do you want to write up a formal job description for me? Do you want to have a panel interview candidates for the job or do you want to handle the interviews yourself?

1. Would you delegate the task of making out the job description? If so, to whom?
2. Would you use a panel interview or a personal interview? Why?

MEMO:

TO: JOHN ENWRIGHT

FROM: JOEL PETERSON, HEAD ACCOUNTANT

Helga Sue (the accounting clerk, responsible for sending out bills) has not shown up for work the last three days. She cannot be reached by phone. The rumor is that she has left town for an abortion. There is a backlog in sending out statements to customers. You know how anxious the president is to maximize income and there is a large amount owed in the accounts receivable ledger. What shall we do?

1. Would you delegate this task?
2. What are the alternatives to the problem?

Figure 11–2. Samples of in-basket forms.

Case Study

The case method was developed by Harvard law professor Christopher C. Langdell. A problem, or case, is presented in writing to a group. Cases are intended to simulate real work situations and therefore include descriptions of the organizational structure and personalities involved. Group members study the problem on their own time, then offer their solutions in the group. Because of group participation, group members are able to get immediate reactions to their ideas, as well as react to the ideas of others. Although groups are often led by a teacher or trainer, the group sessions can be so informal that they get off the track. However, this more experimental approach makes traditional management principles more personally meaningful to group participants.

Determining the problem, *not* the solution

Rather than finding "solutions," which is the basis of the problem-solving method, the case method attempts to use facts to present an effective position based on convincing logic. This method is based on the assumption that in business practice there is no one "right" way. It acknowledges that the "best" solutions often rely on personal preferences.

Although the case method does not increase skills in human relations, it usually deals with problems that affect individuals in organizations. It involves the ability to *justify* management decisions, to give priorities to problems that are important to the company and its employees. For instance, a case study could involve an employee who was fired by a supervisor for using a company car for personal reasons. The employee has appealed to the grievance committee. As a member of the committee, each student would receive pertinent information on which to decide whether to (1) sustain the firing; (2) suspend the employee for a period of time without pay; or (3) reinstate the employee with full rights.

Incident Process

Paul and Faith Pigors developed the *incident process* as a variant of the case method. They say, "Case method takes time, requires skillful leadership in small groups, and traditionally has called for concentrated homework to prepare for discussion."[7]

How to find out the facts

The incident process is based on group discussion. The group is given a problem requiring prompt action, but with the understanding that, as in real-life problems, all the facts are not at hand. The group members are left to determine the *questions* that must be asked in order to make a good decision. The discussion leader provides the facts only on the basis of the questions asked. In summing up the facts, the group must determine what immediate issues are at stake. Members then write out their individual decisions and the reasons for them.

First used in M.I.T. graduate classes, the incident process can be used easily by training groups formed within organizations. The Pigors comment, "You will be thinking and talking with other people in ways which help to make differences of opinion, and diversity of background and experience, productive forces in your organization."[8]

Example of Incident Process

Mr. Teadwell, a highway sheriff, said he *must* have the weekend off, even though he is scheduled to work that weekend. It also happens to be before a major holiday and a few minutes before his work schedule is to begin. If you were the supervisor in charge how would you handle the situation?

ISSUES: What are the procedures and rules of the department to be interpreted? How much determination does the supervisor have in a situation like this? How important is the need for continuous and adequate highway coverage? Why "must he go home"? Would you consider Mr. Teadwell's past, present, and future situation in arriving at a decision? How many other people are likely to be involved in this issue? What message would be given this employee and would it be given to others in the department?

Suppose he refused to report to duty? What recourse does the supervisor have? How important is it that Mr. Teadwell is under contract to give at least two weeks' notice in writing if he wishes to terminate his employment? Suppose he refuses to give the reason for wanting time off—except for such terms as "it's important," "It's very personal," and "I don't want to discuss it"? Each role is acted out, and neither knows how the other is going to play his role. The process may have several scenes before the incident is resolved.

Another Example of the Incident Process

How would the situation be different if it was a female hospital ward attendant, stating she "must" have the weekend off, and you were the Assistant Director of Nursing Services. How would you handle the situation? After working out the issues and some answers to the policy issues, select two people to role-play the parts of the hospital ward attendant and the Assistant Director of Nursing Services.

MANAGEMENT GAMES

Groups compete

A management game is a form of problem solving. At least two teams, each of which represents an organization, make decisions concerning their company's operation. Decisions must be made about production, marketing, and finance. Decisions are based on a set of specified economic theories, presented as a model of the economy. When the model is fairly simple, a referee can be responsible for calculating outcomes. When the model is complex, a computer must be used. The game can be continuous: teams receive all or part of the results of their decisions, on which they make new decisions, thus continuing the game. Figure 11–3 shows a diagram of the steps in a management game.

Good judgment is the key

Simple management games are not based on analyzing complex problems. Instead, emphasis is placed on making good judgments in a minimum amount of time, based on specific problems and limited rules. In simple games, effective strategies can be arrived at without making too many decisions and without having to use large amounts of managerial know-how. These management games may oversimplify business relationships and give the impression that running a company can be easy — when in fact, even the simplest management decisions require the consideration of many factors.

Figure 11–3. Steps in a management game — an important aid in teaching production, marketing, and financial concepts. Teamwork is the key in arriving at decisions.

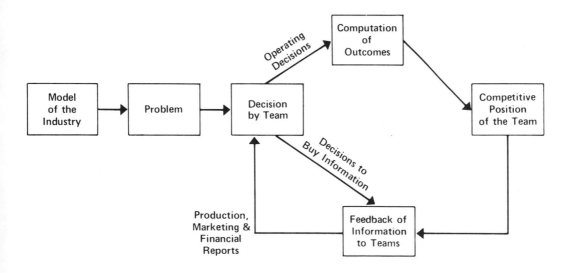

Although limited in scope, simple management games can be challenging and exciting to play. They give players an opportunity to experiment with making a variety of management decisions and to get immediate feedback. It is easier to illustrate the cumulative effect of decisions with management games than with solving case-method problems. Games are popular in management training programs. A game may be used to start out training in a stimulating way, or to relieve the boredom produced by other training techniques. Since teamwork is required in management games, they make it easier for trainees to get acquainted and to learn to work together.

EXPERIENTIAL METHODS

Human relations training

In experiential methods, participants do not pretend they are solving anything. Their goal is to "be" who they are, and to learn about themselves and others through the process of experiencing their relationship to others. Any kind of training in which participants interact and express their feelings is considered human relations training.

Psychology is the most popular game around. Each new "game" leaves a new imprint on our thoughts and language. Each wave etches in its own peculiar vocabulary. The oldest is role playing and close to it is psychodrama, followed by sensitivity training and encounter groups of the 1950s and 1960s. During the 1970s came the new alphabet of T.A., T.M., EST, and A.T. Whether the reader will be caught up with the wave of transactional analysis, transcendental meditation, or assertiveness training is hard to say, but all these methods are based on experiences that each individual will *feel*. That experience can be glowing or damaging to the ego; an afternoon happening that is soon forgotten or a mind-expanding event that will alter one's personality.

Role Playing

Act out a solution

Role playing is an exercise in problem solving, designed primarily to aid in understanding human relations. Role playing works in small groups of two to eight people. Multiple role playing is the name given to breaking up large audiences into small groups to enact roles.

A group is given a situation requiring a decision to be made. Participants are then given descriptions of the attitudes of the people they are to represent, which they develop and dramatize as best they can. There are no lines to memorize—all the characterizations are improvised. The actors and actresses work on the problem until they arrive at a solution that satisfies most of the participants. Some members of the group may act as observers. After each role-playing session, the observers comment on the process, giving feedback on communication skills, supervisory techniques, and attitudes expressed between supervisors and subordinates.

For role playing to be successful, the participants must be able to adopt the specified roles and to react to the decisions of the other players accordingly. Role playing gives people an opportunity to experience the points of view of different employees. In management training courses, managers learn some of the techniques involved in group decision making. They learn to have confidence in employees' judgment when faced with solving job problems; and they learn how to exercise skills in presenting problems to the group.

Norman R. F. Maier and Lester Zerfoss have observed that role-playing sessions "give the participants an opportunity to discover that the way employees behave depends greatly upon the kind of situation the supervisor creates. Thus, both the attitude of the supervisor and his skill in leading the discussion directly determine the outcome of the conference."[9]

Video tape role playing

Another variation is for one role to be played consistently by one person, while another role is played successively by each group member. For example, a trainee plays a personnel director who interviews a particularly talkative job candidate. Application forms are provided and the talkative applicant is well versed in his or her role. A video or audio tape may be used during the role-playing session. Afterward, the trainer and group members discuss the process, thus beginning to change each trainee's attitudes and behavior. Listening or watching the tapes made during the session can help the trainees become more aware of their actions. The author has found the video tape method the most successful way to provide students with helpful insights into interviewing techniques through role playing in job interviews.

Sensitivity Training

How we function in groups

The goal of sensitivity training is for individuals to understand (1) how they function in a group setting, and (2) how a group functions. Sensitivity training is concerned with "sensitivity" to one's feelings and the feelings of others. Sensitivity training differs from psychotherapy groups, whose purpose is to delve deeply into inner motivations. The focus is on observable "here and now" behavior rather than on assumptions about motives.

No stated goal

The T-group, or training group, differs radically from more traditional forms of training in that it has no demonstrable goal. The agenda in a sensitivity group or T-group is whatever people want to talk about. People who have been successful at "getting things done" find this experience frustrating and at first idiotic. With no problems to solve, participants are divested of their worldly status and authority. They are left to deal with other people without their formal relationships to back them up. This means that relating to others must be reexamined, and new ways tried. Gradually group members learn to be more honest in their communication. As they become more open with one another, they trust one another more and accept other points of view. They learn to give and take leadership and make group decisions without using formal authority as a crutch.

Leadership changes

Sensitivity training makes certain assumptions about therapy. One is that people do not need to go back into the past to analyze the effect of events on their lives. Instead, the "here and now" provides sufficient experience to work on. How people "are" in the present is more important than what happened in the past.

Interactions with other people puts the self in touch with feelings. Group members can provide feedback about an individual's impact on others. Understanding others also helps to put people in touch with themselves. The more people under-

Understanding feelings

Figure 11–4. In sensitivity groups members learn to be more honest with each other—they learn to trust each other more and to accept other points of view. *David W. Johnson and Frank P. Johnson,* Joining Together: Group Theory and Group Skills, © 1975, p. 306. Reprinted by permission of Prentice-Hall, Inc.

stand themselves, the more they are able to understand others. The purpose of sensitivity training is to provide a safe environment in which feelings can be unmasked and shared. People are conditioned culturally *not* to share true feelings; T-groups help people to learn how to do this. Another assumption underlying sensitivity training is that it is possible to "let go" of feelings. When feelings are withheld, or held on to, they become nurtured by the self. When they are released, or expressed, they can be "worked through." As with problem solving, when a problem is acknowledged and discussed, it tends to get solved in some fashion. So it is with feelings. When emotions are acknowledged, experienced, and shared, they tend to become more acceptable and more understood—by the self and by others. As a result of such disclosures, changes in behavior often result.

Let feelings come to the surface

Trainers can be important models for T-group members to identify with. Ideally, a trainer should express feelings openly and honestly; should not become defensive and withdrawn under criticism; and should exhibit acceptance and trust of others. Trainers display different leadership patterns, from very directive to virtually nondirective, and from a high expectancy of participants to accept emotional risk to no preconceived notions. These variables should depend not only on the trainer's own preferences, but on the constitution of the group itself. As a result, the styles and results of sensitivity groups vary greatly.

Transactional Analysis (TA)

Transactional analysis, or TA, was developed by the late Eric Berne, a psychiatrist who is best known for his book, *Games People Play,* and was popularized by Thomas Harris in *I'm OK— You're OK.* Muriel and Dorothy Jongeward's book *Born to Win* became a text millions of people could use to apply TA to their personal lives.[10] The leaders of TA believe that everyone's personality is made up of three parts, called ego states. An ego state is a pattern of behavior that a person develops as he grows up based on a network of feelings and experiences he has.

The three ego states

The *child ego state* exists when people feel and act as they did in childhood. The spontaneous expression of internal feelings of joy, frustration, or creative ideas, as well as expressing wishes and fantasies are all examples of the child ego state. The *adult ego state* can be expressed when people are thinking and acting rationally, gathering facts, estimating outcomes, and evaluating results. The *parent ego state* is best likened to how a parent would handle his young children. Rules and laws, tradition, demonstrations of the correct way to do things, and protection can be seen as examples of the parent ego state.

In any of the three stages, you can adopt very different attitudes toward yourself and those you work with. In the *parent state,* you can be an OK supervisor by giving critiques rather than criticism, and know how to be supportive. Or, you can be an OK supervisor in the *adult state* by being responsive and analytical. The *child state* can be seen as being a cooperative supervisor willing to help come up with creative ideas. Table 11–1 shows TA of an adult, a parent, and a child.

Table 11–1. Transactional Analysis of Parent, Adult, and Child

PARENT	ADULT	CHILD
rules and laws	rational	sees, hears, feels
do's and don't	estimating	joy, frustration
truths	evaluating	creative
inconsistency	storing data	wishes, fantasies
how-to	figures out	internal feelings
tradition	explores	
taught	testing	
demonstrates		

I'm OK you're OK

People really express how they feel about themselves and others as being OK or not-OK, whether they are dealing with subordinates or superiors. They also reflect how they feel about others as being OK or not-OK. Further transactional analysis constructs the following classifications of the four possible life positions held with respect to oneself and to others.

1. I'm not OK—you're OK.
2. I'm not OK—you're not OK.
3. I'm OK—you're not OK.
4. I'm OK—you're OK.

By understanding ego states, as well as OK and not-OK attitudes, we can make sense out of the different styles that people use. Some are so common that they are stereotypes. We may not like to use stereotypes, but like a mirror that distorts an image it can still reflect some truth. The OK or Not-OK attitudes can be seen in the three ego states in Table 11–2.

Most supervisors have their own style of handling their subordinates. Since all bosses have some measure of control over others it is not uncommon for supervisors to adopt the *parental ego state* with their employees. This is no surprise, since parents are the first people we know with control over others.

At one time or another we all act out each of the three ego

Table 11–2.   Transactional Analysis of the Not O.K. and O.K. Attitude.

PARENT		ADULT		CHILD	
Not O.K.	*O.K.*	*Not O.K.*	*O.K.*	*Not O.K.*	*O.K.*
Dictator	Supportive	Computer	Communicator	Milquetoast	Negotiator
Do it my way	Informed critic	Always testing	Offering alternatives	Scatterbrain	Innovator

states in the positive and negative manner. It might be fun to tape a conversation and see whether comments can be detected as being from the parent, adult, or child state and whether they can be considered OK or not-OK.

How would you rate the following statements?

1. How about a game of tennis?
2. How long will it take to get the data?
3. You'd better get the job done right!
4. Don't worry about it; it will be all right!
5. What do you think is wrong?
6. Yes, I am trying hard to finish it on time.

Sometimes it is hard to rate a comment without knowing the situation and the other parties to the conversation, but the author rated them as follows.

1. Child state—OK;
2. Adult state—OK;
3. Parent state—not-OK;
4. Parent state—OK;
5. Adult state—OK;
6. Child—not OK.

Transactional analysis is being explored by some companies as a way to increase the capability of employees to cope with problems and deal more sensibly with people. Pan American World Airways, New York Telephone Company, Sears, and General Telephone Company of the Southwest have all tried it with a certain amount of success.[11] Such comments as these are made: "Employees are better communicators particularly in customer contacts." "TA has led to increased productivity."

Some maintain that one of TA's values is its kindling of enthusiasm for many jobs that tend to be monotonous. TA cannot guarantee that human relations problems will disappear, but its role in future organization development programs is likely to be continued for some time.

Assertiveness Training or AT

The term "assertiveness" leads the reader to believe that one is trained to manipulate others. An AT trainer has said, "No one can manipulate your emotions or behavior if you do not allow it to happen. In order to stop anyone's manipulation of your emotions or behavior you need to recognize how people try to manipulate you. That is where the term comes into play."

AT seen as manipulative

This leads one not only to regard assertiveness training as merely a set of defensive techniques, but to slide still further into the belief that the only way to beat manipulation is to be a better manipulator yourself. People who come to workshops say that they feel they're being manipulated and want to be able to stop it. Some workshops try to make them aware of how much they manipulate others, too, and that other people sense it as much as they do.

Perhaps when someone mentions assertiveness training many people think of the "power boys that push people for payoffs." Robert Ringer and Michael Korda popularized the term and gave it a breezy bit of fresh "one-upmanship" in their books, *Winning Through Intimidation* and *Power, How to Get it and How to Use it.* Korda suggests jamming a visitor's chair into a small space to make him feel powerless, and to speak softly to an elderly rival, as it may make him think he is going deaf. Other methods are: Learn to pick out the power seat at meetings and cultivate an appropriate air of mystery about yourself by hinting you have powerful inside information.

A different feeling is expressed by others who believe in AT. The key words are *anxiety* and *authenticity.* Most of the humanistic behaviorists believe that teaching people the basic skills for handling difficult situations serves to alleviate immobilizing anxiety; once people master those skills and feel they have a cushion to fall back on, their self-confidence and spontaneity increase—anxious, scared persons are almost never spontaneous.

Express your feelings constructively

AT's forefather, Andrew Salter, agrees. "It's not one-upmanship," he points out. "The broader definition of assertion refers not only to standing up for your rights, but to expressing all your friendly, affectionate feelings."[12] If both men and women would be warmer and more open, it would eliminate their anxieties about assertion. Straightforward, deliberate, and systematic rethinking is the first step toward a constructive change in our feelings and emotions. For example, we should tell ourselves, "I am upset over the fact that my wife came home late," instead of, "My wife upset me."

HOW TO BE ASSERTIVE

Overcoming the anxiety that prevents us from behaving assertively is the first step. It all comes down to your ability to size up a situation and tackle it without letting the other person's negative reactions sidetrack you. Once you take the risk the worst fears are seldom realized. Here are a few rules.

1. SAY IT DIRECTLY. It is natural to beat around the bush if you don't know how people will react. Recognize the other person's point of view, but be sure to get your own point across.

2. EXPRESS HOW YOU FEEL. If you have been asked to work overtime for at least three days a week for the last couple of months, express that *you are tired of it*. "I think I have done my part; perhaps it is time for someone else to put in their time."

3. BE SPECIFIC WITH A SOLUTION "I don't mind working one night a week, but three is just too much." Besides, I feel if I work overtime just one night a week I can do a better job all around." Ending with a strong positive note makes that request more reasonable and understandable to the listener.

How Assertive are You?

Answer the following statements with *always, sometimes, seldom,* or *never.*

1. I usually make the first move to establish personal contacts with strangers at a party. _____
2. I would complain to the management about being overcharged or given poor service. _____
3. I would leave my usual amount of tip even if the waitress were slow and gave poor service. _____
4. When smoking bothers me, I would say so. _____
5. I can end the conversation comfortably when I think it is dragging on. _____

If the answers show you seldom or never stand up for yourself, you may wonder about your assertiveness. In a training session your trainer may give you a long list of such questions. Responses to such lists might show you that you are a tower of strength at work, but a milquetoast at home or in social situations.

The tendency is more toward integrating both thought and behavior, but with the emphasis on behavior change as the primary means for altering one's self-perceptions and raising self-esteem. As we see ourselves doing something successfully, we feel more confident about trying to do more things. Most assertiveness training groups include a lot of role playing of members' real-life problems. After enough practice in the group to give them some confidence, trainees usually take dealing with the situations in the "real world" as their homework.

Self-awareness

Both self-awareness and social awareness are fundamental to assertiveness. *Self-awareness is looking inside for what you want; social awareness is knowing the consequences of a particular act and being prepared to take responsibility for it.* Personal desire and social consciousness are often seen as opposing forces, but we feel that both are necessary to make a judgment between alternatives.[13]

When assertive (self-enhancing) behavior gains more positive responses from others it leads to positive feedback and to an enhanced evaluation of self-worth; and these feelings in turn result in further assertiveness.

Transcendental Meditation or TM

Eastern psychology

Recently there has been a trend in Western society of indulging in many of the Eastern esoteric psychologies such as Zen, Yoga, and transcendental meditation. Transcendental meditation or TM was first introduced into the United States in 1959 by Maharishi Mahesh Yogi, who was born in India. He revived a lost meditation technique that originated in the Vedas, the oldest Hindu writings.

Silent thinking is undirected

"The technique of TM consists of giving the attention an inward turn by easily thinking a single thought. In this way, the mind remains active but is left undirected. Naturally, attention begins to seek the increasing satisfaction available at quieter levels of the mind."[14] Dr. Benson describes the technique of TM in a more scientific and less philosophical manner:

> TM involves a surprisingly simple technique. A trained instructor gives you a secret word or sound or phrase, called a mantra, which you promise not to divulge. This sound is allegedly chosen to suit the individual and is to be silently "perceived." The meditator receives the mantra from his teacher and then repeats it mentally over and over again while sitting in a comfortable position. The purpose of this repetition is to prevent distraction of thoughts. Meditators are told to assume a passive attitude and if other thoughts come into the mind to disregard them, going back to the mantra. Practitioners are advised to meditate twenty minutes in the morning, usually before breakfast, and twenty minutes in the evening, usually before dinner . . ."[15]

TECHNIQUE OF MEDITATION

In simple terms here are the four steps used to concentrate on meditation. All teachers of the art say that it takes many sessions before the technique can be mastered.

1. QUIET ENVIRONMENT. Ideally, you should choose a quiet, calm environment with as few distractions as possible—a room that is quiet like a place of worship.

2. MENTAL DEVICE. To shift the mind from logical, externally oriented thought, there should be a constant stimulus; a sound, word, or phrase repeated silently or aloud; or fixed gazing at an object. Since one of the major difficulties in the elicitation of the relaxed state is "mind-wandering," the repetition of a word or phrase is a way to help break the train of distracting thoughts.

3. A PASSIVE ATTITUDE. When distracting thoughts occur, they are to be disregarded and attention redirected to the repetition or gazing; you should not worry about how well you are performing the technique, because this may well prevent the act from happening. Adopt a "let it happen" attitude.

4. A COMFORTABLE POSITION. A comfortable posture is important so that there is no undue muscular tension. Some methods call for a sitting position. A few teachers use the cross-legged "lotus" position of Yogi. If you lie down there is tendency to fall asleep.[16]

BENEFITS OF TM

There are physical benefits of TM

The reactions that occur when a person is practicing meditation are mostly controlled by the autonomic or involuntary nervous system, which produces movement in the cardiac and smooth muscle tissue and also controls the activation of the endocrine system. Some research shows the major physiological change associated with meditation is a decreased metabolic rate, which is usually called hypometabolism. This research was taken further to illustrate that autonomic responses can be controlled. Dr. Neil Miller proved that through the technique of biofeedback a person can monitor his brain waves and can learn to control his involuntary functions. This is the basis of mind control and the basis of how meditation operates on your autonomic nervous system. A marked decrease in blood lactate is observed during meditation. It has been observed that there is a relationship between anxiety attacks and blood lactate levels.[17]

Helps to handle stress

Other research has noted that meditation increases tolerance to stress and autonomic stability. Additional evidence has been found that meditation may have an effect on decreasing dependence on various drugs, alcohol, and cigarettes.[18]

Many behaviorists believe that the potentials of meditation are great; we now need more research to prove these beliefs valid before the acceptance of meditation. Have you tried it? Do you know of anyone who practices it? What are their reactions to it?

ORGANIZATIONAL METHODS

Whole company must change

All the methods discussed so far have used the deductive approach. That is, it is assumed that individual training will add to the effectiveness of the company as a whole. Organizational methods, however, assume that an *entire* organization must work for change, rather than only select individuals in it. Organizational methods also recognize the vulnerability of newly trained employees who reenter established work environments. Without continued reinforcement for change, the changes that came about because of the training process will not persist. Thus it is important to find ways for the organization as a whole to support the training that individuals undergo.

Organization Development

Company development

Organization development (OD) has two major objectives: (1) to train people in the specific skills and field of knowledge that make it possible for them to do their jobs well, and (2) to train people in interpersonal and group-membership skills. Capacities are developed in giving and receiving assistance, listening and communicating, and dealing with people and organizational problems. As the name implies, this method aims at developing the organization. OD has been called "a long-term systematic effort to improve an organization's culture."[19] OD advocates maintain that the entire complex organization must be dealt with as a whole. This includes all the personalities and issues that continuously make the organization what it is.

Organizational goals

OD is based on the belief that although organizations begin purposively, as they grow in size and in age, organizational goals give way to individual goals. When this happens, the organization begins to decay. OD theory also recognizes that people have needs and desires that must be considered part of organizational goals. If all members of the organization participate in forming group goals, and in the process subscribe to them, then a great deal of energy is released for employees to move toward a common purpose.

OD theory also assumes that for an organization and its goals to be healthy, individuals within the organization must have the opportunity to grow and be healthy. Warren Bennis stresses that OD methods are practical, and, "the most *practical* approach to nearly any opportunity or problem involving two or more persons requires that all persons act as if they are human beings, not things or parts of human beings. . . . when people work at the tasks involved in a change in such a way that their humanness and entirety is engaged along with other known factors, then they themselves recommence to grow. . . .[20]

But to make this possible, organization developers should not put faith in any one training method. Trainers should use all the methods available that will enhance the welfare of the organization. The assumption should be that what enhances people's lives will enhance the organization's life.

Management By Objectives

MBO   Management by objectives (MBO) grew out of the recognition that organizations must continue to be developed if they are to remain healthy organisms. MBO is the goal-setting phase of OD. It is based on four major ingredients: objectives (goals), time strategies, the coordination of management, and individual motivations. Organizational goals are set to be met within specified periods of time. It is hoped that when individual managers are keyed into overall goals, their participation will motivate them further in their work. MBO theory believes that for organizations to develop objectives, they must have formalized commitments to their goals. MBO is a five-phase process: (1) finding the objective; (2) setting it; (3) validating it; (4) implementing it; and (5) controlling and reporting its status.[21]

Management by objectives tries to clarify the processes of management itself, sometimes much needed and appreciated:

> One Honeywell executive reported that, formerly, managing in Honeywell was unpredictable—almost a game of chance. With the advent of managing by objectives, each manager knew just what was expected of him and how his performance was measured. Job descriptions and job specifications were clarified; instead of generalized duties performed in a number of acceptable ways, specific job results were set forth and performance levels defined. For many managers this changed the job of managing from an almost guessing, or trial and error, method to one involving precise directions, relevant activities, and needed results.[22]

As the title indicates, MBO is for managers—it is not a concept easily applied to an organization's entire staff.

When undertaken seriously, MBO can give a clear overview of company goals and values. Only with this overview is it possible to decide on effective training methods and to know when to use them.

SUMMARY

Training is the practical side of education because it has to do with transmitting information to improve problem-solving abilities. Traditional training is concerned with mechanical and intellectual knowledge, while human relations training is concerned with emotions and attitudes. The main purpose of any kind of training is for learning to take place. Learning occurs when students become different from how they were before training commenced. These differences are demonstrated by changes in behavior.

The effectiveness of training is partially determined by the attitudes accompanying the training: attitudes of students, teachers, and sponsoring companies. For training to be successful, companies must be clear about their training goals, and then pick the training methods most applicable to these goals. In the same vein, it does no good to train employees in new methods only to have them disallowed on the job. The success of training programs is usually measured from the sponsoring company's viewpoint. Trainees may gain a lot personally, but if company goals are not met, the training has not "paid off." So far, there is no reliable way to test for training effectiveness, since training results are often intangible and can take place over a long period of time.

Job orientation is a form of training that can greatly affect new employees' attitudes. Orientation familiarizes new employees with all the matters that don't pertain to performing the job itself. Induction is the term used to describe practical features of the job environment and procedures. Orientation also doubles as the term used to present the company's policies and benefits. New employees must also receive some on-the-job training. Even when they have previous job experience, no two jobs are the same. The success of OJT is up to the trainers, who should have a clear idea of training procedures.

Instructional training includes OJT, and represents those methods that involve an authority who imparts information to students, who are placed in a position of nonauthority. Written material, correspondence courses, lectures, conferences, programmed instruction, and the many kinds of audio and visual aids have, more or less, the instructional concept in common. Instruction is considered the "traditional" teaching method.

Well-known simulation techniques include the in-basket method, the case method, the incident process, management games, and role playing. They share the goal of solving problems that are as close to real-life problems as possible. Simulation methods employ many different styles—but they are always at least one step removed from reality.

Experiential methods advocate learning about the self in order to be more effective at solving problems in human relations. Psychodrama usually works on conflicts within the self or involving one other person. Members of sensitivity training groups, or T-groups, learn to experience themselves and each other in an unstructured group context. Transactional analysis (TA), assertiveness training (AT), and transcendental meditation (TM) all relate to self-awareness and behavior change as people see themselves in a new perspective.

The organizational method is founded on the belief that an entire company must change if change is to be effective. Organizational development (OD) encourages teamwork in order to arrive at company goals, and encourages just about any kind of training that will fit into the company's needs. Management by objectives is another method designed for managers to learn how to analyze company goals and meet them.

CAN TRAINING OVERCOME COMMUNICATION BARRIERS?

Case Study #1

As the division managers of the Sunrise Sporting Goods Corporation departed the conference room, Carl Peterson, the president of the corporation, began considering ways in which to remedy the communication problems experienced during the weekly meetings.

For some time, the ability of the managers to communicate with one another during these sessions has been less than adequate. The purpose of these meetings is to pool the resources of the managers from their various divisions, and through their interaction, to benefit the corporation in all its aspects. This interaction has not been taking place. In many situations, the managers not directly involved do not even bother to listen, let alone contribute to the discussion. Comments made by another manager concerning an action to be taken to improve sales in a particular area are ignored. In other cases, managers wishing to contribute have been cut short, as when the managers of the larger divisions do not consider the opinion of smaller divisions as important enough to be heard.

In Carl's opinion it is time to take action to change the situation. Tempers have been constantly on the rise, and this afternoon's meeting came close to getting totally out of hand over whether smoking should continue during these meetings. One of the managers went so far as to threaten to quit if the ashtrays were not removed at once.

What steps should Carl take in trying to improve this situation? According to Walter Miller, the corporation training director, this breakdown in communications among the managers can be overcome by sending the managers through such programs as role playing, sensitivity training, or transcendental meditation. Would you recommend any of these programs? Or is there a better program you might suggest?

1. Will you remove the ashtrays?
2. Should they be sent to a program separately or as a group?
3. Should it be an in-house program or one conducted by an outside firm?
4. Should participation be optional or mandatory?
5. How many sessions should you have and how long should each session be?
6. Is such a communication training session necessary?

TRAINING GARY FOR PROMOTION

Case Study #2

Recently Don Taber, who is the supervisor of the Auto Repair Department of a large domestic and imported car dealership, was informed that he would be promoted to a position of higher management, that of the vice-presidency of the dealership. He was also given instructions to select the most capable man in his department and to prepare him for taking over his current supervisory position.

There is one man in particular whom Don would like to promote, Gary Kurtz. He has been the lead mechanic for the company for a number of years. Gary is a reliable employee, and has always performed his work with the utmost competence. Don feels that Gary possesses the ability to become a good leader. Along with Gary's knowledge of auto mechanics and his friendly attitude toward helping and training the other men, he is always anxious to accept new responsibilities, and he is a man who enjoys working hard for the satisfaction of accomplishing goals that either he or others have set.

But it will be necessary to work with Gary first before placing him in charge of the department. Although Gary has many good leadership qualities, he does have certain weaknesses that need to be strengthened. In the past, when Don has been on vacation or away on company business, Gary has been placed in charge. On these occasions, when he was actually put in a position of authority, he was nervous and high-strung. When deadlines on repairs were required, he had a hard time scheduling his employees to finish the task. Under stress Gary has handled such situations poorly and has vented his unreasonable frustration upon innocent employees— even customers. During these times he also tends not to listen fully to the ideas of the other men and instead considers his own opinion as final and binding.

It is Don's opinion that these weaknesses can be overcome with proper training, and that he will be able to develop Gary's good qualities to an extent that he will be considered a just and effective leader by both the company and the men who will be working for him.

How should Don go about developing Gary's good qualities and aiding Gary in correcting his poor ones?

1. What training aids or techniques might Don use in developing Gary's leadership ability?

2. Give reasons why certain techniques might develop certain leadership qualities.

Terms and Concepts Students Should Know

learning	management by objectives (MBO)	assertiveness training (AT)
on-the-job training (OJT)	inductive learning	organizational development (OD)
in-basket method	training goals	deductive learning
management games	programmed instruction (PI)	audio and visual aids
transactional analysis (TA)	incident process	
transcendental meditation (TM)	sensitivity training	

Bibliography

1. PIGORS, PAUL, AND FAITH PIGORS, "Learning by the Incident Process," in *Management of Human Resources: Readings in Personnel Administration*, edited by Paul Pigors, Charles A. Myers, and F. T. Malm, New York, McGraw-Hill Book Co., 1964.

2. JAMES, MURIEL, AND DOROTHY JONGEWARD, *Born to Win: Transactional Analysis with Gestalt Experiments*, Reading, Mass., Addison-Wesley Publishing Co., 1971.

3. BLOOMFIELD, HAROLD H., *TM: Discovering Inner Energy and Overcoming Stress*, New York, Delacorte Press, 1975.

4. BENSON, HERBERT, *The Relaxation Response*, New York, William Morrow & Co., Inc. 1975.

Footnotes

[1] Robert F. Mager, *Developing Attitude Toward Learning* (Belmont, Calif.: Fearon Publishers, 1968), p. 8.

[2] *Ibid.*

[3] Norman R. F. Maier, *Psychology in Industry,* 3rd ed. (Boston: Houghton Mifflin Co., 1965), p. 377.

[4] "New Course for Canned Teaching," *Business Week,* 24 July 1965, p. 68.

[5] *Ibid.*

[6] John S. Abma, "Programmed Instruction—Past, Present, Future," in *Studies in Personnel and Industrial Psychology,* rev. ed. edited by Edwin A. Fleishman (Homewood, Ill.: Dorsey Press, 1967), p. 198.

[7] Paul and Faith Pigors, "Learning By the Incident Process," in *Management of Human Resources: Readings in Personnel Administration,* edited by Paul Pigors, Charles A. Myers, and F. T. Malm (New York: McGraw-Hill Book Co., 1964), p. 190.

[8] *Ibid.,* p. 194.

[9] Norman R. F. Maier and Lester F. Zerfoss, "Multiple Role Playing: A Technique for Training Supervisors," in *Studies in Personnel and Industrial Psychology,* rev. ed. edited by Edwin A. Fleishman (Homewood, Ill.: Dorsey Press, 1967), p. 229.

[10] Muriel James and Dorothy Jongeward, *Born to Win: Transactional Analysis with Gestalt Experiments* (Reading, Mass.: Addison-Wesley Publishing Co., 1971), pp. 8–9.

[11] "A New Way to Improve Effectiveness on the Job," *Nation's Business,* July 1975, pp. 65–68.

[12] Paula Landau, "A Guide for the Assertive Book Buyer," *Human Behavior,* May 1976, p. 66.

[13] *Ibid.,* p. 68.

[14] Harold H. Bloomfield, *TM: Discovering Inner Energy and Overcoming Stress* (New York: Delacorte Press, 1975), p. 19.

[15] Herbert Benson, *The Relaxation Response* (New York: William Morrow & Co., Inc., 1975), p. 60.

[16] *Ibid.,* pp. 112–113.

[17] *Ibid.,* pp. 62–67.

[18] Chester Swinyard, "Neurological and Behavioral Aspects of Transcendental Meditation Relevant to Alcoholism: A Review," *Annals of New York Academy of Science,* Vol. 233, April 1974.

[19] Jack K. Fordyce and Raymond Weil, *Managing With People: A Manager's Handbook of Organization Development Methods* (Reading, Mass.: Addison-Wesley Publishing Co., 1971), p. ix.

[20] Warren G. Bennis, *Organization Development: Its Nature, Origins, and Prospects* (Reading, Mass.: Addison-Wesley Publishing Co., 1969), p. 15.

[21] Paul Mali, *Managing By Objectives: An Operating Guide to Faster and More Profitable Results* (New York: Wiley-Interscience, 1972), p. 12.

[22] *Ibid.,* p. 5.

Appraisal and Reward
You are a Great Person ▪ ▪ ▪ ▪ ▪ ▪ ▪ ▪

12

OBJECTIVES

After reading this chapter you should be able to:
1. Discuss the importance of the two basic purposes of performance appraisals.
2. Describe how, ideally, an interviewer should prepare for and conduct an appraisal interview.
3. Define and give the advantages and disadvantages of the following types of appraisal methods:
   A. Essay,
   B. Graphic rating scale,
   C. Critical incident behavior,
   D. Field review,
   E. Ranking,
   F. Management by objectives.
4. Discuss the following errors that supervisors make when appraising employees:
   A. Halo effect,
   B. Personal bias,
   C. Central tendency,
   D. Overemphasis on recent behavior.
5. Discuss the changes that are taking place in employee attitudes toward their jobs, especially in relation to rewards.
6. Describe the various wage incentive plans.
7. Discuss the increasing importance of fringe benefits in establishing better employee/employer relationships.

Here are some more questions to think about while reading the chapter.

Why is a job description important?

What are some of the advantages of appraisals?

What type of appraisal is the most difficult to conduct?

What is meant by management by objectives?

What are some of the "human errors" in rating employees?

What are the various ways of paying a wage or salary?

What are the various forms of fringe benefits? What ones are the most important to you? Why?

What three forms of fringe benefits are most important to the class? Why?

How much should a company contribute a month to a pension plan? What percentage of the employee's pay should be contributed to a person's pension plan?

A LOOK AT APPRAISING AN INDIVIDUAL

Perhaps the most famous and effective performance appraisal of all time was addressed by God to the corrupt, idolatrous King Belshazzar, written on the wall of Belshazzar's palace by a disembodied hand: "You have been weighed in the balance and found wanting" (Daniel 5:27). His poor rating so upset Belshazzar that "he turned pale, he became limp in every limb, and his knees knocked together." He was shortly thereafter terminated.

Throughout history people have evaluated one another's performances, measuring them against the codes of behavior, morals, and values that form the very fabric of society. A process of evaluation is necessary for any sort of understanding and communication. In the job situation, the performance appraisal and interview are equally important to both the employer and the employee.

An employee needs to know if he is doing a good job

All workers must sometimes wonder whether their supervisors think they are doing a good job or not. They may feel that management is either comparing them with other employees or judging their performance against a standard, and the employees are unable to decide which of these two methods of appraisal is more fair.

An employee's attitude will influence to some degree the morale and performance of all the workers. All employees at one time or another wonder what their supervisor thinks of them and every employee is happier when he feels that his work is appreciated. For these reasons it is important that workers know what is expected of them, and also how they will be rewarded or punished if they surpass these expectations, meet them, or fail to meet them. A performance appraisal provides a method of measuring a worker's performance and of letting him know what management thinks. However, it is much more than just a "report card."

PURPOSES OF AN APPRAISAL

Performance appraisals serve many purposes, but they can be sorted roughly into two categories—the administrative purpose and the informative purpose. Appraisals fill certain needs of the employer and certain needs of the employee: a company needs satisfied employees and employees need a prosperous company, and therefore in satisfying the needs of one group, the performance appraisal is also satisfying the needs of the other.

The Administrative Purpose

Seniority system is easy to operate

Performance appraisals are useful for management because they provide a method of allocating the resources of the company. Specifically, they are the means of deciding who is to be promoted, who is to be transferred, and who is to be terminated. In some companies salaries are also determined by performance appraisals, but most companies use a seniority system, not because it is any fairer but because it is easier to operate, usually more objective, and creates less resentment among the employees. Performance appraisals compel the supervisors to do some constructive thinking about both their subordinates and themselves. To some extent any individual's performance is a function of how he or she is supervised; an employee who works best when left alone is unlikely to receive a good rating from a supervisor who watches subordinates closely. The feedback a supervisor receives from an employee in the course of an appraisal interview and the necessity of recording personal prejudices on paper are often educational experiences.

The Informative Purpose

The informative purpose of a performance appraisal, which is more obvious than the administrative purpose, albeit not more important, is to let the employee know whether management thinks he is doing a good job or not; to let the employee know what the company expects from him and what he can expect from the company; to let him know what aspects of his work his supervisor feels need improvement. It is also to bestow recognition on him for those aspects of his work which are outstanding. It is a way of letting him know that his work is appreciated. It is a way to help each employee perform his present job more efficiently and satisfyingly, and also a way to help each employee prepare for possible advancement and promotion.

Advantages and Disadvantages of Appraisals

ADVANTAGES OF APPRAISALS

1. Provides a basis upon which the employee knows he will be evaluated.
2. Motivates the employee by providing feedback on how he or she is doing.

---

3. Provides back-up data for management decisions concerning merit increases, promotions, transfers, and dismissals.
4. Can be constructive rather than critical.
5. Discovers good and bad traits sooner.
6. It is believed that a required periodic appraisal will force the supervisor to face up to the problems of poor performance and deal with them.
7. It forces the superior to communicate to his subordinates his judgment of their performance.

DISADVANTAGES OF APPRAISALS

1. Performance appraisal programs demand too much from supervisors.
2. Standards and ratings tend to vary widely and often unfairly.
3. Personal values and biases can replace organizational standards.
4. Because of lack of communications, employees may not know how they are rated.
5. Managers tend to resist and avoid the task of making formal appraisals, particularly when critical judgments are involved.

Job Description

Job description tells of the duties to be done

Usually, the best way to evaluate an employee is to judge how well the employee's assigned duties are carried out. Before an appraisal can be made, a job description must exist. Often such job descriptions are written, spelling out in a general way the responsibilities and tasks of a position. The job description of a mail clerk might read: "Receives and opens the mail; stamps the date received on each item; distributes the mail to the proper department or individual; picks up the mail from each department, prepares and stamps the necessary envelopes; wraps, addresses, and stamps packages; delivers the mail to the post office." Sometimes the job description is unwritten, but it must nevertheless be understood by both the employee and the supervisor before any performance appraisal can be made. If an employee does not know what is supposed to be done, the job cannot be successfully performed, and if a supervisor does not know what an employee is supposed to be doing, any appraisal will be meaningless.

THE APPRAISAL INTERVIEW

Performance appraisals cannot simply be handed to employees or put in their boxes or mailed to their homes, since they serve as the formal basis for a discussion of the employee's performance between the employee and the supervisor. This discussion is known as the appraisal interview, and it can be one of the most unpleasant tasks of a supervisor, or it can be one of the most satisfying. Which it is depends to a great degree upon how good the employee's performance has been. It can also depend upon how the supervisor handles the interview.

Preparing for the Interview

The supervisor should put his thoughts down in writing as much as possible. He should have the appraisal forms filled out and be prepared to justify each item. He should review the past reports of performance and try to recall what was covered in previous interviews. He should also remind the employee to prepare for the interview, to think about it ahead of time, and to jot down his thoughts. A supervisor should consider what questions he might ask if he were in the employee's place and be prepared to answer those questions. The interview, however, should not be planned too rigidly. It should be flexible, for it is actually as much a discussion as it is an interview.

Plan for a half-hour interview   The supervisor should pick the right day, the right time,

Figure 12–1. The supervisor should select a time for the appraisal when neither he nor the employee is likely to be under stress or tired.
Courtesy of Chino Valley Bank (Photo by Robert Curtis)

Inform the employee in advance

and the right place. He should allow at least a half-hour for the interview, and he should notify the employee well in advance. It is usually best not to have the interview immediately after a disciplinary action or a reprimand. The supervisor should select a time when neither he nor the employee is likely to be under stress or tired; mornings are usually best. The supervisor should arrange not to be interrupted and should provide a private and comfortable place to meet.

How to Open the Interview

If it is the employee's first appraisal interview, he or she should be told something about the general purpose of the appraisal and the interview.

If the performance of an employee has been outstanding, it is often a good practice to make this known at once because the employee will more readily accept any suggestion or minor criticism that the supervisor may want to make. If, however, the appraisal is something less than outstanding, it may be best to avoid a discussion of the employee's overall rating at the beginning. Indeed, it is often best to avoid starting with the past at all. If the supervisor opens with a discussion of the employee's future goals and plans, the interview will naturally go on to areas of improvement in the worker's present performance, and from there will return to and cover the past. If, however, the supervisor opens the appraisal interview with a discussion of the employee's past performance, the interview may bog down in a detailed discussion of a particular item and never get beyond the past.

Discussion Methods

Directive or permissive interviews

An appraisal interview can be either "directive" or "permissive"; that is, either the supervisor or the employee will direct its course. The ideal interview, however, will be neither, for both the supervisor and the employee have something to contribute; the whole discussion is about how the *supervisor* judges the performance of the *employee*, and therefore the participation of both is vital to a successful interview. The supervisor will probably open the interview by asking the employee about his present job and his future plans. He should seek to make the employee comfortable and put him at ease. After that, however, he should pause and encourage the employee to talk about himself and his job. If possible, he should let the employee analyze his own performance; people tend to believe what they have determined for themselves more readily that what they are told. If necessary, the supervisor can check his own understanding of what the employee is saying by summarizing and clarifying his points.

At some point, however, the supervisor does enter into the discussion in a more assertive way. He must let the employee know how he sees his performance and whether it meets the standards of the position. If it does not meet these standards, he must let the employee know in what ways it falls short and how it can be improved.

In the final analysis, the appraisal interview is a joint problem-solving effort, to which the supervisor and the employee both have something to contribute.

Ending the Interview

The interview should close when the supervisor has clarified what he intended to cover and the employee has likewise had a chance to review the issues concerning him. Company practices vary, but most supervisors give a copy of the performance evaluation to the employee immediately after the interview. If, however, the appraisal and the interview have dealt with the employee's objectives and his plans for achieving specific goals, that information is put into the report when the employee is given his copy. The supervisor should also reassure the employee of his interest and his willingness to take up the discussion at another time.

TYPES OF APPRAISAL METHODS

A number of appraisal methods are available, each with its own particular advantages and drawbacks.

Essay Appraisal

The essay appraisal method requires the supervisor to write a paragraph or more about the employee's strengths and weaknesses, the quality and quantity of his work, his present skill and knowledge and his potential value to the company. Such essays, unfortunately, tend to vary considerably in length and content. Although this method of appraisal probably gives a better and more fully rounded picture of the employee, it is likely to be more subjective than a simple graph or form because the supervisor is not as restricted in the terms he can use or the factors he can consider. On a form an employee can per-

"THAT'S THE SHORTEST ANNUAL REVIEW I'VE EVER HEARD."

haps only be "poor" or "average" or "excellent"; in an essay he can also be "above average" or "mediocre." For this very reason, however, an essay is not of much value for the purposes of comparison. In addition, essay writing is difficult and time consuming for the average supervisor. The method is seldom used except to appraise employees in middle- and top-management positions, although it is often employed in conjunction with some other method.

Graphic Rating Scale

A form for graphic rating is usually provided for the use of the appraiser, listing the factors to be considered and the terms to be used. Figures 12–2, 12–3, and 12–4 are examples of such a form.

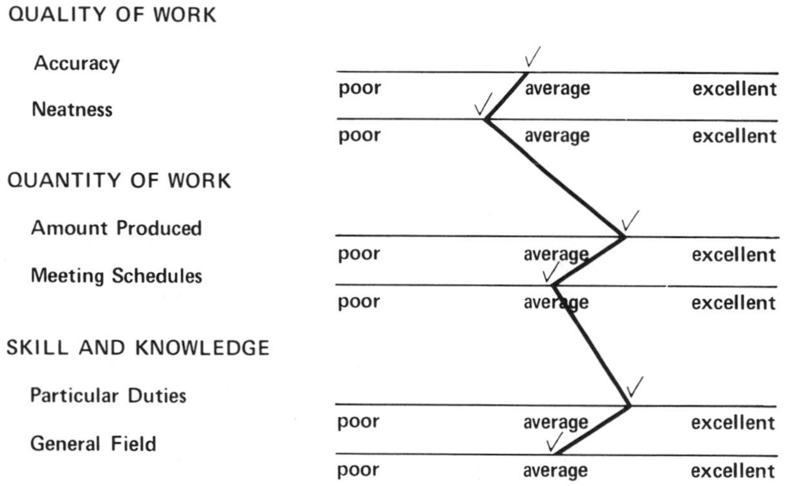

Figure 12–2. Graphic rating scale (or profile rating sheet) showing visually how well an employee is performing on the job (partial rating sheet).

Because the supervisor simply fills out the form, it is easy to prepare. When all the supervisors are using the same form and all the employees are being judged in the same terms, comparisons can be made more easily and will probably be fairer. Although the opinions and prejudices of the appraiser will still influence the rating, this is not necessarily a drawback because the only way the element of subjectivity can be removed from an appraisal method is to eliminate the appraiser. There are some important disadvantages, however. The categories and factors listed often tend to overlap, which makes it difficult for the conscientious supervisor to use the form (e.g., if the quantity and quality of an employee's work is excellent, how can the appraiser say that his skill and knowledge is anything other than excellent?). The method is also rather rigid and does not give a complete picture of the individual. For these reasons, the method is often employed in conjunction with the essay appraisal.

Critical Incident Behavior

Record incident that has happened

When the critical incident behavior method is used, the supervisor records actual behavior he has observed, noting down examples of insubordination or tardiness, and incidents in which the employee used good or bad judgment. Such a method is often used when a supervisor has already more or less decided to recommend that an employee be fired or promoted and company regulations require that he document his recommendations. Keeping such records of all employees, however, demands much of the supervisor's time.

Field Review

Field review or group appraisal is used for middle management

Field review is a method of group appraisal rather than an evaluation by a single person; the group can consist of fellow-employees or several supervisors or a combination of these. It is sometimes used when there is reason to suspect prejudice or bias on the part of the employee's supervisor, or when an employee wishes to appeal an appraisal. The judgment of the group will usually be more fair and valid than that of an individual, but field review is excessively time consuming, and it is not always easy to find a second supervisor who has any real firsthand knowledge of the employee. Some companies use the field method for all middle-management personnel in hopes that they will arrive at a more fair evaluation and overcome the personal biases of supervisors.

Ranking

Ranking means that the employee is compared with other employees. This method is useful and justifiable when several employees are being considered for promotion to a single position. It is also sometimes used when a company finds it necessary to lay off a part of its work force, although seniority more often determines who is laid off. For any other purposes than these, however, a method of appraisal should be used which compares

HOURLY REVIEW FORM

Employee _____Job Assignment_____

Supervisor_____Department_____

Date hired_____ Prior Appraisal Date_____

AREAS OF PERFORMANCE	Outstand-ing 10-9	Above Average 8-6	Average 5-3	Below Average 2-1	Unsatis-factory 0	N/A
JOB KNOWLEDGE: Comment:						
QUALITY OF WORK: Ability to meet standards.						
QUANTITY OF WORK: Ability to effectively use time and materials.						
SAFETY: Result of work under safe/unsafe practices.						

ATTENDANCE: Indicate hours off the job since the date of last appraisal due to:

Personal_____Illness_____Punctuality (tardiness)_____
Comment:

PERSONAL FACTORS	Otg 5pts	A/A 4	A 3-2	B/A 1	U/S 0	N/A
INITIATIVE: How person handles new skills or improvements. Comment:						
ADAPTABILITY: Ability to adjust to new situations. Comment:						
COOPERATION: Ability to get along with employees. Comment:						
DEPENDABILITY: Ability to complete the job. Comment:						

Figure 12-3. Profile rating sheet.

373

an employee to a job standard and not to his fellow employees, for comparing a person with his peers will almost invariably create serious jealousy and bad feeling in a company's work force. Supervisors and appraisers are human beings, however, and all human beings unconsciously tend to compare their associates with one another.[1]

Figure 12–4. Back side of profile rating sheet.

PRESENT EMPLOYEE'S JOB DUTIES_____

_____

COUNSELING SUMMARY

EMPLOYEE'S STRENGTHS   SUGGESTED IMPROVEMENTS

1. _____   1. _____

2. _____   2. _____

3. _____   3. _____

Improvement Activity

Consider how this employee has reacted to the counseling and suggestions which were prompted by the last formal appraisal. What has been accomplished toward the goals and objectives established in the previous interview? If the person has failed to follow through, indicate the reason why.

OVERALL RATING

Comment: _____   _____ Results achieved far exceed the requirements of the job in all areas.
_____   _____ Results achieved were above average
_____   _____ Consistently performed the job to requirements of the position
_____   _____ Results did not always meet the requirements of the position
_____   _____ Results frequently did not meet the requirements of the position.

OVERALL RATING Comment:

_____

_____

Company related extra curricular activity (safety committee, Christmas Party, picnic, etc.)_____

EMPLOYEE'S COMMENT:

_____

_____

_____

_____

Employee's Signature   Date   Supervisor's Signature

Comments by next level of supervision:_____

_____

Manager's Signature

MBO are goals set by both supervisor and employee

Future evaluations are based on MBO

Management by objectives is now widely used and was mentioned in the previous chapter. Under this method the employee and his supervisor set common goals, discussing together what the employee can accomplish during the next evaluation period, and agreeing on what is expected of the employee. This method follows four rules:

1. Both the superior and the subordinate jointly determine the critical elements of the position.
2. Both jointly decide how the performance will be measured.
3. Both jointly develop short-term targets to be accomplished before the next evaluation.
4. The appraisal focuses on the results that have been achieved in accomplishing these goals.

MBO must be measurable

The difficulty of the method is often in the second rule which is, of course, the basic problem of all the appraisal methods listed in this chapter. How do you measure performance? If the goal of a clerk-typist is to be able to type 60 wpm, it is quite simple to tell whether or not the goal has been achieved. Most goals, however, are not so easily measurable. Because it is an achievement-oriented method, management by objectives would seem to be a better instrument for measuring top- and middle-management performance than for measuring the performance of a clerk-typist, but the performance of middle- and top-management is often the hardest to measure.

Nevertheless, middle-management employees are usually more attuned to such approaches, because many have already been introduced to other management performance programs, such as product development plans of Program Evaluation Review Techniques (PERT) and departmental budgeting of Program Planning and Budgeting (PPB). With marketing and production managers using PERT, and business services using PPB, the introduction of management by objectives seems a logical approach to evaluating performance.[2]

FREQUENT ERRORS MADE IN RATING EMPLOYEES

There are a number of common mistakes supervisors make when they fill out performance appraisals, most of them being the sorts of mistakes we all make when we misjudge friends and acquaintances.

Halo Effect

When she is good, she is very, very good

Many people attribute nonexistent virtues or accomplishments to those they are attracted to. This is known as the halo effect. A supervisor may assume that if an employee is above average in one area, he is above average in all areas. Another term for this assumption is the *constant error:* considering the employee to be excellent in one particular area, the supervisor goes on to say that he is excellent in all areas. It is similar to another natural trend, that of rating a person as "excellent" rather than "above average," or flattering a worker rather than leaving room for improvement. The halo effect can also work in reverse. If a man strikes us as unpleasant, we may assume that he is an inefficient worker.

Personal Bias

Personal bias is difficult to avoid. Every human being has prejudices of one sort or another. Preference may be given to employees of the same race or the opposite sex, or to workers who belong to the same club as the supervisor. Intelligent or good-looking persons may receive better ratings than their actual job performances deserve. On the other hand, supervisors are often aware of their prejudices and may attempt to compensate for them, actually giving individuals against whom they are biased better performance appraisals than they really merit.

Central Tendency

Few people are above average

When central tendency prevails, the supervisor completes all the forms in about the same way for all the employees under him and all the employees come out about average. In his efforts to be fair, he does not discriminate among different workers or among the different areas of performance of an individual.

Overemphasis on Recent Behavior

Your performance on the day of evaluation is most important

Supervisors have a tendency to judge an employee's performance for the last year on his actions within the week just before the appraisal. The good or bad incidents of the last week are fresh in his mind; the achievements or failures of a year ago are forgotten. There is also a natural and quite proper hesitation to rehash a recent incident, particularly when it is one in which the employee looked bad. Nevertheless, the performance appraisal is a rating for an entire period. The critical incident technique can help overcome this overemphasis on recent behavior.

376

Mr. Smith is a foreman for the Crummy Concrete Company. The team he supervises consists of Nick, Pedro, and Donald. Nick is the outstanding employee on the team but last week he and Mr. Smith had a bitter argument. Donald, on the other hand, is only an average worker, but during the past week he has volunteered several times to stay a little late and help clean the machinery. Smith is about to submit his semiannual performance appraisal of his work team to top management. He wants to be a fair supervisor, but he will have a natural tendency to rate Donald higher than his overall performance during the past six months deserves, and to rate Nick lower. If he had kept a record of the actual performance of each of the two men on the job for this period and reviewed it prior to filling in the appraisals, his ratings might have been more accurate.

EVALUATING THE PROBATIONARY EMPLOYEE

Many organizations have a probationary period of employment after which the employee is either terminated or granted permanent status. Usually a performance appraisal must be made at the end of the probationary period and the supervisor is required to recommend whether or not the worker be granted this permanent status. This rating is perhaps the most important single performance appraisal the employee will receive. Before the supervisor recommends a subordinate for permanent status, he should have complete confidence that the employee fully meets the performance standards of the position, for it is often difficult to dismiss a permanent employee.

It is harder to get rid of a permanent employee

A probationary employee can be released anytime

Probationary employees can usually be released at any time during their period of probation if, in the judgment of the department head, their dismissal is in the best interests of the company. Should the supervisor have a question in his mind about the fitness of an employee for a position, he should seriously consider the consequences of burdening the firm with an employee who is likely to be a liability rather than an asset. He should also consider that it would probably be a disservice to the employee himself to retain him in a position for which he is not suited.

A plumbing and fixtures company hired George, a college drop-out, as an inspector. George was a physics major until he left college in his junior year because of personal problems. He is not really interested in inspecting fixtures and is not enthusiastic about advancing in the company. But his supervisor, Mr. Brown, feels sorry for George and at the end of his probationary period gave him a good performance appraisal. After a year, however, George becomes more and more embittered and starts to blame the company for his failure to complete college. His bitterness begins to affect other employees in the plant, but the company is unable to fire him because his actual work is about average and the concern's agreement with the union will not allow an average worker with permanent status to be dismissed except on specific grounds. Had Mr. Brown used the probationary appraisal to discuss George's discontent objectively and openly with him in the interview, a serious morale problem could have been avoided.

SPECIAL UNSCHEDULED APPRAISALS

Because of company regulations, union agreements, or state laws, employees may often not be terminated for reasons of unsatisfactory performance unless there is documented evidence of a specific nature. Performance appraisals serve to provide a written record of specified deficiencies during the rating period in which the deficiencies were observed. Often incidents which are not recorded on appraisals cannot properly be used as a basis for dismissal. Similarly, warning may be required before recommendations for demotion, dismissal, or other disciplinary action can be made. These warnings are put in writing on the appraisal form, special forms for the purpose, or written memoranda, copies of which are given to the employee.

Not all unscheduled appraisals, however, are for cases involving unsatisfactory performance. The special evaluation is also an ideal method of recording and commending a particularly outstanding performance.

CRITICISMS OF THE APPRAISAL SYSTEM

Performance review procedures are not without their critics. Such formal appraisals demand too much paperwork and too much time. Too often they deteriorate into rituals. They place too little emphasis on mutual planning and problem solving. They tend to focus too much on the personality of the individual rather than on the requirements of the position. Douglas McGregor commented that the best performance appraisal form he ever saw was a "blank piece of paper."[3] However, performance appraisal is the best system so far for weeding out incompetents, rewarding the outstanding employee, and evaluating the personnel strength of an organization.

EMPLOYEE REWARDS

A profound shift in America's attitudes and way of life is taking place. A reassessment of the American Dream is accelerating as the pursuit of the good life slows down and Americans begin to retrench after the turbulent sixties.

The future seems to point to a more traditionally European way of life, with less abundance of material goods and more attention to human relationships and a relaxed pace of living.

However, the belief that hard work will be amply rewarded still motivates many Americans. Although the task of making a million dollars becomes harder each year, one out of every thousand Americans is a millionaire. Of the estimated 210,000 millionaires in the United States today, roughly 5% are under 35 years of age.[4] In general, they are superachievers who have channeled their ambition to the pursuit of great wealth. In

Figure 12–5. Those who are making a million.
Source: "Now It's the Young People Making Money,"
U.S. News & World Report, February 25, 1974.

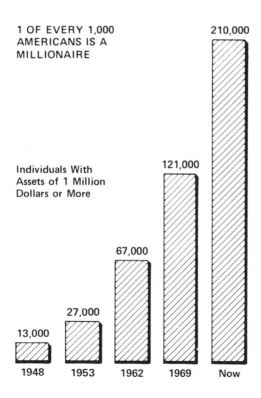

1 OF EVERY 1,000 AMERICANS IS A MILLIONAIRE

Individuals With Assets of 1 Million Dollars or More

1948	1953	1962	1969	Now
13,000	27,000	67,000	121,000	210,000

addition to this drive, the young millionaires are totally dedicated to their work, because the level of job stimulation (creative and intellectual) seems to match the personality needs of each.

The principle of matching job to worker, or developing the job to fit the worker is highly successful in terms of human relationships and worker output. The worker who occupies the niche which corresponds to his own image and assessment of his capabilities and talents will be doing his work as an end in itself, rather than as a duty or chore or simply for the paycheck, and he will get a great deal of personal satisfaction from completing the job.

The standards by which workers judge the acceptability of their jobs have changed radically since the beginnings of the Industrial Revolution. Fast disappearing are the fears of being unemployed and the idea that hard work is a good thing in itself. With the institution of the G.I. Bill and other government programs, higher education is open to many people and with increased education comes greater expectations. In 1922 Henry Ford said of his employees: "Above all [the automobile worker] wants a job in which he does not have to think." But a recent nationwide Department of Labor survey suggests that what working Americans now want most from their jobs is that they be in some way interesting.[5]

In contrast to older workers, today's job holders object to job regimentation, "Big Brother" control from management, and the lack of opportunities to use their own initiative. We see an important phenomenon occurring today—rebellion against job monotony and actual hatred of one's occupation. Boredom on the job and the feelings of irrelevancy that accompany it underline the surreal, hypnotic quality of production work. Management will have more difficult times ahead as workers rebel against the feeling of being unnecessary, of being only a machine, dehumanized to produce quantity, not quality. Workers have the gnawing fear that they are not masters of their machines but slaves to them.

Along with the workers' fear of being psychologically or physically devoured by machines, management and labor have to grapple with the fact that it is becoming increasingly less possible to get something for nothing. Management cannot easily get so-called "cheap labor" because of the minimum wage standards set by the government and the power of unions to organize workers and ask for additional wages and benefits. Labor, on the other hand, cannot expect soaring wages and fringe benefits without an equal rise in inflation, which eats into the buying power of the dollar and, in the end, raises interest rates and weakens the worker's financial gains.

All these shifts in values and attitudes make the already delicate relationship between management and workers even more precarious. Rewards have to be carefully considered and monitored and the whole area of appraisals carefully and continuously thought about.

We might make a comparison here to the well-known fairy tale about the sorcerer's apprentice, who dislikes the boring and menial job of carrying water, so he chants a forbidden spell and brings a legion of broomsticks to life, who carry in buckets of water. The apprentice is pleased with his efficiency until he realizes that he doesn't know the magic words that will stop the broomsticks. Consequently, he is almost drowned by the flood from the waterbuckets, until the sorcerer comes to his sheepish apprentice's rescue. This is why it is sometimes better to give a healthy bonus than a salary increase that extends the life of the employee's tenure.

When the worker feels like a lackey, doing a tiresome, repetitive, and apparently meaningless job, he will almost inevitably look for shortcuts, or ways to get out of doing the job altogether. If the frustration gets too great, the worker may damage the product, intentionally or through carelessness. This is self-defeating for both labor and management.

Stories about boring jobs

Jokes and stories about product deficiencies have become a part of our oral tradition. A college student who worked in a cannery for a summer tells grisly tales of relieving the monotony of the production line by inserting frogs, twigs, bugs, and snakes into random cans.

Sabotage

Poltergeists or ghosts seem to inhabit many new cars. One woman heard a continual rattle in the deep recesses of her car's engine. She took the car to her mechanic, who was obliged to dismantle it in search of the elusive rattle. Finally he reached a twisted pipe with a large, loose bolt inside it. A brief message attached to the bolt read: "I bet you had a helluva time finding *this* one." Incidents like these would in all likelihood almost never occur if workers had truly rewarding jobs. Such sabotage of the company product means that management must take workers' needs for rewarding work seriously. And paychecks are not the answer.

Job enrichment

Although automobile assembly-line work is still monotonous, even since the advent of automation, the Chrysler Corporation has attempted to alleviate the monotony for workers with a "Job Enrichment" program. Chrysler asks its various plant managers to consult the workers for suggestions about improvements, keeping four principles in mind: (1) fix responsibility as far down as possible; (2) give enough authority to go with it; (3) let workers know the concrete results of their suggestions and improvements; (4) create a climate that encourages change. In some plants, as many as 85 percent of the suggestions concerned small practical ways in which the work itself could be done more efficiently.[6]

Other automobile manufacturers are coming up with similar innovations in order to give both management and labor a voice in operations and policies. Foremen attend small-group sensitivity training courses; workers and supervisors meet weekly to brainstorm problems and solutions, and substantial bonuses are awarded for good ideas; workers are allowed flexible time schedules and planned absences (with advance notice.)

WAGES AS A FORM OF REWARD

Being paid a just amount of wages in return for one's time, energy, and skill is a fundamental idea that underlies any modern industrial society. Workers need to satisfy basic material needs for themselves and their families, and wages in the form of cash and fringe benefits enable them to fulfill these needs. Wages, however, are much more than a means of satisfying basic material needs. Human beings, regardless of the form of society in which they live, have similar material wants for food, clothing, and shelter, but primitive societies have other means of gratifying these needs: the barter system, the indenture system, and the slave labor system. But as societies become more sophisticated and complex, wages become not only a material reward but also a form of recognition, of approval for a job well done. Wages give the wage earner status, power, and respect. They are forms of communication; just as we have seen that a good performance appraisal is a way of telling the employee that his employer appreciates his work, a raise is another way of communicating the same information. There are, of course, still other ways of letting an employee know that he is doing a good job: a more important-sounding title, a private office, a space in the parking lot. These are all forms of employee rewards, and indeed they become more and more important when an individual moves upward and his actual financial needs have been satisfied.

Ways of letting employee know he is doing a good job

On most levels of an organization, however, the general procedure that is followed when a supervisor recognizes superior performance is a good performance appraisal followed by a promotion bonus or a raise or a combination of both. The supervisor rewards a high level of achievement over a short period of time with a substantial pay raise which the employee will receive for the rest of his working life. He does so in the hope that the high level of achievement will also continue.

SALARIES

Salaries consist of base pay and fringe benefits. The base pay is more important than fringe benefits, both in practical and psychological terms. An employee must feel that his base pay is fair and adequate: an employer cannot make up in fringe benefits for what is lacking in the basic wages, because a below-average wage plan with good benefits provides security but little substance for immediate necessities. The employee must provide both his basic wants and his luxuries out of his pay. Once these needs are met, fringe benefits can add a most welcome incentive.

Salary can mean purchasing power, status, respect, and appreciation

As we have pointed out, wages mean much more to an employee than simply what he can purchase with them. They mean status, respect, appreciation. Workers need the reassurance that wages can give them; although the company may have been good to them in the past, they need to have their feelings of worth updated periodically. Thus most companies give yearly raises. Indeed, in a great many organizations, except for general pay raises, these are the only raises an employee receives unless he is promoted to a higher position. The employee is practically guaranteed his raise, but status, appreciation, respect, all the intangible benefits that are bestowed with a merit raise are virtually eliminated; the raise simply means that the employee has been there for another year. Given that there are a limited number of positions to which workers can be promoted, this means that other reward systems, such as performance appraisals, become all the more important. There are plans which attempt to link the wages themselves more closely to performance; these are called the wage incentive plans.

WAGE INCENTIVE PLANS

Below are descriptions of eight wage incentive plans, each of which has certain advantages and disadvantages. Many such plans have been devised, only to be abandoned and replaced by others. Any wage incentive plan must take several factors into consideration:

1. The wage paid must be related to the individual's output.
2. The wage plan must make adequate provision for learners and new employees.
3. The plan must be easily administered, easily understood by the employees, and easily related to costs.

Piece Rate

The employee is paid at a set rate for each piece he produces. There may be a guaranteed minimum wage, although such a guarantee is not an inherent part of the plan. Usually the minimum is considerably lower than the average piece rate earnings, thus encouraging a better-than-minimum performance. Often the minimum is only the provision for new employees who are learning the procedure.

Taylor Differential Piece Rate

Exceed the standard and receive a bonus— Taylor method

This system was devised by Frederick W. Taylor, the father of scientific business management. A standard number of pieces is established which an employee is expected to produce in a day. If an employee exceeds this standard, he is paid at a higher rate for each piece he produces. If he fails to meet the standard, he is paid at a lower rate.

Group Incentive Rates

According to this system, employees are divided into different groups, and the output of the whole group determines the salaries of the employees in it. When such a method is used, each group must develop considerable cooperation and teamwork; otherwise, the employees who would work faster under an individual incentive plan tend to slow down to the level of the rest of the group, and slower employees go unnoticed.

Commissions

This system is similar to the piece rate. It is a method whereby the income of salespeople is a percentage of their sales. Many salespeople receive a base salary in addition, while others have a guaranteed minimum wage.

Profit-Sharing Plans

These plans are simply a method of distributing a portion of a company's profits among its employees. Such plans provide an incentive for efficiency, innovation, and cooperation among an organization's work force. Usually the profits are distributed annually, sometimes in the form of a Christmas bonus. Profit sharing is a way of enabling a company to give a pay increase to all of its employees without being saddled with such an increase indefinitely. It has the disadvantage, however, of rewarding all the workers indiscriminately, just as the group incentive rates reward all the employees in a particular group without attempting to differentiate between the efficient and the inefficient.

Scanlon Plan

Scanlon plan means cost reduction

According to this system, increased efficiency in the company's operation is passed on to the employees. The Scanlon plan is not exactly profit sharing, but rather cost-reduction sharing. Unlike profit-sharing plans, the relationship between the wages of the worker and the efficient operation of the organization can be more readily seen, a relationship made even more apparent because the extra cash is paid to the workers as part of their monthly salary. Various incentives are often offered to employees who can suggest ways in which the operation can be made even more efficient, although such a suggestion plan is in no way unique to this method.

Merit Increases

Merit increase means wage increase for excellent performance

These are simply increases in pay given to employees who have received excellent performance appraisals. The system has the advantage of being uncomplicated, and the raises received under such a method probably communicate more of the intangibles (status, appreciation, respect) than raises received under any other system do. Unfortunately, the method also can produce considerable ill will and jealousy; and, because the employee receives raises almost entirely at the discretion of his supervisor, the system is only as fair or unfair as the supervisor is.

Cash Bonuses

Cash bonuses are simply money given to employees for outstanding performance, as a sort of one-time merit increase. Like profit-sharing plans, bonuses have the advantage of not continuing indefinitely.

FRINGE BENEFITS

In every organization the objectives of the firm and the objectives of the employees do not always coincide. There are also conflicts over the division of rewards in a business enterprise. The owners, the management, and the workers are all contenders. Loyalty and mutual respect, however, are necessary in any organization. Just as employees need to feel that the company they work for appreciates their efforts and cares for them, a company also needs loyal employees. One important method of encouraging such loyalty is fringe benefits.

Employees will make sacrifices for a company when they feel that the company, in turn, will make sacrifices for them. Thus a utility crew may take great personal risks to keep telephone service open during a flood. The employees of a store might accept a pay cut when the store is faced with a financial crisis. Less dramatic but no less important is the worker who will stay on the job for an extra ten or fifteen minutes to explain something to his supervisor. On the other hand, when employees are in trouble, they rightly expect the company to make sacrifices also. It is here that fringe benefits come in, for the greater part of such benefits are forms of insurance: medical plans, sick pay, group life insurance, pensions, and credit unions.

During 1972 it was estimated that fringe benefits averaged to more than $50 a week for each employee. Of this amount, $20 was paid for time not worked (vacations, holidays, sick pay) and $30 was paid for other benefits, such as social security, pensions, and profit sharing. In 1971 fringe benefits were more than 100 percent higher than they had been a decade before, although wages rose only 64 percent during the same period.[7]

Fringe benefits cost more than 1/3 of payroll costs

Companies report that fringe benefits are taking a bigger bite out of payroll costs. Employee fringe benefits account for 35 percent of the average employee earnings. A study done by the U.S. Chamber of Commerce shows that a typical company paid out $3,984 per worker (Figure 12–6). The highest money paid out seems to come from the manufacturing companies. Over 36 percent of the payroll of manufacturing companies goes toward fringe benefits.[8] Although the most common benefits seem to be vacations, group life insurance, and medical plans, they range all the way from organ transplants to group auto insurance to company-paid legal fees. The following list is only partial. From your own working experience, can you think of others?

Because of the many available benefits, various large firms have been able to offer their employees compensation packages from which the employees could select the benefits they want.

Figure 12–6. Fringe benefits: gaining twice as fast as wages. (Average cost per employee in industry).
Source: U.S. News & World Report, Oct. 25, 1976.

	1965	1975		
Fringe Benefits	$1,502	$3,984	Increase in "Fringes"	Up 165%
Pay for Time Worked	$5,460	$9,709	Pay Increase Up 78%	
Total Employment Costs	$6,962	$13,693	Total Increase Up 97%	

Such "cafeteria style" packages are tailored to the needs of the individual employee. Different people have different needs and desires. For example, younger employees prefer higher salaries rather than extensive retirement plans. An employee who likes to ski would be interested in membership in a company-owned ski lodge. Women employees, married employees, and employees with children usually consider a medical plan to be the most desirable benefit, especially if it includes maternity benefits. Stock options often appeal primarily to single employees and professional employees. A psychological advantage to these benefit packages is that the employees, by participating in the formulation of their own packages, are more satisfied with their own roles in the programs, and thus the fringe benefits they receive are more "visible" and tangible.

Many workers, especially women clerical employees, feel that organizing for concrete benefits like equal pay, tuition refunds, child care centers, and pensions will also provide the intangible goal of winning respect from their employers because their jobs will take on a more professional status.[9]

PENSION PLANS

Many employee retirement plans are tax deferred

There is a considerable advantage to having money for a pension plan contributed by the firm or withheld from an employee's paycheck before he receives it: the worker does not have to pay taxes on it until he begins to receive the pension, which is usually in his retirement years. Thus, whether it is an annuity plan, a mutual fund or investment program handled by an insurance company, or a stock purchase plan, it is beneficial to the employee not only for his retirement but also as a deferred tax program. He does not, however, receive much interest on that money. If Congress or state legislatures pass laws to make it easier to carry accumulated pension credits from one company to another, employee mobility, at least in upper management, may rise substantially.

NEW BENEFIT PLANS

Preretirement Counseling

The moment of retirement marks a major transition in a person's life. At age 65, a man has an extra forty hours a week to spend as he pleases. All at once he can stay up as late and sleep as late as he wants. He does not have to worry about whether sales in his department are down or whether the assembly line

Table 12–1. Types of Fringe Benefits Provided by Companies

Social Security	Workmen's Compensation
Group life insurance	Supplemental unemployment benefits
Medical plans	Credit unions
Pension plans	Annuity programs
Stock purchase plans	Educational aid
Recreational aid	Vacation with pay
Paid holidays	Paid birthday off
Company discount stores	Profit sharing
Loans	Group dental plans
Flexible time schedules	Child care centers

has broken down again. However, retirement is not always so pleasant; there is a negative side to it. Since he has worked all his life, he does not know what to do with his extra forty hours a week; no matter how much he may have griped about the job, he suddenly finds that it was necessary after all. Suddenly he feels superfluous and unnecessary. Since most of his friends were at the office, he feels "left out" even though he still has contact with them. He feels old—without authority and without respect. Many people feel the need for guidance at this stage in their lives, and many companies as well as the U.S. Civil Service Commission provide both clinics and counseling for those employees approaching retirement. The clinics deal with such areas as financial planning, leisure time activities, the psychological and physical aspects of retirement, employment opportunities, available benefits, and so on. More and more companies are establishing such programs and urging employees drawing close to retirement age to look into them.

Preretirement counseling helps overcome psychological and physical traumas

Action for Independent Maturity (AIM), a national nonprofit organization, trains people to conduct preretirement education and counseling programs for industry. A happy retiree promotes positive public relations.[10]

Sabbaticals

Although teachers have been given sabbaticals for many years, business executives and managers have seldom been granted them. The practice is becoming more and more common today, however, as a means of enabling the executive to gain a fresh and objective outlook on the company's problems. The executive on a sabbatical may teach courses or give lectures in his field, attend seminars and classes, make contacts and renew acquaintances in his particular field, or promote the company abroad and seek new markets. The sabbatical may vary from thirteen weeks at full pay to six months at half pay. While the executive is on his sabbatical, the company will also have an opportunity to place other men in his position temporarily and train them. Perhaps it is for this reason, interestingly enough, that managers and executives themselves often resist sabbaticals, considering themselves too busy or too indispensable.[11]

Shorter or More Flexible Working Hours

In recent years a number of companies have experimented with the shorter work week. In 1973, some 3,000 companies in the United States had adopted the four-day week, compared with an estimated forty in 1970.[12]

Many foreign companies, however, have experimented with flexible working hours. Within limits, employees are permitted to come to work when they choose. In order to guarantee coverage at crucial hours, the workers make whatever arrangements they choose among themselves. Such flexible working hours do much toward making the employee feel like an individual rather than just a piece of machinery which is plugged in at 8:00 and unplugged at 5:00. In addition, flexible hours ease the rush hour traffic crunch and allow the public transportation systems to be utilized more efficiently.

SUMMARY

Performance appraisals serve many purposes. They let management know the quality of the company's personnel; they compel the supervisor to think constructively about his subordinates and about himself; they inform the employee what management thinks about the job he is doing. If a performance appraisal is to be filled out, a job description must exist. The employee and the supervisor must both know what the employee is supposed to be doing. The performance appraisal forms the basis of the appraisal interview, a discussion between the supervisor and the employee covering not only the past performance of the employee but also his future plans, his goals, and possible ways in which he can improve at his job. There are several types of appraisal methods. The *essay appraisal* requires the supervisor to write a paragraph about the employee's performance. The *graphic rating scale* is a form listing a number of performance factors; the supervisor states on the form whether the employee is poor, average, or excellent in a number of performance areas. In *critical incident behavior* the supervisor keeps track of incidents and examples as they occur. The *field re-*

view is a group appraisal of an employee by a number of persons. *Ranking* is a method whereby the employee is compared with his fellow employees. *Management by objectives* places the emphasis upon the employee's goals and the methods whereby those goals can be achieved. Sometimes rating methods are combined: the essay is combined with the graphic rating scale. Each of these methods has its own advantages and disadvantages. In addition to the advantages and disadvantages inherent in each method, there are also a number of errors which supervisors can make when appraising employees. A boss can assume that because an employee is outstanding in one particular field, he is outstanding in other ways too. This is known as the *halo effect.* Supervisors can let their own *personal bias* influence them. They can fill out the forms for all employees under them in about the same way, a *central tendency* which reduces them all to one common denominator. Another kind of error is placing *too much emphasis on recent behavior.*

There are some special types of appraisals. Many companies have a probationary period of employment after which the employee is either terminated or granted permanent status. The performance appraisal made at the end of this probationary period is particularly important because it usually determines whether or not the worker is granted permanent status. There are also special unscheduled appraisals which are used to provide a written record that may be necessary for either termination or promotion. We have seen that the employee, as well as the supervisor, should prepare beforehand for appraisal interviews. Although performance review procedures have been criticized for demanding too much time and work, for often deteriorating into meaningless rituals, for placing too little emphasis on mutual planning and too much emphasis on the personality of the employee, they are nevertheless the best system so far devised for rating employees and strengthening the personnel of the company.

Rewards in the form of wages satisfy much more than simply the basic material needs of employees. They represent status, respect, and appreciation. Wages are given in various ways. There is the simple salary with regular raises, an uncomplicated system. However, when seniority alone is the basis for a pay raise, the raise carries with it little status and is not really considered by the employee to be a token of appreciation. There are also various wage incentive plans, which seek to base the wage on the efficiency and output of the worker. There is *piece rate* in which the employee is paid at a set rate for each piece. There are *commissions* in which a salesman is given a percentage of his sales. Both of these plans often include a guaranteed minimum wage. According to the *Taylor differential piece rate,* the more productive worker is paid at a higher rate for each piece. There are *group incentive rates* in which the output of a whole group determines the wages of the employees of that particular group. In *profit-sharing plans* a portion of the company's profits is shared with the employees; in the *Scanlon plan,* the employees are given a share of the money saved by increased efficiency of operation. There are also *merit increases* and *cash bonuses.*

In addition to ordinary wages of one sort or another, most companies offer their employees fringe benefits. Most, but not all, of these provide employees with security in case of sickness, old age, or other emergencies. They include sick pay, group medical and dental plans, group life insurance, and vacations. Many large companies allow their employees to choose among the various available fringe benefits. Among the new fringe benefits which have lately become widespread are clinics and counseling for retiring employees, sabbaticals for executives and managers, shorter or more flexible working hours, and child care centers.

In this chapter we have seen that the new generation of workers demands more than strictly monetary reimbursement; they want to feel needed by the company, and they want effective communication with management, particularly in performance appraisals; and most of all they want a sense of personal fulfillment from their jobs.

A NEW CAR AS A BONUS?

Case Study #1

An article in a financial newspaper appeared this way: "MOTIVATING WITH MONEY, the Eden Roc Hotel in Miami Beach vows to make its staff 'the best in the world.' The hotel's new owner will give the 'employee of the month' a new Vega. The 'employee of the year' gets $10,000. And if they're still unhappy, he names an 'ombudsman' attorney to represent the 500 workers in dealing with management."

What is your first reaction to this type of reward system? Are there some problems connected with it? Would you use it if you were the new owner of the hotel?

1. What type of appraisal system would you set up to see that the best employee was selected?
2. How could you overcome some of the problems that might arise from this system?
3. If you had the same amount of money available for this bonus program how might you set up a different program?

WHAT REWARDS SHOULD BE GIVEN NOW?

Case Study #2

Bruce Levin is the Sales Manager of the Amcox Corporation, which sells sewing notions to distribution and retail outlets. Bruce has 23 employees in his department and all are paid on commission for their sales in their territories. For the past three years, the market for the company's goods has been steadily growing and the majority of Bruce's men and women have met this growth with increased sales. However, one employee in particular, Jerry Lawson, has not kept up with the pace.

Jerry has been with Amcox for 15 years and is now 59 years old. Jerry is a friendly man and is well liked by both his peers and those to whom he sells notions on a regular basis. The company has always considered Jerry dependable and loyal. Through the years Jerry has been counted as an asset to the company, but at the age of 59 he has gone into a state of semiretirement. Jerry's sales have not increased as the others have, and he doesn't have the determination to acquire a significant increase in sales.

Bruce Levin wishes to change this situation. He wants to motivate Jerry into increasing his sales to match that of his younger peers. To accomplish this Jerry must begin to do more than put in his time, but Bruce is not sure how to go about trying to motivate him. Unlike the majority of the new employees Jerry is an older man, who within a few years will reach the age of retirement.

If you were Bruce what would you do?

1. Would you threaten to fire him?
2. Does your solution involve the feelings of others in your staff?
3. Would you increase his commissions?
4. Would you increase the retirement benefits for Jerry rather than offer him the increased commission rate?

5. Would you offer him more status in the way of a new title, or a new company car or place his desk in a better position in the office?

6. Is there some way in terms of appraisal and rewards that you can motivate Jerry?

FORCED RETIREMENT

Case Study #3

Caswell Industries has a mandatory retirement policy. Paul Armstrong will be 65 in two months and knows that everyone who has reached retirement age in the past has retired. He, however, has decided to talk to Tom Riley, the company president.

"Tom, as you know, I'll be turning 65 in a few months and according to company policy I'll be retiring. Well, I'm not ready to retire! Please listen, I'd like to have my say. You know as well as I do that I'm in fine health. I passed the company's physical less than three months ago with flying colors. I'm not ready to be forced out to pasture yet. If you let me go, you'll be losing a valuable man, and you'll be condemning me to idleness for the rest of my life. Forcefully retiring a person at 65 isn't fair. You can't judge a person's abilities mentally or physically, based solely upon age. I'm in better health than some of the workers in this company younger than 40. I'm asking you to change your retirement policy not only for myself, but for everyone else who faces having to leave their jobs for such a poor reason."

"I know how you must feel, Paul. It's a major point in one's life when retirement is reached, but you must realize that our mandatory retirement policy—and for that matter, society's general retirement policies—are necessary. If we did away with retirement rules how would we offer new job openings to younger workers? How would we offer more promotions to our employees? I don't think that you fully realize the situation of things, Paul. Mandatory retirement is necessary in business. How about meeting the federal mandate to increase the hiring of women and minorities? Can you imagine how hard that would be without anyone being forced to retire? Now, although I admit that you are an exception, there is, I believe, a definite correlation between age and one's ability to work well. The only way that I can see to be fair to older employees is to set a neutral age for mandatory retirement. That age throughout the country is 65. Do you understand now, Paul, why we must stick to our policy?

1. Who would you side with, Paul Armstrong or Tom Riley?
2. Give reasons for your stand.
3. Some companies are strongly encouraging employees to retire at the age of 55 in order to give opportunities of promotion to younger company members? Do you feel this method is fair to the older employees?
4. What suggestions would you make for a retirement program?

Terms and Concepts Students Should Know

appraisal interview	Taylor payment plan	halo effect
graphic rating scale	pension plans	Scanlon plan
field reviews	job description	merit system
management by objectives	critical incident behavior	preretirement counseling
overemphasis on recent behavior	forced choice ratings	

Bibliography

1. LUTHANS, FRED, *Organizational Behavior*, 2nd ed., New York, McGraw-Hill Book Company, 1977, Chapter 19.
2. BITTEL, LESTER R., *Improving Supervisory Performance*, New York, McGraw-Hill Book Company, 1976, Chapter 14.
3. FULMER, ROBERT, *Practical Human Relations*, Homewood Illinois, Richard D. Irwin, Inc., 1977, Chapter 14.
4. BITTEL, LESTER R., *What Every Supervisor Should Know*, New York, McGraw-Hill Book Company, 1974, Chapters 11, 12.

Footnotes

[1] Winston Oberg, "Make Performance Appraisals Relevant," *Harvard Business Review*, January–February, 1972, pp. 61–67.

[2] David Hampton, "The Planning-Motivation Dilemma," *Business Horizons*, June 1973, p. 79.

[3] George Rieder, "Performance—A Mixed Bag," *Harvard Business Review*, July–August, 1973, p. 61.

[4] "Now It's Young People Making Millions," *U.S. News & World Report*, 25 February 1974, p. 4. "The Hot New Rich," *Time*, 13 June 1977, pp. 72–84.

[5] "Boredom Spells Trouble on the Line," *Life*, 1 September 1972, p. 38.

[6] *Life, op. cit.*, p. 38.

[7] Fred D. Lindsey, "Those Whopping Extra Benefits for Employees," *Nation's Business*, August 1972, pp. 58–59.

[8] "The Fringe Fever Keeps Rising," *U.S. News & World Report*, 25 October 1976, p. 83.

[9] Ann Roberts, "Organizing to Organize," *Ms*, August 1974, p. 21.

[10] "Life After Work: Business Moves to Ease Retirement Trauma," *Boston Globe*, 3 October 1976.

[11] "Letting the Boss Take a Sabbatical," *Business Work*, 8 April 1972, pp. 42–43.

[12] *Wall Street Journal*, 30 April 1973.

Four

Humans Must Fit In a Society

Status and the Work Force

" My Dad's Better than Your Dad! " ....

OBJECTIVES

After reading this chapter you should be able to:

1. Discuss the "relativity" of status.

2. Explain why occupations are major channels for rising in social status.

3. Explain how differences in job status are expressed by:
    - A. Job titles,
    - B. Task differentiations,
    - C. Professionalism,
    - D. Hours and pay,
    - E. Work environment,
    - F. Clothing.

4. Discuss the implications of the fact that "the more people desire to move upward, the less accurate their communication upward is.

■ ■ ■ ■ ■ ■ ■ ■ ■ ■ ■ ■ ■ ■ ■ ■ ■ ■ ■

Here are some more questions to stimulate your thinking and open avenues of discussion before you read the chapter.

To which social or occupational class do you aspire?

Do you believe you will remain in the same class as your parents, or do you have upward mobile aspirations?

What is the difference between earned status and status that is donated?

How does each kind of status affect a person's self-esteem?

What personal goals do you have that you believe you have the ability to accomplish?

Will accomplishing them produce more status for you?

What external factors or symbols indicate the status of others?

How aware are you of your own dress standards and habits and what they represent socially?

How would you rate different occupations in terms of status? Do some jobs have more prestige, even though they produce less income than other positions in the marketplace?

"Status is not a thing, but an evaluation. If a man thinks that he has status because he has a new car, he has status."[1] Do you agree with that statement?

THE SOCIAL BASIS OF STATUS

Definition

It is an American ideal to believe that all people are born equal. Behind this concept of equality lies the assumption that all people are *similar* enough to deserve equal opportunities in life. It is also an American practice to observe *differences* among people and to make value judgments about those differences. Americans, like people everywhere, compare themselves to others, as individuals and according to the group standards with which they identify. Whether or not they are proud of it, they are usually ready to admit feeling superior or inferior to others.

Every individual has a status position within every group of which he or she is a member, and every group has a status position within the larger social system. Deep social conflicts have raged concerning the supposed superiority or inferiority of one group compared to another.

Status is ranking by prestige as seen by others

Status is the name applied to the *ranking or ordering of people into relative positions of prestige, and the social rewards offered with such positions.* Status involves a two-way transaction that must include at least two people. One person may claim status, but status is not achieved unless the other person confers it. C. Wright Mills says,

> Claims for prestige, however expressed, must be honored by others, and, in the end, must rest upon more or less widely acknowledged bases, which distinguish the people of one social stratum from others. The prestige of any stratum, of course, is based upon its mutually recognized relations with other strata.[2]

People of similar social status recognize one another by their social similarities, such as speech mannerisms and ways of dressing. People of the same rank consider one another equals. The various status levels are acknowledged and maintained on the basis of social differences that separate people from one another. In the assignment of status roles, certain differences are emphasized, while other differences—as well as similarities—are ignored.

Status ranking can be done based on eight factors

Some of the most common characteristics used to classify people according to status are (1) wealth and possessions, (2) ancestry, (3) education, (4) income, (5) authority (appointed), (6) power (political and economic), (7) occupation, and (8) ethnic religion or race. Which characteristics become the bases for social position depends on what is considered important to a particular society.

For example, in the United States the significance of kinship is less important than it is in China or Great Britain, and ethnic characteristics are more important in the United States than they are in France or Brazil. Certainly education has less significance as a basis of discrimination in the United States than it has in Germany, the Netherlands, or Sweden.[3]

Social Stratification

Social stratification is ranking of people within the society, by others, into higher and lower social positions to produce a hierarchy of respect or prestige. The things people want like money, position, or security, are all in short supply and unevenly distributed.

The status system is a way of recognizing this uneven distribution of social values, a way of according the people at or near the top the respect due them for having the most of what society wants.

Role Prescription and Role Behavior

The things people are expected to do are known as *role prescription;* the things they actually do are known as *role behavior.*

Doing as others expect you to do is playing the role

To the extent that the role behavior matches the appropriate role prescriptions, within a company, for example, an individual is said to be effective or successful. It is assumed that he is in fact contributing to company goal achievement.

The role prescription is the set of expectations that affect a particular role, such as a manager's position. All the different people with whom he comes into contact collectively form his multiple role.

Performance evaluation is essentially a matter of determining the degree to which the role prescription and role behavior match. It is an attempt to put organizational goal attainment down to the level of the individual contribution. What is really important insofar as an organization is concerned is not how much an individual does, but how much of what he does is organizationally relevant as determined by his role.

Socialization forces a person to become part of his society and to share in its culture. It also requires an individual to act in culturally approved ways and to pay lip service to the dominant values of the myriad groups of which he is a part. The

We all have multiple roles to play

mythical James West plays many roles all at the same time. He is (1) a male, (2) an American male, (3) an American male whose family is lower middle class, (4) a policeman, (5) a member of the Methodist church, (6) the husband of Betty, (7) the father of

Steve and Karen, (8) a member of the bowling team, (9) the scoutmaster of Steve's Boy Scout troop. Each of these social roles required James to learn his society's prescription or expectations of him. Society prescribes acceptable behavior for each role. It also prescribes traits deemed undesirable and discourages their development. The outcome of socialization depends on one's cultural and physical environment.

The role is thus the sum total of expectations placed on the person by the supervisors, subordinates, peers, customers, vendors, and others, depending on the person's particular job.

He must be able to integrate these expectations, as well as his own, into a coherent psychological pattern if he expects to perform successfully. If, however, he does not clearly understand these expectations and they conflict with one another or his own expectations, he has "role conflict" and will be unable to satisfy some of these expectations.

When self-expectations and others' expectations differ, "role conflict" develops

Research tends to show that when there is wide divergence between a manager's concept of his role and the employees' role expectations of that job, there tends to be poor motivation and inefficiency. For example, if he sees himself as a mediator and developer of compromises between management and labor, but both management and union alike expect him to be "hard-nosed," there develops a "role conflict."

Even when upper management has learned to live with varying role expectations, many employees find their function in a company much easier when their role prescription is clearly defined. The lack of a job description or role definition sometimes accounts for employees saying, "Oh, I don't know, I just feel uncomfortable on the job. I guess I really don't know what the boss expects of me."

Lack of role expectation leads to uncomfortable feelings

Status Inconsistency and Ambiguities

Thus, there are multiple indicators of status—title, pay, position, and symbols. In a sense each of these is a thermometer which measures a different aspect of status. As long as all these status indicators give approximately the same readings, status is not likely to cause trouble to the individual or the organization. But when such indicators of status give inconsistent measures, personnel unrest and dissatisfaction will occur.

Ambiguous situations in which the status position of an individual or group has not been clearly established can be troublesome. In a sense, status symbols are characterized by a "culture lag," as they do not keep up with technological and organizational changes. Newly created groups obviously suffer status identification, because there is no easy placement using the present status indicator.

At work, people with seniority do *not* always have the highest-status jobs or earn the most money. Office jobs may pay less than factory jobs, even though it is generally agreed that office workers enjoy higher occupational status. Sometimes supervisors earn less than the employees under them.

Several roles have similar expectations

When the various status indicators give inconsistent measures, personnel unrest and dissatisfaction may occur. The more prestigious group members expect to occupy the more prestigious jobs. The longer-service, better-educated employee in a restaurant expects extra respect, but may not receive it. The employee with a prestigious family background and education working in a low status job may feel uncomfortable and may demonstrate aggression. Such samples of social thermometer readings on status indicators are shown in Table 13–1. Those employees who work within an environment that has status consistency are less likely to feel the stress and difficulties than those working within a situation of status inconsistency.

But different status rankings for roles lead to inconsistencies

Table 13–1. Examples of Status Consistency and Status Inconsistency

| Individual Characteristics | STATUS CONSISTENCY | | |
	Level of Education Attainment	Status or Ethnic or Religious Background	Level of Position
MBA, "WASP," executive	High	High	High
High school graduate, Jewish, supervisor	Medium	Medium	Medium
	STATUS INCONSISTENCY		
Ph.D., black, researcher, scientist	High	Low	Medium
Graduate student Episcopalian banker's son, working for the summer as a sweeper	High	High	Low

Relativity

The plumber submitted his bill, only to have the astonished home owner gasp, "Twenty-five dollars an hour? My doctor doesn't charge that much!" To which the plumber replied, "Neither did I when I was a doctor."[4] This joke is funny because status is always relative. It is not possible to be "better" than others without others being "worse." Another way to say this is that "higher" status requires that "lower" status exist. In the Unites States, people are born equal before the law and before

God. But from the moment of birth, the social status of the parents has a profound effect on every aspect of the newborn child's life. Relations within the family itself are status oriented: "We see it in the home, where parents are the superiors of the children, and the older child is superior to or 'ahead of' the younger. And the child looks forward to being an adult, the youngest wants to catch up with the eldest, etc."[5]

In modern life, the status conferred on many occupations changes with geographic location. Consider the experience of Fred Ringley and his family, who moved from Chicago to a farm in central Arkansas. Fred had worked in advertising as a copywriter and salesman. Now, he and his wife own a dairy bar and raise chickens and cattle. Fred comments:

> People say, 'You're wasting your college education.' My ex-employer said to my father, 'You didn't raise your son to be a hash slinger.' I've lost status in the eyes of my big city friends. But where I am now I have more status than I would in the city. I'm a big fish in a little pond. I'm a minor celebrity. I can be a hash slinger . . . and be just as fine as the vice president of the Continental Bank. If I were a hash slinger in the suburbs, they'd ask me to move out of the neighborhood. I said to myself as a kid, What's Mr. So-and-so do? Oh, he only runs a cleaners. He's not a big wheel at all. My personal status with somebody else may have gone down. My personal status with myself has gone up a hundred percent.[6]

One advantage of the fluidity of status rankings is that people who wish to change their status can do so more easily. For instance, racial minorities and women, as classes, have been accorded lower status in the past than white men as a class. Presently they are enjoying status gains throughout the nation. Nevertheless, status lines are still quite inflexible in many areas, often creating "invisible barriers." Especially for those of low status, the status lines in this country are not nearly flexible enough. Burleigh Gardner and David Moore say:

> In fact, the matters of relative status, of where each person fits in terms of it, of how each compares with others, present some of the most interesting and, to those involved, some of the most annoying and painful problems of people at work. Certainly, if no one was ever bothered by the status of himself or others, life would be much simpler for everyone.[7]

The fact that status concepts in America are less rigid and stable than in some other societies has one noticeably negative side effect. Vance Packard points out that "the enjoyment of prestige is often disturbed and uneasy, that the bases of prestige, the expressions of prestige claims, and the ways these claims are honored, are now subject to great strain, a strain which often puts men and women in a virtual status panic."[8]

"Status anxiety"

One can anticipate that "status anxiety" would show itself when an employee is unable to cope with his expected status. Certainly status anxieties are not helped by the fact that the indicators of status are often complex and not easily discerned. For example, the *Wall Street Journal* reported that in 1972 at least four plumbers working for the San Francisco Water Department earned more than the department manager's $35,000, when their overtime pay and benefits were included.[9] Significantly, the studies of Gardner and Moore indicate that in spite of the innumerable factors that complicate status relationships, "there is a feeling that these various status systems *should* be coordinated."[10]

Hierarchies and Groups

As soon as a few individuals form a group, status differences become apparent. Even when status appears to be fairly evenly distributed among group members, prestige distinctions persist. For instance, in a group made up of four students and one teacher, the teacher is automatically accorded the highest status. In a group consisting of all students or all teachers, status ranking will be conferred according to age, experience, or verbal abilities.

Status can be conferred by authority

In organizations, status is conferred by the degree of authority that accompanies job positions within the hierarchy. An organization chart illustrates the status levels of different jobs in terms of responsibility and power over others. The higher the position on the chart, the higher the status of the job. When an assistant engineer is promoted to head engineer, he or she is treated differently and treats others differently because of the newly acquired status. By definition, hierarchies are arranged so that, down to the lowest rank, some people have superior status positions over other people. This does not mean that some people are "better" than others, although that is often the implication.

There tends to be more loyalty towards higher groups

People are more likely to feel loyal to higher-status groups. Social climbers are careful to conform to the norms of the group to which they aspire, rather than comply with the norms of the group from which they want to escape.

Workers who develop strong attachments to individuals of higher status may regard themselves as only temporary members of their own status group. For example, lower-status white-collar workers often identify with their higher-status managers.

But no matter how much people aspire to membership in another group, they must meet that group's standards to be admitted. Vance Packard observed that, "The top power in modern business can be achieved only by those who are accepted by the members of the board and by the company's bankers as sound upper-class men like themselves.[11] If a person is to rise in any system, the values of the system must be understood and applied. Here is how Loretta Hill moved from the "back office" into the "front office":

Associate with the right people

> I began to watch the front office people more closely. They seemed calm and unaffected by their jobs, and I started to realize that it wasn't accumulated knowledge that would get me out. It was a certain way of speaking—polite, cool and calm. A cheerful friendly look on my face, no stray hair out of place or that tight, frantic look that comes with pressure. And above all, association with the right people.[12]

BORN INTO A SOCIAL CLASS

Inherit Class

When a child is born, it inherits, along with its genetic make-up, a social class to which its family belongs. Its family's orientation to life can be viewed in certain ways and then *class*ified into large categories of behavior and thought. Social scientists have found it convenient to designate three major classes in Western industrial nations: the lower, middle, and upper classes. Further divisions occur within these three classes, such as lower-upper, upper-middle, and upper-lower classes. Obviously, the labels "lower," "middle," and "upper" imply status positions. It is natural for some in the "lower" classes to strive to become "higher," and it is natural for the "upper" classes to feel "on top of the world." There is also a complacency belief attributed to the "middle" class that indicates a "middle-of-the-road" mentality—in other words, an attempt to maintain a balance between the extremes of high and low.

Husband's occupation is more important than the wife's

Sociologist Peter Rossi conducted studies based on 1,400 Baltimore households in 1975 and found that the husband's occupation counts twice as powerful a status determinant as the wife's occupation.[13] Occupation is twice as powerful a status determinant as education. The occupation was so important that race and age had little effect on the status level, according to his studies. The children received basically the same status rating as their parents' occupations. Interestingly, most people inter-

Children have the status of their parents

viewed justified paying more to married people with children for the same job than divorced parents. Do you think this feeling would still prevail in your community under today's conditions?

Typically, children grow up to become solid members of the class into which they are born. They learn the aspirations and life style particular to their class upbringing. Class lines overlap—our class system is not a stable one or at all comparable to a caste system, in which a person is born into a class from which it is impossible to depart. However, class lines are strong enough so that "rising above one's class" is considered a feat, demanding devotion and skill. Class origins are not easily erased, even when the upward struggle has been won.

People tend to rate themselves higher than the general public would—why?

One final note in Dr. Rossi's study is the fact that when people were interviewed there was a strong tendency to over-evaluate their own status by 20–30 percent and even consider themselves slightly underpaid. This may be a very natural tendency to have a strong feeling of self-worth, and perhaps stronger than the society as a whole may have of us when it compares us with the rest of the working force.

UPWARD MOBILITY

Occupations provide the major channels for rising in social status. Two factors are essential for a low-status person to acquire a high-status job: (1) education, and (2) the ability to break through the barriers of class prejudice. By acquiring skill, training, and the status that educational degrees automatically confer, it is possible to knock on the doors of employers, who can unlock future status possibilities. For the doors to be opened, however, those in power must accept those who come knocking. Since people of a higher class often feel threatened when members of a lower class attempt to penetrate their ranks, antidiscrimination and fair-employment laws have been enacted to help force open the doors of opportunity.

Members of the same class gravitate toward one another

As a rule, members of the same class gravitate toward one another socially, and these social associations greatly affect hiring and promotions. One vice-president is quoted as saying, "Naturally you have pride if you're socially accepted by your superiors. It does you an awful lot of good. You can have a wonderful personnel system, but the thing that determines where you go in the company is personal contacts."

Occupational status can be envisioned in the shape of a pyramid, with lower-status jobs at the base and higher-status jobs at the peak. This work structure is supported by the class structure of the larger society:

> What matters is that in a class society there is a financial "top" to every area of work; admission to the top is granted largely on the basis of money and class; and the reward for having a top

position is still more money and status. The system is closed and self-perpetuating; the privileged position of the managers and professionals—not to mention the ruling class—is built into it.[14]

This pyramidal status design is shaped according to the capitalistic mold: money, opportunity, and position beget more of the same, just as lack of money, opportunity, and position beget less of the same. People's class destinies depend a great deal on the kind of encouragement they receive to develop talents holding status values. Particularly in the lower-middle and lower classes, parents' expectations are so low that children lose the motivation to develop their natural talents. One source states the matter succinctly:

> There is a constant reinforcement that brings out the "talent" in some, and a denial of reward that very quickly shuts off the talents of others. The young man from the well-to-do family who shows some interest in drawing is, from a very early age, encouraged to develop this talent, first by his family and ultimately by the system that pays inordinate salaries to architects. The more certain you are that you can put your talent to use, the more inclined you are to develop it.[15]

It takes money to make money. The more you have, the more you get. These cliches are still true in this society. It takes money to go to school for an education necessary to qualify for certain jobs. It *is* possible for people to rise within the class system, but not without much effort to *overcome* the tremendous disadvantages wrought by subtle as well as blatant inequality of opportunity based on class. Vance Packard states: "Who you are in terms of religion, ethnic background, and politics, also is important in influencing your possibilities for progressing in many, if not most, corporate hierarchies."[16]

The WASP still seems to get ahead easier

The *Status Seekers*, according to Packard, gave rise to the notion that to be successful in big business you must be born WASP (White, Anglo-Saxon, and Protestant), and it doesn't hurt if you are a Republican.[17]

DOWNWARD MOBILITY

Although the historically acceptable movement among classes is up, the tradition of moving down in class status also exists, and is generally accepted as traumatic. Children born into the upper-middle and upper classes usually meet considerable pressure from their parents to live up to class ideals. The well-born young students of the 1960s who dropped out of Ivy League schools to live in communes in Colorado were called "traitors to their class" by some.

When John Coleman, the president of Haverford College,

spent two months of his summer vacation working as a ditch-digger, dishwasher, garbage collector, and sandwich-and-salad man, some of his academic colleagues thought it admirable.[18] Others in Coleman's social class found it unthinkable, even as a short experiment, to do such menial work. Students who work their way through college probably do not find Coleman's experiment so remarkable. That Coleman's experience is considered extraordinary is but another indication of how far apart the

"HONEY, I WASN'T KICKED UPSTAIRS AFTER ALL!"

classes are in their experience of the workaday world and in their understanding of one another.

Earned and Donated Status

Ideally, those who earn status do so entirely on the basis of their abilities and achievements. Equally ideally, people's images of themselves should match the amount of status they are accorded. Status is a hollow reward when it does not stem from genuine accomplishment. The rewards of status are personally satisfying only when those who receive them feel they have duly earned them.

Status can be faked; ability cannot

While a higher status can be faked, ultimately ability cannot. To some extent, ability is always at the heart of earned status. For instance, people who have a basic aptitude for math may decide to cultivate their tendency. The choice of whether to employ those talents as bookkeeper, accountant, stock market broker, statistician, computer analyst, or researcher depends to some extent on the kind and degree of innate mathematical ability a person has. In any given generation, there are only a few people born with the talent to do original mathematical research. Beyond differences in degree, however, how that basic talent is used depends on class background and expectations, available money and opportunity, personal motivation, and chance. The odds of an American Indian girl, born and brought up on a reservation, becoming a stock market broker are considerably lower than the odds for an Anglo-Saxon boy brought up in New York City—even though both children might have similar mathematical abilities.

Earned status is the social reward for achieving something that others consider useful. *Donated* status is not earned. Unearned status, according to James Diggory, "is ultimately a product of the willingness of somebody else to believe (often on no evidence at all) that we have earned, or could have earned, our position by the successful exercise of ability."[19]

Peter principle

Once status has begun to be conferred because of demonstrated ability, it tends to be donated. One potential result of this willingness to confer status is the *Peter principle,* which states that employees are raised to their highest levels of incompetence.[20] The rise may have been earned, but "in the most rigorous sense, we do not know that a man has the ability to accomplish a job until we have seen him do it."[21]

J. S. Minion was a maintenance foreman in the public works department of Excelsior City. He was a favorite of the senior officials at City Hall. They all praised his unfailing affability.

"I like Minion," said the superintendent of works. "He has good judgment and is always pleasant and agreeable." When the superintendent of works retired, Minion succeeded him. Minion continued to agree with everyone. He passed to his foreman every suggestion that came from above. The results were conflict in policy and the continual changing of plans, which soon demoralized the department. Complaints poured in from the mayor and other officials, from taxpayers, and from the maintenance-workers' union. In short, Minion, a competent foreman, became an incompetent superintendent.

ABILITY

Status is relatively earned. Within every occupation and at every status level, wide differences in individual abilities exist that do not affect status at all. For example, anyone who goes to the trouble of getting a college degree, followed by four years of medical school and two years of hospital internship, is automatically accorded high status for these accomplishments. Everyone who passes this rigorous training program—and this indicates a certain amount of talent—certainly achieves the status that accompanies the title of doctor. But achieved status is not an adequate measure of a physician's ability to heal. There are doctors— like people in every other occupation—who have high prestige but are not particularly good at what they do.

Some individuals, once they have obtained the status of doctor, compete for further recognition among their patients and other doctors. There are others who appear to have little concern for achieving further status.

A moral stand about manipulative means of acquiring status is tenable only when upward mobility is possible through the exercise of job ability. Loretta Hill gained jobs solely on her appearance. Her job abilities were not questioned as long as she looked the part.

> My classier image had improved; it was that image—the clothes, calm manner, etc.—that got me all the jobs that followed during the next ten years. For a while I still worked hard at developing office skills. I can run nearly every office machine ever made, use dictaphone, have solid experience in bookkeeping and general ledger work, years of banking and some years of experience in the car-leasing industry. But it took several jobs to squelch the notion that I would be valued and recognized and rewarded for my job know-how. My concrete knowledge was seldom put to much use. My job applications were seldom more than glanced over, my appearance being the prime qualification . . . .[22]

If Loretta Hill is to be blamed for gaining higher status by exercising her status-getting abilities, so must the people who ignored her true job qualifications. Through no choice of her own, the only way for Loretta to rise in status was through means that were personally limiting and unrewarding. The choice sometimes exists—and sometimes does not—as to whether workers can earn their status on the basis of job abilities, or whether they must use their status-getting abilities to invite the donation of status.

Success and Failure

People who experience failure usually lower their goals

The goals or expectations that people set for themselves change constantly, depending on *feelings* of success and failure. After experiencing success, people generally set themselves higher goals. After experiencing failure, people generally set lower goals for themselves. Individual expectations differ considerably, and can change suddenly. Success and failure are measured in terms of whether an achievement falls above or below the doer's standard or estimation of where it *should* fall. Again, Kurt Lewin provides an example of this process.

> For instance, a person may throw a discus forty yards the first time. The second time he may reach fifty, and feel very successful. After short practice, he may reach sixty-five. If he then throws fifty yards again, he will experience a definite failure in spite of the fact that he got a thrill out of the same achievement but a short time before.[23]

In other words, it is absolutely impossible to correlate objective achievements with consistent feelings of success or failure: one time an action can result in success feelings; the next time, in feelings of utter failure. A sense of achievement depends on the immediate and ideal goals, and recent and past performances.

Reactions of success or failure occur only when tasks are considered achievable. Tasks that appear "too easy" are performed without resulting feelings of success. Tasks that appear "too difficult" do not cause feelings of failure. According to Lewin, "Contrary to the scale of possible difficulties, the scale of possible achievements is not infinite but has a definite upper limit for a given individual at a given time. Both success and failure occur only if the difficulty of the task lies close to the upper limit of achievement.[24]

Real success lies close to the upper limits of achievement

The experiences of success and failure relate specifically to feelings of self-esteem. When some people fail, they tend to deny responsibility for the outcome because it injures their self-esteem. It is sometimes easier to blame failure on an accident, lack of time, inadequate tools, or miscommunication than to admit failure.[25] And, of course, successful outcomes increase self-esteem. Success breeds success—confidence is gained when enterprises meet with favorable responses and feelings of accom-

Failure breeds failure

plishment. Similarly, failure breeds failure—unless realistic goals are set and adequately met, individuals can come to believe that they do everything wrong—all the time. The perception of the self as an habitual failure naturally affects the outcome of further efforts and a vicious cycle of cause and effect is created.

In most cases, high status is a symbol of success, and many people assume they will feel successful when they attain a higher status. In fact, however, achieving higher status brings feelings of true success only when feelings of genuine achievement are experienced. Genuine achievements require constant

Genuine achievement requires constant challenge

challenge. Success is based on a *continuum* of changing goals that can be envisioned, then met. When *successive* challenges are not offered, only stagnation and frustration result. Daniel Bell says:

> The sense of having a fixed place is grinding. And even, as in the large corporations, if one still thinks of moving up, the escalator-like process is slow. In compensation, there is a considerable—and sometimes pathetic—effort, if not to lift oneself, to lift one's occupation by its bootstraps.[26]

JOB STATUS

Subculture

Social class subcultures differ from one another in several dimensions. One way is in terms of beliefs associated with achievement. Basically, there are three value orientations to the motivation of behavior in achievement situations: (1) active versus passive, (2) individualistic versus collectivistic; and (3) future versus present.

The status climber is active, individualistic, and plans for the future

Activism is the belief that one can manipulate the physical and the social environment to his own advantage. *Individualism* is the belief that an individual need not subordinate his own needs to the family group, and *future orientation* is the belief that one should forego short-term satisfactions in the interest of long-term gains. These three are more characteristic of higher social status groups in our society than of groups lower in the socioeconomic spectrum. Likewise a status seeker tends to be more active, individualistic, and plan more for future goals.

Middle-class person or higher plans for a career

Those in professional and managerial occupations, as well as semiprofessional and white-collar occupations, are more likely to believe their lives are under their own control and that occupational achievement and success are a result of their own efforts. The upper-middle-class person fits himself for a career. The notion of a career implies self-actualization. The lower-middle-class person is exposed to experiences that make him look for a job, not a career. He has learned that the values of security, stability, and respectability are his life style.

The levels of job status affect the *ability* to achieve feelings of success. Usually, the lower the job status, the more the work routine is specified. This means that there is relatively little opportunity for creativity, judgment, and initiative to come into play. Usually, the higher the job level, the more opportunity there is to tackle new problems. The motivation to experience increased self-esteem through successfully dealing with *new* problems should not be underestimated. People find subtle and ingenious ways to vary the most monotonous of jobs. Here is how an interstate truck driver does it:

Success is never final

> You have to figure out reasons to keep from going crazy, games to try to beat yourself. After a number of years, you begin to be a better loader. They come with a thirty-thousand-pound coil. If you set it down on the truck three inches forward or backward of where it's supposed to be, you're misloaded. So there's a challenge every time you load. Everybody's proud of that. At the truck shop they'll flash a weight ticket: "Take a look at that." They've loaded a balanced load.[27]

Failure is seldom fatal It is probably best to remember that success is never final and failure is seldom fatal.

Titles and Positions

Job titles provide a way to make status distinctions. An executive has more job status than a shipping clerk; a secretary more status than a typist; a journeyman more status than an apprentice. According to Daniel Bell, "A man will do an infinite amount of physically dirty work . . . if the status and prestige arrangements are right; the physically unpleasant jobs of the doctor, for example, are legion."[28] An assistant professor of a medical-surgery unit at a Midwestern university medical center first says, "That's just a title. I'm an occupational therapist." But then, she goes on to say:

> I do get some mileage out of my title, I hate to admit it. When I'm uncomfortable with somebody new and they ask me what my job is, I make a joke of telling them. But the fact is, I do tell them. It's status, of course. When I'm free of the fear of losing it, I'll be a much healthier person.[29]

Status distinctions sometimes make us forget that many different kinds of work are necessary to the smooth functioning of our total society. They tend to separate us, and to add to existing social and political tensions, particularly in large cities:

The work of the architect who designs a building is, in our distorted society, regarded as more important work than the work of the masons who lay the bricks, and the work of the masons is supposedly more important than that of the hod-carriers who haul the mortar. Neither the architect nor the construction workers could produce the building alone. The fact that the architect was classy enough to go to architecture school is supposed to explain his much higher salary.[30]

In March 1946, the National Opinion Research Center (NORC) interviewed 2,920 people across the nation regarding occupational prestige. Figure 13–2 gives a sample of the occupations ranked in the NORC study.

Table 13–2. Ranks of Occupational Prestige

1	Supreme Court Justice	49	Small store manager
2	Physician	50	Bookkeeper
7	College professor	51	Insurance agent
10	Banker	55	Policeman
12	County judge	57	Mail carrier
14	Minister	59	Auto repairman
15	Architect	60	Plumber
17	Dentist	65	Factory machine operator
18	Lawyer	66	Barber
19	Large corporation director	67	Store clerk
20	Nuclear physicist	70	Milk route man
22	Psychologist	74	Filling station attendant
24	Airline pilot	75	Night club singer
26	Owner of factory employing about 100 people	76	Farm hand
27	Sociologist	77	Coal miner
28	Accountant for large firm	78	Taxi driver
31	Author	79	Railroad section hand
32	Army captain	80	Restaurant waiter
33	Building contractor	82	Night watchman
36	Public school teacher	83	Clothes presser
38	Railroad engineer	84	Soda fountain clerk
39	Farm owner	85	Bartender
40	Official, international labor union	86	Janitor
41	Radio announcer	89	Street sweeper
42	Newspaper columnist	90	Shoeshiner
44	Electrician		

Source: NORC Survey No. 244, in Logan Wilson and William L. Kolb, *Sociological Analysis* (New York: Harcourt, Brace & World, 1949), Chapter 13.

Smaller, later studies indicate that job status in the United States has remained fairly stable. For instance, an update of the Ranks of Occupational Prestige study was done in 1964 at the University of Michigan by Paul Siegel, and there was little difference between the two studies in fifteen years.

The name of a job may have more status than the task indicates. A billing clerk in one company may do exactly the same tasks as the bookkeeper in another. The manager of a small, renowned firm may perform a job quite similar to a department head in a large company.

The same job title can carry differences in status caused by the status of the organization or the supervisor. The salesperson for an international company has a "better" job than the one working for a local manufacturer. The secretary to the senior vice-president has more status than the one to the sales division manager. The architect who designs huge office buildings can be more influential with his colleagues than the one who designs only small dwellings.

The secretary's status is determined by whom she works for

In complex organizations, it is common for workers to advance their careers by doing essentially the same job tasks but moving to higher levels in the organizational hierarchy. The position changes—the job does not. For example, the stenographer to the sales division can become the secretary to the sales manager, then the private secretary to the vice-president, then the executive secretary to the president. Such advancement is in accord with the seniority system, but the basic nature of the job has not changed. The power of seniority is based on the belief that the more time employees work for a company, the more entitled they become to higher-ranking jobs.

Seniority can lead to promotion

Task Differentiations

Occupational status is usually based on a range of criteria having to do with the technical skills and learned behaviors necessary to perform the job. Table 13–3 indicates six separate distinctions from which status is derived.

One study done by sociologists at the University of Chicago assigned status ratings to occupations according to skill

Table 13–3. Fundamental Job Behaviors on which Status is Based

RANGE	
Higher Status	*Lower Status*
1. Mental work	Physical work
2. Skilled, unrepetitive work	Unskilled, repetitive work
3. Creative work	Routine work
4. Individual responsibility and exercise of judgment	Minimum responsibility and standardized work
5. Complex tasks	Simple tasks
6. Long training and education	Short training and education

Source: Adapted from Robert Dubin, *The World of Work: Industrial Society and Human Relations* (Englewood Cliffs, N.J.: Prentice-Hall, 1958), pp. 64–65.

and responsibility. They analyzed data from 3,880 households in the Chicago area and rated some 300 occupations on a status scale of one to seven. Table 13–4 gives examples of the ratings by group.

Table 13–4   Occupation Rating Based on Skill and Responsibility

First Status Group: Lawyers, doctors, dentists, engineers, judges, high-school superintendents, veterinarians, chemists, regional and divisional managers of large companies, certified public accountants, gentlemen farmers.

Second Status Group: High-school teachers, trained nurses, chiropodists, chiropractors, newspaper editors, librarians (graduate), businesses valued at $20,000 to $75,000, assistant managers and office managers, accountants, real estate and insurance salespeople, ministers.

Third Status Group: Social workers, grade-school teachers, optometrists, librarians (not graduate), auto salespeople, bank clerks, cashiers, postal clerks, secretaries to executives, supervisors of railroad, telephone, etc., contractors.

Fourth Status Group: Stenographers, bookkeepers, rural mail clerks, salespeople in department stores, factory forepeople, electricians, plumbers, carpenters who own their own business, butchers, sheriffs, railroad engineers.

Fifth Status Group: Dime store clerks, hardware salespeople, beauty operators, telephone operators, carpenters, plumbers, timekeepers, linepeople, barbers, firepersons, policepersons, cooks in restaurants, bartenders.

Sixth Status Group: Moulders, semiskilled workers, night policepersons, taxi drivers, waiters in restaurants, small tenant farmers, truck drivers.

Seventh Status Group: Heavy labor, migrant workers, odd job men, miners, janitors, scrubpeople, newspeople, migrant farm laborers.

Source: W. Lloyd Warner, Marchia Meeker and Kenneth Eells, *Social Class in America, The Evaluation of Status* (New York: Harper & Row, 1960).

Professionalism

Sometimes the only difference between an "occupation" and a "profession" is the social status accorded to various jobs. Attempts to "upgrade" or "professionalize" occupations are attempts to gain greater social recognition for certain kinds of work. Sometimes the nature of the work warrants such desires to raise status—sometimes it does not. As Daniel Bell says:

Professionals are experts

> The garage becomes the "lubritorium"; individuals do not say "I sell pots and pans" but "I am in selling"; the janitor becomes the "superintendent"; the hospital superintendent turns into the "administrator"; the secretary becomes the "executive assistant"; and the minister, if he is unable to rise to bishop, measures his success in terms of the social class of his parishioners.[31]

**The more professional,
the less they are
questioned**

**Licensing helps
establish the status
and the profession**

Professionals are "experts" whose decisions tend to go un-challenged. The more professional the standing, the less the expert's authority is questioned. Both time-honored and brand new professions have established their own schools and licensing programs, not only to assure high standards of expertise, but also to establish criteria on which status can be based.

Certain tactics are employed to confer professional status in many jobs. They are: (1) to drop activities that do not enhance prestige and, at the same time, (2) to claim as part of the job the performance of tasks that already have status; (3) to restrict the job to those with recognized "professional" training and credentials; (4) to make sure that the professional is consulted in an early stage of decision making.

The strictly managerial aspects of the executive's job have lost prestige in recent years. Leonard Sayles suggests that the reason is that the human relations skills necessary for good management have low prestige and interfere with the professionalization of management.

STATUS SYMBOLS

Attaining power and rank are considered normal work goals and play important roles in organizational incentive systems. In fact, the privileges attached to high-status positions are sometimes even more important to workers than the money they earn. Generally, it is a matter of considerable importance to *all* workers that their status be recognized. Secretaries do not like to be thought of as typists, just as executives don't like to be mistaken for shipping clerks. A lower-echelon worker might be amused or pleased at being mistaken for someone of higher status, but a mistake the other way around would cause displeasure. As a result, different work groups have established various ways—sometimes too subtle to be observed by outsiders—to distinguish status levels.

**Status must be
recognized**

The more observable the tasks are, the easier it is to discern status. In physical or manual work, the levels of skill and responsibility a job requires are readily apparent. In offices, however, everyone shuffles papers; and, because jobs tend to look similar, more obvious external signs of status are needed. The importance of jobs, then, remains to be judged by the symbols attached to them.

**Importance of jobs are
often determined by the
symbols**

Resistance to change can often be traced to managerial misuse of status symbols: Placing a new employee's desk next to a desirable window or in a larger room; bypassing another's seniority and promoting a less experienced employee; showing favoritism that doesn't conform to the established company customs—these matters can greatly upset workers and cause in-security and bitterness.

Generally speaking, the larger the organization, the more preoccupied its workers are with status symbols. Vance Packard observed that large organizations operate much like the army with highly visible status symbols operating as a way of communicating authority.[32] Because of the close personal contacts usual in small companies, where everybody knows who has power, symbols of authority are not as necessary. Packard contrasts the style of self-made successful business people with their corporate counterparts:

> . . . I found the ways of operating of these lone wolves startlingly
> different from the hundreds of corporate executives I have
> interrogated, over the years, behind their neat, polished desks.
> Several of the entrepreneur-multimillionaires worked in such
> modest cubicles that I couldn't believe I had reached my
> destination when I faced them. One shared a secretary with his
> two assistants. Another had odds and ends of furniture; a third
> had a "board" room less than ten feet square. Most impressive,
> at least eight relaxed by putting up their feet on their desks as
> they talked. I have strained my memory and I can remember only
> one executive of a large corporation who ever did that. He was a
> president, and even he did it uneasily.[33]

Hours and Pay

Salary has more status than wages—why?

Hourly workers who are required to punch time clocks do not have the same amount of status as those who receive fixed salaries—even though the hourly employees may earn more money. Within the same company, obvious status distinctions exist between employees paid monthly and those paid semimonthly or weekly. Daily wages can only indicate that the employee's worth is temporary and replaceable. As a matter of convenience, the payroll department may pay groups of employees on different days; but that convenience is not often without an awareness of each group's status.

Fixed working hours have less prestige

Working during fixed daily hours usually carries less prestige than being paid to complete specific projects. Only "important" employees are given the freedom to work around the clock or not show up at all. Employees often indicate their high status by being casual about the hours they work: arriving late, leaving early, taking long lunch hours and breaks, and randomly leaving work stations to chat with other workers. Lower-status employees must observe rigid work schedules and strict eating and resting periods. So-called hourly employees can actually be paid for minutes worked, and may even have to request permission to go to the bathroom. General Motors pays its hourly workers in six ten-minute segments for each hour on the job.[34]

Within organizations, differences in rates of pay usually conform to levels of job importance. For example, according to a Dartnell Corporation survey of executive compensation, when the president's salary is rated at 100 percent, the top marketing executive's salary is usually 60 percent of the president's, the financial executive and top production executive both make about 54 percent, and the industrial relations executive receives about 37 percent.[35] Even minor pay differences can mean changes in status. Payroll clerks may feel they have an edge over typists because they make three cents more an hour. To minimize status conflicts, many companies have a "top secret" policy about pay scales.

An office worker has more status than a laborer

Laborer may earn more than an office worker

We often work for status, not wages

Relative pay standards within organizations do not apply consistently within the larger society. A relatively high wage may indicate monetary *compensation* to make up for low status. For example, a construction worker doing manual labor usually has less social prestige than an office clerk. Yet construction workers make two to three times more money than office clerks. Sometimes, the inequities and inequalities of our wage systems can justifiably be called absurd. Vance Packard comments that, "any reward system that year after year pays a wailing crooner approximately one hundred times as much as the Chief Justice of the United States Supreme Court is somewhat out of balance."[36]

Work Environment

Status can be conferred by any agreed-upon formula. The placement of a machinist's machine, the location of a parking spot, the location of a personal locker—all can carry status significance. Working near the end of the production line usually carries more status than working near the beginning. Working on the eighth floor with the salespeople can imply less status than working on the tenth floor near the manager's office.

The aspects of the work environment that go beyond meeting utilitarian needs are usually placed there for the sake of status. Just about any environmental factor can be incorporated into creating a desired image: size of facility, layout and size of work areas, furniture, colors, decorations, temperature, humidity, ventilation, noise, and lighting are all status indicators.

Table 13–5 gives a list of the furnishings allowed the various occupations in a small research firm in California. In this company the furnishings obviously indicate precise levels of status.

Within organizations, the value of certain status symbols

Table 13–5. Office Furniture Allotment

1. *Department Head or Equivalent*
   desk/table/credenza/swivel chair/4 to 6 arm chairs/12' chalkboard/files as required
2. *Section Head*
   desk/table/swivel chair/4 to 6 side chairs/8' chalkboard/2 bookcases/files as required
3. *Supervisor*
   desk/table/swivel chair/2 side chairs/bookcase/chalkboard space/4-drawer file
4. *Scientist or Engineer*
   desk/swivel chair/side chair/chalkboard space/bookcase/4-drawer file cabinet
5. *Secretary/Clerical, etc.*
   desk/swivel chair/file/furniture as authorized by Department Head
6. *Draft, Tech, Hourly, etc.*
   no furniture

Corner offices have a higher premium

depends on high demand and limited supply. If all the offices are already plush, then the size and location of work areas will indicate the relativities of status. For example, in most companies the few corner offices have premium status, followed by the rarely available offices with windows. Windowless offices are more numerous and, hence, lower in status. In offices with no windows, windows are not, of course, used as a status criterion. If office space and furnishings are equally provided the symbols of status become more subtle—importance may be attached to the newness of a stapler, the thickness of a rug, or the design of an ashtray.

Because whatever is in least supply usually has the highest status, status symbols become more and more exclusive. Large companies sometimes maintain expensive, private dining rooms for their executives, while lesser employees must eat in the company cafeteria. Providing separate eating facilities according to status is similar to the military tradition of the Officer's Club and the Mess Hall.

Although still prized by some executives, being presented with a key to the executive bathroom has been widely satirized as an exaggeration of the absurd ways in which status is sometimes bestowed. But consider this account of a typist who was transferred from the office to the shop: She expressed her disdain for her fall in status by refusing to use the nearby shop bathroom, choosing instead to walk across the building and up a flight of stairs to use the office bathroom.[37]

Working near the end of the production line carries more status than working near the beginning, for the finished product, it is claimed, is more valuable and the job carries more responsibility. Do you agree?

Even foods have status. The status of food handlers was established according to the food they handled. Parsley, chives,

420

and celery as the luxury or decor items, were given top billing, while carrots costarred, with potatoes and onions given bottom listing. The onions smell and stain the hands, so obviously the lowest person on the ladder should handle them.

Better working conditions — higher status

Normally, higher status is attached to the people having better working conditions. The better the working conditions, the higher the status. That is why white-collar jobs usually carry more status than blue-collar jobs of equal skill and pay. Most people seem to prefer the white-collar surroundings to those of the blue-collar environment. Because they are sought and there is limited supply relative to the demand, they receive higher status. In this respect the status value given to different conditions has a supply and demand effect similar to that in economics. When supply is adequate relative to demand the status value will be less than when demand exceeds supply. For example, if there were a great demand for plumbers and carpenters and few trained, their status would go up; likewise if the demand for nurses and druggists were low, the status of these professions would drop.

Clothing

Throughout history, dress has been an important way to determine people's status. The mass production of clothing in the twentieth century has eliminated many traditional status distinctions based on dress. Today, everyone wears standardized street clothing. Status distinctions must now be made on the basis of expense or quality rather than on style.[38] Aldous Huxley comments:

> In recent years, and above all in America, the revolution in clothing has entered a new phase. As well as cleanliness, elegance is being placed within the reach of practically everyone. Cheap clothes are mass-produced from patterns created by the most expensive designers. Unfashionableness was once a stigma hardly less damning, as a symbol of inferiority, than dirt.[39]

Dirt, not fashion, remains the determining factor in the different attitudes white- and blue-collar workers have about their work clothing. Blue-collar workers get dirty in their work environments; white-collar workers don't. Consequently, the basic dress distinction between the two groups is that white-collar workers can wear fashionable street clothes to work, and blue-collar workers must wear clothes to protect them from dirt.

Lab technicians, nurses, waiters and waitresses, police persons, and many other people employed in service industries wear uniforms to work every day. Many people expect the po-

**Career apparel can
affect morale**

lice, airline stewardesses, and nurses to wear readily identifiable clothing on the job. Some banks, public utilities, and insurance companies are also providing "work clothes" for employees. The advantage of career apparel is that it tends to boost employee morale for a while, it improves the public image, it is tax deductible for the employer or the employee, and the cost is small when compared to what a person would normally pay for a work wardrobe during a year. The disadvantage is that the cost usually ranges from $75 to $200 per employee outfit; there is a loss of individuality, and the apparel program can become old and dull after a few years.[40]

White-collar workers enjoy the freedom of greater individuality. But clothing fashions have become so standardized that most clothing worn to work might just as well be uniforms. Imagine what would happen if executives, professionals, or white-collar workers wore shorts and sneakers to work, instead of suits and ties and dresses and stockings. This unthinkable behavior would be ridiculed, reprimanded, and probably punished.

In a study done by William Form and Gregory Stone to determine the clothing attitudes of American working men, male

Figure 13–1. Many people expect the police, airline stewardesses, and nurses to wear readily identifiable clothing on the job.
Courtesy of Santa Barbara City College (Photo by Rob Reilly)

subjects were asked what might happen to a foreman who is promoted to a position in the office and fails to change his dress habits to meet white-collar standards. Sixty-one percent said he would be fired, demoted, or transferred. Fourteen percent said he would either quit his new job or volunteer for a demotion. Over nine-tenths of the respondents believed that by failing to meet the white-collar dress requirements, the foreman's job future would be adversely affected.[41]

In the Form and Stone study, blue-collar and white-collar workers alike were aware of the status value of the foreman's clothing. However, in regard to their own dress, blue-collar workers cared most about its durability and usefulness. In spite of the fact that workers were sensitive to ridicule by fellow workers, and felt that if they deviated from group norms they would incur direct group disapproval, clothes were not viewed as status symbols.[42]

Clothing is important

Clothing plays a much more symbolic role for workers with higher-status jobs. Although the popular stereotype has it that men in this culture do not attach much importance to their clothing, more than half of the men in the Form and Stone study found clothing important. Their degree of dress awareness was directly proportionate to the type and status of their occupations.[43]

These white-collar males with higher-status jobs generally held clothing in high esteem. They saw clothing as an aid to impressing other workers and supervisors. They thought that "dressing up" for a job interview was socially necessary to impress the interviewer. Over one-half of the respondents knew someone who had been given a higher-status job because of dress style or thought it was possible to win a promotion on such grounds. Fully one-sixth of those studied consciously dressed for work with a promotion in mind. These white-collar employees and businessmen were afraid that deviating from traditional dress standards would elicit disapproval from the public, their customers, or other employees. Unlike the direct co-worker disapproval blue-collar workers expected, the white-collar men saw their dress habits as controlled by more indirect and impersonal social forces.[44]

Realistic differences in status can be measured by clothing budgets. White-collar workers must set aside a portion of their salaries to buy appropriate clothes. After late adolescence, for instance, women clerks spend a good deal more on clothes than women working in factories for similar wages. To a lesser extent, the same is true of men.[45] In the Form and Stone study, more white-collar than blue-collar workers complained that they did not make enough money to purchase the clothes required to dress properly for their jobs.[46]

A white-collar job requires the right wardrobe

To some people, the status codes serve more as restrictions than as prestige symbols. It is virtually impossible to get a white-collar job without having an appropriate wardrobe. Standard items of white-collar women's work clothing are particularly unsuitable for daily wear. High-heeled shoes hurt the feet. Stockings snag and tear easily. Wearing socially approved short skirts causes some women to feel more like sex objects than valued employees. Women in white-collar jobs have had to battle for the right to wear pants to work. Even when pant suits are permitted, jeans and other casual attire are not.

New era requires a new dress code

One of the more interesting experiments in status and its relationship to clothing was demonstrated in 1969 during the frequent college riots. Next to the University of California at Santa Barbara is the community of Isla Vista, where the majority of the students live. The bank there represented the "establishment" and the personnel who worked there dressed accordingly. The gentlemen wore suits and the women wore dresses appropriate to their white-collar positions. The clients of the bank were often barefooted, wearing overalls, only Levis, bathing suits, or other forms of casual wear.

New dress code at the bank

Looking back through history it is easy to see that the casual wear of the bank customers did not seem to fit the formal environment of the bank. After the students burned down the bank in protest against the "establishment," a temporary building was built. Also a new code was tried—that of casual wear. The tellers wore slacks and pant suits, and the men no longer wore ties and seldom sport coats. The tension eased and a new bank was built. The new fad became the permanent dress code. How does this experience reflect the attitude of status within the community?

In recent years, white-collar dress standards have loosened up a bit. Many young, male executives have challenged the traditional rules about how long they can wear their hair.[47] Some of their challenges have been moderately successful. The average acceptable hair length for a male white-collar worker is several inches longer today than it was some years ago.

HOW STATUS AFFECTS COMMUNICATION

Status affects the manner in which people communicate with one another. For example, in one experiment, three senior staff members were given 165 separate instructions or orders by a department manager. However, the three executives interpreted 81 of the orders as merely advice or information. Their high-status self-images compelled them to respond negatively to obeying orders and to use their own judgment instead.[48]

Similarly, when a worker consistently asks a co-worker for

assistance or advice, differences in informal status are created. Frequent requests of this sort imply a belief in the co-worker's superiority or expertise.[49]

The ability to move upward in the organizational hierarchy greatly affects the nature of communication. Talking with a supervisor, even about the job, is a form of socialization often used to gain favor with supervisors. Employees may minimize actual disagreements with their supervisors to put themselves in a favorable light.[50] A study done in three large industrial organizations found that information communicated to supervisors is heavily filtered when it reflects incompetence and thus threatens the security or progress of subordinates. The study discovered that the more people aspire to move upward, the less accurate is their communication upward.[51] Another study concluded that when low-ranking members of an organization are in a position to move upward, they are exceedingly guarded in their relations with those of higher rank who can interfere with their progress.[52]

To some extent, upwardly mobile workers are hostile to one another because they represent a competitive threat to one another. Nonmobile workers tend to discuss information that is irrelevant to the job and are often hostile to superiors. On the other hand, employees who consider themselves capable of moving up in the hierarchy tend to "stick to business" and communicate more job-relevant information to the upper-status levels.[53]

The ability to communicate well can itself be status-producing. In one experiment, thirty-two groups of four college undergraduates discussed two problems in human relations. After discussing the first problem, group members picked out (A) the most talkative and (B) the least talkative people in each group. Then, the groups were given the second human relations problem. Both A and B people were given the solution to the second problem, unknown to the other group members. When the A people presented the solution, the groups accepted it more than two-thirds of the time. When the B people gave out the same information, it was rejected two-thirds of the time. From these results, the researchers concluded that higher status—and therefore greater credibility—was accorded to the most talkative individuals.[54]

> **The more one wants to move up, the less accurate the communication**

SUMMARY

Status is rated according to relative rank. Status positions are rewarded in different ways according to rank. While higher status can be claimed by someone, it does not actually exist unless it is acknowledged by others. Society establishes

specific behaviors and symbols by which status is acknowledged. Status values depend on the entire value system held by
the reference group to which an individual belongs. Relative to
some other cultures, the American status system is flexible, but
not as flexible as the "American Dream" would have us believe.
People are glad to have opportunities to rise in status, but they
also want the system to operate by fair rules.

Groups always form status relationships, and generally
choose members from "their own kind," i.e., those of similar
class and status. Class membership is usually for life, although
changing class is not rare. Occupations are a major vehicle for
"moving up the ranks." The individual is responsible for acquiring the necessary education and skills to move upward, but
employers are responsible for providing equal job opportunities.

Status should be based on ability and achievement—it
should be earned. Often status is donated—sometimes because
people prefer to base their decisions on the *appearance* of status
rather than on actual talent, and sometimes because people want
to confer status on those they believe deserve it.

Self-esteem is the value and success one attributes to one's
self. Achieving higher status indicates that one's social value
has been recognized. Self-esteem interacts with other basic human needs, often in status-giving forms: the acquisition of material goods; love and respect from others; and the ability to act
creatively. People tend to evaluate themselves in terms of the
social status they have achieved.

Status is based on social values. When social values
change, status hierarchies also change. One way of defining
"value" is in terms of usefulness. In this country, status serves a
useful purpose, which can be measured by the extent to which
people of high status are taken seriously by others.

Immediate and ideal goals are influenced by personal
abilities and group pressures. The nature of an individual's present-day goals depends on the experiences of success or failure associated with previous goals. The ability to succeed affects self-
esteem. Achieving higher status is perceived as a sign of success
only when the individual has set a goal and met it, gaining status
in the process. Self-worth is so important that workers in the most
mundane jobs find ways to achieve a sense of success.

Job titles separate people by status levels. In fact, status
ranks are rather clearly defined. One of the most common ways
to gain status in complex organizations is by doing the same job
tasks for higher-ranking individuals in the hierarchy. Job status
is based on practical criteria of job content. The more mental,
skilled, creative, responsible, and complex the job, and the more
training and education the job requires, the more status the job
holds. Jobs gain status when they qualify as professions. One

way to be considered a professional is to "act" like an expert and to tailor the job so that "nonprofessionals" cannot do it.

Status symbols are convenient ways of distinguishing differences in status. When the relative importance of job tasks are apparent, status symbols are hardly required. Large companies depend on status symbols more than small ones. At work, status is designated by (1) the amount of pay and how it is calculated, and the rigidity of working hours; (2) the location of work stations within the organization, plushness of offices and furnishings; and (3) accepted modes of dress.

Status affects the quality of communication. People with high status are in the habit of making their own decisions. Workers who are upwardly mobile mask their disagreements with higher-ups and cast as little negative light on themselves as possible. Upwardly mobile employees talk about work to their superiors. Workers who do not expect to rise in status talk among themselves about personal matters, and are often hostile to those ranked above them. Very articulate people gain immediate status in groups—groups tend to choose "talkers" as their leaders.

STATUS REVERSAL

Case Study #1

How would you feel if a man who had worked under you for a long time suddenly became your boss, taking a job you had wanted and for which you felt qualified? Doubtless you would have feelings of disappointment, competitiveness, anger, and insecurity.

Status reversal is a frequent problem at all levels in organizations. But when it occurs at the pinnacle of a complex organization, which badly needs the optimum talent and experience of both people, it represents a problem of considerable consequence.

A difficult relationship problem between two key officers need not be felt with the same intensity by both parties to cause damage. In this case, each executive was highly ambivalent about the other prior to the reversal of their status. When the status reversal was announced, Alan McLean, the man who had been senior found negative attitudes. By contrast, the new superior, Norman Menninger, became more positive, tolerant, understanding, and caring toward his former boss.

In this instance both parties concerned recognized that they had to do something. Their experience and norms of their organization were such that they felt that in the best interests of human relations and the company something should be done. So they came to you.

1. Is this a short-term problem or a long-term problem?
2. Is it best to bring in an outside consultant on the problem?
3. Should counseling take place and if so, what kind of counseling?
4. What specific steps can be taken to solve this problem?

Terms and Concepts Students Should Know

social stratification	occupational prestige	active vs. passive
status inconsistency	status symbols	future vs. present
status seekers	status and communication	professionalism
individualistic vs. collectivistic	role prescription	work environment
	upward mobility	salary vs. wages

Bibliography

1. HAYAKAWA, S. I., *Symbols, Status and Personality*, Harcourt Brace and World, 2nd ed., 1964.
2. MILLS, C. WRIGHT, *White Collar: The American Middle Classes*, New York, Oxford University Press, 1951.
3. TERKEL, STUDS, *Working*, New York, Pantheon Books, 1974.
4. PACKARD, VANCE, *The Status Seekers*, New York, David McKay Company, 1959.
5. APPLEWHITE, PHILIP, *Organizational Behavior*, Englewood Cliffs, N. J., Prentice-

Hall, 1965.

6. LONGENECKER, JUSTIN, *Principles of Management and Organizational Behavior*, 4th ed.,

Columbus, Ohio, Charles E. Merrill Publishing Company, 1977.

Footnotes

[1] S. I. Hayakawa, *Symbols, Status and Personality* (New York: Harcourt, Brace & World, 2nd ed., 1964), p. 64.

[2] C. Wright Mills, *White Collar: The American Middle Classes* (New York: Oxford University Press, 1951), p. 241.

[3] Shils, "Class," *Encyclopaedia Britannica*, Vol. 5, 1960, p. 766.

[4] "Time is Out of Joint," *Wall Street Journal*, 16 February 1973, p. 12, col. 1

[5] Burleigh Gardner and David Moore, "Status and Status Hierarchies," in *Organizations: Structure and Behavior*, Vol. 1, 2nd ed., edited by Joseph A. Litterer (New York: John Wiley & Sons, 1969), p. 189.

[6] Studs Terkel, *Working* (New York: Pantheon Books, 1974), p. 536.

[7] Gardner and Moore, "Status Hierarchies," p. 189.

[8] Vance Packard, *The Status Seekers* (New York: David McKay Co., 1959), p. 240.

[9] "Time Is Out of Joint," p. 12, col. 1.

[10] Gardner and Moore, "Status Hierarchies," p. 192.

[11] Packard, *Status Seekers*, p. 124.

[12] Lynn O'Connor, Walter Russell, and Pat Mialocq, *The Office Workers' Manifesto* (New York: Freeway Press, 1973), p. 17.

[13] Peter Rossi, "Judging People—It's the Job that Counts," *Psychology Today*, July 1975, pp. 24–28.

[14] O'Connor, Russell, and Mialocq, "*Office Workers' Manifesto*, p. 32.

[15] *Ibid.*, p. 32.

[16] Packard, *Status Seekers*, p. 122.

[17] *Ibid.*

[18] "Theory and Practice," *Wall Street Journal*, 26 June 1973, p. 16, col. 1.

[19] James C. Diggory, "Status, Ability, and Self-Esteem in the Process of Supervision," in *The Frontiers of Management Psychology*, edited by George Fisk, (New York: Harper & Row, Publishers, 1964), p. 112.

[20] Laurence Peter and Raymond Hull, *The Peter Principle* (New York: William Morrow & Co., 1969).

[21] Diggory, "Status, Ability, and Self-Esteem," p. 114.

[22] O'Connor, Russell, and Mialocq, *Office Workers' Manifesto*, pp. 17–18.

[23] Kurt Lewin, "The Psychology of Success and Failure," in *Readings in Managerial Psychology*, edited by Harold J. Leavitt and Louis R. Pondy (Chicago: University of Chicago Press, 1964), p. 26.

[24] *Ibid.*, p. 29.

[25] *Ibid.*, p. 31.

[26] Daniel Bell, "Work and Its Discontents," in *The End of Ideology: On the Exhaustion of Political Ideas in the Fifties*, rev. ed. (New York: Free Press, 1962), p. 257.

[27] *Ibid.*

[28] *Ibid.*

[29] *Ibid.*

[30] O'Connor, Russell, and Mialocq, *Office Workers' Manifesto*, p. 32.

[31] Bell, "Work and Its Discontents," p. 257.

[32] Packard, *Status Seekers*, p. 116.

[33] *Ibid.*

[34] Bell, "Work and Its Discontents," p. 233.

[35] Dartnell Corporation, *Executive Compensation* (Chicago: Dartnell Corp., 1961).

[36] Packard, *Status Seekers*, p. 113.

[37] Gardner and Moore, "Status Hierarchies," p. 193.

[38] Mills, *White Collar*, p. 241.

[39] Aldous Huxley, "Hyperion to a Satyr," in *Tomorrow and Tomorrow and Tomorrow and Other Essays* (New York: Harper & Row, 1972), p. 172.

[40] "Career Apparel: New Fringe Benefit," *Administrative Magazine*, August 1973.

[41] William H. Form and Gregory P. Stone, "Clothing and the Man at Work," in *Human Relations in Administration*, 3rd ed., edited by Robert Dubin, (Englewood Cliffs, N.J.: Prentice-Hall, 1968), p. 316.

[42] *Ibid.*, pp. 315–316.

[43] *Ibid.*

[44] *Ibid.*

[45] Mills, *White Collar*, p. 241.

[46] Form and Stone, "Clothing," p. 316.

[47] Judson Gooding, "The Accelerated Generation Moves into Management," *Fortune*, March 1971, p. 51.

[48] Philip B. Applewhite, *Organizational Behavior* (Englewood Cliffs, N.J.: Prentice-Hall, 1965), p. 60.

[49] *Ibid.*

[50] *Ibid.*

[51] *Ibid.*

[52] *Ibid.*, pp. 95–96.

[53] *Ibid.*, p. 60.

[54] Coleman and Ramwater, "Making It in America," *Newsweek*, 5 January 1976.

Job Discrimination

"Now Give Me a Chance" ■ ■ ■ ■ ■ ■ ■

14

■ ■ ■ ■ ■ ■ ■ ■ ■ ■ ■ ■ ■ ■ ■ ■ ■ ■ ■ ■

OBJECTIVES

After reading this chapter you should be able to:

1. Define and discuss the meaning of prejudice and discrimination.
2. Explain why women and minorities often have such poor self-images.
3. Discuss some of the ways it is possible to see and measure discrimination in the business world.
4. Discuss the psychological and economic roots of prejudice.
5. Describe and give examples of some of the ways in which discrimination can be overcome.
6. Discuss some of the ideas of "affirmative action" in relation to the following:
   A. Goals and objectives,
   B. Hiring and promotion policies,
   C. Recruitment,
   D. Job restructuring.
7. Discuss the problem of discrimination in relation to unions.

It might be well to discuss some of these questions with others before you read the chapter. Maybe some different feelings will develop as a result.

What is meant by prejudice?

What is meant by discrimination?

Do we inherit or learn prejudice, and how do we exhibit our discrimination in everyday life?

What group is discriminated against most in your area? What are some of the social, economic, and personal reasons used?

Which social class exhibits the greatest discrimination? Does it seem to be a social class other than the one to which you belong?

Is society giving more opportunities to minorities now as compared to three years ago?

How do we discriminate against the physically and mentally handicapped?

Some years ago a paper was written on personality traits of prejudiced persons. Do you believe there is some truth in the statements below?

1. A prejudiced person has a tendency to be a moralist.
2. A prejudiced person has a need for definiteness.
3. A prejudiced person has an ambivalence toward parents and authority.
4. A prejudiced person has a strong love and worship for institutions.

BACKGROUND TO PREJUDICE
AND DISCRIMINATION

Discrimination is a continuous human relations problem for both management and workers. Most people are familiar with the overt, violent acts of political and racial discrimination that are reported by the public media. Other kinds of discrimination, however, are often much less recognizable, and for this reason difficult to overcome. Nevertheless, because it affects so many people in the job market, and because people need to work in order to live, even mild discrimination deserves serious attention.

Prejudgments

Prejudgment is normal Making a prejudgment is normal, for we cannot freshly handle every event in its own right. If we did, what good would past experience be? Although prejudgments help give order to our daily living, our mind has a habit of assimilating as much as it can into categories by which it prejudges a person or event. By overcategorizing we tend to form irrational rather than rational categories and this is when the danger of prejudices comes in.

We know all women are not incompetent at math, all Chinese are not inscrutable and industrious, and all blacks are not suffering in exotic misery. People are more complicated, more varied, more interesting. They have more resiliency and survivability than we might think.

A person acts with prejudice because of his personality, which has been developed by socialization, or his learned behavior taught by his family, school, and neighborhood environment. It is in his environment that his attitudes are shaped and can be reshaped.

What is Prejudice?

Prejudice is an attitude, not an act A definition was given of prejudice as "being down on something you're not up on." Prejudice is an attitude, not an act; it is a habit of mind, an opinion based partially on observation and partially on ignorance, fear, and cultural patterns of group formation, none of which have rational bases.

One of the trademarks of prejudice is that a prejudiced person tends to think of a group of people as being all the same, without considering individual differences. This kind of thinking gives rise to stereotypes. A stereotype can be thought of as a

434

set of prejudices, a group of attitudes about a group of people. Stereotypes, like prejudices, are based partially on observation and partially on ignorance and tradition. For example, a person who assumes that most or all women are clumsy, vain, illogical, overly emotional, and spiteful is subscribing to a widely held stereotype of women.

Stereotypes are hard to overcome

Stereotypes are difficult to overcome because they have developed over long periods of time and because so many people share them, giving them an illusion of rationality. However, many people today are trying hard to rid themselves of stereotyped thinking about other people, and the effort shows in a general, growing consciousness that people are individuals and can and should be treated as such. For example, the film and television stereotype of the black person as servile, clowning, and stupid has vanished. We now have television programs that show independent, strong, capable blacks in lead roles.

Stereotypes still exist, but people are more frequently and effectively breaking out of such rigid thinking. They are asking themselves if an individual who is a member of a group that is often stereotyped is really exactly like the stereotype. People are also beginning to question whether the group as a whole fits the stereotype. Education is also helping to break down the stereotypes and prejudices on which discrimination is based. Eventually, nothing but the facts remain, without an overload of emotional distortions: black people can be singled out on the basis of color—but they are not all one color, any more than white people are. Women *are* different from men in terms of sex and a few minor sex-related characteristics—but they are not a whole different species from men. The differences among people make our lives rich; and it is important to remember that as human beings we have much in common.

THE WIZARD OF ID   by Brant parker and Johnny hart

THE WIZARD OF ID by permission of Johnny Hart and Field Enterprises, Inc., 1975.

What is Discrimination?

Discrimination is an act; prejudice is a feeling

The term discrimination has at least one meaning: "The practice or act of making distinctions among people or groups of people." For example, a discriminating employer may make a distinction between white and black applicants for a job, and choose only white applicants.

Perhaps to understand job discrimination we must look at the roots of prejudice that lie behind it. We all are likely to have some feelings of prejudice against those who are different from us and certainly a stronger feeling against those we don't understand. We may show a tendency to mistrust those who are different and even display our hostility through actions in the form of discrimination. Therefore by definition, prejudice is an attitude and discrimination is an overt act demonstrating our prejudices.

Prejudice Works Both Ways

It is also important to point out that all people are prejudiced in one way or another, not simply members of dominant cultural groups. We all hold stereotypes about other groups of people. Furthermore, groups that are traditionally thought of as objects of prejudice and discrimination are usually also prejudiced themselves. Black people, for example, hold stereotypes about white people, and women hold stereotypes about men. The prejudices that people hold are usually met with equal prejudices from the other side, like reflections in a mirror. This process is one of the reasons that prejudice tends to spread throughout society.

The prejudices that people hold become serious human relations problems when they are translated into action, into discrimination. A person who holds a prejudice but who does not discriminate, is tolerant—capable of allowing other people to live freely. Our society values freedom of thought highly, which is why most efforts to deal with discrimination are directed at persuading people to be tolerant—to avoid harming other people—not at legislating ways of thinking.

Prejudice and Culture

Many powerful social values and traditions support prejudice and discrimination in American culture. People who have no particular reason to be prejudiced, who in fact know very little about the groups of people they dislike, still subscribe to the stereotypes. Why? Because "everyone knows that . . ."—and out comes a stereotyped description of a group of people without regard for the individuals involved, or for the facts.

Culture rests on group identity

Culture also rests on a huge complex of group identifications. People are naturally friendly and seek contact with other people, preferably people like themselves—they form groups to fill these needs. Group membership is highly valued by the individual and by the culture as a whole. The trouble with groups is that they involve exclusion as well as inclusion. If one is forming a union, for example, employers are excluded, an exclusion based on a relatively rational principle. But people will also form groups on irrational principles, in order to have the kind of support and self-identification that goes along with group membership. Frequently, a group will be formed along discriminatory lines—whites band together and exclude blacks and vice versa. Each group reinforces its own members and therefore also reinforces the rules for exclusion.

The in-group and the out-group

The status that the *in-group* (the group that is discriminating) achieves by discriminating against the *out-group* (the group that is being discriminated against) is supported most strongly by those members of the in-group who would have a low social status if they were not in the group. For example, in their massive study on discrimination, Simpson and Yinger noted that women tend to serve as culture carriers for prejudice because they hold low status themselves.[1] Women, like most groups that are discriminated against, are also educationally disadvantaged, which means that they have less access to facts about other minority groups, and therefore tend to accept stereotypes more easily. Furthermore, women traditionally bring up the children and pass on to them the cultural pattern of prejudice. Fortunately, this condition is being modified as more women identify with the out-groups, gain more access to education, and are less rigidly confined to the child-rearing role.

Prejudice and Self-Image

One of the arguments offered for prejudice and discrimination is that people in the out-group in some way deserve what they get. An employer may say that he does not hire blacks because they are unreliable, but there is a hidden factor in this kind of justification: the fact that discrimination becomes a closed circle, creating its own facts and producing them as solid evidence. The fact is that discrimination effects a self-fulfilling prophecy. Blacks, and for that matter, Chicanos, Asians, native Americans, and women, may actually prove unreliable in many situations because they are expected to be so. The minority shares cultural traditions with the majority or dominant group, including the tradition of prejudice. They too develop prejudices, not only against the in-groups and other out-groups, but also against themselves. They tend to accept the image others hold of them, to be ambivalent about their own self-worth, to fulfill the stereotypes, and to suffer from lack of confidence. All of these effects tend to provide reasons to discriminate against them as workers and make attempts to help them very difficult.[2] An employer who wishes to change the situation must be prepared not only to completely avoid discrimination, but actively help encourage employees to overcome it.

Employers and workers alike can become more sensitive to the problems of self-image that minority people and women face by "putting themselves in the other person's shoes." Role playing is a very useful technique for learning how discrimination affects people. A white supervisor (or, for that matter, a black) who is an object of discrimination, even if only for a short training session, can experience real changes in attitude and action as a result of experiencing the change in role. One of the most interesting studies of such a role shift was made by a white sociologist, John Howard Griffin, who changed his skin color with a series of chemical and ultraviolet treatments. He passed himself off as a black man in the South, and wrote a book about the experience called *Black Like Me.* The most vivid effect of the adventure was that he found the rejections accumulating in his self-image, until he found himself fearful, clumsy, and self-rejecting. His conclusion was, "You place the white man in the ghetto, deprive him of educational advantages, arrange it so he has to struggle hard to fulfill his instinct for self-respect, give him little physical privacy and less leisure, and he would after a time assume the same characteristics you attach to the Negro. These characteristics don't spring from whiteness or blackness, but from a man's conditioning."[3]

A white man travelled as a black man

Man's action may arise more from situation than skin color

The general movement against discrimination has made great changes in the self-image of minority people and women. Slogans such as "Black is Beautiful" have positively expressed and affected the way black people are seen by others as well as by themselves. Other out-groups have developed similar slogans and experienced similar changes. The effort to achieve and maintain self-respect has affected on-the-job relations so much that the employer may even be faced with a reverse problem occasionally—oversensitivity to and rejection of constructive criticism. In such situations, the employer should be guided by the understanding that movement often proceeds by extremes, and that this specific extreme may well be necessary to achieving balance.

Black is beautiful

KINDS OF DISCRIMINATION

What kinds of discrimination are most common in the United States? Sometimes it is not easy to tell, because at any given moment the public media may be emphasizing one kind over another. During the beginning of our national history, religious discrimination was at the forefront because early settlers often came to America to escape religious persecution in Europe. And, because prejudice and discrimination along religious lines affect minorities as well as majority groups, religious rivalry accompanied the settlers to their new home. Discrimination based on religious beliefs and groups is no longer as strong as it once was.

RELIGIOUS DISCRIMINATION

From the time our founding forefathers set foot on the American soil to establish the basic principle of freedom of religion, a new faith has sprung up in our nation. However, those of certain religions have had a more difficult time in obtaining employment than those belonging to the Protestant faiths. Catholics, Jews, Mormons, Buddhists, all have been subject to ridicule in various parts of the United States and more violently during certain times in history. While the practice is still common, religious discrimination has not received as much attention of late as perhaps other more overt forms of discrimination.

RACIAL DISCRIMINATION

The United States was divided from the beginning by racial tensions. White settlers drove out the native Americans and set up a system of labor based on black slavery. These two types of racism are still with us today. The native Americans were decimated, so that statistically the problem is not as great as with black Americans, who are the largest ethnic minority in the United States, approximately 10 percent of the population. However, the lot of native Americans who survived was hardly better than that of many black Americans.

Approximately 10% of the population is black

The United States also expanded into areas held by Spanish settlers and extended discrimination to the second largest ethnic minority, the Mexican-Americans or Chicanos. Asians, who first came here in large numbers to serve as cheap labor in the West, also suffer from discrimination. Originally many other ethnic groups who immigrated here, such as the Irish, the Germans, and the Italians, were the object of ethnic prejudice as well, although this is no longer a major problem.

The subject of racial discrimination is an emotional issue and perhaps a few facts may help give us all a common ground for further discussions. Black Americans number more than 22 million persons, or about 10 percent of the total U.S. population. The birth rate of blacks is increasing faster than that of whites,

Approximately 5% of the
population is Mexican-
American

about 20 percent as compared with 12 percent. There are some 9,230,000 Americans, nearly 5 percent of the total U.S. population, who identify themselves as having an origin in a Spanish speaking country.

A review of the historical events seems to show that society is moving to overcome racial discrimination, but at a slow pace. Review of dates listed below and the landmark events that happened during those years gives an interesting spectrum to the problems of racial discrimination.

1863 — Emancipation Proclamation frees slaves in rebel states.

1896 — U.S. Supreme Court establishes "separate, but equal" doctrine.

1905–1910 — Black Americans organize NAACP.

1954 — Supreme Court rules that "separate education facilities are inherently unequal" and orders schools desegregated.

1963 — Widespread civil rights demonstrations. More than 250,000 blacks and whites march in Washington. Medgar Evans and William Moore assassinated.

1963 — President John F. Kennedy assassinated.

1964 — Race riots in Northern cities.

1964 — Civil Rights Act of 1964 passed establishing the Equal Employment Opportunity Commission

1965 — Race riots in Watts, California.

1968 — Assassination of Reverend Martin Luther King, Jr.

1970 — Presidential Executive Order 11246 sets detailed guidelines for fair employment practices for all government contractors. Revisions later include women as well as minority groups.

1972 — Congress passes law strengthening Power of EEOC.

Certainly many of the "crisis" events that have occurred in the last two decades have forced the public to focus on racial discrimination. The blacks were the first to recognize that protests and demonstrations did have a part in forcing public recognition. Their pushing for new laws, better education, and government pressure have brought about some change.

Black Pride

The term "Black Pride" can bring self-respect to some and fear to others. One store owner in Watts said, "Black Pride means self-determination. That a black can determine his own destiny and his own future. This in a way is a great slogan for blacks, and instills a fear in some whites." Not knowing what a black will do if he has his own way can generate fear in a caucasian for several reasons.

Certainly blacks could not forget their color even if they wanted to. Individuals need not necessarily see something good or bad when they perceive an object with color, but they are likely to see color. Bill Cosby in films and lectures had pointed out how our myths and fairy tales are full of the "white knight" and the "black witch of the North." We look at sweet white sugar and talk of black as the absence of color—and we are all afraid of the dark.

Such self-pride has been seen in the change of black advertising. The Afro hair style is accepted by whites as well as blacks. One magazine layout for Afro-Sheen, a hair preparation that is supposed to enhance the natural, curly look carries the headline: "A beautiful new product for a beautiful new people." That is quite a change from the wording of older ads for cosmetics intended to bleach skin and straighten hair.

A new stronger self-pride has helped the black cause in the search for a better place in society and for job opportunities. However, there are two problems that are beyond the capacity of business or blacks alone to handle and need government assistance. The number of families headed by black women, a most critical welfare problem, has grown over the decade to more than a million. Second, a number of older, unskilled blacks are having an even more difficult time getting work.[4]

Figure 14–1. A new, stronger self-pride has helped the black cause in the search for a better place in society and for job opportunities.
Courtesy of A.T.&T. Co.

The bulk of the 14 million Mexican-Americans are found in the Southwestern part of the United States, from Texas, New Mexico, Arizona, and the entire state of California. Unless you live within this geographical area, you are not likely to know of the problems of discrimination that Mexican-Americans may face. The same is true with the fact that few Californians are aware of the problems of Puerto Ricans or Cubans living in Florida or New York.

The term *brown* is a militant term to some Mexican-Americans and *Chicano* is a new proud term for the young adults born in Los Angeles, but the same term Chicano can be derogatory to a Mexican-American over forty years of age raised in Los Angeles. "I am a proud Mexican, but also an American. I am not a punk of a Chicano Indian from the barrio."

Historically, there are several differences between the blacks and the Mexican-Americans. In the last three decades blacks have congregated in the inner-cities or the urban areas of the United States. For more than a century Mexican-Americans have traditionally been found in the rural areas of the West.

Cesar Chavez and United Farm Workers

Agriculture was the strongest agent to bring the members of the Latinos together. The United Farm Workers Union formed by Cesar Chavez became a focal emphasis for identification and enduring spirit when it was formed in 1965. Mexican-Americans may have ambivalent feelings about migratory workers in the farming community. Allowing people to come from Mexico to work as aliens, either legally or illegally, does put more people available on the employment rolls. They know that a large supply of workers can keep the wages down for all of them. On the other hand, the Mexicans who are U.S. citizens often want to bring their relatives into the United States. This ambivalence to the problem creates the feeling that Chicanos want Mexicans to come into the United States and also want to keep them out. The fact that migratory workers are not covered under the National Labor Relations Act makes the situation more of a problem that has to be settled locally.

La Raza

The two million Mexican-Americans in Los Angeles makes La Raza (the race) a powerful group that has influenced the development of the West. The Spanish language is a powerful tool that allows the Latinos to converse with one another while only a few Caucasians can understand them. The ballots are now printed in both English and Spanish so all can understand the issues to be voted on.

Culturally La Raza appears to be more paternalistic, meaning the family is governed more often by the father than the mother. By tradition, the Mexican-American family is more likely to be of the Catholic faith. All of these facets make the

Mexican-Americans different as a group from the blacks. Their problems and goals are different because their background and culture are different.

The Indian Nation

A basic issue for many groups is how to integrate with the majority of society for the good of all, but still maintain the unique individual cultures that can easily be lost forever if there is total simulation into the mainstream of America.

Many Indian leaders agree that unity of the native Americans or American Indians is in a large part the result of recent activism. Emerging from the quiet disorders, tribal officials say that the new determination among the nation's 800,000 Indians is to "work within the system" through lawsuits to bring about legislation for their rights.

Three goals of native Americans   Their major goals include three long-range proposals: greater Indian control of the Bureau of Indian Affairs, establishment of an independent federal unit of lawyers to oversee Indian legal affairs, and more direct supervision of federal funds by local tribes.[5]

The Oriental View

Every major city has an oriental section or "Chinatown." However, the substantial oriental population is more spread out within the United States. They can be found in rural areas as well as in the big cities. Orientals appear as a race to experience less discrimination than any other minority skin color. Why?— certainly the "coolies" of San Francisco and the railroad builders of 1850 were treated much like slave labor. Can one reason be that as a group they are the most educated group in America— even more educated than the Caucasians? The proportion of Japanese and Chinese men with a college degree is nearly 90 percent greater than it is for white men. With regard to occupational status for men, both Chinese and Japanese rank higher than whites.[6]

THE OLDER WORKER

The emphasis of late has been on the retired person, since every tenth American is over 65 years of age, however little attention has been given to the older workers. Certainly age does affect the characteristics of an employee. Some become slower and less adaptable, but compensate by improving their quality of work, dependability, and attendance. On the whole the job performances of older workers and younger workers are about the same.

Certainly the number of older workers is increasing because of better health conditions. The age of forty arbitrarily seems to classify employees as older workers. Although thirty-five is over the hill for most sports figures, sixty can still be young for tool and die makers. The age of retirement minus ten or fifteen years usually marks the beginning of the "older worker cycle." The attitude of the individual, his skill, and union and company policies are all factors that tend to fix the age range for the older worker.

Job engineering and job reassignment

Job engineering and job reassignments are two things companies can accomplish to help the older worker. Job engineering is redesigning the work station so that work can be done in a way that is less taxing on the employee. It may be planning the work so it can be done sitting down, providing different power equipment, reducing body movement or changing the flow of work. Job reassignment is moving the person into a different position, in which the task does not demand so much in terms of dexterity or speed, but is hopefully just as rewarding. Older workers can become good trainers and set-up men, as well as rework rejects from the production line.

Obtaining Positions after Forty

Some of the reasons that make finding employment after forty more difficult are:

1. Seniority and policies of promotion from within tend to protect the employed worker, but make it difficult for the unemployed worker to get a job at anything other than the entry level, which is below his ability and pay need.

2. The decline in self-employment and small businesses has forced the older worker to look for positions with middle-sized or large companies.

3. Phased-out industries or closing of plants force older workers to learn a new trade or move to other plants. The new technology has forced the fireman out of the railroad lines and some key punch operators out of the office. It has forced older workers into new areas for which they are not trained, and many resist learning a new trade.

4. The lowering of retirement age to fifty-five in some firms has shocked the self-confidence of the older worker rather than raised it.

Psychologically, this period can be just as difficult for the older employee as the early years of employment are for the younger person. During this period he faces his last promotion. He may be motivated to work harder, up to the point when he knows he cannot reach that last promotion. Thereafter motivation may operate to maintain the worker's status quo rather than to propel him toward self-realization. Some social behaviorists say this point is reached at retirement age minus three years.

Quickly following this period comes the preretirement syndrome, or "What the hell shall I do when I retire?" Preretirement counseling seems to be necessary regardless of how astute the older worker may be. The fixed age of 65 for retirement was established by Social Security, but the military, public-service agencies, and many companies are now granting pensions at 55 or earlier. Retirement is moving to a sliding scale that allows employees to select a time that is easiest for both the worker and the firm.

Some firms allow busy executives to become accustomed to retirement by lengthening their vacation to two months at age 62 and having them work mornings only after 65, with compulsory retirement at age 72. Another plan is having two retirees working half time to fill one position. The idea of hiring retired specialists or executives for one-year contracts affords companies a certain flexibility.

Perhaps one of the best ways to end this segment is to relate a story of one man's zest for life and a company's confidence in the man: conductor Leopold Stokowski, at the age of 94, signed a six-year recording contract with Columbia Records.

THE EMPLOYMENT OF WOMEN

Possibly the new era for women started January 5, 1976, when *Time Magazine* selected "Woman of the Year" instead of a man as having the most influence on history and everyday living for the year. The cover of the magazine pictured such people as Carla Hills, then head of the Department of Housing and Urban Development, Barbara Jordan, the black Texas Congresswoman, Billie Jean King of tennis fame, and Betty Ford, then First Lady.

"It isn't how much time you spend with your children, but how well you spend it," says Mrs. Letty Cotting Pogrebin, author of *How to Make it in a Man's World.* She is convinced that if you prefer working at a challenging job to doing housework, then by all means keep the job and you will be happier in the long run.

Although no women have been named to the Supreme Court and there is as yet no Amazon playing halfback for the Los Angeles Rams, there is a definite long-term trend for more women to enter the working world. Many jobs are opening for

Figure 14–2. As yet no Amazon is playing halfback for the Los Angeles Rams, but many jobs are open for women that were once taboo, such as truck driving, telephone line work, and auto repair.

Courtesy of Santa Barbara City Collge (Photo by Rob Reilly)

women that were once taboo, such as truck driving and telephone line work. The greatest discrimination against women is most evident in industries such as steel, banking, finance, mining, and railroads. On the other hand, women have found little discrimination in advertising, high fashion retailing, medical fields, marine biology, dentistry, and physics.

Forty-five percent of the women are in the work force

In 1940, 27 percent of the women over 16 years of age were working, and in 1975, there were 45 percent working-age women in the labor force. A federal survey showed that the average woman employed in a full-time job earned only $3.00 for each $5.00 paid to a man with a similar job. However, according to *Time Magazine* of March 20, 1972, in order to have a situation of equal pay for equal work, the total wages for women would have to be increased by a shocking 109 billion dollars (Figure 14–3).

Social Changes have Altered Women's Roles

New public attitudes toward the "pill" and other forms of birth control, divorce, housekeeping, child rearing, and abortion have all influenced women's self-concept and quickened their journey

446

into the business world. Perhaps the last two decades have influenced women's role in society more than the last hundred.
Today child support is now a shared responsibility between husband and wife. In most states, a spouse seeking a divorce must
charge specific cruelties such as abandonment, adultery, or mental
abuse. But divorce laws are changing drastically. California, for
example, in 1970 passed a no-fault divorce bill whereby the
court now will grant divorce or a dissolution of marriage
based on "irreconcilable differences": there needn't be an accu-
ser and an accused. Women are more subject to paying alimony
in divorce cases than ever before.

Aims of Women's Liberation Groups

NOW leads the way for women

Some of the far-reaching attitudes of women that will influence
business have been taken up by the women's liberation groups
such as NOW (the National Organization for Women), The National Women's Political Caucus, and the Women Equity Action
League. The strongest demand is naturally equal pay for equal
work, but other causes have significant impact on business also,
such as:

1. CHILD CARE CENTERS

Since we have moved from split-level living to split-family living, there need to be child care centers while the single parent
is working. There are about 2 million mothers in the labor force
who are divorced, separated, or widowed. Working mothers are
usually too busy with their family's needs to be involved in the
fight for women's rights.

Low-income families are faced with the greatest difficulty.
Fewer than 300,000 children get free or low-cost care in non-

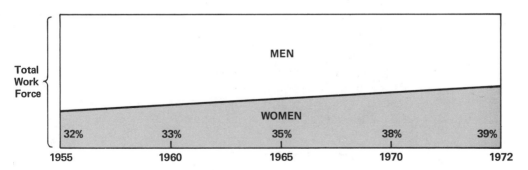

Figure 14–3. Women are a growing part of the work force. Almost 45% of the
work force is composed of women.

profit day care centers in the entire country. Those not poor enough to get subsidized care and not rich enough to get quality care are faced with an equal dilemma, as day care can run as high as $3,000 a year per child.

2. BIRTH CONTROL AND PLANNED PARENTHOOD

The widespread use of the "pill" and intrauterine devices is only part of the issue. The male accepting the responsibility in birth control through vasectomies has also been strongly encouraged and is on the increase. Several companies are granting a day's leave for their male employees to have a vasectomy.

Some women workers are taking up the cause of "maternity lib." They want to choose, without interference from the company when they quit work to have a baby and when they will return. They want disability pay while unable to work. "Maternity lib" enjoys support from many women's organizations.

3. ABORTIONS

Unwanted and unplanned childbirths have led to the acceptance of abortion by some women's liberation groups. It should be noted that because of the last two issues many Catholics have not joined the women's lib bandwagon.

4. EDUCATION

Many women are encouraged to further their education beyond high school and not in the traditional areas of secretarial skills, but in fields pursued by males, such as accounting, law, and medicine. In ghetto areas special courses are offered for mothers during the day, so they are not faced with walking to school at night. Short-term programs and television courses are all attempts at meeting the demand of women for more education.

5. POLITICS

"It is time for women to make policies and not coffee." Rather than acting as hostesses for political candidates, women are moving to the forefront by running for political office. Shirley Chisholm was the first serious female candidate for the presidency in 1972. Today there are several women senators, representatives, and judges, as well as two women generals in the armed services.

Problems for the Businesswoman

There are several unnoticed factors that face the working woman in her daily routine.

1. The discomfort for the women to buy lunch or a drink for a male client.
2. Women hate to ask their husbands to move when a promotion for her comes along.
3. Traveling alone and eating alone on business trips, as well as the lack of female executive washrooms.
4. The income earned by a wife is often discounted when a couple seeks a home mortgage. If the wife's income is taken into account the bank may ask for an embarrassing statement as to whether either the husband or wife is sterile, or if they practice birth control.
5. Women routinely have no credit rating following a divorce. Even if the husband drank and gambled while she kept the credit good, he gets the good rating and she gets none.

THE EMPLOYMENT OF THE HANDICAPPED

Early in 1977 the physically handicapped let the country become aware of their needs through a national convention in Florida. While thousands of firms are willing to hire the handicapped, thousands will not. Among the latter, reluctance to hire is largely based on fear of extra expense. Here again there are fallacies about hiring people. Insurance companies apparently are not aware of any increased costs related to employment of the handicapped.

Hiring the handicapped does not increase insurance premiums

One insurance company stated, "We believe, and our actuarial studies reinforce this belief, that physically handicapped persons who are full-time active employees not only do not increase Group Life, Disability or Medical Care insurance cost, but actually exert a slight but not measurable reduction in costs. We believe the reason for this is that physically handicapped employees are aware of their condition, are somewhat more careful in their work and play habits . . ."

Mainstream aids the handicapped

A second item of expense is remodeling. Mainstream Inc., a nonprofit organization dedicated to getting handicapped persons into jobs, is finding that the costs of making a building free of architectural barriers are not that expensive. When Kaiser Aluminum & Chemical Corporation decided to revamp its 27-story headquarters building in Oakland, California to help disabled workers, it was concerned that the cost would be hundreds of thousands of dollars. Mainstream Inc., sent in architects who showed that the work could be done for less than $8,000.

All it takes to help a blind person is to spend about $3 to put braille numbers on every selection button in an average elevator. And it's a simple matter to install a two-tone bell system that indicates whether the elevator is going up or down.

It is estimated that between 25 and 40 million Americans have physical or mental disabilities which qualify them as handicapped. Since the passage of the Rehabilitation Act of 1973, any company that does more than $2,500 in business annually with Uncle Sam is required to take affirmative action to hire the handicapped. The law also applies to institutions, including schools and hospitals, which accept federal funds.

Rehabilitation Act of 1973

CULTURAL STEREOTYPES

The cultural traditions of discrimination against women also marked our nation's founding. No one even considered giving women the vote when the Constitution was first written. The culture has also discriminated against prisoners, ex-convicts, homosexuals, and other people whom society considers offenders against the mainstream of social values. Physically handicapped people, deaf, blind, paraplegics, epileptics—even midgets, dwarfs, and overweight people—are discriminated against. The mentally disadvantaged are likewise affected. Even young people and older people experience discrimination, in their case because the culture holds certain stereotypes about people of their age groups.

We are now involved in a period in which all types of discrimination are being challenged. The social protest wave that began in the 1960s has greatly improved the position of minorities in our society.

PSYCHOLOGICAL ROOTS OF PREJUDICE

C. G. Jung, one of the three founders of modern psychology, along with Freud and Adler, also suggested that prejudice is a projection onto other people of feelings we repress in ourselves. For example, if a person is angry and doesn't want to feel angry, he may repress it in himself and project it onto other people.

Jung also suggested that projection most often occurred when the person involved was dealing with the unconscious part of himself or herself.[7]

Meerloo, another noted investigator in the field of prejudice, suggests that "Every war is a dramatization of man's [and woman's] inner war, the externalization of its own conflicts. Man feels temporarily relieved of tensions when there is outside trouble in the world. He can postpone finding a solution to his own conflicts as long as the outside world offers a more stirring emotional drama in which he can play a role."[8] Politicians know that one way to unite a constituency is to present the people with an enemy. Meerloo implies that this mechanism also operates for individuals. By providing oneself with a fearful enemy, one can feel whole and not divided against oneself. In business, as in other aspects of life, one can frequently meet individuals who blame their shortcomings on other people. A woman worker who blames all her incompetence on men, for example, is making that kind of projection and is not dealing with shortcomings by seeking education and advancement on her own.

Why are some people more prejudiced than others? Bettelheim and Janowitz suggest that hostility is linked to feelings of deprivation, anxiety, fear of imminent war, fear of losing one's job, sense of achievement, feeling trapped in one's job, etc.[9] Whenever people are worried or bothered about something, they are likely to look for a scapegoat, someone who can be made responsible for their difficulties. The emotions are then displaced onto the scapegoat, so that anxiety about losing one's job becomes anxiety that group X is trying to take away one's job. This effect explains why so often disadvantaged people are themselves highly prejudiced, especially against other disadvantaged people.

The personality, like any other system, has an ecology of its own. The system always tries to balance itself—to achieve the state of equilibrium known as *homeostasis*. Being prejudiced and discriminating against other human beings, while solving some problems, creates others, which are often worse than the original ones. Sociologists feel that society as a whole must be and is becoming aware that the long-term costs of prejudice are greater than the temporary and illusory benefits.

THE ECONOMIC ROOTS OF PREJUDICE

Prejudice and discrimination also have economic roots. Such economic fears are rational; it is a fact that if there are not enough jobs to go around, people will be competing for the jobs that are available. There are also not enough high-paying jobs, and people will compete for good wages. If one group of workers can be singled out, on the basis of some difference such as color, sex, ethnic background, or language, and if prejudice can be built up against such a group, then other workers will have a slightly better chance of getting the available jobs. This is one reason why workers develop and maintain prejudiced attitudes—to express economic insecurity and to justify job discrimination that operates in their favor. This is also why discrimination permeates the unions to nearly the same extent that it permeates the economy as a whole—because competition for jobs is part of our economic system, and there are rarely enough for everyone.

Competition for jobs feeds prejudice

There is also a macroeconomic gain for employers in aiding and abetting discrimination in the work force. Competition for jobs among workers can help employers push wages and working conditions down. Employers often threaten striking workers with the prospect of being displaced. And there are always members of minority groups, having previously had little or no chance at jobs, and needing to survive like everyone else, who are willing to take jobs that pay poorly or who will even scab to make a living. The situation then ripens for social unrest. Until we have an economy that can assure jobs and a living wage for everyone, competition for survival will tend to express itself in prejudice and discrimination.

Unskilled workers keep production down

Add to these figures the loss in human resources, which is directly reflected in the GNP (Gross National Product), and the cost of prejudice and discrimination becomes staggering. For one thing, as the United States learned from its own experience with slavery, a discriminated-against minority is not skilled, and is therefore not usable as a work force in a highly industrialized nation that requires a high level of skill in its workers. South Africa is currently trying to maintain its apartheid system as well as industrializing—but the workers are too oppressed to be highly productive.[10]

Smaller families

Discrimination also works to render useless minority members who are skilled; the prejudice against women renders potentially productive workers helplessly idle, unable to add to the nation's prosperity. The *Manpower Report of the President* (1973) projects that the current shift from a three-child to a two-child family average in the 1970s will add 1.7 million women to the labor force by 1980.[11] And the increase in older workers (45 to 60 years of age) will be about 30 percent in the 1990s.[12] That is a huge number of willing workers to be assimilated. In order to grow economically, the United States will simply be forced to drop discriminatory barriers in employment. Forward-looking businesses are making efforts to reach out to these newly powerful consumers. For example, J. C. Penney Company has begun

Credit cards for women

to offer women credit cards in their own names in an effort to win the market by dropping the discriminatory practice of denying women credit unless their credit is guaranteed by the income of a man.[13]

Minority members have also launched successful business ventures that must be reckoned with. *Commerce Today* reports that "Black-owned businesses . . . by 1980 will total 240,000 businesses with aggregate receipts of $11 billion."[14] The Feminist Federal Credit Union, in Detroit, has $82,000 in assets; the First Women's Bank & Trust Co. (New York) has $4 million.[15]

International trade

These business ventures are small, but growing at a phenomenal rate, given their youth, and present a solid challenge to the business world.

Finally, as the United States becomes more involved in the international market, businessmen are increasingly becoming aware that discrimination can make a disastrous impression on potential buyers and sellers abroad. We need many products that we cannot supply for ourselves; these products are becoming limited as natural resources become more scarce. Our bargaining power abroad depends heavily on the good will that our democratic principles engender. But when we practice discrimination and preach democracy, our credibility is lost. The United States is now trying to establish trade relations with African peoples, on a democratic basis, which will be very difficult if we do not break down our own double standard at home, as well as guard against exporting it to our business ventures abroad. Establishing oil trade with Nigeria becomes a more complex issue when their people see us discriminating against blacks.

FIGHTING DISCRIMINATION

One of the areas of fighting discrimination is within the individual—a process of reexamining prejudice and discrimination in the light of modern psychological theory. Self-knowledge is one of the most powerful weapons against prejudice. This sounds like such benign advice, yet any ideas listed here are only guidelines and certainly no magical satisfactory solution can come about so simply by following them.

Education and Awareness

Another area is *education*. Much of the inertia that allows discrimination to exist is based on ignorance supported by tradition. Education is helping to break down old beliefs in the superiority of men over women, whites over nonwhites, the English language over Spanish, Japanese, and Chinese, one religion over another, and so on. Much of this battle against old patterns is taking place in the schools, but it is also affecting the public in the form of public media, higher-level training and research, and on-the-job training.

PROGRAMS OF AWARENESS

If we distrust that which we know little of, then it is time to learn more of the cultural background of the disadvantaged. The increase of multicultural awareness is being tried in colleges, through ethnic study programs. Likewise companies are attempting to educate employees through small study groups and sensitivity programs. Training programs for the hard core unemployed and testing procedures for applicants, as well as special supervisory training courses for minority groups, are focusing on the need for a new awareness.

MORE INTERGROUP CONTACT

As more intergroup contact is achieved, the realities of how people think and act will tend to overcome the myths and pseudo-scientific lingo that has formed people's prejudices. The movement of minority groups into the suburban areas has influenced white attitudes. Likewise, the flood of women into management positions has altered age-old myths of working females.

Legal and Legislative Action

The battle against discrimination is also being waged on the legal front. Laws, of course, like education, do not substantially alter a society's general behavior—both systems reflect the trend of the majority and serve only to guide or coerce the minority into the general trend. It is important for businessmen to understand the nature of the laws, in order to avoid prosecution and even more importantly, to use the laws as an indication of current trends in society.

The most important antidiscrimination bill of the many that have been passed in the last two decades is the Civil Rights Act of 1964, which made discrimination illegal if it was based on national origin, ethnic group, sex, creed, age, or race. Easy-to-read explanations of the laws pertaining to discrimination can be found in two books published by the National Civil Service League (NCSL): *Federal Mandates for Affirmative Action: A Guidebook for Public Employers*[16] and *Judicial Mandates for Affirmative Action: A Guidebook for Public Employers.*[17] The first describes the law and gives excerpts from relevant materials; the second describes the court cases that have tested specific provisions of the laws. Many of the cases have been brought to the courts by the Equal Employment Opportunity Commission (EEOC), the federal agency established to enforce such laws. These cases define the areas in which the federal law applies and serve to rectify situations in which discrimination is being practiced. Since the law is continuously being clarified and modified by the court decisions, it is not possible to present completely up-to-date information. For example, the current EEOC emphasis has not been fully tested before the Supreme

Civil Rights Act of 1964

EEOC

Court, and several cases protesting reverse discrimination in affirmative action programs have yet to be heard and judged. The businessman should try to stay abreast of new legal developments, and should be aware as well of whatever state and local laws have been developed to guide the antidiscrimination movement.

Two million dollars in back pay ordered by court

It is possible, however, to give a general overview of the kinds of judicial mandates that have been handed down. For example, in May 1974, the United States Labor Department won a suit against a private employer in which $2 million in back wages were ordered paid to 160 employees over the age of 40 who were laid off for reasons of age between 1971 and 1973.[18] This decision defines at least a lower limit to age discrimination, although upper limits remain unclear.

Another area clarified by the courts has been testing for new job applicants. The case of *Griggs* vs. *Duke Power Company*, at Draper, North Carolina (1971), resulted in a decision that "(1) If any employment test or practice has a disparate *effect* on persons on the basis of race, sex, religion, or national origin, for example, a test with a higher percentage of black failures than white failures, *and* (2) that test has not been proven to be job-related and an accurate predictor of job performance, *then* that test constitutes unlawful discrimination under Title VII of the Civil Rights Act of 1964."[19] Another area has indicated that seniority systems, while not in themselves discriminatory, may serve to extend discrimination in industries that have discriminated in the past: "U.S. District Court Judge Fred J. Cassibry . . . ruled in New Orleans that Continental Can Co. and a Louisiana local of the United Steelworkers violated civil rights laws by using seniority as the *sole criterion* for laying off workers. . . ."[20] This kind of ruling is helpful to clarify the scope of affirmative action programs, which have hired minority members and women, only to find that the newest members of the work force were the first to be laid off under the rules of seniority when times got bad. For example, all 120 women hired at the Mercury automobile plant in Detroit since April 1972 were fired in February 1974 and 1,300 out of 2,700 black people were fired, because the seniority system permits people with more seniority to keep their jobs.[21] Such suits serve not only to define the law, but also to enforce it by exacting stiff penalties from offenders. The EEOC and the Justice Department are constantly pressing suits against employers for discriminatory practices. Which practice is currently in vogue today, that of laying off the most recently hired (thus disfavoring women and minorities), or that of laying off the senior employees (thus disfavoring older, more skilled workers)?

DISCRIMINATION IN BUSINESS

Although it is true that the law and education are helping to push and pull social institutions into conformity with a majority trend, the fact remains that coercion is not a highly successful form of motivation. One of the clearest indications of this fact is that affirmative action programs succeed or fail depending on the interest and self-motivation of the organization involved, not on the formal investigation and enforcement of such programs by the EEOC and other human relations agencies. And business, like any other sector of society, is moving with the trend away from discrimination mainly under its own steam. Business is in the process of reexamining its goals, and many businessmen feel that it is time to add social concern to the profit motive. For example, Mobil Oil Corporation ran an advertisement in the *San Francisco Chronicle,* stating "Businessmen are pragmatists, and with their daily feedback from the marketplace, they readily abandon dogma whenever their survival instinct tells them to. It has become less and less a question of what they might *want* to do or might *like* to do, but of what their common sense and survival instinct tell them they *have* to do. . . . Because it is keyed so closely to the marketplace and is so responsive to it, private business is necessarily the most effective instrument of change. Some would call it revolutionary. Many of those who attack business fail to comprehend its constructive contributions to responsive change. And this sort of change is one of the basic reasons business manages to survive.

Not *all* businesses survive, of course. The record is replete with companies that expired because they didn't adapt rapidly enough to a new milieu."[22]

Affirmative Action

Investments of this sort are relatively easy projects; it is far more difficult to eliminate discrimination on the job. For this reason, the major emphasis in business for the last decade has been affirmative action. What does the term mean? The NCSL states that

> In its simplest terms, affirmative action is a comprehensive effort by an employer to:
>
> (1) Identify all barriers in the personnel management system which limit the ability of applicants and employees to reach their full employment potential, without regard to race, sex, religion, national origin or other extraneous factors.
>
> (2) eliminate all such barriers in a timely, coordinated manner.

(3) undertake whatever special programs are needed to accelerate the process.[23]

As of 1972 the law extended affirmative action to public employers, and a great deal of information is now available about such programs because public agencies are like glass houses — everyone can see in. The NCSL, in addition to preparing the guides to federal laws and related court decisions, has issued a guide to setting up affirmative action programs for public employers, most of which serves equally well for private employers, who are usually more reticent about the workings of their own programs. The NCSL suggests that:

> An affirmative action program should include *not just some* but *all* of the following:
>
> (1) Commitment from the Chief Executive Officer.
>
> (2) Designation of an Affirmative Action Coordinator and assignment of specific responsibilities to the personnel department, civil service commission, human rights agency, operating agencies, and other agencies.
>
> (3) Outreach recruitment.
>
> (4) Job analysis, and where needed, job restructuring.
>
> (5) Validation and revision of examinations, educational requirements and all other screening criteria.
>
> (6) Upgrading and training programs.
>
> (7) Internal complaint procedure.
>
> (8) Supervisory training.
>
> (9) Employment census and progress report system.
>
> (10) Manpower planning.[24]

Where should an employer begin? The NCSL suggests that the program should begin simultaneously on all fronts, as all are interrelated. For example, a good job analysis is required for test validation, and test validation is required for effective outreach hiring. The establishment of on-the-job training programs is required to help disadvantaged workers; supervisory training in human relations is required to establish good training programs, to get a good job analysis, and to administer hiring practices successfully.[25]

Goals and Objectives

In outlining a new affirmative action program, try to develop detailed, specific objectives for the organization. If your goal is to bring employed minority percentages up to the national

Company goals should
be realistic

norm, state in writing what the present percentages are, what the national norm in each category is, and by what date you wish to achieve your goal. Objectives should be realistic. Be prepared for the fact that hiring the disadvantaged means that they will need support in the form of training programs to remedy lack of skills and lack of confidence. One of the problems that affirmative action programs have run into is unchanneled enthusiasm—poor planning can sabotage the best of intentions. Developing a set of objectives that breaks down the major goals by months, and even years, is essential. If you want to meet your goal in three years, set subgoals for achievement and evaluation at six-month intervals. Beginning small but solidly will allow you to apply experience to bigger steps later.

Objectives should be
set by months

Involvement

Get everyone involved, especially top management. Formalize involvement by getting official approval and by establishing lines of responsibility. Specific responsibilities should be assigned to other departments by a central coordinator, particularly to the personnel and human relations departments. Put responsibilities in writing, and hold meetings to educate and to request help in formulating objectives. Participation in the development of any program helps to involve people in its success or failure.

Involvement should not end with the development of the program. All departments and personnel should be kept informed of the program's progress and should be periodically surveyed or called together to give their opinions and suggestions on how to smooth over rough edges. The introduction of minority members and women into the organization may arouse fear and anger on the part of other employees, and opportunity to express these feelings can go a long way toward resolving them. Employees should be assured that their jobs will not be threatened, and that whenever possible their personal feelings about the situation will be respected. Clear, detailed information about proposed changes can help squash destructive, unsettling rumors among the workers.

Hiring and Promotion Policies

Traditionally, discrimination in business begins at the point of entry—hiring. Some of the forms it takes are arbitrary educational requirements, such as a high school diploma for a manual labor job; unvalidated tests that require skills not related to the job (such as the ability to solve problems in trigonometry for jobs that involve only simple arithmetic); and the requirement that an applicant write English, although spoken instructions could be adequate. Of course, there are also more clearly discriminatory requirements, such as that only white people or men should be hired. These latter requirements are easier to spot and eliminate than less visible barriers to equal employment opportunity.

Recruitment

Personnel officers working on affirmative action programs frequently find that even when there are job openings, minority people and women do not apply. Sometimes they do not believe they can actually get the job, or they do not know about the job openings. Jobs that are affected by affirmative action programs should be advertised in minority group publications as well as in the standard public media, and special efforts should be made to indicate that applications are being actively sought and that fair employment practices are promised.

Job Restructuring

One of the ways in which business has made room for minority members and women has been through the restructuring of jobs. Employees can be involved in this process in a way that can help dispose them favorably toward the program. For example, if a secretary can take over excess work from an overloaded supervisor, and is given a promotion and raise in pay, she can restructure her job to give simpler jobs to a trainee. The promotion and pay raise serves to ease the fear of displacement, and the participation in the restructuring can involve the older worker in the success or failure of the program. Jobs can also be restructured to eliminate requirements such as the writing of English; for example, if a trucker's job normally involves the writing of reports, the establishment of a records clerk job to help fill out reports can make it possible to hire workers who do not write well, but are excellent truckers.

DISCRIMINATION OF OTHER TYPES

Would you hire a "gay," a mentally handicapped, or one over 65?

While some businesses are making noble efforts to overcome society's prejudices, there are other types of discrimination being practiced today. What are your feelings about companies failing to hire the physically handicapped, those over sixty-five, homosexuals, or foreigners. Are these acts justified?

There are strong concerns over public reactions to hiring a cripple, an "old gent," a "gay fellow," an Arab, or a Nigerian. This strong public concern causes some managers to find artificial excuses for not including the person as a potential applicant for a position.

SUMMARY

Discrimination is the active expression of prejudice, the stereotyped, exclusionist, negative perception of people in an out-group. Prejudice is deeply rooted in the economic history of the United States, in our cultural values, and in the structure of the individual personality. Recently, in the last two decades, a social movement to combat discrimination based on prejudices has gathered force, especially in the field of equal employment opportunity.

The prejudiced individual may be trying to project internal tensions and self-doubts onto another person or a group of people. He or she may also gain a sense of group solidarity or individual identity by following cultural patterns of prejudice against other groups or individuals. But the personal costs of prejudice are also high: guilt, tension, and the fear of retaliation.

The economy may benefit from discrimination, too. Employers who wish to depress wages may be motivated to keep certain groups unemployed or underemployed and to use the threat of hiring such people against demands for higher wages from currently employed workers. The costs of discrimination to the economy, however, are even greater than the benefits: disadvantaged workers are not skilled, and unemployed workers are blocked from contributing to the nation's productivity. Furthermore, international trade relations are hampered by discrimination.

Business in the United States is recognizing that discrimination must be dealt with—that the costs of maintaining it are greater than the costs of allowing it to collapse. Like all other sectors of society business is permeated with discrimination and is also working hard to eliminate it. The major emphasis in business (as reflected in legislation) has been on affirmative action programs designed to actively find and destroy barriers to equal employment.

Affirmative action programs should be based on a thorough analysis of minority and female representation in various levels of the company, compared to their representation in the country as a whole. Disparities should be remedied by the achievement of a set of specific goals and objectives over a given period of time, in stages. Responsibilities for the program should be clearly established, and ongoing evaluations should be made from time to time.

The program should seek to involve all employees, especially top management. Clear, comprehensive information should be made continually available to alleviate fears of job insecurity among current employees. Hiring and promotion policies should be reviewed and revised. Tests should be validated for the job requirements, and unnecessary educational requirements should be dropped.

Recruitment should be active, and should involve advertising in minority media as well as standard media. Social welfare agencies are frequently able to refer qualified applicants. The company should clearly state that it intends to apply equal employment practices.

Affirmative action programs are currently being emphasized as a means of actively combating discrimination. Whether or not they will prove effective is not yet known. Nevertheless, the drive that underlies such efforts is gathering impetus from personal, social, and economic pressures, and promises success.

DISCRIMINATION AGAINST A WOMAN STOCKBROKER

Case Study #1

Diane Patterson is employed as a broker by Johnson and Hunt, a large metropolitan brokerage firm. Diane was promoted to this position five months ago when the company lost a few of its brokers to a competing firm. Diane had previously worked for a number of years as a secretary to Scott Pitts, one of the brokers in the firm, and he recommended her for a promotion when a vacancy arose.

Although Diane assumed her duties with enthusiasm, Cliff Stevenson, the office manager, soon felt it necessary to question Diane on her deteriorating performance. Cliff suspected the reason for Diane's poor performance. When Diane assumed her duties as broker, Cliff had heard some of the men speak against her, as if they resented her taking on the job of broker. He also knew that Diane was losing customers for no apparent reason other than the fact that she was female.

When Cliff questioned Diane on this, she replied, "I don't like being the only female in the department. I feel as if everyone is against me here." And she added, "Many of my male clients seem to think that because I'm a woman, I'm not qualified to be a broker."

Diane also mentioned that perhaps a new start in another department would enable her to carry out her duties as a broker more effectively.

Cliff knows that Diane is capable of performing her duties, even though she has few clients, and with the shortage of brokers in Cliff's department, he does not want to lose her. Cliff decides to ask Scott's opinion on the problem.

"The men feel threatened by Diane," Scott replied. "They feel that being a broker is a demanding job, and should belong to men only. One of the men said that she has no right to fill a position that may be needed by a man to support his family."

"I find that a bit hard to believe," replied Cliff.

"Believe it, Cliff, even Harry Morgan mentioned something about not only having to worry about younger men taking over his job, but now he'd have to worry about his secretary."

Now, understanding the problem that exists, Cliff must decide what course of action to take. If you were Cliff, what would you do?

1. Would you let Diane go?
2. Discuss the problem with the men separately?
3. Discuss the problem with Diane present?
4. How could you as manager enhance Diane's status?
5. What is the best course of action for all concerned?

PROBLEMS IN PROMOTING A BLACK

Case Study #2

The executives of the Omega Computer Tape Company began to assemble for the bimonthly committee meeting. Wayne Baker, president of the Omega Company, knew that this particular meeting would be a touchy one. The first item on the agenda, the one that he was concerned about, dealt with the proposed promotion of Jad Lloyd, a black resident of the community, to the position of supervisor of the shipping and receiving department.

For some time, the Omega Company has been without a minority member in a management position. Although the company has had minority members in management positions before, the last member left the company more than five years ago for a higher paying job in another city. When Brad Hall, the supervisor of the department under discussion, became eligible for promotion, this dispute began.

Bill Moore, Head of the Personnel Department and former civil rights activist, feels that Jad Lloyd should be promoted to the supervisory position, because he is a minority member. He knows that Mr. Lloyd has been with the company for a good number of years, and from reports that he has received feels that Lloyd is qualified to handle a supervisory position.

Richard Speer, administrative assistant, who is in charge of the shipping and receiving department, plus others, thinks otherwise. He feels that regardless of the fact that the company needs minority members in management positions, the best qualified man should be promoted. It is his opinion that Mr. Lloyd is not the most qualified. He feels Mr.

Manachek is more qualified and has more years with the company.

When the meeting begins and the discussion is opened on the topic, Bill Moore states, "If Mr. Lloyd is not promoted to this supervisory position, then we are failing in our obligation to insure that minority members have an equal standing in this company."

"I'm all for giving minorities a fair shake," replies Mr. Speer, "but I won't stand for a man to be promoted over another just because of his color, black or white, as I feel you want done in this case."

"It's time minority members were treated fairly around here, and it's high time we had one promoted to a management position!"

"Are you saying that regardless of ability, if it comes to promoting a black or a white, we should promote a black?"

"In this case, that is exactly what I am saying."

"That is reverse discrimination and I won't stand for it."

The meeting is obviously getting out of hand and Wayne Baker calls the discussion to a halt.

1. As president Wayne Baker, how would you handle the meeting?
2. Should he continue the meeting? If so, in what way?
3. Do you feel Mr. Lloyd or Mr. Manachek should be promoted? Why?

Terms and Concepts Students Should Know

prejudice	cultural stereotypes	birth control
black pride	job restructuring	women's liberation
Chicano	discrimination	affirmative action
NOW	older worker	EEOC
planned parenthood	United Farm Workers	

Bibliography

1. SIMPSON, GEORGE E., and YINGER, MILTON, *Racial and Cultural Minorities: An Analysis of Prejudice and Discrimination*, New York, Harper and Row, 1965, 3rd ed.
2. GRIFFIN, JOHN HOWARD, *Black Like Me*, Boston, Houghton, Mifflin, 1960.
3. *Models for Affirmative Action: A Guidebook for Public Employers*, National Civil Service League, Washington, 1973.
4. HALEY, ALEX, *Roots, The Saga of an American Family*, Doubleday & Company, Inc. Garden City, New York, 1976.
5. KOSSEN, STAN, *The Human Side of Organizations*, New York, Canfield Press, 1975, Chapters 11, 12, and 13.

Footnotes

[1] George Eaton Simpson and J. Milton Yinger, *Racial and Cultural Minorities: An Analysis of Prejudice and Discrimination*, 3rd ed. (New York: Harper & Row, 1965), p. 116.

[2] *Ibid.*, p. 51.

[3] John Howard Griffin, *Black Like Me* (Boston: Houghton Mifflin, 1960), p. 96.

[4] "The Black Message, Business Must Do More," *Business Week*, 22 January 1972, pp. 79–80.

[5] "An Indian 'Nation' is Gaining Unity, Respect—and Results," *U.S. News and World Report*, 25 February 1974, p. 60.

[6] Calvin F. Schmid and Charles E. Nobbe, "Socioeconomic Differentials Among Nonwhite Races," *American Sociological Review*, December 1965, pp. 909–922.

[7] Carl G. Jung, M.L. von Fraz, Joseph L. Henerson, Jolande Jacobl, and Aniela Jaffe, *Man and His Symbols* (Garden City, New York: Doubleday & Company 1973), p. 172.

[8] Joost A. M. Meerloo, *That Difficult Peace* (Great Neck, New York: Channel Press, 1961), p. 16.

[9] Bruno Bettelheim and Morris Janowitz, *Social Change and Prejudice* (New York: The Free Press, 1964), pp. 70–71, 162–163, 184, 220–221, 280.

[10] Simpson and Yinger, p. 66.

[11] Manpower Report of the President (United States Department of Labor's Manpower Administration and United States Department of Health, Education and Welfare's Office of Education, 1973), p. 59.

[12] *Ibid.*, p. 66.

[13] "Women Win More Credit," *Business Week*, 12 January 1974, pp. 76–77.

[14] "Progress Seen in State of Black Economy," *Commerce Today*, 28 May 1973, p. 11.

[15] "We Will Not Discriminate Against Male Customers," *Business Week*, 12 January 1974, p. 77.

[16] *Federal Mandates for Affirmative Action: A Guidebook for Public Employers* (National Civil Service League, Washington, 1972).

[17] "Judicial Mandates for Affirmative Action: A Guidebook for Public Employers" (National Civil Service League, Washington, D.C., 1973).

[18] "Age Discrimination," *Administrative Digest* 9 (July–August, 1974), p. 4.

[19] *Federal Mandates for Affirmative Action*, p. 6.

[20] "Last Hired, First Fired, Takes it On the Chin," *Business Week*, 9 March 1974, p. 166.

[21] "Women: Last In, First Out in Detroit," *Business Week*, 16 February 1974, p. 51.

[22] "Capitalism: Moving Target" (Mobil Oil Corporation Advertisement), *San Francisco Chronicle*, 5 September 1974, p. 10.

[23] *Models for Affirmative Action: A Guidebook for Public Employers* (National Civil Service League, Washington, 1973) p. vi.

[24] *Ibid.*

[25] *Ibid.,* p. viii.

Employees and the Union
"Power to the Little People" ......

OBJECTIVES

After reading this chapter you should be able to:

1. Explain why trade unions became an important force in the American economy.
2. Relate the functions and difficulties of the shop steward and the company foreman in the labor-management relationship.
3. Define *collective bargaining.*
4. Compare the basic negotiating procedures in collective bargaining from the union's and the management's point of view.
5. Discuss "grievance procedures" and the types of arbitration that are used when no decision can be reached.
6. Explain union power from the point of view of:
   A. Politics,
   B. Mergers,
   C. Government controls.

Again here are some questions that you might think about as you read this chapter.

Do you think unions have become more powerful in the last five years?

Do you think unions are more beneficial to society now than they were 20, 50, 100 years ago?

Are there more strikes now than five years ago? Why?

What is the difference between a mediator and an arbitrator?

Do you think public employees should be members of a union and be allowed to strike?

What is the difference between an open union and a closed shop?

What is a yellow-dog contract? A boycott? A lockout?

A LOOK AT THE UNIONS

Union membership is at a record high in the United States today. As of 1970 the total number of union members was 20 million and the figure has doubled since 1960.[1] The country's two largest unions are the International Brotherhood of Teamsters, which has almost 2 million members, and the United Auto Workers, which has more than 1½ million. One of the fastest growing unions and one of the ten largest, with substantial concentration of employees in the food and drug chains, is the Retail Clerks International Association.[2] Since the unions represent a large portion of the working society, it is necessary to discuss labor-management problems.

Public employee unions are the fastest growing

Public employee unions have been the fastest growing of any segment of unionism. This segment includes teachers, policemen, firemen, and county employees. Even the middle-class workers have rushed to join unions. There are now more than 3 million white-collar workers in unions. Despite their growth, however, labor organizations have not kept up with the growth of the labor force. This is due in part to management's offering the same benefits to nonunion employees that union members would receive. Another reason why labor organizations have not grown is because they are not flexible enough for the concerns of today's youth.[3]

A CLASH OF GOALS

With few exceptions, every company in the United States, regardless of size, has been faced with the fact that unions and union organizing are here to stay. For managers, dealing with unions can be frustrating, tedious, and, in some cases, almost impossible. There are no precise formulas to make dealing with unions easy, no directions on the back of union contracts to help management come to an understanding of how a union works or why it is necessary in the first place. Yet it must be remembered that unions often have trouble dealing with management. Too often, both the company management and the union forget that the other is made up of people and that working with and understanding people takes more time and effort than mastering a complicated computer language. Computer languages are logical and always consistent; people rarely are. Management sees the union as a corporate body, much like itself, a business which is in opposition to management goals. Unions see management as a profit-monster that will take no time or expense to attend to the needs of the workers who feed it.

Management vs. unions

Jack London, a writer and Socialist, wrote:

The working men . . . furnish the labor. The stockholders furnish the capital. By the joint effort of the working men and the capital, money is earned. They divide between them this money that is earned. Capital's share is called "dividends." Labor's share is called "wages."[4]

The relationship between capital and labor is hand in glove. One cannot survive without the other, but a struggle between the two has been going on for hundreds of years.

THE ROLE OF MANAGEMENT

The goals of management are varied, including profit making, market development, and efficiency of the company. By concentrating on efficiency and profit the management of many American companies neglected personnel problems for a long time, leaving such problems to the foremen and shop superintendents. Faced with the union challenging their authority, that was company's inherent right to make all decisions, employers have in the past generally been opposed to unions. They dealt with them only if forced to do so by the National Labor Relations Act of 1935, which stressed collective bargaining for the settlement of differences between workers and employers.

Relationship between unions and management

Prior to the National Labor Relations Act many employers encouraged pseudounions under company domination. Many American employers at the present time have come to accept unionism and forms of collective bargaining. But a few are bitterly opposed to the principle of unionism. The typical attitudes of employers can be classified from *exclusion* to *cooperation* with intermediate steps of *containment, acceptance,* and *accommodation.*

When the employer's policy is that of union *exclusion,* management tries to discourage workers from joining unions by coercion or by trying to provide the wage and fringe benefits that the competitors grant through collective bargaining.

Faced with a law compelling them to deal with unions, many employers grudgingly acted accordingly, but did everything possible to wean the loyalty of the workers away from the union. Under *containment,* all relations with the union are kept on a strictly "legal" basis, and the scope of collective bargaining is kept as narrow as possible. By doing so the company hopes to eventually rid itself of collective bargaining.

Another attitude toward unionism is that of *acceptance* and *accommodation,* in which the employer recognizes the union as part of the industrial scene and tries to use collective bargaining to improve its relations with its employees.

Finally, there is the relationship of *cooperation* in which the management actually seeks the assistance of the union in production problems which are not usually the subject matter of collective bargaining. The acceptance and accommodation situation is more prevalent than either that of exclusion or cooperation.

Sensitivity to the total situation rather than standing on management's rights is likely to be the best guide for management. Supervisors cannot be certain that industrial relations policies, no matter how carefully planned, will guarantee a satisfactory relationship with the union. However, management often holds the initiative that can influence the collective bargaining relationship more than unions. Another advantage for the firm is the fact that employees are generally anxious to be on good terms with their employers and will eventually react against union leaders who refuse to meet management halfway in the solution of joint problems.

Labor's Reaction to Management

The history of the labor movement in the United States is marked by months and years of destruction, death, and degradation on both sides of the factory fence. The bloodiest days of those first years are unknown to many young workers. Today's wage earner often fears that the company holds all the keys to his well-being and, rather than lose what he has, would accept what the company offers on any ground to protect what he has won in the past for himself.

Employees don't own what they produce

From the Middle Ages to the present, the wage-earning laborer has believed that the factory owners have it in for him. Since money is basically the only gain the worker expects from his labors, the money holders have all the power. Laborers, craftsmen, and skilled workers no longer own what they make as many of them did in the Middle Ages. They do not control the production or sale of their wares. Their labor and only their labor is contracted out to the factory. The factory or company is

Employees sell their services

sole owner of everything produced by the workers. Since workers cannot claim ownership of what they produce, the only thing they can claim is ownership of their labor. If they sell their labor to a company, most laborers feel that they have the right to bargain over the price of their labor, just as the company has the right to haggle with the buyers of their product over its wholesale cost.

Costs of production rise when the cost of raw materials rises, so the company, in order to maintain a level of profit, must raise its prices. Likewise, if the cost of living rises, the laborer must raise his prices in order to maintain a standard of

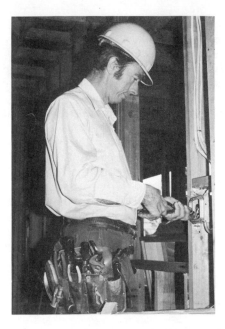

Figure 15–1. Most laborers feel that they have the right to bargain over the price of their labor, just as the company has the right to haggle with the buyers of their product.

(Photo by Robert Curtis)

National Labor Relations Act—1935

living. Until the National Labor Relations Act of 1935, workers had no legitimate means of bargaining with the company for increased wages. There was no guarantee that a worker's salary would be raised even after years of service to the company. It was possible for the company to lower his salary to cover losses caused by production failure or financial difficulties. Workers wanted job and wage security, so they formed unions to protect themselves in the same way that the company was protected.

Unions did not simply appear along with the factory, and they did not spring up without reason to harass the well-intentioned company management. Unions have a history that dates back to the 1700s, one hundred years *before* the factory system became a reality. The first protests against the practices of capital occurred when artisans and craftsmen were threatened by the "new policy of buying labor, like the raw material of manufacture, in the cheapest market."[5] All restrictions on the hiring and payment of labor were swept away so that manufacturers could produce their commodities at an expense far below that of the self-employed artisan or craftsman.

A separation occurred between the laborer and the management when "the great bulk of the workers had ceased to be independent producers, themselves controlling the processes, and owning the materials and the product of their labor, and had passed into the condition of lifelong wage-earners, possessing neither the instruments of production nor the commodity in its finished state.[6] At this point, the trade unions began and became an important force in the economy.

The Differences and Similarities

Both management and workers have a vested interest in the product of a given company. The management provides the directions and supervision of the company's operations and workers provide the manual execution of those operations. Whether or not the company is successful is the responsibility of all concerned. If the company fails all suffer in some way. If the company is successful, all benefit to some extent. Consumers are frequently baffled when they hear of yet another strike in industry. "Why can't they work together for their mutual benefit?" consumers ask. "If the workers go on strike, the company can't run itself, right? No one makes any money on it, do they?" And it always seems that the people most affected and inconvenienced by strikes are the uninvolved third party, the consumers.

The reasons for industrial conflict are strongly linked to ordinary human behavior and human needs.

SATISFACTION

Unlimited wants and limited means

All partners in the conflict have *unlimited* wants, but the means by which those wants can be satisfied are *limited.* Higher wages and higher profits are the basic respective desires of labor and management. Raising wages lowers profits if the price of the commodity cannot be adjusted. Each side would prefer to benefit itself, but since the source of income from the product is limited, they must share in some way, though the agreement will rarely be totally agreeable to both parties.

POWER

Someone must always be in *control,* while others must always be *controlled.* The conflict inherent in the management–union relationship stems from the basic human desire to run things according to individual whim. *Managers* have the power to direct operations and move people. The *managed* would like the same power. In any situation, the opposing sides vie for control.

In the case of management and unions, management has the upper hand, so the union contends for its share of the power.

CHANGEABILITY

Because the conditions of industrial operations are constantly changing, a satisfactory division of profits at one time can be completely *unsatisfactory* at another. That is, profit margins fluctuate almost daily, and if negotiations are completed between management and the unions at a point when the profits are low, then, when and if they rise, the union is dissatisfied with the settlement. If the settlement was made when profits were high and they have since dropped, management is dissatisfied.

INDEPENDENCE

Checks and balances

In order to maintain survival as separate forces within the industrial society, management and unions must assert their independence through conflict, setting up a system of *checks* and *balances* so that neither is made to submit to all the demands of the other. If one is in total agreement with the other all the time, it is committed to self-destruction. Just as an individual cannot exist as a full and complete human being if he constantly allows himself to suppress his own drives and desires to the will of others, so must union and management contend with each other to maintain their separate identities.

Dual Loyalty

Dual loyalty or divided loyalty

With employment and union membership comes a problem unique to the worker. His wages come directly from his employer, but the protection of his rights and privileges as an employee comes from the union. Some personnel managers and union officials believe that employees will give their loyalties to the side that benefits the *individual* most, without considering the overall impact of their actions on the actual problem, society, or the economy.

Public reaction can give support to one side

News media may favor one side

Neither unions nor management can count on blind support from their members or employees, as they could in the past. So many more aspects of a labor problem are brought to public attention now, that union employees cannot help but know the effects of their proposed actions even before they are taken. Workers are forced to take public reaction into account because the general public, through television, may know about the strike or walk-out even before some of the workers do and public reaction will be instantaneous. In the past, news of strikes wasn't heard until the following day or by word of mouth. Also, television news broadcasters have a habit of analyzing an event for the benefit of the public within minutes of its occurrence. Public sympathy for a strike for higher wages or increased fringe benefits cannot be gained by simply making the facts known, no more than management can get the public on its side by claiming low profits and increased costs.

SUB

To attract employee support some companies have offered SUB or Supplementary Unemployment Benefits. For every hour an employee works the company puts two or three cents into a fund for the employee for the time when he is not working. This is an attempt to match the unions strike fund and gain the employee's loyalty.

I owe my soul to the company store

In a copper mining community in Arizona strikes frequently lasted six months. During such periods union members obtained funds from the union strike fund and charged at the company stores. A personal friend of the author was able to pay his three-year strike debt to the company stores just one month before the miners went out on a nine-month strike. It is hard to believe the expression, "I owe my soul to the company store," could be true as late as the 1960s.

Employees, more often, see themselves in the middle of the dispute, actually the base from which unions and management build. Workers have a better sense of their importance to production than they did in the past. They no longer consider themselves the ineffectual pawns in the factory *or* union hall and will make themselves heard above the clamor of management and union alike.

Two in the Middle

The foreman and shop steward are caught in the middle

There are two positions within the structure of the typical company whose occupants are answerable to more officials, managers, workers, and boards than any other positions, including company president. These two are the shop steward and the company foreman. Though on opposing sides, their functions are similar and each is situated in the hierarchy of either the union or management so that they are one step above any worker on the floor. Each has the unenviable position of being answerable to higher-ups who sometimes have no *practical* knowledge of the work floor.

SHOP STEWARD

The shop steward represents the employee

On the union side, the shop steward has direct contact with the workers and is, generally, elected by the workers in his or her department. The steward is an employee of the company and works by the side of the men and women he represents. Provisions are usually made in the union contract that allow the shop

The elected steward reflects the attitudes of the employees

steward time off to conduct union affairs. His attitude toward management is a reflection of the attitude of the workers who elect him.

If the union is new and the members are militant, they may elect a person whose main quality is his expertise in rallying support against the company. This antagonism, if recognized by management as severe growing pains and uncertainties about how far the workers can go, can be dealt with by establishing management credibility. Many of the problems coming from the growth of a new union are related to the workers' general suspicion of management. Tensions are high during periods of organizational change and the insecurity of the workers in regard to their jobs and the strength of their union may cause them to place a great deal more blame on management than is warranted. Creating credibility may change the attitude of the steward or convince the workers to select a steward at the next election who is more open-minded.

The steward hears the employees' complaints

The shop steward functions as a safety valve in most cases. He represents individual employees in grievance hearings with management. He listens to employee complaints and advises on whether an employee is justified in taking the complaint to management. On occasion, the foreman may bring a problem to the shop steward which the steward forwards to the individual involved. He is *not* a messenger for management *or* the union. He is more or less a lay lawyer, skilled or unskilled in the various articles of the union contract, effectively versed in the fine points of grievance procedures. His effectiveness is largely based on the strength of the union itself within the company.

Training programs for stewards

Large national unions usually have shop steward training programs which instruct stewards in the fundamentals of labor law, economy, human relations, and technical skills to protect the interest of the membership and the union. They are also trained in labor–management relationships because their effectiveness depends on fair and equitable dealings with the foreman and management.

A weak union may misconstrue the function and strength of the shop steward to the extent that he is made completely useless to union members.

A mistake of a union

During a civil service employees' wildcat strike, a number of the younger workers who went out with the union and were not union members were told: "Protect yourselves against arbitrary firing. Join the union." The union membership comprised only 5 percent of all the employees, but the young people, inexperienced in strikes or unions, signed up. When it became obvious that their cause was hopeless, most of the employees returned to work. But the union did offer further protection. Most of the striking employees were *appointed* to positions of shop stewards, the idea being that a shop steward in every unit would let management know that they would have trouble if any disciplinary action was taken. The new shop stewards wore their badges for two weeks and then abandoned the position, keeping the badges as mementos of their first strike. Legitimate shop stewards lost considerable prestige with foremen and management because their union was poorly informed of the duties of their shop stewards. It became laughable to see six and seven shop stewards in every group of ten employees.

COMPANY FOREMAN

A realization of the importance of the foreman in labor–management relations has brought about critical changes in the selection and training of foremen by American management. Some time ago, foremen were selected primarily for their ability to produce and for their industrial skill. The emergence of the union as a force in business has caused a severe reduction in

Figure 15–2.   The union adds an additional formal organization to the employment relationship.

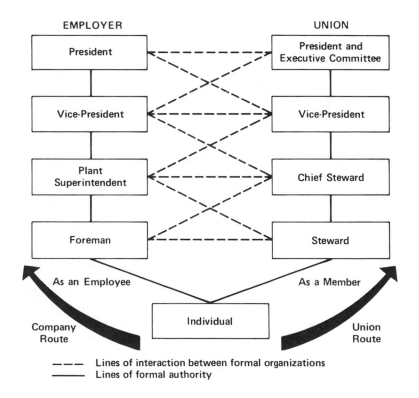

the power of the foreman, forcing the qualities of leadership and ability in personal relationships to take precedence over manual skill in the selection of new foremen.

A training program for foremen is needed

An increasing number of companies have instituted training programs to teach their foremen elemental psychology, leadership skills, and group dynamics. Foremen who were accustomed to absolute authority over the workers in their departments have found the transition to the demands of collective bargaining difficult. Even the most carefully designed training program sometimes fails to overcome the old system of unquestioned authority and the foreman must either learn to satisfy the needs of management, as well as coping with the workers' new status as a bargaining force, or lose his position. The strain on the foreman to meet the requirements of management, without causing the workers to call in the shop steward, is great. Some, if they mainly see their job as getting the work done, will lose ground with their subordinates. Others, who see their job as working with the employees, and thus tend to identify with them in relation to management will lose ground with the higher-ups.

Emotional strain on foreman

During collective bargaining the duties of the foreman may be given to the shop steward or to union representatives by management. As a result the shop foreman can lose power with employees, and with the union. What power they lose is not given up willingly, but handed over to unions without the foremen being given a voice in what is happening to their jobs. As a result, many foremen become as resentful of management as the workers are and either quit the company altogether or go back to being wage-earning employees.

Union strength can undermine the supervisor's authority

Union power is, in many cases, so strong—involving discipline, work assignments, seniority, transfers, and so on—that frequently the foreman feels he doesn't have the authority to deal properly with the people under him. He may think that his only function is to stand to one side and watch. As he becomes more acquainted with the union and its functions, the foreman may realize that the shop steward, who was once regarded as the uncooperative antagonist, can be useful in maintaining discipline, screening unwarranted complaints, counseling employees on personal problems and work habits, and communicating with management about employee problems.

Developing mutually beneficial communications can result in a foreman—steward relationship that would alleviate many of the difficulties inherent in the labor-management conflict. The shop steward is also a leader and is often influential in determining the opinions of the wage earner concerning management. A mutual understanding, as well as open lines of communication, is imperative between the steward and the foreman.

While this is not always easy to attain, it should be worked for whenever possible.

UNION INTERACTION WITH MANAGEMENT

The day-to-day relations of management and unions at the plant level center around the written collective bargaining agreement. The vast majority of the contracts are written for a fixed period of time, usually three years. A provision of the contract is the "union security" clause that may provide for a **Union shop** *union shop* under which all employees covered by the agreement must join the union after a brief probationary period, or **Closed shop** lose their jobs. Federal law forbids the *closed shop* agreement under which only union members are hired, and the same federal law delegates to the states the authority, which some of them have exercised, to bar union shops. Such state laws have **Right-to-work laws** become widely known as *right-to-work laws* and are strongly opposed by organized labor.

Another clause may provide that union membership must be maintained during the agreement. Many companies agree to deduct union dues from the workers' wages and pay them directly to the union treasurer. By this "check-off" system management avoids having dues collection taking place during work time and the union avoids the nuisance of seeking out individual members in order to gets its income.

Some managements insist that agreements clearly state that management has the responsibility in directing the working force including the hiring and firing, assigning jobs, and determining production schedules.

Collective Bargaining

Though considered by some to be a contract of legalistic proportions, the collective bargaining agreement is much more flexible **Bargaining agreement** than a contract. It does have some of the properties of the con-**is legal, has time limits,** tract: (1) it can be enforced by law; (2) it has a time limit; and **and is complete** (3) it is complete in itself. However, provisions for change are built into the agreement which allow one or the other of the parties to interpret and apply the clauses on a continuing basis. It is a working document of resolution of conflict and, as such, is subject to renewed debate should conditions not covered by the agreement arise at a later date. Because the collective bargaining agreement is flexible, it is also interpreted in many different ways. In the opinion of some, it merely controls union–

management day-to-day relations. This is a limited interpretation and covers only a small portion of the intended purpose of the agreement.

The collective agreement can be divided into three sections: (1) binding provisions, which include clauses by which little or no change is anticipated by either party, i.e., wages, union security, and the duration of the contract itself; (2) "contingent" clauses governing actions taken by union or management concerning new conditions not present at the time of agreement, i.e., promotion, transfer, change in operation techniques, governmental legislation; and (3) grievance procedures should disputes arise concerning interpretation of the agreement.[7]

The foundation of the collective bargaining procedure is to make equitable the respective strengths of unions and management. It limits the authority of management. It recognizes the ". . . inequality of bargaining power. . . . The private ownership of means of production implies, at once, that the economic liberties of workers are circumscribed . . ."[8] and that, therefore, ". . . the job-dependent worker finds employment only if the employer anticipates profit from production."[9] As was stated earlier in this chapter, the worker barters only his labor, and his survival is contingent upon the availability of work. In such a position, he easily fumbles into individual employment agreements with companies and, without collective bargaining, would have no redress should the agreement *not* guarantee employment. Such agreements are now superceded by the collective labor agreement, though they would not be nullified. In case of conflicting rules, the rules set forth by a collective bargaining agreement would take precedence over those of individual employment agreements.

MANAGEMENT PREPARATION

Clearly understand the issue

1. A clear understanding of the issues is necessary. The issues may be wages, severance, conditions of work, the criteria for promotion, seniority rules, discipline, delays in the settlement of grievances, or a dispute over interpretation.

2. If the dispute involves procedures, it should be made clear that the disagreement concerns the ways of attaining goals. Formulating criteria and agreeing on how to evaluate procedures must be spelled out clearly in operational terms.

3. Management should be acquainted with the unions, their leaders, structure, policies, and style of negotiation. The basic attitudes of how union leaders *or* managers accept or reject ideas, trust or suspect each other, will directly determine the degree of success at the bargaining table.

4. Negotiators should know, as part of their preparation, what they want to get and what they are indifferent to getting. What they will concede, cannot concede, and could possibly concede are important tools of compromise. They should also be aware of the alternatives available to them in case agreement cannot be reached. They should be prepared to negotiate at a future time for fringe benefits or changes that cannot be made at present.

NEGOTIATING PROCEDURES

1. Prior to the actual negotiations, both parties should agree on a time and place. There should be a central table for confrontation between the opposing sides, as well as two separate areas so that each side can confer separately.

    Because negotiations often begin in an atmosphere of distrust and hostility, attitudes of courtesy and reserve are important. The shape of the table may also have bearing on the negotiations. As in diplomatic confrontations, a round table is preferable because there is no head or foot and one party cannot seem to take precedence over the other.

2. Either of the parties may make the opening statement on the matters in dispute. Unless copies of this statement are made available, a complete record should be kept by the other party. Frequent recesses may help minimize emotional reactions and encourage a problem-oriented discussion rather than angry debate, filled with charges and countercharges.

Negotiations are often tense

3. Negotiations are frequently tense and emotional, and the strong feelings must be dealt with. Condescending attitudes can never be tolerated; they simply promote the feeling that the other party has the upper hand. Dealing with the issues and not the emotions is generally best for the success of the entire procedure. Answering emotional outbursts with an attitude of reason and logic can sometimes lead to increased hostility from the emotional opponent, especially if reason and logic are offered in parental or superior tones. Withdrawing from negotiations for a short period of time may cool some tempers and allow both parties to take into full consideration the effects of their attitudes.

Remaining cool is a key point

Just as in the boxing ring, it does not do to lose one's cool in the negotiating room. Likewise, just as the judo expert uses the thrust of an opponent's attack to floor him, so one can withdraw or retire in order to encompass an opponent more effectively. As a general rule, clinical coolness allows for a more rapid rational appreciation of a situation and makes possible an effective response.

Never discuss personal values

There should not be any discussion of *principles* because they are closely related to personal values and tend to evoke strong, unproductive feelings in people. Always keep in mind *particular* facts and particular conditions of the issues being discussed.

4. Never go up faster than the opponent comes down, when discussing wages or demands. If one party gives in too easily on a particular issue, the other party may assume that the opponent is willing to agree to everything it demands. It should be remembered that, in a sense, bargaining is making a trade. Each demand may produce a counterdemand so that what is accomplished is that both parties eventually receive something from the bargaining process, even if it is only to trade higher wages for mandatory overtime.

In effect the negotiating process should not be a zero game—the more I win, the more you lose, but the more I gain, the more you gain also. However, the negotiation process seems to be ruled more by human nature than by logic.

Experience and systematic observation sometimes can reveal the cues of serious commitment. A story is told of a union representative who always glanced at his watch when he had made his really final offer. His managerial opponent always lit a cigar when he had made his last offer.

TACTICS

Strikes are used only when there appears to be no alternative

Strikes are a show of power. If union leaders and members believe that a strike will make management more inclined to bargain than resist, they will strike, but, generally, only if there is no other alternative. Unions have used craft unions (highly skilled laborers) to restrict the production of new workers by long apprenticeships, training, and licensing provisions. Insurance, relief, and retirement funds help to strengthen the individual worker as well as improve the union's striking power.

Slowdowns, jurisdictional and wildcat strikes, mass picketing, boycotts

Slowdown strikes, jurisdictional strikes (forcing the company to recognize one union over another), wildcat strikes, mass picketing, informational picketing, and boycotts can all be used by the union to influence the negotiations.

Blacklisting, injunctions, yellow dog contracts

The company has at its disposal the lockout (the company itself prevents its employees from working); blacklisting (a list of troublemakers available to other companies; employment is not given to blacklisted union organizers); injunctions (court orders aimed at preventing the union from interfering with production); the yellow dog contract (signed as a condition to secure employment with a guarantee that the worker will not join a union); and strikebreakers.

All the aforementioned tactics have been used by either unions or management at some time in the history of the labor movement. Some are still being used and are "respectable" in the sense that they are effective, if not always productive. Some, like the jurisdictional strike and the lockout (if it comes under the national emergency regulations of the Taft–Hartley Act as amended by the Landrum–Griffin Act), are against the law. The tactics used by unions today are generally aimed at production and hence, the company's financial resources. Management uses tactics aimed at the resources and solidarity of the union or the bank accounts of the workers. With very few exceptions, labor disagreements today are relatively mild compared to the bloody confrontations of forty years ago. Nevertheless, these disagreements can have powerful economic repercussions if not dealt with promptly and effectively.

Grievances

Grievance procedures are usually outlined in collective bargaining agreements. They follow a similar pattern in most companies, beginning with an employee complaint to the foreman and then continuing on up the managerial and union hierarchies until some settlement, agreeable to both, is reached. Beyond the employee or shop steward–foreman stage, the grievance begins to take on proportions that encompass more than the individual employee's dissatisfaction. It can become an issue of arbitration that will affect not only the individual, but his co-workers and management as well.

As Figure 15–3 illustrates, the chain of grievance procedures extends beyond labor–management control. If the grievance isn't settled by the highest levels of company and union, an outside arbitrator is called in.

At the beginning of the grievance procedure, the foreman may have decided that disciplinary action was warranted by the violation of a company rule. If he decides to settle the problem without consulting someone on the next level, he must first "be aware that if the employees in his department are unionized, practically all formal disciplinary action by him will result in a union grievance. . . . Therefore, the supervisor must be sure that the disciplinary action is well within the prescribed limits of that labor contract."[10]

Foreman's discipline must be within the union contract

The employee involved may go to the shop steward for advice or help in formulating a formal grievance. The shop steward's first objective is to determine the strength of the worker's complaint. If he decides that it warrants investigation, he will approach the foreman, which means that the shop steward must know the terms of the labor agreement. If the foreman and shop steward cannot come to terms, the grievance is called to the at-

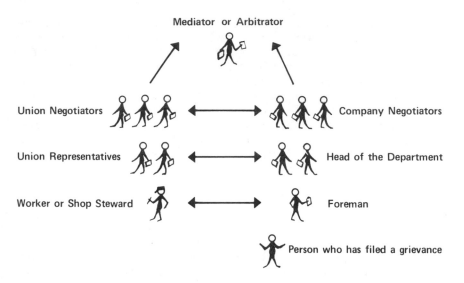

Mediator or Arbitrator

Union Negotiators ⟷ Company Negotiators

Union Representatives ⟷ Head of the Department

Worker or Shop Steward ⟷ Foreman

Person who has filed a grievance

Figure 15–3. The chain of grievance procedure. After a grievance has been filed with the foreman and shop steward a solution is attempted at each level. If a resolution cannot be reached the problem moves to a higher level, until a solution is reached by a mediator or arbitrator.

tention of the general manager or the head of the department, and so on until it reaches the ears of union officials and the company management. Should either continue to insist on its own interpretation of the collective labor agreement, the grievance goes to an arbitrator, and his decision becomes final interpretation of that part of the labor agreement.

Arbitration

Personnel directors often set the tone

Wise personnel directors must make up their minds how they will react to complaints and grievances. Some employers regard grievances as individual nuisances; others see them as symptoms of problem areas that may be necessary to discuss with the union. Some managements will determine to be very legalistic and stick to the letter of the contract, forcing each grievance to arbitration unless the union accepts the administrative interpretation, yet others take pride in almost never allowing a difference to go to arbitration.

As the grievance is taken to higher steps in the chain, it becomes a group problem. Since the collective bargaining agreement is subject to interpretation, both sides may be firmly set in their own reading of the contract. The role of the arbitrator is to make a decision about the meaning of the present contract. His decision may be an interpretation that neither side has foreseen, or he may side with one or the other. In any case, his decision is final and remains the binding decision until the labor agreement is negotiated again at the end of its duration.

Voluntary arbitration

There are two types of arbitration. Voluntary arbitration is preferable because it indicates a willingness on the parts of labor and management to work together to solve mutual problems. Both sides agree to accept the decision handed down by the arbitrator.

Compulsory arbitration

Compulsory arbitration involves the government and usually means that the labor—management dispute is threatening to, in the words of Section 206, the Taft-Hartley Act, "(i) affect an entire industry or a substantial part thereof . . . and (ii) will, if permitted to occur or to continue, imperil the national health and safety." The government then dictates that a binding decision must be agreed to by both sides for the good of the country and the economy or both.

Some unions and companies retain the services of a permanent arbitrator or mediator, but the majority selects them on a temporary basis. A mediator in a dispute is an outside person or "disinterested third party" who listens impartially to both sides and makes a compromise decision between the demands of one and the demands of the other. The mediator, however, has no binding authority, but can only suggest solutions to the dispute. The arbitrator, also a "disinterested third party," has been selected to act as a judge in the dispute and makes a decision binding on both parties involved in the conflict.

TODAY'S UNIONS

The working class of today is vastly different from the workers of even ten years ago. The American worker has opportunities for advancement and change that his or her parents couldn't have imagined. Today's workers are not particularly concerned with job permanence, are less inclined to conform to the decisions of higher authority, and are less likely to put up with uncomfortable working conditions. Workers' attitudes are in part responsible for current changes in unions, but there are other reasons.

Politics

The union labor movement in this country is deeply involved with politics and politicians. The union has become a tremen-

Union support
influences elections

dous force in government. When the AFL-CIO gives its support to a political candidate, there is little doubt that the candidate's opportunity for election has been enhanced. A majority of the members of the Senate and the House of Representatives are elected with union support and "have voted 'right' more than half of the time on organized labor's checklist of federal legislation." Unions are a strong influence in the appointments made to administrative positions in all public agencies and "the importance of judges who favor unions is not being overlooked by their leaders." George Meany, president of the AFL-CIO, said: "Much of the progress we make in the next decade will depend on our ability to get the legislation we want." Business interests have their lobbyists as well, but labor is just beginning to show its strength in the political arena. Business has been there for a long time.

SOCIAL CHANGE

More urban unions

More acceptance to
bargaining

More blacks in unions

There has been a growing public sector of "urban unions" composed of teachers, hospital workers, policemen, firemen, and sanitation workers. Currently these groups have a more difficult time at the bargaining table, but personnel executives and middle managers believe that the receptiveness to collective bargaining is increasing.[14] Such unions are becoming increasingly black, adding a different social base and political outlook, which is considerably different from some of the more "stand-pattism" of skilled workers' unions in the building trades.

INTERNATIONALISM AND UNIONS

More often foreign
unions are more
socialistic and lack
strong central support

The new multinationalism has led American businessmen to deal with foreign labor unions, and certainly they cannot be dealt with in the same way as American unions. By and large, foreign unions are more steeped in tradition, are more socialistically oriented, and lack strong centralized power. It seems that more often American businessmen wish to change the union system than deal with it as it is.[11] Workers have not always agreed with their union leaders on the stress to place on collective bargaining or political action, but generally speaking American unions have opted for collective bargaining, while unions in many other countries have relied more on political action.

In 1973 a study of automobile manufacturing companies in the United States, Italy, Argentina, and India was conducted. The results showed that in all the countries the workers usually approved of their union's actions, regardless of the officers' political stand.

It is interesting to note that, in this study, the American workers at Oldsmobile ranked the improvements of working conditions as the most important, even over securing higher wages, while the workers with less complex machinery, those at Fiat in Italy and IKA of Argentina, ranked economic benefits as the most important.[12]

Union Issues

WAGES

The part of the collective bargaining agreement of most concern to the employees naturally is wages. With few exceptions the direction of wages has been upward and the burden of the arguments for the change has been carried by the unions. The employers are not usually arguing against wage increases, but against the amount of union demands. Metaphorically speaking, the union members are the offensive football team carrying the ball, and management is the defensive team holding the line. For the past ten or more years, the cost of living has been the base for most wage demands. For most United States industries the post World War II decades have been a period of high activity and good profits. The inability to make a substantial wage increase resulted from the threat of nonunion competition and foreign imports, according to management.

The general amount of wage increases for an industry is usually determined by settlements arrived at by the leading unions and large companies. Whatever settlement is made between the United Auto Workers and whichever employer of the big three automobile manufacturers they negotiate with first becomes the "pattern" for the industry. Sometimes one firm in a locality is recognized as the pace setter and other settlements follow it in much the same way.

Fringe benefits is a misnomer for the pension, hospitalization, supplementary unemployment, holidays and vacation package, which now runs about 30–35 percent of the per employee cost paid by the employer. In order to make comparisons with what other employers and unions are doing, estimates of benefits are calculated on a per hour expense — so benefits have a dollar value. Such comparisons of employee costs between companies should include benefit expenses.

MANDATORY OVERTIME

Mr. Tiegen, a tall broad-shouldered man who is in his 50s, doesn't want to work seven days a week, although he likes the extra money. He receives double-time for Sundays, time-and-a-half for most other overtime. Proudly he will show a paycheck that lists gross wages of $430 for one week; he says he is tired of all the overtime. But he has to work, because under the United Automobile Workers contract with the major auto

Union members are the offensive team

Leading unions set the trend for wages

30–33% of the employer's wage cost is in fringe benefits

Who makes the decision to work overtime, the company or the employee?

manufacturers workers he must put in overtime whenever the company chooses to schedule it.

Auto workers aren't the only union members subject to mandatory overtime. Postal workers, for example, are subject to similar rules. Members of the International Union of Electrical Workers at General Electric Company have worked under a mandatory overtime policy for ten years, even though their contract doesn't specify it. G.E.'s right to compel "reasonable" overtime was established in a series of arbitration cases.

Leonard Woodcock, the UAW's president once said in response to mandatory overtime, "It's not so much 'by God, we're not going to work overtime,' but I'll make that decision if I give up my Saturday or Sunday or work three or four hours beyond eight, not the company."

How would you feel about such a situation if you were the employee? What if you were the employer? What is fair?

FLEXIBLE WORKING HOURS

The four-day work week

"The Bible says the Lord worked six days and rested on the seventh. That may have been good enough for the Lord, but young people these days won't accept it at face value. We have to re-examine all our premises and get away from the 200-year tradition of shopkeeping." In mid-1971 600 firms offered a four-day week to some workers. The firms were largely Eastern and Central, predominately manufacturing, and generally nonunion. The four-day work week was found in such areas as hospitals, banks, retailing, and the police departments. By staggering the hours and shifts, maximum numbers of police officers can serve in what is termed "critical hours." Members of the Long Beach Police Department were asked in a survey if they wanted to return to the five-day week and 95% said no.[13]

The 4–40

The ten-hour day reverses the 100-year-old trend toward shorter workdays won after a long union struggle. The trend for larger blocks of leisure time is seen in the rapid extension of paid vacations and legal rearrangements of national holidays for more three-day weekends. As recently as 1965 the four-day forty-hour work week (4–40 plan) was virtually unknown, although a few economists and labor leaders had predicted that it would come soon. The four-day work week evolved for many different reasons, but mainly as a means of improving production schedules and efficiency.[14]

Morale has risen, there is less absenteeism and fewer job changes. It has given a chance for better delivery and service, and offers more time for the customer's convenience.

For the employee the "usable leisure appeals to them as well as the reduction in transportation time and cost by 20%, plus less for lunch and child-care costs.[15]

But not all is rosy in this 4–40 plan. At one company 20 percent of its female force quit when the 4–40 program was initiated, citing fatigue and overlong hours when added to their home duties. Transportation problems developed for those in car pools, and family schedules were upset with earlier morning and later evening hours. Some union leaders are opposed to the four-day week, because it leads to moonlighting and taking of jobs that could otherwise go to unemployed persons. Last, the one thing that management fears is that when it becomes an accepted thing production will drop. Nevertheless by the end of 1973 more than 3,000 firms had come to adopt some form of flexible scheduling.[16] And the figure increased in 1977.

MERGERS

The power of mergers vs conglomerates

The unions' power will continue to grow if they consolidate into fewer and larger unions, with more centralized control. The combination of all transportation industry workers into the United Transportation Union has been the biggest step to date toward a powerful and united front against the conglomerates and multinational corporations of business. The same difficulties that are involved in corporate mergers are evident in union mergers as well. Old rivalries and animosities often combine with ordinary merger problems to cause further delay. However, since the merger of the American Federation of Labor and the Congress of Industrial Organizations twenty years ago, the realization that union strength can be increased by a broad political base has impressed more and more union leaders.

Government Controls

In 1973, over 4.5 million workers were bargaining for higher wages. As unions become more powerful, their ability to bring government around to their way of thinking increases. "The unionists' goal in the next decade is to dominate government at all levels, in all areas of responsibility, and to use government as a prime source of power to win economic and other aims." [17] With government backing and support from the state and national legislators, there is, conceivably, no limit to the future gains of American unions.

While the government has occasionally placed restrictions on the coercive practices of unions (specifically the Landrum-Griffin Act) it is, nevertheless, very much aware of the influence the union has on over forty million people, union members and their families, and uncounted millions of union supporters. And, considering that the majority of the working people in this country are blue collar, though not all are union members, it seems, by sheer numbers, that the labor forces have a passage into the *thoughts* of politicians that business cannot match.

SPIRIT OF COOPERATION

Perhaps the element of conflict is everpresent between union and management, but maybe a spirit of cooperation can be developed. Sensitive observers increasingly call our attention to the fact that humans are not machines, that they have feelings and emotions which must be respected in order to get the highest degree of cooperation in the work place and in labor–management relations. The present emphasis on the study of individual and group relationships is a recognition that along with the solution of technical problems, there must be increasing concern for human elements in production.

Below are some ideas that have been developed by the National Planning Association in hopes of developing a spirit of cooperation.

1. The company should consider a strong union as assistant to management.
2. The union fully accepts private ownership and operation of industry, and recognizes that its members depend upon the profitable operation of the firm.
3. The company stays out of union's internal affairs, and does not seek to alienate the workers' allegiance to their union.
4. Mutual trust and confidence should exist between the parties for the easiest and fastest solution to problems.
5. Neither party to bargaining should adopt a strong legalistic approach to a solution.
6. Grievances should be settled promptly with as much flexibility and informality as possible within the procedures.[18]

Collective bargaining is still relatively young and growing into other areas of the working world. The basic outlines are established, but certainly today the variety of relationships is so great that it is clear much change is yet to come.

SUMMARY

In the last forty years, unions have become a potent force in labor—management relations and dealing with them requires considerable time and thought from management. Because the positions of foreman and shop steward are closely related in their functions, they are important to consider when a foreman is chosen or a labor dispute is imminent. The difficulties of contending with an equally powerful opponent at the bargaining table is probably the most important problem with which management must come to terms. It is no longer a matter of raising wages or firing unnecessary employees. There are now fringe benefits and profit motives, court-sanctioned strikes, and everchanging attitudes of the workers about working conditions which require management to change its own attitude toward employees.

The shop steward is sometimes a powerful adversary on the floor and can have a direct effect on the attitudes of the workers. The foreman also affects the attitudes of the workers. If a foreman misinterprets his relationship with either the shop steward or the workers, it can mean a serious breakdown in his working relationship. Should the foreman think that the union has more power on the floor than he does, his ability to direct operations will be undermined, and the workers will not respect his authority or accept him as a supervisor. On the other hand, if the foreman adheres to the old attitude of complete and unquestioned authority, the employees will grow increasingly resentful of him and their attitude toward the company itself will suffer. A good foreman understands his relationship with the workers as one in which he has the authority to ensure that the work that has to be done is done, but not the authority to arbitrarily decide that some of the workers are transfered to other areas or shifts, or the power to discipline an employee without that disciplinary action being questioned by the shop steward.

A shop steward is the workers' advocate in disputes about discipline or working conditions. He is the direct line to the union leaders. His function on the floor is to make sure that the labor agreement signed by both management and labor isn't violated by the foreman or by directives from middle management. In disciplinary actions, he presents the worker's side. The shop steward's relationship to the foreman is important to the entire floor. If the shop steward works under the assumption that his opinions and attitudes are reflected by the workers who elected him, he may become a threat to the foreman's authority. He may believe that his function is to create a condition in which there is constant friction between workers and management. This can be countermanded by the fairness with which the foreman treats the employees and hears the shop steward's complaints. A trained shop steward often reflects the policies and attitudes of the union. The foreman can determine the course of the shop steward–foreman relationship by discovering how the shop steward relates to the workers.

Collective bargaining is probably the most complicated area of labor–management interaction. The tensions involved are frequently excessive on both sides of the table. Without a good understanding of the demands of the other, neither of the opponents will be able to come to terms with the issues. In almost every instance where there are conflicting interests and goals, there will be arguments, excitement, tension, and fear. Cooperation on both sides may curtail a number of the problems, but cooperation is not the only attitude that plays a part in the effectiveness of the bargaining.

The general attitude of management about the advent of unions as a bargaining force may have considerable effect on the success of the bargaining. Occasionally, management considers the union a usurper and approaches the bargaining table as if it is about to engage in a battle for power rather than a trade of responsibilities and benefits. Unions may also behave as if they were going into battle. The purpose of collective bargaining is to set up an equitable position for both management and labor. Management's position is somewhat limited by the collective bargaining procedures, but this limitation simply ensures that the workers have an opportunity to obtain what they need without fear of jeopardizing their jobs.

If management understands the needs and desires of its employees, even though there are conflicting interests, it will be able to approach the bargaining table in a more reasonable frame of mind. If management is reasonable in its demands, it is safe to say that the union will also be reasonable. Bargaining can be considered a trade. A demand is met by a counter-demand, and the result is an exchange that benefits both parties. What cannot be agreed upon at one session can be held over until another, when changes in the market make it possible to discuss the disagreement without one side having to relinquish more than it safely can.

Negotiations occur on the average of every three years, depending on the length of the agreement. Important to the success of bargaining are the pains to which each party goes to meet the tensions and issues with fairness and intelligence.

As unions gain in strength, their influence is felt in all areas of business and government. They are no longer at the back door. Unions should not be underestimated because they wield considerable weight at the bargaining tables and in the legislatures, although overestimating them would be an error as well.

FIREHOUSE UNION

Case Study #1

Culver is a small and pleasant town with two modern and attractive fire stations. Most of the firemen employed at these stations grew up together and now live within the city limits. They all get along well and frequently have family get togethers. In spite of these conditions, the firemen are far from happy.

For quite some time the firemen have been in conflict with the City's Board of Administration over obtaining a wage increase. The men feel that their wages are too low and that the board is spending money unnecessarily. They feel that this money is being spent on fire equipment to impress the community instead of paying the men a reasonable salary in line with the amount being paid neighboring communities.

Previous attempts to obtain a significant wage increase from the board have been futile. The only occasion when the firemen managed to obtain an increase over 2½% was when the men hired a lawyer for an evening during negotiations that cost $400 of their own money.

Tomorrow the men will go into negotiations

with the board. There is talk among the ranks that if their request for a 6% wage increase is turned down, as it is expected to be, they will contact the local Teamsters Union and request an election for union representation.

Those who speak in favor of joining the union state that the union would have a great deal more leverage in dealing with the board. If the board refuses to cooperate with the union, the firemen could go on strike with the financial support of the union. In addition, the union could stop all trucking in the town to support a firemen's strike if need be.

The men who are speaking against joining the union point out that the union requires what they consider high fees and that the firemen might be called upon to strike in support for other union members in the town. Additionally, a neighboring community fire station recently went on strike and in that community, hostility was being expressed against the firemen.

If you were one of the firemen, what would you do?

1. Recommend hiring another lawyer?
2. Recommend accepting the wage increase offered by the board?
3. Recommend joining the union?
4. Quit and find a better fire station in some other community?

UNIONS VS. MINORITY RIGHTS

Case Study #2

Management decided that due to a decline in business, the Rayon Furniture Plant would reduce the number of positions in the Finishing Department by twelve persons. After receiving the union's consent on the matter, the plant management gave the twelve men

with the least seniority their notice of termination.

Shortly after these events occurred, Tom Hale, head of the Personnel Department, contacted Bill Norton, the plant manager. Their discussion concerned the employees who received termination notices. Nine of these twelve men were black, and they contacted the Fair Employment Practices Commission and filed a complaint against the company for discriminating against them. The complaint centered on the fact that only the Finishing Department was being forced to cut back, and that only the Finishing Department was predominantly black. The men saw this as discriminatory.

"I am aware that the majority of those to be laid off are black," stated Bill, "but we've been ordered to reduce that department, and we must follow the seniority provision of our union contract."

"Yes, I know," replied Tom, "but the seniority provision could well be contested. A few months ago, the Waltan Corporation laid off some men based upon seniority, and after a complaint of discrimination similar to our own, the F.E.P.C. won a case of discrimination in court."

"Well, what do you propose we do about it?

Violate our union contract?"

"Can't we cut back in the Assembly Section and the Cutting Room too? That way, instead of laying off the twelve men in one department, we could lay off four men from each. Then it wouldn't seem discriminatory. There would be more whites laid off than blacks."

"But we don't need to cut back in the Assembly Section or the Cutting Room," Bill replied. "Besides, we have the men with the greatest seniority of the entire company in the Assembly Section. Why, Fred has been with us for twelve years and he has the least seniority of anyone in the department."

"What do you think about transferring the majority of the twelve men into other departments, then?"

"That doesn't solve the problem; the company is cutting back to save money, not to play musical chairs with the men. As far as I'm concerned, the problem is out of our hands. Let's let the union handle it."

1. Whose solution to the problem do you think is best, Bill's or Tom's?
2. Are there other options to this problem?
3. Is there a compromise to this problem? Should there be a compromise?

Terms and Concepts Students Should Know

urban unions or public unions	blacklisting	slowdowns
dual loyalty	yellow dog contracts	wildcat strikes
shop foreman	arbitrator	boycotts
union shop	National Labor Relations Act	injunctions
right-to-work laws	SUB	grievance
negotiators	shop steward	compulsory arbitration
jurisdictional strikes	closed shop	
mass picketing	collective bargaining	

Bibliography

1. BLOCKHAUS, ARTHUR, *Grievance Arbitration, Case Studies,* Boston, Massachusetts, Cahners Books, 1974.
2. DAVIS, KEITH, *Human Behavior at Work,* 5th ed., New York, McGraw-Hill Book Company, 1977, Chapter 17.
3. BEACH, DALE, *Managing People at Work,* 2nd ed., Macmillan Publishing Com-

pany, Inc., 1975, Part VIII, "Collective Bargaining."
4. BURSTEIN, HERBERT, "Labor's Next Decade," in *Unions, Management and the Public,* E. Wight Bakke, Clark Kerr, and Charles W. Anrod, eds., New York, Harcourt, Brace and World, Inc., 1967.
5. *Monthly Labor Review,* current journals.

Footnotes

[1] "Unions Slip From Past Gains," *Business Week,* 2 October 1971; see also Bureau of Labor Statistics, 1970.

[2] *The Retail Clerk* (New York: Wiley, 1962).

[3] "Is the Labor Movement Losing Ground?" *U.S. News and World Report,* 21 February 1972.

[4] Jack London, *The Iron Heel* (New York: Bantam Books, 1971), p. 20.

[5] Sidney and Beatrice Webb, "The Divorce of Capital and Labor," in *Unions, Management and the Public,* E. Wight Bakke, Clark Kerr, and Charles W. Anrod, eds. (New York: Harcourt, Brace and World, Inc., 1967), p. 45.

[6] *Ibid.,* p. 44.

[7] Leo Kotin, "Labor Agreement in Collective Bargaining," in *Unions, Management and the Public,* p. 301.

[8] Herbert Burstein, "Status of the Collective Bargaining Agreement," in *Unions, Management and the Public,* p. 302.

[9] *Ibid.*

[10] Kotin, "Labor Agreement in Collective Bargaining," p. 301.

[11] "They Carry Less Clouts Overseas—Unions," *Business Week,* 18 September 1971.

[12] William H. Form, "Job Vs. Political Unionism: A Cross-National Comparison," *The American Sociological Review,* Vol. xxxvii, December, 1972, pp. 224–238.

[13] *Los Angeles Times,* 6 June 1971.

[14] "The Four-Day Work Week is Coming Sooner Than you Think," *Business Management,* April 1971. Jon Jones, "Try it, You'll Like it, Says the Four-Day Week Firms, *Los Angeles Times,* 9 April 1972.

[15] "A Look at the Four-Day Workweek", *Monthly Labor Review,* October 1971.

[16] Alvar O. Elbing, Hermand Gadon, and John Gordon, "Flexible Working Hours, It's about Time," *Harvard Business Review,* January–February 1974.

[17] Herbert Burstein, "Labor's Next Decade," in *Unions, Management and the Public,* E. Wight Bakke, Clark Kerr, and Charles W. Anrod, eds. (N.Y.: Harcourt, Brace and World, Inc., 1967), p. 720.

[18] "Ideas from the National Planning Association," *Cause of Industrial Peace Under Collective Bargaining,* A Final Report, Case Studies (Washington D.C.: U.S. Government Printing Office, 1953), p. 93.

Intercultural Relations
"the World Is Getting Smaller Every Day" ∎

OBJECTIVES

After reading this chapter you should be able to:

1. Discuss the importance of establishing good intercultural relations before embarking on an international business venture.
2. Discuss how the following frames of reference affect business relationships with other countries:
   A. Political,
   B. Economic,
   C. Language,
   D. Cultural.
3. List the basic ingredients that make up a cultural frame of reference.
4. Discuss the importance of the hidden languages of space and time in cross-cultural business relationships.
5. Recognize how the relationship between touch and friendship differs from one culture to another.
6. Discuss the language of agreements in relation to each of the three basic types of rules that usually apply to business contracts.

■ ■ ■ ■ ■ ■ ■ ■ ■ ■ ■ ■ ■ ■ ■ ■ ■ ■ ■ ■

Again it is time to ask questions of ourselves. This time, about the field of intercultural relations—how do we feel about foreigners and those with cultural backgrounds that are different from ours? How can we relate and work effectively with people in foreign lands?

Why do we feel uncomfortable with foreigners—even if they speak English?

Is time more important to us than most foreigners?

Since we are one of the most advanced societies in the world, should we teach other countries to handle sales contracts like we do?

Do we have a responsibility to "third world" countries? If we do, what might it be and why?

What nonverbal actions have you observed about a particular foreign group that is different from your group of friends?

What is an "inner circle" and how does yours compare with others in your class? What racial group is likely to have the tightest "inner circle?" Why?

Is space more important to us or to foreigners?

Our society has certain "rules" about touching people. When is it all right to touch people in public? Those of the same sex and those of the opposite sex?

Is it more acceptable for men to touch men or women to touch women?

Are there certain cultural taboos in our society that are more acceptable in other countries?

Is the reverse also true? What are some of the acceptable mores in our culture that are really "no-no" elsewhere in the world?

A LOOK AT THE SHRINKING WORLD

The world is getting smaller. Technology has made communication and travel not only easier, but essential for two reasons: first, technology has made it possible for nations to hold the threat of death over one another to an extent never before possible, and second, technology has made demands on the material resources of the earth that threaten it with scarcity if its population does not cooperate and share. Unfortunately, the peoples of this world have had a history of not being able to share and cooperate. The problems of war and scarcity directly involve the business world in intercultural relations. First, many people look to business to satisfy their material needs. Moreover, they are increasingly looking to business to help solve social needs, or, at the very least, not to interfere with or obstruct the satisfaction of social needs. Business is often one of the first links established between peoples that have previously been separate and even antagonistic. Business was one of the first links between the United States and Japan in the nineteenth century; business was one of the first links between the United States and Japan after World War II.

Business becomes one of the first links between countries

It is one of the first links being established between the United States and China now, after years of antagonism. These business links will have a far-reaching effect on relations between the American and the Chinese people: both will begin by offering each other material goods not available through other channels. At first these goods may seem tokens: a store in San Francisco run by the People's Republic of China is now offering a scanty selection of Chinese clothing, Communist-inspired calendars, caps like those worn by Chinese workers, and baskets. Very few of these goods are actually needed by the American people to fill material needs, but the store serves a purpose in acclimatizing the city to the new relations between the two countries: it makes Americans familiar with what Chinese people may wear or make. Even the fact that the goods offered are not so very different from clothing worn here or baskets woven here and elsewhere in the world serves to establish familiarity with a people who were once described by hostile Americans as the "Yellow Peril."

The fear of the unknown is thus being alleviated by business dealings, which will serve to pave the way for business dealings of much greater import for both the United States and the People's Republic of China. The food and fuel crises that have plagued the United States in the seventies have reminded this country that it has needs that can only be met by cooperation with other countries. For this reason, if business is to fulfill its job of providing material needs, it must learn how to deal

The fuel crisis of 1974
changed our ways of
thinking with other cultures in a way that satisfies the material and social needs of both parties. The fuel crisis of 1974 was an object lesson in many ways. It became apparent very quickly that people were dependent on fuel and the world would have to become aware of the Arab culture in order to deal with the suppliers of the needed commodity.

The international businessman must be prepared in a special way to overcome the obstacles to peaceful trade that are set up in the form of political, linguistic, social, religious, economic, and human differences. This book cannot provide the kind of intensive training that a businessman seeking to trade with foreign countries will need, but it can suggest the areas with which he must concern himself and in which he must educate himself to be successful. In the discussion of cultural differences and intercultural relations that follows, the reader should not lose sight of the fact that we are all human—that beneath the external barriers to understanding, we are all people. We all have the same physiology and psychology—90 percent of each of us is like everyone else in the world; this is the bond that helps us respect and understand the 10 percent of individual differences that remain as obstacles to cooperation.[1]

THE UNITED STATES AND THE WORLD

Until fairly recently, the American economy developed along a path that was unique and enviable in world history. The United States began as a nation rich in natural resources, highly developed in human resources, and virtually self-sufficient in terms of providing its people with the world's highest standard of living. Its geographical isolation from Europe and Asia inclined its people toward political and economic isolation. It must have appeared that we could go on indefinitely creating a better life for ourselves, oblivious and independent of the rest of the world. This attitude became firmly rooted Appearance of
isolationism in the national consciousness. It was labeled *isolationism,* and it applied not only to politics, but to business, economic, and cultural relations and development.

Ethnocentric Attitude

This century has toppled our isolationism, but has not necessarily toppled our naive ethnocentrism, meaning that the feeling that our attitude is the only right attitude, the only way, the natural, normal way. Incidentally, this attitude is found all over the world, originating in the process of enculturation; as long as we are taught just one way, and know no other, we tend to accept that way as the right way.

We must become increasingly aware of our ethnocentric attitude. As we learn of the existence of other different ways, and become conscious of the nature of enculturation, we can recognize and understand the ethnocentric attitude in ourselves and others.

Sometimes we develop a reaction against ethnocentrism— we discover the principle of cultural relativity, which holds that there are no absolute standards for judging customs, that a society's customs and ideas should be viewed in the context of that society's culture. A commonly drawn conclusion is that all cultures and cultural practices are equally valid, and that therefore we should have tolerance and respect for other cultures and cultural practices, even if they happen to differ from ours.

A stage sometimes occurs at about this point which we call "reverse ethnocentrism"; it holds that our ways, rather than being better than others, are actually *worse* than others. This stage is not uncommon among some college students.

Last Traces of Isolationism

World War II ended most traces of isolationism in the United States. Again, the end of the war resulted in more American businessmen and more American dollars flowing into Europe, and this time also into Asia. Parts of Asia had also experienced a Communist revolution. With large areas of the world sharply divided along political and economic lines, the United States was forced to consolidate its position by entering more wholeheartedly into the life of the world.

The development of the "third world nations"

The split of the world along Capitalist-Communist lines has in postwar years brought the United States into close relations with certain nonaligned, emerging nations, known collectively as the Third World (although these nations are not a unified political or economic bloc). American investments and foreign aid was one way to assure that such nations would remain friendly. This kind of contact also served to widen the horizons of American business and the American people. The impact on Americans going for the first time into conditions of widespread deprivation in other countries has had great ramifications in our relations with the rest of the world. Our social consciousness, our awareness of the problems of other people, and even our perception of our own situation, has been vastly altered by the experience of trying to do business and make friends abroad.

The slow creation of a united European economy after World War II has also increased the respect that American businessmen have for the foreign market. The European Common Market has emerged as both a threat and an unparalleled opportunity for improving American–European business relations. The Common Market is another example of the ways in which a display of real economic strength outside has served to drive home in the United States the necessity for developing good business and cultural relations with other parts of the world.

And finally, in recent years Americans have had a taste of scarcity. We have begun to realize that our material resources have natural limits. Our expanding population has made and will continue to make demands on our ability to produce, which cannot be met. The food and fuel crises of the seventies have impressed on us that we need economic and political cooperation with other nations not only to survive under political and military pressure, but also to survive and fill the needs for food, adequate shelter, light, and fuel. Good intercultural relations are therefore no longer a luxury but a necessity.

THE UGLY AMERICAN OR THE PROTECTIVE FATHER IMAGE?

The image of the impolite, inarticulate, ill-mannered, patronizing "ugly American"—barging through foreign countries like a barbarian at a tea party—is legendary; that is, it contains some truth and some error. But the image does tell us something about the problems associated with attempting to establish good business and human relations with the people of other countries. It suggests that Americans need to modify and adapt their approach to other cultures, particularly in the realm of business, where success or failure hinges on cooperation.[2]

The recent growth of multinational corporations, the majority of which are American owned, points up more than ever before the need to prepare American businessmen for dealing with foreign cultures and business practices. "Coca-Cola" is a word that has crept into almost every language spoken on earth, and "IBM" (International Business Machines) are initials that are understood in business conversations around the world. Of course, many of the multinational corporations are foreign-owned, which requires American businessmen to treat the import/export market with increasing respect.[3] The German and
Japanese automobile industries have recently emerged as trend-setters for Detroit. The highly efficient rotary engine, disc brakes, radial tires, torsion bar suspension, and electronic fuel injection systems are all innovations of the Japanese and European markets—innovations that the United States has followed.[4]

Of the thirteen major innovations in the steel industry in recent years, including the electric furnace, not one originated in the United States. Such technological achievements compel respect in our highly developed technological society.

The increasing interdependency fostered by the development of the multinational corporation and by the rapidly rising technological level of foreign economies has brought American businessmen to realize that the image of the ugly American must be changed. How can they go about changing that image? How do they perceive other cultures, and how must they learn to interact with them to gain their cooperation?

Subtle Differences

American businessmen sometimes remark that the "pace" of business in, for example, San Francisco is different from the pace in New York, or that negotiation techniques that work in Detroit may utterly fail in Atlanta. Yet the United States is relatively homogeneous in terms of culture. Abroad, cultural differences may be much more acute between areas that are much closer together. Not only are the manners different, but the very language is different. So are the religion, the culture, the history, the social graces, the politics, the education, and probably the work ethic. Even the motives for doing business may vary. An American capitalist seeking a profitable contract for a private firm may encounter a host of communication problems when he sits down at the conference table with a dedicated socialist who does not respect the profit motive.

Cultural differences go deep but are subtle

The differences go deep. Even the language of gestures is culturally defined. Ask a question of a Greek, and he may reply in the negative—by clicking his tongue and nodding his head. A gesture that is friendly in one culture may be interpreted as hostile in another; an innocent gesture can be an insult. These subtle *cues to action* complicate the problems of international business relations in a way that cannot be deduced from business experience in the United States.

The businessman who is faced with such subtle cultural differences as gestures and tone of voice is experiencing a frame of reference that is different from his own. Since communication always takes place within a frame of reference, the international businessman must make sure that he can communicate in one that is not his own. The broad outlines of a culture are marked by the political and economic frames of reference, and these are the frames with which the businessman must familiarize himself first.

When we watch the stock market fluctuate with every major or minor crisis in our political life, we are aware of the close relationship between politics and business. The political climate of our nation is largely determined by its economic well-being. Major decisions in business and industry affect political movements and vice versa. This is also true on an international scale. Naturally, Americans know more about American politics than about foreign politics, a tendency which in the past has been the result of isolationism, but which is decreasing as the United States enters into greater involvement in the world. But American businessmen need much more education in the political structures of other nations if they are to operate successfully.

For example, with the fluctuating political detente with the Communist world, American businessmen have been establishing trade agreements with most of Eastern Europe and China. One of the lessons that we have learned is that the political structure of those nations is far more bureaucratized than the organizational structure of American business. Trade agreements must be passed through dozens of government bureaus and officials and may take three times as long to complete as similar transactions among private firms. An American businessman seeking a contract with a Communist trade agency must learn how to operate within a political framework that is intrinsically foreign to him.

Foreign political structure is more bureaucratic than in the U.S.

Another political problem facing the multinational corporation has been the risk of nationalization, a problem that has been particularly acute in South America. American copper companies suffered severe losses in Chile when the regime of Salvadore Allende came to power, and all American enterprises in Cuba except for the Guantanamo naval base were nationalized during the Cuban Revolution. The multinational corporation frequently runs the risk of being considered imperialist by the countries in which it operates, and the international businessman must be alert to changes in the political atmosphere.

Multinational corporations may be called imperialists

Tendencies toward nationalism have made it difficult for Americans to manage foreign workers, too. Some companies have sought to counter this problem by hiring managers from a third nation. This practice helps reduce tensions arising from the presence of Americans in an emerging nation. The practice is augmented by hiring local managers from the country in which the corporation is operating, people who know the customs and the laws and who speak the language. Furthermore, when local nationals head up the branches of a multinational corporation, the company is relatively immune from political expropriation or nationalization.

504

One of the first things that an American businessman traveling abroad may become aware of is the difference between the standards of living that he is accustomed to and those that he is now experiencing. These differences in economic capacity seriously affect the course of business dealings in foreign countries.

Standard of living varies greatly

The standard of living throughout most western European countries has improved dramatically in the last twenty years and is now pretty much on a par with that of the United States. For instance, the buying power of the average European has increased at two to three times the rate that the average American's income has increased. While the income and other measures of affluence, such as ownership of luxury items like cars and washing machines, still lag behind the United States, the rate of increase abroad is much greater than here. Naturally, the rate of increase must be understood in context: the levels of productivity in these countries were in some cases so low that dramatic increases were easy to achieve. In the United States, it would be far more difficult to achieve growth at such high rates because the United States was already operating at the upper limits of productivity relative to possible growth and technology.

The United States is still more productive and wealthy than most of Europe, however, and the difference affects business relations there. Workers in Europe are accustomed to working longer hours for less money than American workers are. Cheap labor is one of the inducements to business to set up branches in Europe and elsewhere. The foreign worker is also accustomed to taking less time off work. Such differences are rapidly being eliminated, however.[5]

Differences in quality of life style become much more marked as we move away from Western Europe and Japan. In the underdeveloped nations incomes are extremely low, so low that the basic necessities of life are frequently beyond the reach of the poorest citizens. The poorer the economy, the less developed technology and modern methods of industry and business are likely to be, and the more complicated international business dealings become. Poor economies usually also indicate cultural isolation, and therefore human relations are more difficult to manage.

Poor economies usually indicate cultural isolation

The underdeveloped nations, for example, having little experience of a highly developed level of technology, tend to have work forces who find it difficult to adapt to quality control systems, tight schedules, and performance standards. The American manager of foreign workers who does not adjust his frame of reference frequently makes the mistake of considering such workers lazy or sloppy. They are not; they simply have not experienced the development of technology and the consequent modifications of work behavior with which we are familiar here. They may, in fact, feel—with some justification—that the American worker has been reduced to the level of a machine by efficiency and time-and-motion studies.

The low level of economic development in many of the emerging nations is aggravated by high birth rates and even higher rates of inflation. Both factors discourage saving, which is one of the prerequisites for capital accumulation necessary for investment and expansion. The workers of such countries are essentially trapped by the cycle of low income, large families, and inflation that encourages spending rather than saving. Little money is available from local business and governments for training and relief of crisis situations, and foreign aid is usually inadequate for more than stopgap measures.

The multinational corporation, however, has both the resources and the responsibility to help break the vicious circle that such workers find themselves in. In return for business profits realized from cheap labor and easy access to local natural resources, the multinational corporation can and should contribute massive training programs to help develop the human resources of its host nation. The ability of a nation to increase its productivity is directly proportionate to the amount of training the work force gets. Hopefully, of course, a trained work force will demand more money for its skills—but it will also bring in more profits for the corporation that trains and employs it.

A few economic factors must be mentioned when one considers dealing with foreign countries.[6]

1. During the decade of the seventies, the concept of international relations has come to rest heavily on the shoulders of American businessmen. The year 1971 brought the first foreign trade deficit since 1875. The years of 1971 and 1972 produced the revaluation of the American dollar that hit the front pages of newspapers, but the concept could only be understood by a few.

2. The United States exports only about 6–10 percent of its Gross National Product, but several European nations export up to 50 percent of their Gross National Product and are highly vulnerable to international crises.

3. A number of nations have less than a $600 annual income per capita and are not increasing their income by more than 1 percent per year. Yet with income so low a native employee is likely to spend his money as quickly as he earns it, because he

must survive inflation. Inflation in some Latin American countries has been greater than 10 percent annually over a period of years. Saving seems impractical because the longer a worker saves his money, the less it is worth.

The Cultural Frame of Reference

This chapter has suggested that the many variables in the political and economic structures of both the developed and the underdeveloped nations are challenges that must be met by adaptation of American business methods to the foreign market. When "the American way" is transplanted to foreign soil it must bend and twist, give and take, absorb and develop according to local expectations and traditions. In the process a third "way" to do business will be formed, one that borrows from both parties and aims at filling the needs of both. This process requires that the American businessman become versed not only in the economics and politics of a country, but also in its culture, and in its manners. He must steep himself in the language, religion, institutions, and personal relations of the host country. He must learn to understand and respect its way of life.

Language is a major barrier   Language is the foremost barrier to good international relations. Although English is still commonly accepted as the international business language, foreign businessmen usually frown on the inability of Americans to converse in the native language. Mark Twain once observed, while traveling in France, that the French were astonishingly bright. "Even the smallest children speak fluent French," he remarked. Twain's satiric observation suggests that Americans feel English should be the universal language, all others being secondary. In fact Americans have found it difficult to acquire other languages easily, which has made people of other countries feel that Americans do not make an effort to communicate. It is perhaps understandable that Americans do not acquire languages readily because the United States is both homogeneous and isolated linguistically, and foreign languages are generally spoken only in small enclaves in the large cities and in some parts of the Southwest. Europeans, on the other hand, are in close and constant contact with people who speak other languages and sharply differentiated dialects. Switzerland, for example, has four national languages: French, Italian, German, and Romansch!

The effect of America's isolationism and subsequent entry into world politics as the most powerful nation has so far meant that Americans abroad did not need to acquire other languages. Most countries offer English as a second language to students, often beginning instruction in the primary grades. America, however, may be losing its preeminence as well as its self-sufficiency in economics and politics. Russian and Chinese dialects are taking their place as second languages around the world. In the future, American businessmen will need to communicate in the language of their host countries, both by necessity and as a mark of good will.

Religion is reflected in one's culture

In much of the world formal religious observances have lost their power in the areas of politics and trade, although religious and philosophical assumptions still play a role in determining the cultural interactions of peoples. The American work ethic, for example, is sometimes called the Protestant work ethic, because it is associated with the simultaneous rise of capitalism and Protestantism in Europe. The idea is that people who work hard are virtuous and are rewarded with material goods. We now feel that such an idea is rather harsh, but it remains an undercurrent in American business thought, and more powerful because it is invisible or at least not openly incorporated into conscious religious observance. Abroad, this underlying belief may lead an American businessman to feel that people who are poor deserve to be so because they have obviously not worked hard enough. Such an attitude can seriously undermine human relations with people from other countries who do not share in the Protestant tradition.

Most of us know little about the Islamic, Buddhist, or Hindu religions

Religious traditions are accompanied by various degrees of formal religious observance in most countries, including the officially antireligious Communist nations. Therefore, religion may play a key role in determining how business is transacted. This is particularly true in the Islamic nations of the Middle East and among the Buddhist and Hindu populations of the Far East and India. If an American businessman is assigned to a managerial team in India, for example, he should acquire at least a rudimentary knowledge of the religious customs and beliefs of that country. One of them is that Hindus consider the cow a sacred animal, and someone who harms a cow is committing a serious offense.

An American businessman who has never examined his own religious beliefs may feel that he has none, but most people have some religious tradition that helps determine their behavior or system of values. To understand one's own relationship to religion, and the sensitivity of religious issues, is the first step toward respecting the religious behavior of other people. Furthermore, even if one does not hold religious beliefs themselves in high regard, it is very important to understand the relation of religion to the development of culture as a whole. Investigation of the rise of specific religious beliefs frequently shows that such beliefs are vital to the survival of the people who hold them.

HIDDEN LANGUAGES

Language and religion are only two of the more obvious frames of reference in which business takes place. A basic understanding of them allows the American businessman to negotiate on a roughly equal footing with his foreign associates and helps the American manager of foreign workers to motivate and understand his employees. There are many other languages by which people communicate, however, and these may be more difficult to acquire. These are the unspoken, hidden languages of time, space, familiarity, agreements, touching, and friendship. These languages vary from culture to culture, are often incredibly complex, and are usually as important as the spoken language in establishing good communication and human relations abroad.

The Language of Time

Time is more important to Americans than any other cultural group

Such an unspoken language of time appears informal, but the rules governing its interpretation are surprisingly ironbound. In the United States a delay in answering a communication can mean to the person waiting that the decision has a low priority on the part of the other person. In Ethiopia, the time required for a decision is directly proportional to its importance. The more money involved the longer it will take to arrive at a decision. In the Arab East, the time that is required to accomplish something depends on the relationship between the two parties involved. More important people receive faster service from less important people and conversely, less important people receive slow service from important people. Close relatives take absolute priority, while nonrelatives are kept waiting. Foreigners may be kept waiting for a long time.

Deadlines can be rude and pushy

In the Middle East to meet a time deadline, a way of indicating a degree of urgency, is a cultural trap, because to give a person a deadline in this part of the world is to be rude, pushy, and demanding. An Arab's evasiveness as to when something is to happen does not mean he does not want to do business, it only means he is avoiding unpleasantness and sidestepping possible commitments which he takes more seriously than we do.

In certain countries of the Orient — certainly not Japan — a delay of years does not mean that the people have lost interest in the project, only the urgency of time is not as important to them as it is to Americans. "Americans have one terrible weakness; if they are made to wait long enough they will agree to anything," said one oriental businessman. The delays in arriving at agreements in the Vietnam Peace Treaty seem to show our sense of urgency versus the oriental's patience.

From Microseconds to Antiquity

There is no country in the world where time is more important than in the United States. Telegrams were not fast enough for businessmen, so telephones have become the most common form of communication. The automated society has brought the terms of *microsecond* and *nanosecond*. The microsecond is equal to one millionth of a second and a nanosecond is equal to one billionth of a second. Such sophistication of time, in the words of one Chilean, is "rushing us to our graves."

Foreigners feel we are rushing to our graves

A significant fact is that many cultures have had little opportunity to accept modern technology and its relationship to time, as we know it in the United States. People of an agrarian culture usually have a low tolerance for perfection, time, schedules, performance standards, and demonstrate little employee initiative. The acceptance of responsibility for work done by others rather than by themselves is a concept some have not had to accept before. The American demand for punctuality, regularity, and discipline of the job would find many foreigners quitting their jobs in a U.S. plant before they could become accustomed to the culture changes and sending employee turnover skyrocketing.

We have two hundred years of history; the Orient has many centuries

Our country has barely two hundred years of history, and the European countries have many hundred years of written history, while the Orient has many centuries of recorded history. In the language of time most cultures other than ours may seem to be tied with antiquity and the time lag we may associate with it.

The Indians of South Asia have an elastic view of time, indefiniteness does not mean they are evasive. When the Chinese Communists moved into Tibet, the Western world believed the last stronghold of semidemocracy was lost there forever. However, the people of Tibet were not as concerned as we were. The spiritual leader, the Dalai Lama, escaped into India in 1959. As long as the spiritual leader lives the war is not over. In terms of the game of chess, there is no "check-mate"—the game is not over until the king is captured. The Tibetans are willing to wait ten, twenty, or a hundred years if necessary before the Dalai Lama returns to his homeland.

Americans must learn that time is not something fixed in nature, but that it can be experienced in many different ways.

The Language of Space

Americans always want more space

In everyday life, the manipulation and use of space have many meanings that vary considerably among different cultures. For instance, in the American business office, space is allocated according to hierarchy. Lower-echelon workers may have a small space in the middle of a crowded room shared with other workers. The top executive usually has an office to himself. The amount of space we receive is an indication of status.

Japanese rooms often seem uncluttered to Westerners, because objects tend to be placed in the center of the room, while we tend to place objects around the edges and against the walls. The Japanese sense of privacy can be assured by the thinnest of paper screens, which do not give us a sense of being alone. Germans may require thick concrete walls that screen out the noise from other people's living space in order to feel private. If the American businessman does not understand cultural differences in the use of space, he may feel very uncomfortable or may make his hosts very uncomfortable.

The office of an Arab businessman may seem small, crowded, and confused to an American, and he may fail to give himself the confidence necessary to arrive at a contract. Such a strange environment may cause the American to wonder if he can trust such a man with a million-dollar contract.

SUPERVISION AND SPACE

U.S. status requires more space and less control

In the United States, our pattern calls for the president or chairman of the board to have the largest office in the company. Each person's office space is determined by his status. The operative manager may have an area fenced by a four foot barrier. If he is more important he is given more space and his office is completely walled in. A foreigner may wonder how a manager can supervise when he is unable to see his subordinates. The ultimate, of course, is to move the executive up to another floor, so he will not see his subordinates for days. The French are much more likely to lay out space as a network of connecting points of influence, activity, or interest. The French supervisor is usually found in the middle of his subordinates where he can control them. What Americans see as crowded, most foreigners would see as spacious.

VERTICAL SPACE

U.S. status is height

In the United States the executive suites are on the top floor and the relative rank of vice-presidents are placed along "executive row." The top floor in Japan is frequently seen as the place for the average worker. Why should the executive spend his time going to the top floor? The privilege of class is for the first and second floors. Likewise, the top floor in a Japanese department store is not reserved for furniture, but the "bargain roof." One wonders how many customers get off the elevator on a floor before they reach the roof to purchase an item, when really their purpose was to find a bargain on the top floor.

The hilltop home or the estate high on the Santa Barbara Riviera holds more prestige to Americans than the home down on the "flatlands." The concept of looking down on people is a part of our culture. Tall people have a psychological advantage in the United States because of this attitude. Rio de Janerio, by contrast, is a city that represents an opposite attitude. The higher one lives up Sugarloaf Mountain, the poorer the person. The peon has the view, but the aristocrat has the conveniences by living in the heart of the city.

Brazil uses the opposite view to status and height

FAMILIARITY BREEDS USE IN THE UNITED STATES

Americans tend to use or claim what they are near

In the United States, because of our tendency to zone our activities, nearness carries rights of ownership. As a child, I never thought of asking permission to use the neighborhood vacant lot to play baseball. Because it was close and not in use I felt justified in using it. The streets were community property and children's games were frequently played there. Cars are parked in front of your home and few people are concerned. By contrast, in England nearness entitles you to nothing. You have to make an appointment for your children to play with the child next door. Frowns or verbal reprimands are given to those who park in front of a home without permission. My children, to the dismay of some neighbors, taught the local British children the wonderful world of play outside their fenced yards, the world of "hop-scotch," on the sidewalk and doing "wheelie's" on their bikes in the street.

OUR "INNER CIRCLE" OR SOCIAL SPACE

Americans require more visual space between speakers

Sociologists have also found that different cultures keep different social distances—the distances between people that correspond to the degree of comfort they feel in each other's presence. The distance we keep between others and ourselves is known as our "inner circle" or our personal space. We allow people to step into our space only if we want them. We frequently step backward to prevent someone else from coming too close to us and invading our social space. Americans normally keep a distance of about four to six feet during business conversations, but other cultures are more inclined to reduce that distance, sometimes to three or four inches. An American businessman may be confused and disturbed by what he feels is undue intimacy (or threat), but his hosts may feel that he is cool and perhaps disdainful by keeping his distance. There is a sensitivity training method that demonstrates the amount of social distance people require in order to feel comfortable: two people stand about fifteen feet away and are asked to move toward each other until they begin to feel uncomfortable. If one

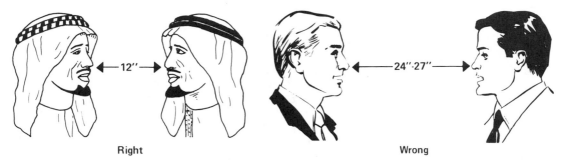

Right   Wrong

Figure 16–1. Body language speaks. The normal conversational distance between Arabs is 12 to 14 inches, about half the distance that Americans use. When approached, don't flinch or laugh. Learn to like it. Don't expect as much eye to eye contact; such a practice is not a comfortable one for them.
Source: Glen O'Brien, "How To Make it Nice with the Arabs," Esquire, *August 1975, pp. 75–81.*

person moves closer than his partner, his partner may begin to feel acutely disturbed by the experience.

Space speaks

Space speaks. When a businessman arrives in a foreign country he must try to be sensitive to what space tells him. Some useful advice to a newcomer: try to be aware of where people stand in relation to you, and don't back up. This, in itself, can greatly enhance people's attitudes toward you.

The Language of Touch

We also communicate by the frequency and manner in which we touch each other, customs which differ radically from culture to culture. American men rarely go beyond a formal handshake. If they happen to be old friends, they may slap each other on the back. Infractions of these rules are fraught with tension: if someone refuses to shake a hand that is offered him, he implies a serious insult or rejection. The man who is an indiscriminate back-slapper is usually viewed with either distaste or some fear, since the act implies intimacy without consent.

The custom of "nontouching" is common in the U.S.

The taboos of touching in the American culture are very strict. American men avoid excessive touching, as it is seen as an expression of emotionalism or homosexuality. It is all right for an athlete to pat a fellow teammate on the back or on the bottom on the basketball court or on the football field, but this behavior may not be acceptable elsewhere on the campus. An

Men touch each other less than women

American father will no longer put his arm around his son after he reaches a certain age, yet in foreign cultures the holding of hands by members of the same sex is not uncommon.

In the United States when two men ride a motorcycle together the rider will sit a few inches away from the driver and put his hands anywhere but around the waist of the driver. "The right masculine image seems more important than safety," said an Italian cycle driver of our culture. The various methods of tactile contact in countries along the Mediterranean Sea may seem too intimate or rude to us, but are accepted ways of communicating there. An American is apt to be shocked if a Frenchman kisses him on the cheek, or if an Italian pats his cheek or embraces him. Some of his shock may come from the heavy taboo (heavier between men than women) on touching between members of the same sex in our culture, which is often not so frightening to people of other cultures.

The relationships between men and women in other cultures are also sensitive to touching metaphors. The ease with which American women enter into touch may be interpreted as promiscuous by other cultures; in yet other cultures, American women may be seen as cold and unfriendly. The women of many Islamic and Hindu countries are only recently emerging from a tradition of purdah, the custom that a woman must be veiled in the presence of men. An involuntary or innocent infraction of social rules may result in serious consequences for both her and for the man who is involved. And anything in the realm of serious sexuality is sensitive and even dangerous for all cultures, including our own.

The American businessman must remember that, as with space and time, touch is a language that has developed in the midst of specific cultural needs. The correct use of this language depends not only on the people involved, but on the place and the time.

The Language of Friendship

A story of reciprocity

An experience I once had with a woman from India may illustrate the difference between cultures on how friendship is expressed. During a dinner party, I had casually commented how much I admired the necklace she was wearing. "Then it is yours," she said matter-of-factly, slipped it over her head and handed it to me. I protested that I really could not accept it; and then discovered that I had hurt her feelings. To make amends and to find a way to solve the problem, I then accepted the gift on the condition that she allow me to pay for it. At this the woman was shocked and deeply hurt. She had given something of herself, openly and freely, as a gesture of friendship. My offer to pay came across like a degradation of her gesture. Similar encounters

You do me a favor, and I will return a like favor

abroad have made some foreigners feel that Americans approach all human relations with the cynical and cold feeling that "everything has a price." The American abroad should be careful to distinguish between friendship and business relations, and to find out what gestures are significant in matters of friendship and hospitality. The offering of food, for example, is a universal gesture of friendship — to protest that one is on a diet may be interpreted as an unwillingness to "break bread together" — as a rejection of friendship and good relations.

Reciprocity does not exist in some cultures

The philosophy expressed above is one of giving freely of oneself and the good feeling one has about his own psyche after giving. Most often our culture manifests itself in the belief of reciprocity. When we give something or perform a favor we expect one in return — some time in the future. Reciprocity does not exist in some cultures.

In most foreign countries, friendships tend to be deeper and more complex than in the United States. We are a very mobile population and often do not establish long-lasting friendships. Instead we encounter them in a casual way and drop them as casually. Other cultures, which are less mobile and perhaps less alienated and fragmented, tend to develop closer, longer-lasting relationships that involve real obligations. An American who is offered such a friendship may feel incapable of handling the intimacy required, or may feel that the relationship is uncomfortably demanding.

TIPS FOR THE WORLD TRAVELLER

1. Don't call all people of the Middle East Arabs. It is like calling a Mexican an American. Sure he is an American, but not from the United States, he is from Mexico. So — the Iranians are Aryans, not Arabs.

2. Our old friends, the English, are still more formal than the Americans. In the U.S. families more often meet through their children. The children meet to play and introductions then come between the parents via their children. In England children were encouraged to play with mine only after the parents were formally introduced.

3. Women may be liberated in the United States, but remember you have come a "long way, baby" only in the United States. If a woman is out on the street unaccompanied by a man in Saudi Arabia, she is liable to be hassled. In Latin American countries she is not likely to get the "respect" that she would in the United States.

4. Unions in many developed countries are stronger, not from the national level, but from the "grass roots" level. National union leaders cannot encourage, predict, or direct their membership as well as here in the States. In England shop stewards and

     managers alike frequently spend half of their day on labor disputes.

5. People of the third world find that their loyalties must change frequently, because of changes in government leaders. This often confuses U.S. businessmen, because the American feels he understands the attitude of his foreign contact—when suddenly his attitude changes.

6. In most of the Arab world—as well as in the Latin American countries—appointments are rather approximate. No matter how important you are, be prepared to wait hours, if not days, so take a book.

7. Remember many work days begin around 8:00 a.m. Lunch and siesta are anywhere from two to four or five. In the hot spots, they may not go back to work. Elsewhere, business goes on into the evening and the streets are hopping till around ten o'clock, when dinner is served.

8. Douglas Fairbanks, Jr., said, "In America, the workingman will see someone drive by in his Cadillac and he'll say, 'That guy has a Cadillac and I don't. Some day I am going to have two Cadillacs.' In Britain, the instant reaction is: 'That man has a Rolls-Royce and I don't. He is going to come down to my level.' "

9. The "people from down under" often feel closer to Americans than the British. They use dollars and follow the American 100 cents to a dollar, rather than the British pound.

10. It must be remembered that all the world knows more about Americans than we do of any country. That is because of all the TV reruns of "I Love Lucy" and hundreds of TV shows, plus thousands of movies—not to mention such magazines as *Playboy* on every European newsstand. Even the Stock Exchange in London displays the largest sign of all—the current U.S. Dollar-British Pound exchange rate. U.S. culture and influence is felt everywhere throughout the world.

11. In some countries don't expect to make a deal on the first appointment or even on your first trip to the country. You may make a few trips before you really talk turkey. Don't try to make a deal before friendly relations are established.

12. You need an interpreter. Don't pick up the first bilingual person you meet in your foreign country. If you feel you need help in making a contact there are hundreds for hire in the States. Get to know him before you need to rely on him. If you want to play it safe, consult the international department of your favorite multinational bank.

The Language of Agreements

For any society to produce on a highly commercial level, a complex set of rules must be developed and widely accepted on

Here are the "unwritten" ground rules for contracts

which agreements can be reached. The language of agreements may be absolute or flexible, sophisticated or informal, but in any event it must be clearly understood by both parties to the agreement. Differences in cultural approaches to agreements can cause serious difficulties in business.

Usually, agreements are based on one or a combination of three types:

1. Rules that are technically spelled out as demonstrated by law or regulation.
2. Moral practices mutually agreed on and taught as a set of principles.
3. Informal customs to which everyone conforms without being able to state the exact reason or rule.

Naturally, informal, unstated rules can cause a lot of trouble for an uninformed American.

Americans are particularly unfamiliar with the practice, and unspoken rules, of bargaining, since in our own economy goods and services do in fact "have their price." In other economies, prices may be flexible—goods may have to be sold rapidly because there is no place to store them at the end of the market day, and therefore the price may come down. The American confronted with a confusion of different prices for the same product has to deal with the situation of the moment, which may include a number of social variables. If he offers too low a price, the seller may be insulted. If the seller suggests an exorbitant price, the American may not realize that the seller is willing to bargain downward.

A woman may have no legal right in a foreign country

A verbal contract may be more binding than a written contract

In the Arab world, a man's word is considered as binding as his legal signature (a woman may have no legal rights in business at all, however). To require a Moslem to sign a formal contract runs the risk of violating his sense of honor. However, since 1974 many Arabs have adopted American customs regarding contracts. On the other hand, to a Greek, a contract may only represent a sort of way station along the route of negotiations, to be modified periodically until the work is completed. If an American complains about such a procedure, the Greek may exclaim, "Take me to court." But there is no court to settle international business disputes, and mutual satisfaction is reached only through mutual respect and understanding of the various meanings of the agreement. For this reason the American businessman must not only understand that the laws governing trade in the United States no longer apply on the world market, but that the laws of the host country may not protect him. His only security is in structuring a business deal so that guarantees of fulfillment are intrinsic, and the terms of the agreement are firmly based on informal as well as formal rules. The best guarantee, of course, is good human relations, the building up of a

Some written contracts have no value

relationship in which both parties willingly cooperate to reach common goals of exchange.

SUMMARY

Technology has made the world smaller by introducing rapid communication, travel, machines that boost productivity and hence allow for greater productivity, weapons that have enormous range and power, and the realization that the natural resources of the world have limits. We are now aware that for our survival in military matters, as well as in matters of food, fuel, and other resources, we must become a more outgoing nation.

The first unofficial ambassadors to other countries are frequently businessmen, and the multinational corporation is becoming so common on the international market that it bears the brunt of establishing good intercultural relations abroad. American businessmen must learn how to relate successfully with people from other cultures in order to fulfill the role of business in our economy—to procure for the United States the things it needs. American businesses from the wealthiest nation in the world have a human responsibility to other peoples who have less than we. That responsibility might best be fulfilled by training and developing the human resources of other countries.

The American businessman seeking to establish good business relations abroad must educate himself in the political and economic frames of reference of his host country. Conflict with local politics or a lack of understanding of the predominant economic structure and level of development can mean the ruin of successful business ventures. Good trade relations with the People's Republic of China, for example, will require careful study and adaptation of American business motives and political relations to the Communist economic and political environment.

Language and religion are especially sensitive areas in intercultural relations. The American businessman should make an attempt to learn the language of his foreign associates and employees, both as a means of making information more readily available to both himself and to them, and as a gesture of interest and good will. Religious customs and beliefs frequently have a bearing on business as well as general human relations, and should be understood and respected.

In addition, there are a number of hidden languages with which a successful international businessman must be familiar. The languages of space, touching, friendship, and agreements all involve informal, often almost unconscious, but extremely expressive communication among people. The American life style is affected by the amount of living space we are accustomed to, the mobility that fragments our friendships, and by an economy that develops habits of precision in time, controls, price, and legal sanctions and guarantees in business. Consequently the American abroad must overcome an image of being arrogant, pushy, speedy, and cold.

All these cultural differences, however, can be worked out if he keeps in mind the basic common bond of humanity, understands that his own values are not universal, but local to his own culture, and makes a serious effort to respect and understand the cultural differences in the countries in which he operates. The businessman abroad is involved in an exciting venture into broadening his own cultural horizons, as well as in a process on which depends our ability to survive in an increasingly interdependent world.

INTERNATIONAL BRIBERY

Case Study #1

Henry Cordero works for Maytax Industries, a large multinational corporation with production and research facilities in several foreign countries. Henry is in charge of one of the facilities in a South American country.

Henry was recently informed by a member of the country's government that if Maytax wished to remain operating in the country, it was strongly suggested that the corporation begin contributing to their country's medical research association. Somewhat shocked, Henry asked if the order was official. He was told by the individual that although the order did not come officially from the government, it could easily be enforced.

Well aware that bribery payments were being demanded, Henry returned to the corporation's home office to discuss the matter with the corporation's vice-president, Mr. Manoushek. After filling in Mr. Manoushek on the details of the demand, Henry was asked what should be done concerning the matter.

It's my opinion," stated Henry, "that we shouldn't become involved in making bribery payments. Aside from the fact that such payments are against our moral ethics and our system of free enterprise, the American public and our government take a pretty dim view of such matters."

"I agree with you there, Henry," stated Mr. Charles Manoushek, "but I don't think you understand the realities of the problem. In countries such as the one we're dealing with, bribery has been an accepted custom for years and years. Although our country is against this type of thing, many countries abroad are not. We are a corporation that does the majority of our business abroad and we must deal with these countries on their own terms. If we don't, some other company will."

"But if we begin paying these bribery payments every time someone suggests it, where will the demands end?" retorted Henry. "On the other hand, when we begin offering these payments on our own initiative, like Lockheed, Exxon, Gulf or ITT, and the public finds out, we will be no better off for it. I know company images suffer when the American public finds out about their affairs. If it was my choice, I'd back out of the country if necessary."

"Our duty, Henry, is to our shareholders first, and that duty is protecting our investments abroad. If we must contribute to a country's medical research association to protect our investment, then that is what we must do."

1. Whose side do you favor—Henry Cordero's or Charles Manoushek's?

2. Give reasons for your stand.

3. Is giving small gifts acceptable? When does it stop being a gift and become a bribery payment? At what point do you make the distinction? Is there a dollar value?

4. Should there be more government agencies to audit overseas operations? Can it legally be done?

5. If codes should be established, who will say what is ethical?

6. Companies have stated that there will be no "unusual payments." What is considered unusual?

A PROBLEM OF CULTURAL COMMUNICATION

Case Study #2

Harold Underhill walked into the office of the Latin American Country's Commercial Attache for help. Harold had arrived two weeks earlier from the United States for the purpose of securing a several million dollar production order. Harold is the Sales Manager of a large corporation that produces communications systems.

When Harold first arrived in the country he had been under the impression that his business would take no more than a few days, and then he could take a few days vacationing before returning within his allotted seven day period.

Upon arriving in the country Harold immediately contacted the Minister of Communications, whom he needed to have sign the production order. He was then instructed that Minister Munoz would see him that afternoon. When Harold arrived he was forced to wait in the outer office for a considerable amount of time and then only to be greeted briefly, but politely by the minister before being ushered out without any business being discussed. Harold was then informed that the Minister would see him next Wednesday for lunch. Although upset about the delay Harold accepted the invitation.

When Harold and Señor Muñoz did meet the following week for lunch Harold soon realized that the minister had no intentions of talking business. Somewhat in a panic he tried pressing the fact that he needed the order signed. As a result of this the minister politely cut short the business conversation and invited Harold to meet him again in a few days.

As a result of these events Harold asked the Commercial Attache for his advice. "You must understand," stated the attache, "that business relations are not the same here as they are in the United States. Things are not always done overnight here. Latin Americans feel a need to spend more time completing business transactions and to get to know who they are doing business with. You should not rush things—let them take the initiative. When you are in their country you must follow their rules of behavior."

When Harold met again with the Minister of Communications they took a walk in a memorial park near the minister's office. As Señor Muñoz commented on the beauties of the park Harold failed to recognize the statue of Simon Bolivar, and then he compounded his error by stating that he had never heard of him. Insulted, the minister decided that the pushy, rude American was not the person whom he wanted to do business with and informed both Harold and his employer that he didn't wish to continue negotiations.

1. Identify the American's problem.
2. Name several errors in Underhill's approach.
3. How could Underhill's company have better prepared him for the business transaction?

Terms and Concepts Students Should Know

ethnocentric attitude	cultural shock	women's liberation in the world
language of space	moral customs vs. laws	working hours in foreign lands
supervision and space	isolationism	the world knows of America
language of touch	inner circle	how much do we know of the
language of agreements	status and vertical space	world?
management of waiting	language of friendships	formal vs. informal customs
world union trends	universal language	

Bibliography

1. ROSENFELD, LAWRENCE, and JEAN CIVIKLY, *With Words Unspoken, the Nonverbal Experience*, New York, Holt, Rinehart and Winston, 1976.

2. JOHNSON, DAVID W. and FRANK P. JOHNSON, *Joining Together*, Englewood Cliffs, N.J., Prentice-Hall, Inc., 1975.

3. ADLER, RON and NEIL TOWNE, *Looking Out, Looking In, Interpersonal Communication*, New York, Holt, Rinehart & Winston, 1975.

4. DAVIS, KEITH, *Organizational Behavior, A Book of Readings*, New York, McGraw-Hill Book Company, 1977, Chapter 15.

5. DAVIS, KEITH, *Human Behavior at Work*, New York, McGraw-Hill Book Company, 1977, Chapter 20.

Footnotes

[1] "Those Unwritten Social Rules," *Fortune*, January 1971, p. 31.

[2] "Politics of Envy," *Time*, September 15, 1975, p. 61.

[3] "Doing Business Overseas: The Handsome American," *Business Management*, April 1970.

[4] "U.S. Marketeers Can Learn From European Innovators," *Harvard Business Review*, September–October 1972, p. 89.

[5] "The Big Gap in Wages Between U.S. and Others Has Started to Narrow," *The Wall Street Journal*, May 11, 1972.

[6] "Upstairs/Downstairs at the Factory," Britain/Special Report, *Time*, April 12, 1976, pp. 58–60.

Index

X

Y

Z